A HANDBOOK FOR THE JEWISH FAMILY

Understanding and Enjoying the Sabbath and Holidays

By ALEX J. GOLDMAN

NEW YORK
BLOCH PUBLISHING COMPANY

ISBN 0-8197-0085-1
Library of Congress Catalogue Card Number: 58-12938

First printing 1958
Second printing 1962
Third printing 1968
Fourth printing 1983

Published with the assistance of Books for Jewish Education, Inc.

PRINTED IN THE UNITED STATES OF AMERICA

For
ROBERT
and
PAMELA

Table of Contents

vii

Preface

You may have heard this commentary on the American family: Some families make swimming, tennis, literature, even the synagogue (or church), a part of family life. They all go into it together. But some fathers and mothers sit at the edge of the pool, and bid their children, "Go on." Is it any wonder that so many children fail to realize the beauty of great music and great literature and great faith? Too many of us are at the edge of the pool, urging, "Go on"; too few of us are *in* the pool, saying, "Come on!"

The purpose of this Handbook is to provide greater incentive and opportunity to American Jewish parents to say, "Come on" to their children, in an age crying for togetherness. It is designed to help recapture the Jewish family spirit with meaningful, joyous observance of Jewish life through the beauty of the Jewish holidays. Every Jewish festival has family aspects which this Handbook emphasizes and whose observance it encourages.

The need for such a book became increasingly evident to me while serving as rabbi to a vigorous, newly organized Jewish community, like the hundreds which have sprung up in the last decade or are in process of formation. The families which make up these communities are seeking home stability and spiritual security. They want to establish continuing family traditions. Young mothers and fathers have been asking many questions. What do we need for the holidays? What do we do? Where do we begin? How do younger children participate? What does Yom Kippur mean? Sabbath? Sukkos? How can the family observe these holidays? How do we prepare for and conduct a Seder? Where can we find one book to suggest what to do with our children on the holidays? These questions and innumerable others are familiar to every rabbi in America. They represent the seeking of a whole generation of young Jewish families in new homes, with children who have need for family ties and traditions and for lasting and unifying religious experiences.

Let me take you around the Jewish calendar, and pause at every holiday, and offer your family the wonderful experience of religious participation in Sabbath and festive days, and the feelings of family warmth, reverence, gaiety, and fellowship. Permit me to introduce you to, or reacquaint you with, the rich heritage of the Jewish people. I will explain concisely the meanings of every holiday, how it is observed in the synagogue, the manner of your family observance, and detailed instructions for the needed preparations; the parts mother and father and children play, the songs to sing, the games to play, the decorations to prepare, the services to conduct at the table and in the home, and the stories to read and tell.

I have treated each holiday as a separate and complete unit, without relying on cross-references. Transliterations are extensive so that even those unacquainted with the Hebrew may participate fully in every holiday ceremony. The Haggadah developed offers a new family approach to the conducting of and sharing in the Seder; father's explanations have been made part of the Haggadah service. The Birkas Hamozon, Grace after meals, is a condensed version, retaining however, the four traditional benedictions. A complete Grace after meals has also been added.

I have included in this Handbook, which is designed to help also teachers of all faiths interested in gaining a perspective of Jewish family observance, a special section with pertinent information for ready reference: a Home Consecration Ceremony, The Bible and its Parts, Childrens' Prayers for Varied Occasions, Hebrew Names for Your Children, and a Glossary of Terms and Explanations.

Many have been involved in this undertaking, and to them I must acknowledge my debt. To Ruth and Martin Bell of Margate City, New Jersey, for their encouragement and suggestions. To Mrs. Malgert Cohen, whose original ideas for home decorations and table settings are incorporated because they lend warmth and beauty to the holiday observance. To Mrs. Alex Maissel, art teacher at the Elkins Park Junior High School in Elkins Park, Pennsylvania, for directing the art work enclosing every poem and holiday introduction; this work was done by her most promising students, thirteen year old girls, who have been able to capture the spirit of the holidays, Jean Cassel and Joan Reisbord. To Shalom Altman, Music Director of the Council on Jewish Education in Philadelphia, for his help with the songs and music which appear here. To Rabbi Abraham Burstein of New York City for his careful editing of the manuscript and many valuable suggestions. To Mrs. Neil Josephson of New Britain, Connecticut, Miss Emily Solis-Cohen of Philadelphia, and Mrs. Maurice Hahn of Elkins Park, Pennsylvania for their generous help. To Mr. Solomon Kerstein, Vice President of Bloch Publishing Company, for his personal interest in the many facets which comprise this volume.

I must direct profound appreciation to Dr. Maurice Jacobs of Maurice Jacobs, Inc., for the blessing of his friendship and confidence during the writer's twelve years in Philadelphia. I am also deeply grateful to the members of his staff, especially Dr. Menahem G. Glenn, whose vast knowledge and erudition are evident in this book, Mrs. Margaret R. Jacques, who helped make the volume more valuable, and Mr. David Skaraton, who patiently guided its physical composition and format.

Though they are not directly involved in this work, I want to offer the gratitude of a son to my parents, Rabbi and Mrs. Julius D. Goldman of Chicago, for the basic home education and environment and love of tradition, from which sources I have drawn.

And lastly, it must be admitted that this book is due, more than I can express in words, to the unstinting effort and loyal cooperation of my dear wife, Edith, who has been its guiding spirit from idea to draft after draft, to publication. It was she who, day after day during the years of preparation, not only helped write, rewrite, and guide the style and format which evolved, but also motivated, encouraged, and inspired every step in the development of this volume. This venture has been a joint effort and, with all my love, I heartily share with her any credit which may accrue.

ALEX J. GOLDMAN

THE FAMILY PLANS AHEAD
A TEN YEAR CALENDAR OF JEWISH HOLIDAYS

(Note: All holidays begin at sunset on the evening before date mentioned)

Holidays	5744 1983	5745 1984	5746 1985	5747 1986	5748 1987
Rosh Hashanah (New Year)	Sept. 8 Sept. 9	Sept. 27 Sept. 28	Sept. 16 Sept. 17	Oct. 4 Oct. 5	Sept. 2 Sept. 2
Yom Kippur (Day of Atonement)	Sept. 17	Oct. 6	Sept. 25	Oct. 13	Oct. 3
Sukkos (Feast of Tabernacles)	Sept. 22 Sept. 23 to	Oct. 11 Oct. 12 to	Sept. 30 Oct. 1 to	Oct. 18 Oct. 19 to	Oct. 8 Oct. 9 to
Shemini Atzeres (Eighth Day of Assembly) and	Sept. 29 and	Oct. 18 and	Oct. 7 and	Oct. 25 and	Oct. 1 and
Simchas Torah (Rejoicing of the Law)	Sept. 30	Oct. 19	Oct. 8	Oct. 26	Oct. 1
Chanukah (Feast of Lights)	Dec. 1 to Dec. 8	Dec. 19 to Dec. 26	Dec. 8 to Dec. 14	Dec. 27 to Jan. 3	Dec. 1 to Dec. 2
	1984	1985	1986	1987	1988
Tu Bi-Shevat (New Year for Trees)	Jan. 19	Feb. 6	Jan. 25	Feb. 14	Feb. 3
Purim (Feast of Lots)	Feb. 17	Mar. 7	Feb. 23	Mar. 15	Mar. 3
Pesach (Passover)	April 17 April 18 to April 23 April 24	April 6 April 7 to April 12 April 13	April 24 April 25 to April 30 May 1	April 14 April 15 to April 20 April 21	April 2 April 3 to April 8 April 9
Lag Bo-Omer	May 20	May 9	May 27	May 17	May 5
Shovuos (Feast of Weeks)	June 6 June 7	May 26 May 27	June 13 June 14	June 3 June 4	May 22 May 23

MONTHS OF THE JEWISH CALENDAR

Tishri, תִּשְׁרִי; Cheshvan, חֶשְׁוָן; Kislev, כִּסְלֵו; Tevet, טֵבֵת; Shevat, שְׁבַט; Adar, ר
*Adar II, אֲדָר שֵׁנִי; Nisan, נִיסָן; Iyar, אִיָּר; Sivan, סִיוָן; Tammuz, תַמּוּז; Av, אָב; Elul, לל

* Added in leap year.

THE FAMILY PLANS AHEAD
A TEN YEAR CALENDAR OF JEWISH HOLIDAYS

(Note: All holidays begin at sunset on the evening before date mentioned)

Holidays	5749 1988	5750 1989	5751 1990	5752 1991	5753 1992
sh Hashanah (New Year)	Sept. 12 Sept. 13	Sept. 30 Oct. 1	Sept. 20 Sept. 21	Sept. 9 Sept. 10	Sept. 28 Sept. 29
n Kippur (Day of Atonement)	Sept. 21	Oct. 9	Sept. 29	Sept. 18	Oct. 7
kkos (Feast of Tabernacles)	Sept. 26 Sept. 27 to	Oct. 14 Oct. 15 to	Oct. 4 Oct. 5 to	Sept. 23 Sept. 24 to	Oct. 12 Oct. 13 to
emini Atzeres (Eighth Day of Assembly) and	Oct. 3 and	Oct. 21 and	Oct. 11 and	Sept. 30 and	Oct. 19 and
nchas Torah (Rejoicing of the Law)	Oct. 4	Oct. 22	Oct. 12	Oct. 1	Oct. 20
anukah (Feast of Lights)	Dec. 4 to Dec. 10	Dec. 23 to Dec. 30	Dec. 12 to Dec. 19	Dec. 2 to Dec. 9	Dec. 20 to Dec. 26
	1989	1990	1991	1992	1993
Bi-Shevat (New Year for Trees)	Jan. 21	Feb. 10	Jan. 30	Jan. 20	Feb. 6
rim (Feast of Lots)	Feb. 19	Mar. 11	Feb. 28	Feb. 18	Mar. 7
sach (Passover)	April 20 April 21 to April 26 April 27	April 10 April 11 to April 16 April 17	Mar. 30 Mar. 31 to April 5 April 6	April 18 April 19 to April 24 April 25	April 6 April 7 to April 12 April 13
g Bo-Omer	May 23	May 13	May 2	May 22	May 9
ovuos (Feast of Weeks)	June 9 June 10	May 30 May 31	May 19 May 20	June 7 June 8	May 26 May 27

MONTHS OF THE JEWISH CALENDAR

shri, תִּשְׁרִי; Cheshvan, חֶשְׁוָן; Kislev, כִּסְלֵו; Tevet, טֵבֵת; Shevat, שְׁבָט; Adar, אֲדָר; r II, אֲדָר שֵׁנִי; Nisan, נִיסָן; Iyar, אִיָּר; Sivan, סִיוָן; Tammuz, תַּמּוּז; Av, אָב; Elul, אֱלוּל.

Added in leap year.

Acknowledgments

BARTON'S CANDY CORPORATION, New York.
Stories: *The Most Precious Thing* and *The Beautiful Willow.*

BLOCH PUBLISHING COMPANY.
Jewish Holiday Party Book, by Lillian S. Abramson and Lillian T. Leiderman, New York, 1954 — "Ideas for Holiday Parties."
So We Sing, by Sara C. Levy, Beatrice L. Deutsch, and Anita Rogoff, New York, 1954 — Songs: "The Shofar Man," "To the Sukkah," "Simchas Torah," "Chanukah Presents," "Make a Hamantash," and "The Mezuzah."
Around the Year in Rhymes, by Jessie E. Sampter, New York, 1920 — Poems: "A Dream" and "Questions."
Star Light Stories, by Lillian S. Freehof, New York, 1952 — Story: "The Lopsided Challah with the Crooked Crown."
What Danny Did, by Sadie Rose Weilerstein, New York, 1932 — Story: "The Chanukah Lights."

CENTRAL CONFERENCE OF AMERICAN RABBIS.
The Union Hymnal, Cincinnati, 1932 — Songs: "Come, O Sabbath Day" and "Sabbath Blessing."

MARK DAVIS, Philadelphia.
Song: "Chanukah."

RABBI ISRAEL GOLDFARB.
The Jewish Songster, Brooklyn, 1948 — Songs: "Sholom Alaychem" and "Sabbath Eve Kiddush."

HEBREW PUBLISHING COMPANY.
Hamillon Hamaasi, Practical Hebrew-English Dictionary, by Menahem G. Glenn, New York, [1947] — List of Hebrew names of men and women [selected].

HOUGHTON MIFFLIN COMPANY.
Poems of Emma Lazarus, Boston, 1899 — Poem: "The New Colossus."

JEWISH EDUCATION COMMITTEE OF NEW YORK.

The Songs We Sing, by Harry Coopersmith, New York, 1950 — Songs: "My Draydel," "Yom Tov Lawnoo," "I Love the Day of Purim," "Lawmaw Sookaw Zoo," "O Chanukah," "Passover Kiddush."

World Over Story Book, edited by Morris Epstein, New York, 1952 — Stories: "Passover Dream," by David Einhorn, "Hermit of Lag Bo-Omer Hill," by Morris Epstein, "The Date Tree," by Judah Steinberg.

JEWISH PUBLICATION SOCIETY OF AMERICA.

Songs of A Wanderer, by Philip M. Raskin, Philadelphia, 1917 — Poem: "My Chanukah Candles."

NATIONAL JEWISH WELFARE BOARD.

The Jewish Center Songster, edited by Bernard Carp, New York, 1949 — Songs: "Siman Tov" and "Mi Y'malayl."

NATIONAL WOMEN'S LEAGUE, UNITED SYNAGOGUE OF AMERICA.

The Adventures of K'tonton, by Sadie Rose Weilerstein, League Press, New York, 1947 — Stories: "How K'tonton Drove Satan Out of the Shofar," and "How K'tonton Masqueraded on Purim."

The Singing Way, by Sadie Rose Weilerstein, League Press, New York, 1946 — Poems: "For a Good and Sweet Year," "Fasting," "Seven Times Around," "The Trees' New Year," and "A Poem for Lag Bo-Omer."

PRAYER BOOK PRESS.

Sabbath and Festival Prayer Book, United Synagogue of America and Rabbinical Assembly of America, edited by Rabbi Morris Silverman, New York, 1946 — Quotations of prayers.

Prayerbook for Summer Camps, edited by Rabbis Morris Silverman and Hillel Silverman, Hartford, Conn., 1954 — Quotation of night prayer for children.

ANITA ROGOFF, Cleveland.

Sketch: for the "Sabbath Firefly" story.

UNION OF AMERICAN HEBREW CONGREGATIONS.

Jewish Festivals in the Religious School, edited by Elma E. Levinger, Cincinnati, 1923 — Poem: "About Purim," by Miriam Myers.

Purim Entertainments, edited by Elma E. Levinger, Cincinnati, 1924 — Poem: "An Old Fashioned Purim" (fifth stanza omitted).

If You Cannot Read Hebrew

If you cannot read Hebrew, you can still participate fully in all the home experiences developed in this Handbook.

The transliteration system adopted, that is, the method by which you may read the Hebrew selections and sing the songs in English characters, is the Ashkenazic. This is the manner of pronunciation followed by most Jewish people, especially in religious services. Here is a key to help you understand it.

LETTERS OR CONSONANTS

All Hebrew letters are easily printed and sounded in English, except the following:

1. Both ח and כ or ך we print as CH and sound as in Chanukah.

2. צ or ץ we print as TZ and sound as Tzah-deek.

VOWELS

1.	ָ	is	AW	as in crawl.
2.	ַ	is	AH	as in hurrah.
3.	ֵ	is	AY	as in day.
4.	ֶ	is	EH	as in led.
5.	ִי	is	EE	as in deer.
6.	ִ	is	I	as in bin.
7.	ו or ֹ	is	O	as in rose.
8.	ו or ֻ	is	OO	as in moon.
9.	ַי	is	AI	as in aisle.
10.	ָי	is	OY	as in boy.

In most cases, the English letter "a" is sounded as "ah," and the letter "e" as "eh." Where there was doubt in the author's mind as to whether the word would be correctly sounded, the letter "h" was added to the "a" and to the "e."

The Sephardic (Israeli) and Ashkenazic Systems

In Israel, the Sephardic method of pronunciation is employed. Here are the basic differences:

1. In the Sephardic, the letter ת, with or without the dot, or דָּגֵשׁ (dawgaysh) as it is called in Hebrew, is always pronounced T. In the Ashkenazic, the ת with the dot is pronounced T, and without the dot, S.

2. All the vowels are the same in both systems, except:

   a) The ֵ (צֵירָה — tzayreh), pronounced in Ashkenazic "ay" is, in Sephardic, closer in sound to "eh," ֶ (סֶגֹל — sehgol). For example: סֵפֶר, say-fehr (book), is almost like seh-fehr.

   b) The וֹ or ֹ (חוֹלָם — cholawm), pronounced in Ashkenazic "o" is, in Sephardic, sounded "aw." For example: בֹּקֶר, bo-kehr (morning), is sounded as baw-kehr.

   c) Generally, the vowel ָ (קָמַץ — kawmatz), sounded in Ashkenazic "aw" is, in Sephardic, pronounced "ah" as in father. When it is a קָמַץ קָטָן (short kawmatz), however, that is, a kawmatz without an accent, or a ָ (חַטָף־קָמַץ — chahtawf-kawmatz), the pronunciation is like the Ashkenazic, that is, "aw." For example: כָּל, kawl (all), אָזְנִי, awz-nee (my ear), or אָנִיָּה, aw-nee-yaw (ship).

   You can recognize a short kawmatz in these two ways:

   1) When it is followed by a שְׁוָא נָח (shvaw nawch), that is, a shvaw (ְ) which closes the syllable, as for example, the word תָּכְנִית, tawch-neet (plan), and 2) when the letter

following the ָ (kawmatz) contains a dot, as for example, רָנִּי, raw-nee (sing).

A good example illustrating the difference between the two systems of pronunciation is: הוּא שָׁבַת בַּשַׁבָּת (he rested on the Sabbath), pronounced in Ashkenazic, hoo shaw-vahs bah-shah-baws, but in Sephardic, hoo shah-vaht bah-shah-baht.

In this volume, we have retained in the Sephardic those songs which have come from Israel, and also words and terms commonly expressed in Sephardic.

Rosh Hashanah

ROSH HASHANAH

Our wishes for a happy year
Resound and fill the atmosphere.
Apples, honey, all things sweet
Provide a special New Year treat.

The new beginning will afford
A blessed time to thank the Lord
For every hour of usefulness,
For every year of happiness.

We go to synagogue, there to pray,
We greet our friends along the way:
L'shaw-naw to-vaw ti-kaw-say-voo!
May you be inscribed with good, we
    pray you!

Rosh Hashanah

As the summer season wanes and we feel saturated with its hot sun and balmy evenings, we begin to plan for our children's return to school and the Jewish New Year. Many other thoughts come to mind. We think about attending High Holy Day services with our parents and children, of registering the children in Hebrew or Sunday School, or consulting our budgets for new holiday attire. New Year cards must be ordered, perhaps with personal imprint, and sent to our friends to wish them the year's best. The coming New Year creates an exhilarating new spirit.

You will want to know about this New Year, this Rosh Hashanah, as it is called in Hebrew, what it means, the customs which surround it, and how you can help your family enjoy it.

Rosh Hashanah means the beginning ("head") of the year. It falls on the first day of Tishri, first month in the Jewish calendar, usually in September. All Jews, whatever their personal religious views, observe Rosh Hashanah. Orthodox and Conservative Jews celebrate it for two days, and Reform Jews for one day. In Israel, where most of the holidays are observed for one day, the New Year is an exception, because it is considered a *Yomaw Ahrichtaw* — a long or continuous day.

Many of us do not know that when Rosh Hashanah arrives it has already been heralded for a full month. Twenty-eight days before, on the first of Elul, the last month in the Jewish calendar, and every morning thereafter (until the last day of the month), the shofar, ram's horn, is sounded at synagogue services announcing the approaching holy season. On the Saturday night before Rosh Hashanah, a special midnight service is conducted which is called Selichos (Penitential Prayers), developed from a passage in the book of Jeremiah: "Arise and sing out into the night at the beginning

3

of the watches." Most of the prayers and chants are drawn from the liturgy of the Day of Atonement, perhaps because they help prepare the worshiper for the coming season of reverence and self-appraisal. Selichos services are being reinaugurated throughout the country and many communities arrange for a social hour to either precede or follow the services.

You will understand the meaning of the holiday better from the names by which it is known. Each indicates a special characteristic, and the combination offers a total picture. Some of these names are mentioned in the Bible; others have been added through the ages.

First, Rosh Hashanah is the New Year. It marks the renewal of the Jewish calendar. In addition, it celebrates the birthday of the world. "This day the world was called into being," says our liturgy.

Secondly, Rosh Hashanah is the Yom Hadin, the Day of Judgment, when every man passes before his Creator, his past actions are evaluated, and his future judged. This thought is magnificently portrayed in one of the more beautiful prayers called *Oo-n'sah-neh To-kef*. Here is a brief quotation. "All who enter the world dost Thou cause to pass before Thee, one by one, as a flock of sheep. As a shepherd musters his sheep and causes them to pass beneath his staff, so dost Thou pass and record, count and visit, every living soul, appointing the measure of every creature's life and decreeing its destiny."

Thirdly, Rosh Hashanah is termed Yom Hazikoron, the Day of Remembrance. This emphasizes that God remembers His covenant of days gone by and His promises for a better and more peaceful world. And on this day every man can bring to mind his own deeds and actions of the year, review the events of the past, and use the opportunity for self-examination and self-analysis.

Fourthly, Rosh Hashanah is the Yom Teruah or Zichron Teruah, the Day of Blowing the Shofar. These names are specified in the Bible itself.

Many of us remember standing alongside our parents waiting eagerly for the shofar ceremony, the central feature of the entire service. In olden days this was conducted in the early morning, but it was later changed so that children too might be able to hear the trumpet blasts. The shofar or ram's horn was the instrument used to announce major national and religious events in Jewish life, and the means whereby the congregation of Israel was called together. The source is found in the account of the binding of Isaac, and of Abraham's unswerving faith and trust in God. You can read the story in the 22nd chapter of Genesis, first book of the Bible.

If you listen carefully to the three times the shofar is blown in the traditional service by the *Baal Tekiah* (the man who sounds the shofar), you will count one hundred blasts. You will also detect three distinct sounds: *tekiah*, a straight, strong blast; *shevorim*, a combination of three broken notes; and *teruah*, a quick succession of short trills, staccato.

Now that you know the various names and the central feature of Rosh Hashanah you will also want to be able to recognize the three essential themes of the day's service, which provide the pattern of the ritual. They are sectioned into *Malchuyos*, prayers of God's kingship; *Zichronos*, prayers of God's remembrances; and *Shofros*, prayers dealing with the shofar. Each is introduced by a beautiful prayer emphasizing its theme, followed by ten selected passages from the Pentateuch, Prophets, and Writings (the three parts of the Bible), and concluded by another prayer underscoring the same theme, which is then climaxed by sounding the ram's horn. All these prayers have been developed into beautiful chants by cantors throughout the ages and have become familiar to many of our congregants.

If you have gained the impression that Rosh Hashanah is a very serious day, one of moral responsibility, and of synagogue attendance, your understanding is correct. At the same time, the

holiday is a joyous and hopeful occasion because of the good feeling
it engenders among members of the family and friends, and because
of our prayers for renewed efforts for doing good, so that the year
may be filled with brightness and cheer.

CUSTOMS AND PRACTICES

Like all holidays, Rosh Hashanah is clothed with a number of
customs and practices which reflect its character, and add delight
and interest. You are probably acquainted with a few of these.

Sending greeting cards to family and friends wishing them a
year of health and happiness is perhaps the most prevalent and
popular custom. Generally, when you purchase the cards, you will
find them printed with Hebrew words. They say:

לְשָׁנָה טוֹבָה תִּכָּתֵבוּ וְתֵחָתֵמוּ

L'shaw-naw to-vaw ti-kaw-say-voo v'say-chaw-say-moo

"May you be inscribed and sealed for a good year in the Book of
Life." This phrase is also used in personal greetings at the synagogue,
and upon returning home. Many people simply mention the first
two words, "L'shaw-naw To-vaw — a good year."

The custom of Tashlich on Rosh Hashanah is not observed
today as in the past. This is the custom of visiting the adjacent
river or sea on the first day (or the second day when the first occurs
on the Sabbath) and there, with appropriate prayers, symbolically
casting the sins into the flowing waters.

Wearing a white gown or *kittel* in the traditional synagogue
was not limited to the rabbi and cantor. Other congregants, too,
joined in donning the garment on the New Year. This custom was
symbolic of the ideals of purity of thought and heart associated
with this holy period.

Honey cake and wine on Rosh Hashanah intensify the meaning
of holiday joy. This is the cherished custom of home visits following

the services for Kiddush (blessing over wine). The purpose is to offer good wishes for the coming year to friends and neighbors in the warm and tender environment of home. Honey cake and wine are both indicative of a "sweet" year. In some communities the custom of sending jars of honey to members of the congregation prevails.

Rounded challahs or bread loaves replace the regular twists or braided white loaves because they present the idea of roundness or completeness. In Hebrew, the word *shalom*, peace, which we use for greetings and salutations, really means *complete*, and the rounded challahs exemplify the hope for a year of completeness, peace, and unbroken happiness.

In Our Homes

Every important festive occasion in our lives assumes added meaning with previous planning and preparation. The same is true of the New Year. We have to create the spirit of the holiday by telling our children it is coming and including them in planning its welcome.

The first step is to bring the family together in the warmth and closeness of the living room, talk about Rosh Hashanah, and consider what may be done in unison to make the holiday a happy and enjoyable one.

These are some suggested projects:

Sending New Year Cards

These cards can either be purchased or made by the family. If they are purchased, the children can be asked to select them, choose the people to whom they are to be sent, address the envelopes, and add personal greetings. If the cards are home-made, we can capture the children's imagination by describing holiday symbols, such as the shofar, honey jars, bees, rounded challah or bread loaves. Even the symbols of the synagogue service, the Scroll (Torah), adornments such as the crown or breastplate or pointer used to direct the reading, can be recommended for greeting card pictures.

In addition to original cards the following suggestions may be helpful:

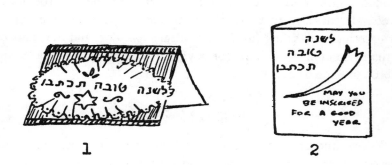

1. Cut a piece of colored construction paper or cardboard to desired size.

2. Paste a ready-made, fancily cut, paper doily, (or cut paper in a design) to colored paper.

3. On a plain piece of paper print the message and cut out in thin strip. Paste on top of cut paper.

4. Stars may be cut from aluminum foil and added to card.

5. Another card may be made by cutting a shofar from aluminum foil. Paste to white card and letter with gold paint.

Around the Dinner Table

The atmosphere about the dinner table on Rosh Hashanah evening is very important. Your children can share in creating the holiday spirit by making a shofar to be placed or suspended near the table and by decorating the tablecloth in this way:

To Make a Shofar:

1. If one large piece of cardboard is not available, use two smaller sheets, like shirt cardboard. Place as in 1, and cut according to pattern.
2. Tape cut sections together in back with masking tape or scotch tape.
3. Draw a curved line from corner to corner at wide end of shofar to represent opening. Cut a curved piece of aluminum foil as wide as desired, but longer than opening of shofar.
4. Attach foil across end, mouthpiece, and center by taping to back of shofar with tape.
5. Tack or tape to wall and hang New Year greeting cards in a formal or informal design around shofar.

To Decorate Tablecloth (Use white or solid colored cloth):

1. Cut lengths of colored decorative sticking tape — 6 lengths — about 6 inches long, for each star.
2. Stick to tablecloth in even row around edge or scattered.

WHAT YOU NEED TO WELCOME THE NEW YEAR

With the approach of Rosh Hashanah evening, the family can welcome its arrival in a beautiful home ceremony. You will find a rich experience awaiting you, and you will see the delight of your children sharing eagerly in the various phases of the ceremony.

These are the items needed:

Holiday candlesticks and candles

Wine and wine decanter

Wine cups for every member of the family

Two rounded challahs (you may use regular twists or bread if the rounded challahs are not available in your area)

Challah cover (a cover can be purchased, or you can embroider one, and include a Jewish symbol in the embroidery design)

Holiday bread knife

Jar or dish of honey

Cut or sliced apples

Flowers (a fresh bouquet may serve as centerpiece on the table, with a small cardboard-shofar in the flowers to further create the New Year atmosphere)

THE HOME CEREMONY

1. *Blessing the Holiday Candles*

With the children seated about the table, freshly scrubbed and dressed for the occasion, mother blesses the holiday candles:

בָּרוּךְ אַתָּה יְיָ, אֱלֹהֵינוּ מֶלֶךְ הָעוֹלָם, אֲשֶׁר קִדְּשָׁנוּ בְּמִצְוֹתָיו וְצִוָּנוּ לְהַדְלִיק נֵר שֶׁל (*On Sabbath add* וְ) שַׁבָּת וְ) יוֹם טוֹב:

בָּרוּךְ אַתָּה יְיָ, אֱלֹהֵינוּ מֶלֶךְ הָעוֹלָם, שֶׁהֶחֱיָנוּ, וְקִיְּמָנוּ, וְהִגִּיעָנוּ
לַזְּמַן הַזֶּה:

Baw-rooch ah-taw Ado-noy, Elo-hay-noo meh-lech haw-o-lawm, ah-shehr ki-d'shaw-noo b'mitz-vo-sawv, v'tzi-vaw-noo l'hahd-leek nayr shel (*On Sabbath add:* Sha-baws v') yom tov.

Baw-rooch ah-taw Ado-noy, Elo-hay-noo meh-lech haw-o-lawm, sheh-heh-cheh-yaw-noo, v'kee-y'maw-noo, v'hi-gee-aw-noo, la-z'mahn ha-zeh.

Blessed art Thou, O Lord our God, King of the universe, who hast sanctified us by Thy commandments and granted us the privilege of kindling the (Sabbath and) holiday candles.

May this coming year, O God, be for our dear ones and for all our people, a year of health and plenty. May these holiday candles bring peace within our souls, cheer within our home, and happiness within our family.

Blessed art Thou, O Lord our God, King of the universe, who hast granted us life, sustained us, and brought us to this festive season. Amen.

2. *The Kiddush or Blessing of Wine*

Father rises as he leads the family in chanting or reciting the Kiddush. Each member of the family holds his wine cup in his right hand.

On Sabbath, add first paragraph and words in brackets:

וַיְהִי עֶרֶב וַיְהִי בְּקֶר

יוֹם הַשִּׁשִּׁי. וַיְכֻלּוּ הַשָּׁמַיִם וְהָאָרֶץ וְכָל צְבָאָם. וַיְכַל אֱלֹהִים בַּיּוֹם
הַשְּׁבִיעִי מְלַאכְתּוֹ אֲשֶׁר עָשָׂה, וַיִּשְׁבֹּת בַּיּוֹם הַשְּׁבִיעִי, מִכָּל מְלַאכְתּוֹ
אֲשֶׁר עָשָׂה. וַיְבָרֶךְ אֱלֹהִים אֶת יוֹם הַשְּׁבִיעִי, וַיְקַדֵּשׁ אֹתוֹ, כִּי בוֹ שָׁבַת
מִכָּל מְלַאכְתּוֹ, אֲשֶׁר בָּרָא אֱלֹהִים לַעֲשׂוֹת:

When holiday occurs on weekday, begin here:

בָּרוּךְ אַתָּה יְיָ, אֱלֹהֵינוּ מֶלֶךְ הָעוֹלָם, בּוֹרֵא פְּרִי הַגָּפֶן:

בָּרוּךְ אַתָּה יְיָ, אֱלֹהֵינוּ מֶלֶךְ הָעוֹלָם, אֲשֶׁר בָּחַר בָּנוּ מִכָּל עָם,
וְרוֹמְמָנוּ מִכָּל לָשׁוֹן, וְקִדְּשָׁנוּ בְּמִצְוֹתָיו. וַתִּתֶּן לָנוּ, יְיָ אֱלֹהֵינוּ, בְּאַהֲבָה,
אֶת יוֹם [הַשַּׁבָּת הַזֶּה וְאֶת יוֹם] הַזִּכָּרוֹן הַזֶּה, יוֹם [זִכְרוֹן] תְּרוּעָה [בְּאַהֲבָה]
מִקְרָא קֹדֶשׁ, זֵכֶר לִיצִיאַת מִצְרָיִם. כִּי בָנוּ בָחַרְתָּ, וְאוֹתָנוּ קִדַּשְׁתָּ
מִכָּל הָעַמִּים, וּדְבָרְךָ אֱמֶת וְקַיָּם לָעַד. בָּרוּךְ אַתָּה יְיָ, מֶלֶךְ עַל כָּל
הָאָרֶץ, מְקַדֵּשׁ [הַשַּׁבָּת וְ] יִשְׂרָאֵל, וְיוֹם הַזִּכָּרוֹן:

On Saturday night, add the following:

בָּרוּךְ אַתָּה יְיָ, אֱלֹהֵינוּ מֶלֶךְ הָעוֹלָם, בּוֹרֵא מְאוֹרֵי הָאֵשׁ:

בָּרוּךְ אַתָּה יְיָ, אֱלֹהֵינוּ מֶלֶךְ הָעוֹלָם, הַמַּבְדִּיל בֵּין קֹדֶשׁ לְחֹל, בֵּין אוֹר לְחֹשֶׁךְ, בֵּין
יִשְׂרָאֵל לָעַמִּים, בֵּין יוֹם הַשְּׁבִיעִי, לְשֵׁשֶׁת יְמֵי הַמַּעֲשֶׂה. בֵּין קְדֻשַּׁת שַׁבָּת לִקְדֻשַּׁת יוֹם טוֹב
הִבְדַּלְתָּ, וְאֶת יוֹם הַשְּׁבִיעִי מִשֵּׁשֶׁת יְמֵי הַמַּעֲשֶׂה קִדַּשְׁתָּ. הִבְדַּלְתָּ וְקִדַּשְׁתָּ אֶת עַמְּךָ יִשְׂרָאֵל
בִּקְדֻשָּׁתֶךָ. בָּרוּךְ אַתָּה יְיָ, הַמַּבְדִּיל בֵּין קֹדֶשׁ לְקֹדֶשׁ:

בָּרוּךְ אַתָּה יְיָ, אֱלֹהֵינוּ מֶלֶךְ הָעוֹלָם, שֶׁהֶחֱיָנוּ, וְקִיְּמָנוּ, וְהִגִּיעָנוּ
לַזְּמַן הַזֶּה:

On Sabbath, add first paragraph and words in parentheses:

Va-y'hee eh-rehv, va-y'hee vo-kehr.

Yom ha-shi-shee: Va-y'choo-loo ha-shaw-ma-yeem v'haw-
aw-retz, v'chawl tz'vaw-awm. Va-y'chahl Elo-heem ba-yom
ha-sh'vee-ee m'lahch-to ah-shehr aw-saw, va-yish-bos ba-yom
ha-sh'vee-ee, mi-kawl m'lahch-to ah-shehr aw-saw. Va-y'vaw-
rech Elo-heem ehs yom ha-sh'vee-ee, va-y'ka-daysh o-so, kee vo

haw-vahs mi-kawl m'lahch-toh, ah-shehr baw-raw Elo-heem
a-ah-sos.

When holiday occurs on weekday, begin here:

Baw-rooch ah-taw Ado-noy, Elo-hay-noo meh-lech haw-o-
awm, bo-ray p'ree ha-gaw-fen.

Baw-rooch ah-taw Ado-noy, Elo-hay-noo meh-lech haw-o-
awm, ah-shehr baw-chahr baw-noo mi-kawl awm, v'ro-m'maw-
oo mi-kawl law-shon, v'ki-d'shaw-noo b'mitz-vo-sawv, va-ti-ten
aw-noo, Ado-noy Elo-hay-noo, b'ah-ha-vaw, ehs yom (ha-shah-
aws ha-zeh, v'ehs yom) ha-zi-kaw-ron ha-zeh, yom (zich-ron)
'roo-aw (b'ah-ha-vaw) mik-raw ko-desh, zay-chehr lee-tzee-ahs
nitz-raw-yeem. Kee vaw-noo vaw-chahr-taw, v'o-saw-noo ki-
dahsh-taw mi-kawl haw-ah-meem, oo-d'vawr-chaw eh-mehs v'ka-
rawm law-ahd. Baw-rooch ah-taw Ado-noy, meh-lech ahl kawl
aw-aw-retz, m'ka-daysh (ha-shah-baws v') Yis-raw-ayl, v'yom
a-zi-kaw-ron.

On Saturday night, add the following two paragraphs:

Baw-rooch ah-taw Ado-noy, Elo-hay-noo meh-lech haw-o-
awm, bo-ray m'o-ray haw-aysh.

Baw-rooch ah-taw Ado-noy, Elo-hay-noo meh-lech haw-o-
awm, ha-mahv-deel bayn ko-desh l'chol, bayn or l'cho-shech,
ayn Yis-raw-ayl law-ah-meem, bayn yom ha-sh'vee-ee, l'shay-
hehs y'may ha-ma-ah-seh, bayn k'doo-shahs shah-baws li-k'doo-
hahs yom tov hiv-dahl-taw, v'ehs yom ha-sh'vee-ee mi-shay-shes
'may ha-ma-ah-seh ki-dahsh-taw. Hiv-dahl-taw v'ki-dahsh-taw
hs a-m'chaw Yis-raw-ayl bi-k'doo-shaw-seh-chaw. Baw-rooch
h-taw Ado-noy, ha-mahv-deel bayn ko-desh l'ko-desh.

Baw-rooch ah-taw Ado-noy, Elo-hay-noo meh-lech haw-o-
awm, sheh-heh-cheh-yaw-noo, v'kee-y'maw-noo, v'hi-gee-aw-noo,
a-z'mahn ha-zeh.

Heavenly Father:

As we share in the sweetness of this wine, symbol of joy and gladness, we thank Thee for the blessings of life and health. W pray Thee, grant that the coming year be for us one full of happines and abundance and delight. In gratitude to Thee for Thy goodnes to us and to those who are near and dear to us, we thank Thee a we recite the blessing over wine:

Blessed art Thou, O Lord our God, King of the universe, who createst the fruit of the vine.

Blessed art Thou, O Lord our God, King of the universe, who hast granted us life, sustained us, and brought us to this festiv season. Amen.

3. Washing the Hands

The traditional home service suggests washing of hands before dinner. The custom is reminiscent of the act of preparation and consecration which priest performed before they began their functions in Temple days of old. The blessing recited is:

בָּרוּךְ אַתָּה יְיָ, אֱלֹהֵינוּ מֶלֶךְ הָעוֹלָם, אֲשֶׁר קִדְּשָׁנוּ בְּמִצְוֹתָיו, וְצִוָּנוּ
עַל נְטִילַת יָדָיִם:

Baw-rooch ah-taw Ado-noy, Elo-hay-noo meh-lech haw-o lawm, ah-shehr ki-d'shaw-noo b'mitz-vo-sawv, v'tzi-vaw-noo, ah n'tee-lahs yaw-daw-yeem.

Blessed art Thou, O Lord our God, King of the universe, who hast sanctified us by Thy commandments and granted us the privilege of partaking of Thy blessings of food and sustenance after the symbolic washing of the hands.

4. Breaking Bread Together

Father removes challah cover and leads the family in the Hamotzee prayer as he slices the challah.

בָּרוּךְ אַתָּה יְיָ, אֱלֹהֵינוּ מֶלֶךְ הָעוֹלָם, הַמּוֹצִיא לֶחֶם מִן הָאָרֶץ:

Baw-rooch ah-taw Ado-noy, Elo-hay-noo meh-lech haw-o-lawm, ha-mo-tzee leh-chem min haw-aw-retz.

Blessed art Thou, O Lord our God, King of the universe, who bringest forth bread from the earth.

Each member of the family receives a slice of challah, dips it in salt, and partakes of it.

5. *Prayer for the New Year*

(With the approach of Rosh Hashanah the Jew prays that the year ahead may be one filled with the blessings of life, health, happiness, and joy. It is an old tradition, on the eve of Rosh Hashanah, as the family is seated about the holiday table and after the Kiddush has been chanted, for all the members of the family to take apples, challah, or bread, dip into honey, and recite the following prayer beseeching God to make the year arriving one of sweetness and goodness for the family, for our people, and for all mankind.)

בָּרוּךְ אַתָּה יְיָ, אֱלֹהֵינוּ מֶלֶךְ הָעוֹלָם, בּוֹרֵא פְּרִי הָעֵץ:

Baw-rooch ah-taw Ado-noy, Elo-hay-noo meh-lech haw-o-lawm, bo-ray p'ree haw-aytz.

Blessed art Thou, O Lord our God, King of the universe, who createst the fruit of the tree.

יְהִי רָצוֹן מִלְּפָנֶיךָ, יְיָ אֱלֹהֵינוּ וֵאלֹהֵי אֲבוֹתֵינוּ, שֶׁתְּחַדֵּשׁ עָלֵינוּ
שָׁנָה טוֹבָה וּמְתוּקָה:

Y'hee raw-tzon mi-l'faw-neh-chaw, Ado-noy Elo-hay-noo vay-lo-hay avo-say-noo, sheh-t'chah-daysh aw-lay-noo shaw-naw to-vaw oo-m'soo-kaw.

May it be Thy will, O Lord our God and God of our fathers, to renew unto us a sweet and good year.

We pray Thee, O God, that by our thoughts and deeds we may be worthy of Thy continued blessings and goodness, and that health, happiness, and joy be given to us, our dear ones, our families, our people, and all mankind.　Amen.

6. *Dinner is served.*

7. *Singing holiday songs.*

Either during the meal between courses or following dinner, the family can join in singing songs appropriate to the New Year holiday. Here are a few well known melodies:

V'TAHAYR LIBAYNOO

וְטַהֵר לִבֵּנוּ — O, PURIFY OUR HEARTS

O, Purify our hearts that we may serve Thee in truth.

וְטַהֵר לִבֵּנוּ לְעָבְדְּךָ בֶּאֱמֶת.

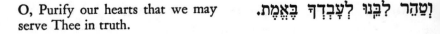

AWVEENOO MAHLKAYNOO

אָבִינוּ מַלְכֵּנוּ — OUR FATHER, OUR KING

Aw - vee - noo mahl - kay——— noo,——— chaw-

nay-noo vah-ah-nay—— noo,—— Aw - vee-noo mahl-kay-noo, chaw

nay-noo vah-ah-nay-noo, kee   ayn baw- noo   mah-ah - seem.——

Fine

Ah - say   ee-maw - noo,—— ah - say   ee-maw -

noo,—— ah - say   ee - maw- noo,   ts-daw-kaw vaw-cheh - sed,

1. v' ho - shee - ay - noo.——   **2.** Ah - noo.——   *D. C. al Fine*

Our Father, Our King, be merciful to us, for we have no deeds to commend us.

אָבִינוּ מַלְכֵּנוּ, חָנֵּנוּ וַעֲנֵנוּ
כִּי אֵין בָּנוּ מַעֲשִׂים.
עֲשֵׂה עִמָּנוּ צְדָקָה וָחֶסֶד,
וְהוֹשִׁיעֵנוּ.

THE SHOFAR MAN

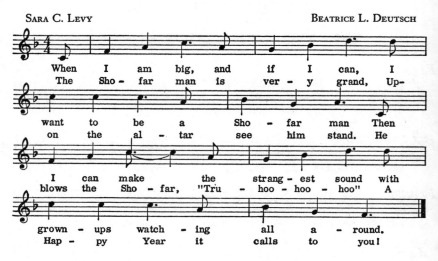

SARA C. LEVY   BEATRICE L. DEUTSCH

When   I   am   big,   and   if   I   can,   I
The   Sho - far   man   is   ver - y   grand,   Up-

want   to   be   a   Sho - far   man   Then
on   the   al - tar   see   him   stand.   He

I   can   make   the   strang - est   sound   with
blows   the   Sho - far,   "Tru - hoo - hoo - hoo"   A

grown - ups   watch - ing   all   a - round.
Hap - py   Year   it   calls   to   you!

8. *Grace*

Father leads the family in reciting grace, thanking God for His bounty.

Father: רַבּוֹתַי, נְבָרֵךְ.

Ra-bo-sai, n'vaw-raych

Family: יְהִי שֵׁם יְיָ מְבֹרָךְ מֵעַתָּה וְעַד עוֹלָם.

Y'hee shaym Ado-noy m'vo-rawch may-ah-taw v'ahd o-lawm.

Father: יְהִי שֵׁם יְיָ מְבֹרָךְ מֵעַתָּה וְעַד עוֹלָם. בִּרְשׁוּת מְשַׁפַּחְתִּי,
נְבָרֵךְ שֶׁאָכַלְנוּ מִשֶּׁלּוֹ.

Y'hee shaym Ado-noy m'vo-rawch may-ah-taw v'ahd o-lawm. Bi-r'shoos mish-pahch-tee, n'vaw-raych sheh-aw-chahl-noo mi-sheh-lo.

Family: בָּרוּךְ שֶׁאָכַלְנוּ מִשֶּׁלּוֹ וּבְטוּבוֹ חָיִינוּ:

Baw-rooch sheh-aw-chahl-noo mi-sheh-lo,   oo-v'too-vo
chaw-yee-noo.

Father: בָּרוּךְ שֶׁאָכַלְנוּ מִשֶּׁלּוֹ וּבְטוּבוֹ חָיִינוּ:

Baw-rooch sheh-aw-chahl-noo mi-sheh-lo,   oo-v'too-vo
chaw-yee-noo.

Father: Let us join in thanking God, of whose bounty we have
partaken.

Family: Blessed be our God, of whose bounty we have partaken
and through whose goodness we live.

Family:

בָּרוּךְ הוּא וּבָרוּךְ שְׁמוֹ.

בָּרוּךְ אַתָּה יְיָ, אֱלֹהֵינוּ מֶלֶךְ הָעוֹלָם, הַזָּן אֶת הָעוֹלָם כֻּלּוֹ בְּטוּבוֹ,
בְּחֵן בְּחֶסֶד וּבְרַחֲמִים. הוּא נֹתֵן לֶחֶם לְכָל בָּשָׂר, כִּי לְעוֹלָם חַסְדּוֹ.
וּבְטוּבוֹ הַגָּדוֹל תָּמִיד לֹא חָסַר לָנוּ, וְאַל יֶחְסַר לָנוּ מָזוֹן לְעוֹלָם וָעֶד.
בַּעֲבוּר שְׁמוֹ הַגָּדוֹל, כִּי הוּא אֵל זָן וּמְפַרְנֵס לַכֹּל, וּמֵטִיב לַכֹּל, וּמֵכִין
מָזוֹן לְכָל בְּרִיּוֹתָיו אֲשֶׁר בָּרָא.
בָּרוּךְ אַתָּה יְיָ, הַזָּן אֶת הַכֹּל:

Baw-rooch hoo oo-vaw-rooch sh'mo.

Baw-rooch ah-taw Ado-noy, Elo-hay-noo meh-lech haw-o-
lawm, ha-zawn ehs haw-o-lawm koo-lo b'too-vo, b'chayn b'cheh-
sed oo-v'ra-chah-meem, Hoo no-sayn leh-chem l'chawl baw-sawr,

kee l'o-lawm chahs-do. Oo-v'too-vo ha-gaw-dol taw-meed lo chaw-sahr law-noo, v'ahl yech-sahr law-noo maw-zon l'o-lawm vaw-ed. Bah-ah-voor sh'mo ha-gaw-dol, kee hoo Ayl zawn oo-m'fahr-nays la-kol, oo-may-teev la-kol, oo-may-cheen maw-zon l'chawl b'ree-yo-sawv ah-shehr baw-raw.

Baw-rooch ah-taw Ado-noy, ha-zawn ehs ha-kol.

Father:

Blessed art Thou, O Lord our God, King of the universe, who providest food for all. Through Thy goodness food has never failed us. Mayest Thou provide sustenance for all Thy children at all times for the sake of Thy great Name.

Family:

We thank Thee, O Lord our God, for our liberation from bondage, for the heritage of Eretz Yisroel, for Thy Torah which Thou didst reveal and impart unto us, and for the life of grace and blessing which Thou hast bestowed upon us.

וְעַל הַכֹּל, יְיָ אֱלֹהֵינוּ, אֲנַחְנוּ מוֹדִים לָךְ, וּמְבָרְכִים אוֹתָךְ, יִתְבָּרַךְ שִׁמְךָ בְּפִי כָּל חַי תָּמִיד לְעוֹלָם וָעֶד: כַּכָּתוּב, וְאָכַלְתָּ וְשָׂבָעְתָּ וּבֵרַכְתָּ אֶת יְיָ אֱלֹהֶיךָ, עַל הָאָרֶץ הַטּוֹבָה אֲשֶׁר נָתַן לָךְ.

בָּרוּךְ אַתָּה יְיָ, עַל הָאָרֶץ וְעַל הַמָּזוֹן:

V'ahl ha-kol, Ado-noy Elo-hay-noo, ah-nahch-noo mo-deem lawch, oo-m'vawr-cheem o-sawch, yis-baw-rahch shi-m'chaw b'fee kawl chai taw-meed l'o-lawm vaw-ed. Ka-kaw-soov, v'aw-chahl-taw, v'saw-vaw-taw oo-vay-rahch-taw, ehs Ado-noy Elo-heh-chaw, ahl haw-aw-retz ha-to-vaw ah-shehr naw-sahn lawch.

Baw-rooch ah-taw Ado-noy, ahl haw-aw-retz v'ahl ha-maw-zon.

Father:

Have mercy, O Lord our God, upon Israel, Thy people, and upon Zion, and hasten the day of peace for all mankind.

וּבְנֵה יְרוּשָׁלַיִם עִיר הַקֹּדֶשׁ בִּמְהֵרָה בְיָמֵינוּ. בָּרוּךְ אַתָּה יְיָ, בֹּנֵה בְרַחֲמָיו יְרוּשָׁלָיִם. אָמֵן:

Oo-v'nay Y'roo-shaw-la-yeem, eer ha-ko-desh, bi-m'hay-raw v'yaw-may-noo. Baw-rooch ah-taw Ado-noy, bo-neh b'ra-cha-mawv Y'roo-shaw-law-yeem. Aw-mayn.

בָּרוּךְ אַתָּה יְיָ, אֱלֹהֵינוּ מֶלֶךְ הָעוֹלָם, הָאֵל, אָבִינוּ, מַלְכֵּנוּ, אַדִּירֵנוּ, בּוֹרְאֵנוּ, גּוֹאֲלֵנוּ, יוֹצְרֵנוּ, קְדוֹשֵׁנוּ, קְדוֹשׁ יַעֲקֹב, רוֹעֵנוּ, רוֹעֵה יִשְׂרָאֵל, הַמֶּלֶךְ הַטּוֹב וְהַמֵּטִיב לַכֹּל, שֶׁבְּכָל יוֹם וָיוֹם הוּא הֵטִיב, הוּא מֵטִיב, הוּא יֵיטִיב לָנוּ. הוּא גְמָלָנוּ, הוּא גוֹמְלֵנוּ, הוּא יִגְמְלֵנוּ לָעַד, לְחֵן וּלְחֶסֶד וּלְרַחֲמִים וּלְרֶוַח, הַצָּלָה וְהַצְלָחָה, בְּרָכָה וִישׁוּעָה, נֶחָמָה, פַּרְנָסָה וְכַלְכָּלָה, וְרַחֲמִים וְחַיִּים וְשָׁלוֹם, וְכָל טוֹב, וּמִכָּל טוֹב לְעוֹלָם אַל יְחַסְּרֵנוּ:

Baw-rooch ah-taw Ado-noy, Elo-hay-noo meh-lech haw-o-lawm, haw-ayl, aw-vee-noo, mahl-kay-noo, adee-ray-noo, bo-r'ay-noo, go-ah-lay-noo, yo-tz'ray-noo, k'do-shay-noo, k'dosh Yah-ah-kov; ro-ay-noo, ro-ay Yis-raw-ayl, ha-meh-lech ha-tov v'ha-may-teev la-kol, sheh-b'chawl yom vaw-yom, hoo hay-teev, hoo may-teev, hoo yay-teev law-noo; hoo g'maw-law-noo, hoo go-m'lay-noo, hoo yig-m'lay-noo law-ahd, l'chayn oo-l'cheh-sed oo-l'ra-chah-meem oo-l'reh-vahch, ha-tzaw-law v'hahtz-law-chaw, b'raw-chaw vee-shoo-aw, neh-chaw-maw, pahr-naw-saw v'chahl-kaw-law, v'ra-cha-meem v'chah-yeem v'shaw-lom, v'chawl tov, oo-mi-kawl tov l'o-lawm ahl y'chah-s'ray-noo.

Family:

Blessed art Thou, O Lord our God, King of the universe. Thou art our God who showerest kindnesses upon all Thy creatures. Every day dost Thou grant unto us the blessings of Thy hand. Thou art kind and dost deal kindly with us. Thou hast bestowed upon us Thy blessings, yielding us lovingkindness, grace, sustenance and support, mercy, life and peace. We pray Thee, withhold not Thy blessings from us.

Father: May God sustain us in health.

Family: Amen.

Father: May God bless all assembled at this table.

Family: Amen.

Father: May God send plentiful blessings upon this house, and all who are near and dear to us.

Family: Amen.

(On the Sabbath)

Father: הָרַחֲמָן, הוּא יַנְחִילֵנוּ יוֹם שֶׁכֻּלוֹ שַׁבָּת וּמְנוּחָה לְחַיֵּי הָעוֹלָמִים:

Family: אָמֵן: — Amen

Father: May this Sabbath eve bring its message of rest and peace to us.

Family: Amen.

Father: הָרַחֲמָן, הוּא יְחַדֵּשׁ עָלֵינוּ אֶת הַשָּׁנָה הַזֹּאת לְטוֹבָה וְלִבְרָכָה:

Family: אָמֵן: — Amen

Father: May the New Year bring us life, health, and happiness.

Family: Amen.

Family:

מִגְדוֹל יְשׁוּעוֹת מַלְכּוֹ, וְעֹשֶׂה חֶסֶד לִמְשִׁיחוֹ, לְדָוִד וּלְזַרְעוֹ עַד עוֹלָם.
עֹשֶׂה שָׁלוֹם בִּמְרוֹמָיו, הוּא יַעֲשֶׂה שָׁלוֹם עָלֵינוּ וְעַל כָּל יִשְׂרָאֵל,
וְאִמְרוּ, אָמֵן:

Mig-dol y'shoo-os mahl-ko, v'o-seh cheh-sed li-m'shee-cho,
l'Daw-vid oo-l'zahr-o ahd o-lawm. O-seh shaw-lom bi-m'ro-mawv,
hoo yah-ah-seh shaw-lom, aw-lay-noo v'ahl kawl Yis-raw-ayl
v'i-m'roo, aw-mayn.

May He who creates peace in His celestial heights, grant us
peace and contentment this coming year. Amen.

HOW K'TONTON DROVE SATAN
OUT OF THE SHOFAR*

By Sadie Rose Weilerstein

K'tonton was talking to Sammy, the sexton's boy. He often talked to Sammy in the synagogue between the afternoon and evening prayers. Sammy would sprawl on a bench and K'tonton would sit on a reading stand looking down at him.

"So you'd better watch out, K'tonton," Sammy was saying. "If you commit the tiniest little sin, Satan will pick it up and carry it straight to God. He watches especially near Rosh Hashanah."

K'tonton glanced toward the shadows gathering in the corner. "But, Sammy," he said, "how do you know?"

"How do I know? My father told me, that's how I know."

"Oh!" said K'tonton. If Sammy's father had told him, there was nothing more to say. Wasn't it Sammy's father who blew the shofar, the ram's horn, on Rosh Hashanah?

Sammy had once told him about the shofar. "Do you know why you blow the shofar so loud, K'tonton?" he had asked. "To confound Satan! There is Satan before God's throne telling all the sins of Israel. All of a sudden there comes a great sound. T'kee-aw-aw, T'ruaw-aw, T'kee-aw-aw!" Sammy imitated the notes exactly. "Satan is so upset he forgets everything he was going to say and begins to stutter. So what does Satan do next time? He goes down to earth and tries to crawl inside the shofar to stop the sound."

"Did he ever really stop it?" asked K'tonton.

"I don't remember," said Sammy, "but he might. If it weren't for Satan, we would be in Eretz Yisroel already. The Messiah would have come long ago."

K'tonton thought about what Sammy had said as he lay awake

---

* The character K'tonton is best described as a little imp, a Jewish Tom Thumb.

in the dark that night. He thought of it the first thing he openeᴅ his eyes in the morning.

"Mother," he said, "could Satan get inside a shofar?"

"Stop troubling your little head about Satan," said his mother, "and come and try on your new suit."

K'tonton went to his father.

"Father," he said, "do you suppose that Satan could get inside our shofar?"

Father was reading his paper.

"He has gotten into too many shofars already," he answered without looking up.

All that day K'tonton went about worrying whether Satan could get into the shofar. After that he forgot all about him. There were too many pleasant things to do. New Year's greetings to write out, rosy apples to shine, the big round challahs to sniff as they came out of the oven. And then it was Rosh Hashanah night. K'tonton got into his brand new suit and hat and shoes, to "renew the year" you know. He went to synagogue and wished everyone L'Shawnaw Tovaw, Happy New Year! He sat at the table before mother's shining candles and dipped apple in honey for a sweet year.

It was not until the next morning in the synagogue when the shofar was blown that K'tonton remembered Satan again. Then he gave him no more than a thought. He was too busy counting the blasts. Father had said there would be one hundred shofar blasts and K'tonton was counting to see whether he was right.

"T'kee-aw-aw, sh'vaw-reem t'ruaw, t'-kee-aw!" called the rabbi.

"T'kee-aw-aw, t-t-t-t-t-t-too, t'kee-aw-aw!" answered the shofar, now clear and ringing, now broken like a sigh, now bold and clear again.

All morning K'tonton counted the notes carefully on his fingers; thirty after the reading of the Torah, ten and ten and ten again during the additional prayers, more of them toward the end of the service. "Seventy, eighty, ninety," counted K'tonton; and then, "ninety-five, ninety-six, ninety-seven, ninety-eight, ninety-nine."

It was time for the final note, the great triumphant blast, the Tekiah Gedolah. K'tonton sat up tense and waiting. But no sound came — nothing but a muffled "pf, pf, pf." Sammy's father shifted the shofar sidewise to his lips. He blew again. He puffed and panted. His face grew red with the exertion. All that came was a broken, stuttering t-t-t-t-t.

A buzzing and whispering rose in the synagogue. People leaned over the benches and whispered to one another. Someone behind K'tonton was speaking quite loudly.

"Satan has gotten into the shofar!"

Satan! Satan in the shofar! Sammy had said he sometimes got inside, but K'tonton had not thought he would really do it, not in their shofar at least! Suppose he stayed there! Suppose he stayed the whole Rosh Hashanah. Suppose they couldn't blow the shofar at all! How would the people be forgiven? How could they be written down for a good year?

Suddenly a thought came into K'tonton's head. It grew and grew until it was so big it filled his whole mind. *He, K'tonton, would get inside that shofar and drive Satan out.*

K'tonton hardly knew what was happening during the rest of the service. His mind was so busy with his plans. Services were over at last. Father folded his prayer shawl and carried it to the little back room. On a table near a pile of prayer books lay the ram's horn. K'tonton slipped from his father's arm and hid. Father walked out of the synagogue, not even noticing that K'tonton had been left behind.

The last footsteps passed. Voices died away. K'tonton was alone.

Cautiously he crept from behind the prayer books and approached the shofar.

He stooped and peered into its deep mouth. Somewhere among those shadows Satan was lurking — Satan the adversary, the enemy. Who was he, K'tonton, to fight the dread angel? He trembled, but he did not turn back. Firmly he stepped into the mouth of the shofar and groped his way. The darkness grew; the walls drew closer. He stopped and stretched out his hand. He could scarcely see it in the blackness. Suddenly something clutched his arm. He felt his shoulders held fast. The enemy!

"Shema Yisroel!" K'tonton called, wrenching himself free. He stepped back. He struck out against the enemy. He gave blow upon blow fiercely without stopping.

"Kra Soton! Rend Satan!" he cried.

Steps were approaching in the room outside. A voice spoke. "Sammy," it said, "I'd better try the shofar and see what's wrong."

The shofar was lifted.

But K'tonton inside the shofar was so absorbed in the struggle he neither heard nor felt. He knew nothing until suddenly through the narrow end of the horn came a blast like a whirlwind. It lifted K'tonton up. It shot him out of the shofar, across the room, out through the open window. He landed on something soft. It was his father's shoulder.

"K'tonton," said his father, "what have you been up to? I've been all the way home and back." K'tonton smiled and shut his mouth tight.

*   *   *

Next morning at services the shofar rang out so clear and bold, everyone remarked about the difference. Anxiously K'tonton listened to each blast, lest some sign of Satan appear. But no! Each note came clearer than the one before. At the end, the Tekiah Gedolah rang out so loud and held so long, the people gasped with wonder.

"K'tonton," said Sammy after the services, as K'tonton sat waiting for his father, "do you remember what I told you about Satan getting into the shofar? Yesterday I saw him. I was in the back room with my father. He shot out of the shofar like a rocket. I saw him with my own eyes."

K'tonton nodded and smiled. He didn't tell Sammy who it was who had driven Satan out of the shofar.

THE LOPSIDED CHALLAH WITH
THE CROOKED CROWN

By Lillian S. Freehof

Gloria and her mother had been baking bread, and now five round Challahs stood in a row on the kitchen table waiting to go into the oven.

They were baking these Challahs for Rosh Hashanah, the New Year. And on the New Year all the bread was made into round loaves, to wish everybody a happy new year, with good luck rolling into everyone's life.

The dough, because it had yeast in it, had been rising all the day before. And now Gloria and her mother finished shaping each round loaf, making them as round as circles. And on the top of each one they added a little crown made out of braided dough. There were five of these Challahs, one for each of Gloria's and Allen's relatives, and one for themselves.

Now the oven was hot and ready for the bread and all the Challahs were glad of it, especially the Middle Loaf. He was feeling cold because Mother had just finishing brushing him all over with the beaten yoke of egg. Now Mother opened the door of the stove and into the oven went all of the Challahs.

"Ah," said the Middle Challah. "This is fine. I feel warmer already. Hey there, folks," he said to the other Challahs. "You're crowding me. A little more room there, please."

The second Challah said, "I can't help crowding. I'm getting fatter."

The other Challahs paid no attention to him. In the good comfortable heat of the stove, they were getting bigger and rounder and higher.

"I'm in the middle," the Middle Challah said. "And you're all squashing me. Watch out there. You're pushing me out of shape."

And indeed, that's just what was happening. The stove was large, but not quite large enough for five Challahs to grow in. So the poor middle one was being squeezed from the right and squeezed from the left. He was being squashed out of shape! His nice roundness was being pushed and shoved, and once more he cried out.

"Please, folks. Less shoving, there. Oh, look what you're doing to me. You're squashing me from round to square! Help, help!"

"He doesn't like the shape he's in." The First Challah laughed.

"Don't bother me," the Third Challah said. "I'm busy puffing up."

"And I'm busy changing color," the fourth Challah said.

"Quiet, please," the Second Challah said. "Let us get baked through and through so we'll be delicious to eat on the New Year."

"That's just the trouble," wailed the Middle Challah. "I'll never be in shape for a New Year Challah, if you don't give me more room. A New Year Challah is supposed to be round, and I'm being pushed square. Oh, what will happen to me?"

The other Challahs, busy baking, did not answer him. So he tried to help himself. He pushed to the right, he shoved to the left, but he couldn't budge an inch. Instead, he felt himself growing narrower and taller.

"Oh," he wailed. "Look at my crown. It's getting all crooked."

"Yes, it's way over to one side of your head," the Second Challah said, smiling to himself because *his* crown was on most securely.

The oven was getting hotter and hotter and all the Challahs could feel their dough drying up and baking into bread. They were changing from pasty white to a rich, golden brown, and so they were very happy.

All except the Middle Challah. Oh, he was baking all right, and he was becoming the right color. But look at his shape! Now he was long and narrow and tall, instead of round.

"Oh, this is the worst thing that could have happened to me," sobbed the Middle Challah. "I started out in life to be a round Challah for the New Year. Now who would use me for Rosh Hashanah? No one, I'm just a square, just a lopsided Challah."

"Don't worry," said the Third Challah kindly. "The family can use you for a Sabbath Challah."

"Oh, it's nice being a Sabbath Challah, of course," whimpered the Middle Challah. "But I had my heart set on being a New Year Challah. This is the saddest day of my life."

The other Challahs felt sorry for him, but they just kept on steaming and puffing, and baking and browning. To himself, the Lopsided Challah grieved and grieved as he baked and browned and got in the wrong shape.

Soon Mother began taking the Challahs out of the stove and placing them on the kitchen table. One by one the four round Challahs came out, glad now of the cool air, feeling their crowns nice and tight on their heads. Then out came the Lopsided Challah, so embarrassed to be square instead of round, he half-hid his crown from sight.

"Oh, Mommie," Gloria cried. "Look what happened to this poor Challah. It isn't round! It's lopsided! And its crown is all crooked."

"Isn't that too bad," Mother said. "Put it to one side, dear."

And then the Lopsided Challah was really unhappy. Exactly what he feared, was happening. The family didn't want any Lopsided Challah for their New Year and he was being pushed aside. He didn't weep any tears, it was too late for that. What was done, was done. But he *was* glum. And he sat way over in the corner watching Gloria and her mother wrap each one of the round Challahs first in shiny wax paper, then in white napkins.

Allen came running in from school, and Mother said, "Now the Challahs are ready, children. You and Daddy may deliver them."

Daddy came in and picked up two of the round Challahs, Allen picked up one, and Gloria the fourth, and they all went out of the kitchen. Mother turned off the light and the Lopsided Challah with the Crooked Crown was left all alone in the dark.

Daddy took the four round Challahs wrapped in the snowy white napkins and piled them into the back seat of the car. Then he and Gloria and Allen got into the front seat, and they drove away.

First they went to Grannie's and Grandad's, then to Teresa's, and then to Jerry's and Lorrie's, and last to David's, and at each house they left one of the round Challahs.

Back home in Gloria's and Allen's house, the poor forgotten Lopsided Challah sat on the corner of the table, sighing very deep sighs. Mother was in the dining-room, setting the table for the New Year dinner. He tried to call to her but, of course, no one had ever heard a loaf of bread talk, so Mother didn't hear him. But he kept on begging, "Please use me for Rosh Hashanah. You made me for the New Year. Use me. Please use me."

But Mother was putting forks and knives and spoons on the table, and didn't hear. Suddenly, Gloria and Allen and their Daddy rushed into the house.

"Mommie, Mommie," Gloria cried. "We had the lovliest time. Daddy and Allen and I took all the four round loaves to Grannie and Grandad and Teresa . . ."

". . . and Jerry and Lorrie and David," Allen said. "And everybody was glad to have a nice round Challah for the New Year."

"Thank you for delivering the Challahs," Mother said.

"Oh, may I help set the table?" begged Gloria.

"Yes, dear. Go into the kitchen and get the jar of honey, please."

Gloria ran into the kitchen and turned on the light. And the Lopsided Challah yelled in its doughy voice,

"Gloria! Gloria! Don't forget me!"

No one knows if she heard the Challah but she called out.

"Oh, Mommie. What will we do with this poor Lopsided Challah? It's pushed all out of shape."

Her mother called back to her, "We'll decide about that later, dear. Just bring the jar of honey now."

"Not later," gurgled the Lopsided Challah. "Decide now."

But the little girl picked up the jar of honey and ran into the dining-room. And the Lopsided Challah sank back on the table, and sighed.

Gloria and her mother set the table with a white cloth and beautiful cream-colored plates, and the silverware and clear crystal glasses. In front of Daddy's place, they put the beautiful silver cup for the wine. And then in the center of the table Mother placed white candles in silver candlesticks and a bowl of white flowers.

"The table looks just beautiful!" Gloria said, clapping her hands. "Everything is so perfect. The silver is polished. And the flowers are just so pretty. And the apples and the honey are ready. But Mommie, we haven't got a Challah. What will we do without a round Challah?"

"All we have is this lopsided loaf," Mother said. "After all the work we did to bake those loaves, now we have none left for ourselves. I feel as sad as you do, Gloria."

"Maybe," said Gloria, "maybe we should ask Grannie to give hers back to us."

"Oh Gloria," Allen said. "How can you do that? Once you give a gift, you *never* take it back."

"I'm sorry," Gloria said. "I guess it wouldn't be nice to take it back from Grannie. But Mommie, what will we do?"

The Lopsided Challah on the kitchen table yelled, "Use me, please! I bet I taste delicious. Please use me."

But no one heard its yells. They all came into the kitchen, and Mother said, "I guess maybe we'll have to ask Daddy to drive to the bakery and buy a round Challah."

"Oh, poor Challah." Gloria was looking at the Lopsided Challah with the Crooked Crown. "I feel sorry for this poor Challah, Mommie. We made it round for the New Year. And you know, Mommie, I just bet this poor Challah feels very sad because we're not going to use it for Rosh Hashanah."

"Don't be silly," Allen said. "I don't think a Challah thinks thoughts. I don't think a Challah has feelings."

"I don't agree with you, Allen," Gloria said. "Just because you're older, you always think you know all the answers. But I know better than you this time. I think this Challah does have thoughts and I think it does have feelings, and I think it must be feeling very sad."

She put her little hand on the Crooked Crown of the Lopsided Challah and said, "Listen, Mommie, don't send Daddy to the bakery. Let's use this Lopsided Challah. We made it *round* and it isn't the Challah's fault if it came out lopsided. So let's use it."

"Yes, yes," shouted the Challah, "use me! Once I was round, and I'll taste just as good. Please use me."

"I guess Gloria is right, Mom," Allen said. "Let's use this Lopsided Challah with its Crooked Crown."

"All right," Mother said. "I'm willing."

"Oh, thank heavens," sighed the Lopsided Challah. "Thank the Lord. Now I'm going to be used for Rosh Hashanah. Now the father will make the New Year blessing over me. I promise to taste as good as I possibly can."

The mother put the Lopsided Challah with the Crooked Crown on a silver breadplate, and covered it with a white satin Challah cover. And Gloria carried it into the dining-room.

And now it was a happy Challah. It was a proud Challah and held itself as straight as it could, even if its crown was crooked.

The family was ready to begin its New Year meal. After the mother lighted the candles, the father recited the blessing for the apple and the honey and gave Allen and Gloria each a piece of the apple dipped in honey, then a piece to Mother, then one for himself, and said —

"I hope we'll all have a sweet year."

Then he made a blessing over the wine, and they each took a little sip.

Mother took off the white satin Challah cover, folded it up, and the Lopsided Challah with the Crooked Crown knew that his great moment had come. His coat was shiny and brown and crisp. And he sat square in the center of the silver plate, a Challah for the New Year.

Daddy made the blessing over the bread, and when he finished by saying,

"Blessed art Thou, O Lord, Who bringest forth bread from the earth," the Lopsided Challah with the Crooked Crown yelled with all his might,

"Amen! And may good luck roll around to each one of you. Happy New Year! Happy New Year!"

FOR A GOOD AND SWEET YEAR

By SADIE ROSE WEILERSTEIN

Bees, bees,
Give us your honey!
Give us your honey, please.
We have special round bread,
Apples too, round and red,
That came from orchard trees.
We'll eat them with honey,
All golden and sunny,
When Rosh Hashanah is here;
Honey, apples, and bread,
When the blessing is said,
For a good and a sweet New Year.

Yom Kippur

YOM KIPPUR

With feelings solemn and sincere
We know Atonement Day is here.
One prayer fills every heart and soul
To make amends; our hope, our goal

We humbly heed Kol Nidre's chant,
Our deepest plea: forgiveness grant
For selfishness, for love withheld,
We search our souls, our wrongs
    beheld.

Our humble plea to God ascends,
We're sorry, and we'll make amends
And as we fast and chant and pray,
We strive to make a better day.

Yom Kippur

Having celebrated Rosh Hashanah in any or all the ways suggested, attending services with the family, listening to the blasts of the shofar, dipping apples into honey, welcoming the holiday with wine and honey cake at Kiddush, wishing all the year's best, you have begun the New Year aright. You have opened the door to rich home experiences in a kind of glow which can carry you and your family through a glorious year of sustained Jewish living.

And riding the crest of Rosh Hashanah in the high tide of spiritual elation, we are transported to the more serious and the more contemplative day of the season, Yom Kippur, the Day of Atonement. It falls on the tenth day of the month Tishri to mark the end of the period known as the Ten Days of Repentance, Asehrehs Y'may T'shoo-vaw.

This Sabbath of Sabbaths, as it is called in the Bible, is best explained and understood by the locale of its observance. Yom Kippur is not a home festival; it is a synagogue day. At the same time we can help our children sense its meaning and spirit through home preparations for its arrival, as well as in our synagogue attendance, where we and our fellow Jews fast and pray, and express the feelings of our hearts and the thoughts of our minds on this holiest day in the Jewish calendar.

And it *is* the holiest day because the thoughts are distinctive, different, with an aura of nobility about them. The thoughts come from the majestic themes of the service: penitence, sincerity of heart and purpose, reconciliation, and harmony. Underlying these themes is the basic idea of forgiveness. On Yom Kippur, we ask forgiveness of God and men for wrongs we may have committed.

Of the two, we are first to ask forgiveness from our fellowmen before we can with full hearts approach God in prayer.

Yom Kippur is the annual Jewish opportunity to erase any ill feeling we may be harboring against others. To say, "I'm sorry," or "Let's forget it," and at the same time affirm our faith in God and rededicate ourselves to Him and to His people, is the quintessence of Atonement. We thus rearm ourselves on this Great White Day with spiritual strength and sustenance as we offer our prayers that we be sealed in the Book of Life.

THE SYNAGOGUE SERVICE

The solemn day begins with the beautiful Torah pageant. As dusk shadows the day, all the Torahs (Scrolls), adorned in all their glory, the white velvet mantles, the sparkling silver crowns, breastplates, and pointers, are withdrawn from the Ark, and the more pious of the congregation are given the honor of holding them ahigh. With the Torahs in hand, the cantor, surrounded by this aura of white, begins chanting the most stirring melody in the Jewish liturgy, Kol Nidre. The melody of Kol Nidre is infinitely more captivating than the contents of the paragraph being sung. Through the text the worshiper prays that he be absolved from promises and vows made to God. The music is sublime. In it one can sense the entire history of the Jew, his varied experiences, good and bad, the changing and contrasting moods of the plaintive song, the progress from the minor key of sorrow and complaint into the more resolute note of faith and hope. The drama of the Jew is relived in the chant; the congregants become more intimately attached to God and holiness.

The eve of Yom Kippur has assumed the name Kol Nidre night, the first of five services conducted on the Day of Atonement, one more than on any other festival. The others are:

Shahcharis, (Morning), Musaf, (Additional), Minchah, (Afternoon), and Neilah, (Closing). In all except the last, Neilah, a series of confessional prayers are offered by the congregants. These prayers for forgiveness, it should be noted, all appear in plural form, not singular, to teach us an important Jewish principle. As Jews and as human beings we are responsible not alone for our own actions, but also for those of our fellows. When we admit these wrongs we are, in effect, asking forgiveness for all who have deviated from the paths of goodness and righteousness.

Memorial services called Yizkor, which means "May God remember the souls of our departed," are recited on Yom Kippur as on every religious holiday. During the afternoon service the book of Jonah is chanted, revealing its message of the omnipresence of God.

The day-long period of prayer is brought to a close by Neilah. We do not know whether the term refers to the closing of the gates of the Temple of old, to the allegorical closing of the gates of heaven to prayer, or the idea of the closing service itself. In any case, Neilah is introduced by a chant which differs from previous melodies of the day. This is a more assured and confident one because of the feeling of assurance that the prayers have been answered and that the year ahead looks good. There is a significant change in one word of the service. That word is "sealed" or "seal," which replaces "inscribed" or "inscribe." On Rosh Hashanah we recite prayers asking God to *inscribe* us in the Book of Life, and now with Yom Kippur drawing to a close, we pray that the inscriptions be finalized by the seal of God in the Sefer Hachayyim, the Book of Life.

Some twenty five hours after Kol Nidre was chanted there is a long, uninterrupted shofar blast (Tekiah Gedolah), proclaiming the end of the solemn day.

IN THE HOME

We know that Yom Kippur is primarily a synagogue day. But for our children's understanding we should create a spirit of solemnity at home by talking, on their level of comprehension, about the ideas of right and wrong, about forgiveness, being able to say "I am sorry" or "Please forgive me." You can read the story about Yom Kippur here included, which presents the theme of apologizing for not having done the right thing. You may also describe parts of the Yom Kippur service which they would appreciate, the importance of Kol Nidre, and the significance of having one day set aside for setting ourselves straight with the world.

The Family before Kol Nidre

A fine Jewish tradition tells us that it is as much a positive duty (Mitzvah) to eat a good meal on the eve of Kol Nidre as it is to abstain from food on Yom Kippur itself. A family dinner is therefore customary before going to services. Honey and apples are again served as on Rosh Hashanah. The dinner should be made as festive as possible and with full holiday regalia. Dinner is begun with the Hamotzee prayer and Grace follows the meal. (See page 18.)

When the meal is over the family should ready itself for services because Kol Nidre generally begins before sundown. This is true in Orthodox and Conservative synagogues. In the Reform temple the service usually begins at a later hour.

Be sure to have your children attend and hear the Kol Nidre services. Your community may have arranged children's services for them. Yom Kippur is one family synagogue day retentive of spiritual value for the entire year. To see the magnificent pageant in the synagogue, to share in its spirit, is so very important for our youngsters, who find themselves part of a great stream of people, a collective unity praying together. They feel that they and their loved ones are part of the larger family of families.

Before leaving for the synagogue, Mother takes the children about her and recites the blessings over the candles:

בָּרוּךְ אַתָּה יְיָ, אֱלֹהֵינוּ מֶלֶךְ הָעוֹלָם, אֲשֶׁר קִדְּשָׁנוּ בְּמִצְוֹתָיו וְצִוָּנוּ

לְהַדְלִיק נֵר שֶׁל (On Sabbath add) שַׁבָּת וְ) יוֹם הַכִּפּוּרִים:

בָּרוּךְ אַתָּה יְיָ, אֱלֹהֵינוּ מֶלֶךְ הָעוֹלָם, שֶׁהֶחֱיָנוּ, וְקִיְּמָנוּ, וְהִגִּיעָנוּ

לַזְּמַן הַזֶּה:

Baw-rooch ah-taw Ado-noy, Elo-hay-noo meh-lech haw-o-awm, ah-shehr ki-d'shaw-noo b'mitz-vo-sawv, v'tzi-vaw-noo, 'hahd-leek nayr shel (*On Sabbath add:* Sha-baws v') yom ha-ki-poo-'eem.

Baw-rooch ah-taw Ado-noy, Elo-hay-noo meh-lech haw-o-awm, sheh-heh-cheh-yaw-noo, v'kee-y'maw-noo, v'hi-gee-aw-noo, a-z'mahn ha-zeh.

Blessed art Thou, O Lord our God, King of the universe, who hast sanctified us by Thy commandments and granted us the privilege of kindling the lights of (Sabbath and of) Yom Kippur.

Blessed art Thou, O Lord our God, King of the universe, who hast granted us life, sustained us, and brought us to this festive season.

We pray Thee, O God, as this solemn day approaches, remember us unto life, seal us in the Book of Life, and bless our family and all our dear ones with health, happiness, peace, and contentment. Amen.

After blessing the candles, the family should make an offering to charity. In the older synagogues, when one went to the afternoon (Minchah) service, plates (Kaarohs) were set in the vestibule with the names of various charitable institutions. The worshiper would make contributions to these charities. Some families contribute the sum of $.18 or $.36 on behalf of children. In Hebrew, which has numerical values for all the letters, the equivalent for the English word "life" is "chai — חַי." "Chai" is composed of two Hebrew letters; the first is "ches — ח" or 8 in numerical value, and the other is "yod — י" which is 10. Thus, the two equal 18 or "chai." To contribute 36 is to offer twice the hope for life. The principle applies to all coins: cents, nickles, dimes, etc.

A beautiful old tradition suggests that father bless the children on Yom Kippur eve. The blessing is on page 324.

As your children are with you at the onset of the holiest day of the year and during the day itself, they should also be at your side when sundown approaches, and the congregation awaits the final sound of the shofar, heralding the conclusion of Yom Kippur.

And then back home again. The break-the-fast dinner should become a satisfying family experience, reliving some of the feelings of the day, discussing the occurrences during the services, the rabbi's sermons, the cantor's singing, and the stories heard at the children's services. All these will indelibly impress our minds and gratify us that the family as a unit has observed the Great White Day.

THE MOST PRECIOUS THING*

A Yom Kippur Fantasy

I've never seen an angel. I've never even heard one speak. But I've heard stories about the angels and some of them are very beautiful. . . .

It seems that once (I don't even know if it was very, very long ago or just long ago) a young little angel did something it shouldn't have done. I suppose it's possible for an *angel* to do something it shouldn't have done — at least, according to this story. . .

And just as with us humans, the Lord decided that He must punish the little angel for doing wrong. And what was the punishment? It was assigned a task — to come down to earth (that's some punishment in itself, in a way) and stay here until it found the most precious thing in the world! Once the angel found it, it was to bring it back to the Lord. Only then could it stay in Heaven with all the other angels.

Now, when the poor little angel heard the sentence of the Lord, it sighed a long, deep sigh.

"Oh, my! Oh, my!" it thought. "How shall I ever know what the most precious thing in the world is? And if I don't know what it is, how shall I ever find it?"

The poor little angel was indeed greatly troubled. But there was nothing it could do. The word of the Lord was Law — and that was that!

And so it was that one sunny morning, a worried little angel appeared on earth — although no one could really see it. The angel looked around and gazed wonderingly at this strange world of ours. It took quite a time for our little angel to get accustomed to its surroundings. But once it did, it set out to perform its task. "I wouldn't want to spend too much time here," it said to itself.

---

* Reprinted by permission of Barton's Candy Corporation, New York City.

The little angel wandered for many days — through fields and woods, through villages and large cities. And the angel learned many things in a very short time. (It found out, for example, that gold and silver and diamonds weren't very precious after all. Wise men, the angel saw, didn't waste much time seeking such things. Power, too, the angel learned, wasn't especially precious — for it never lasted long and was usually lost through much violence.) The angel learned and learned. But still could not find something that was really precious. Until one day. . .

It was on a battlefield. Thousands of soldiers stood facing each other, deadly weapons in their hands and murderous hate in their eyes. Suddenly, there was an attack! The soldiers that were invading the country swarmed in great numbers towards the soldiers that were defending their homeland. For a while it seemed that the invaders would be victorious. Nothing could stop them.

But in a moment, everything was changed. The attack stopped, the invaders were driven off. When all was quiet again, the angel looked for the cause of this sudden reversal. And there, in a narrow pass, it saw the fallen body of a soldier who had thrown himself against the invaders and valiantly saved the day. The brave soldier lay there dying, having given his life for the defense of his country. Quickly, the angel rushed to the side of the dying man and scooped up his last drop of blood. Surely, this must be the most precious thing in the world — the life-blood of a man who bravely and unselfishly sacrificed himself to save his comrades and his countrymen.

The angel appeared before the Lord.

"Yes, yes, My little angel, this is indeed very valuable, a great and noble thing. But it is not the most precious thing in the world. You must go back, My little angel, and try again."

Sadly, the little angel turned away and came back to earth. How much longer would it be until. . .

But this time, it hardly took any time at all. Almost as soon as it arrived, the angel happened to pass a hospital. Inside, in a bare little room on a narrow bed, lay a young nurse. She, too, was sick.

Investigating, the angel discovered that the nurse had spent a whole year caring for a man who had a dangerous and contagious disease. The man was now cured. But, while curing the man, the nurse had caught his disease herself. After caring for the sick man so lovingly and devotedly, she now was sick from his illness.

The angel now rushed quickly to her side, too, and caught up her last gasp of breath. And again the angel appeared before the Almighty.

"Surely, My Lord, now. . ."

"Yes, yes, My little angel," the Lord interrupted, "you have brought me a very precious thing, much more precious than blood spilled in the heat of battle. But still, it is not the most precious. . ."

The angel knew without any further words from the Lord. It must go back. Back to earth. Back to search. "Will it never end? Will I ever find it?" the angel began to wonder.

Weeks went by. And the weeks turned to months. The little angel had almost given up hope of ever returning to the Heavenly Paradise.

And as it sat in the woods one day, bewailing its sad fate, a black faced villain rode by on a galloping horse. The dust and clatter of the horse and his rider and the mean, fierce look on the villain's face awakened the little angel's interest. This was something to look into.

The little angel quickly followed the galloping pair. Angrily muttering to himself, the villain was unknowingly telling his story to the angel.

He was, it turned out, a poacher, hunting and killing animals in this forest, which was part of the king's estate. But lately, a newly appointed and very efficient forester was guarding the king's animals exceptionally well, foiling the poacher's plans more and more every day. The villain therefore decided to kill the forester and be rid of this meddlesome man, once and for all. As a matter of fact, this very minute he was on his way to the forester's hut to carry out his desperate plan. The angel could only follow, powerless to stop him — for an angel can only perform the mission he was sent for and nothing else.

Soon they arrived at the forester's hut. The poacher dismounted from his panting horse and crept quietly to the single window in the one room cabin. The forester was nowhere to be seen. He would have to wait, thought the poacher, until the forester returned.

But as he stood there watching through the window, he noticed the forester's wife. Tenderly and lovingly she was putting their only child to sleep. With the deep happiness of a mother, she was singing a soft lullaby, gently stroking the baby boy's blond curls. The look on her face said, more clearly than words, that this was her chief joy in this lonely forest.

Suddenly, a thought flashed across the poacher's mind. If I kill the forester, this lonely woman will become a widow — and this poor, innocent little baby will be an orphan! Who will care for them? How can I cause them so much pain and grief? Look what has become of me — a cruel, cold-blooded murderer!

And the poacher was sorry he had ever planned to kill the forester. A tear of repentance trickled down his weather-beaten face, something that probably never happened before.

The little angel didn't waste a moment. Before the tear had a chance to dry, he scooped it up and rushed with it to Heaven.

"My Lord, My Lord," it gasped breathlessly, "I think . . . I have . . . is this . . ."

"Yes, yes, My little angel," the Lord said, smiling, "you have found it. *The Tear of Repentance is truly the most precious thing in the world.*"

And the little angel sighed with happy relief.

A DREAM

By Jessie Sampter

I shall not taste of food today,
  Nor think of food at all,
But all the day I mean to pray —
  Although they say I'm small —
I mean to pray among the crowd,
That ask forgiveness low or loud.

Last night I heard Kol Nidre sung;
  The cantor's voice was deep,
And back and forth the people swung —
  I think I fell asleep;
I dreamed my Mother took my hand
And led me through a desert land.

But on the ground were cookies round,
  As white as milk and sweet;
Enough for all the day I found,
  I seemed to eat and eat.
Then Mother said, "By this 'tis known
Man does not live by bread alone."

"Awake, my pet," my Mother said,
  When all the prayers were through.
"I know the Lord who gives us bread
  Will grant us pardon, too."
I shall not wish to eat today;
My dream will feed me while I pray

FASTING

By SADIE ROSE WEILERSTEIN

I'm hungry when it's breakfast time;
   I'm hungrier at noon;
And when it's time for supper
   I could almost eat the moon.

But next week on Yom Kippur
   I'm going to try to fast
'Til suppertime — or noon time —
   Or at least 'til breakfast's past.

Sukkos

SUKKOS

Gathered fruits and greenery,
Harvested from field and tree,
Beautify our festive roofs
Built for Sukkos, "Feast of Booths."

Temporary dwellings, these,
Symbols of humility.
Reminders of the years of str
And wandering in the wilder

Lulov, esrog, willow sprigs,
Added to the myrtle twigs,
Are blessed in temple every day
Throughout this harvest holiday.

Sukkos

From the solemnity of Yom Kippur day we are quickly transported to the more jubilant festival of Sukkos, which comes but five days later. The seriousness of the year's beginning, welcomed with so much anticipation, gives way to the gaiety of the "festival of rejoicing," one of the names of this festival.

Sukkos, you will learn shortly, is unusually rich in symbolism and in the colorful ceremonials of the autumn season. God, Torah, man, and nature, all revolve around the Sukkah. Learning about this Festival of Booths or Tabernacles will make us realize how intimate a part of nature we are, how grateful we should be therefor.

Sukkos comes exactly two weeks after Rosh Hashanah (15th of Tishri) and is celebrated on the same days of the week. It continues for nine days in the Orthodox and Conservative ritual and for eight in the Reform ritual. The first and last two days, (or the first and last day in Reform), regarded as holidays, are separated by what we call Chol Hamoed, intermediate days.

Like many of our holidays, Sukkos has different names and varied meanings. The Sukkah is the central idea of the season; it means a hut or tabernacle. It is erected immediately after Yom Kippur (as if the builders were seeking for a pleasanter task, a lighter observance) and it is reminiscent of the days when our forefathers, wandering in the wilderness, lived in flimsy structures like these. The Sukkah must be built for a temporary purpose only, teaching the idea of the transitoriness of life and the dependency of man upon God. Elsewhere in our history, our fathers of old resided in these little huts while the harvest was being brought to the granaries.

There are numerous laws, into which we need not go, detailing the place and manner of Sukkah architecture. An entire tractate of the Talmud is devoted thereto. It is important to point out that the Sukkah, embellished with seasonal products of the earth and other adornments, its roof covered with greenery but permitting us to see the stars from within, is the major feature of this autumnal festival.

We know Sukkos, too, as the Feast of Ingathering or Harvest (Chag Haw-aw-seef); for it also celebrates the conclusion of the agricultural season and the time to bring in the harvest for the winter days ahead. Thanksgiving Day, celebrated in November, is Sukkos on American soil. It is the American derivative of our harvest time festival. If you have read the story of the pilgrims, their trials and problems, and the prayer of gratitude they offered God when blessed by His bounty, you will see clearly that Sukkos is the source of Thanksgiving Day, so acknowledged by the leaders of the colony.

The synagogue or the community will erect a Sukkah in a conspicuous place for all to admire. The booth will be handsomely adorned with seasonal decorations, corn stalks, vegetables, flowers, and foliage of varied kinds. To admire the Sukkah from the outside will not suffice. You will want to enter it, see the decorations, and appreciate the many meanings it holds for our people and for us. Kiddush, the blessing over the wine, and a special prayer for the honor of dwelling in the Sukkah, reliving our ancestral experiences, are recited under the green ceiling, on the eve of the holiday as well as during the day.

IN THE SYNAGOGUE

In the morning's service you will witness one of the most fascinating scenes in the Jewish ritual, the Procession of the Lulovim. Here are the components and meanings of the ceremony:

On Sukkos we take four different species of nature's products, and combine them into one unit which we may call the Sukkos bouquet. This consists of a) a citron or *esrog*, a member of the lemon family; b) a palm branch or *lulov*; c) myrtle branches or *hadasim*; and d) willows of the brook or *arovos*. The last two are bound together and to the lulov by a palm branch strip. The group of three is then placed in the right hand, the citron in the left, and a blessing is recited thanking God for the fruit of the earth, or literally for the privilege of holding the lulov.

Many imaginative accounts are found in Jewish legendry which offer symbolic meanings for these four species. One of the better known looks upon them as representative of major bodily parts — the lulov symbolic of the spine, the esrog the human heart, the hadasim the eyes, and the arovos the lips. We are given to understand that total man, with all his might, heart, perception, and speech, thanks God for the sustenance with which he is blessed at harvest time.

When the four plants are thus held together during the service called Hallel (Hymns of Praise, Psalms 113–118) a waving ceremony is conducted. To the theme of the service, "Give thanks unto the Lord, for He is good," the Sukkos bouquet is waved in all directions, denoting gratitude to God wherever He may be found — in other words, everywhere. Following the Musaf (Additional) service, the Torah is taken from the Ark and the rabbi leads all holding the four species in the Procession of the Lulovim, accompanied by special chants of benediction. In some synagogues the procession is conducted before the Torah reading service.

THE SUKKAH IN OUR HOMES AND GARDENS

If at all possible, there should be a family project of constructing a Sukkah. The children should share. Perhaps it is more reasonable to suggest that a group of families join in erecting a community Sukkah which all may use.

Decorations can be made, expressive of family as well as individ
ual artistic ability. The walls may be designated for specific purpose

such as one devoted to pictures, maps, and drawings depicting events in American Jewish life, Jewish book jackets, and the like. A second wall may display Israeli events, pictures of farms, settlements, or religious observances in Israel, America, and other lands. A third can be directed to individual creativity by the children, finger-painting, tempera pictures, or Jewish symbols such as the Torah or a synagogue. The fourth may be devoted to the creations of the parents. The earth's produce should help blanket the walls with the season's bounty.

Knowledge that the Sukkah requires adornments will induce the children to begin cutting out and saving appropriate pictures from magazines and newspapers well before the arrival of the holiday. Occasional tokens or encouragement for their efforts will make them feel part of the Sukkah planning.

From the ceiling, seasonal products can be suspended — strings of grapes, cranberries, crabapples, in the shapes of symbols, like the Magen David and the Menorah. For preservative purposes, the vegetables and fruits can be shellacked. Jars of honey, oil, water, and wine, each symbolizing a wish for the coming year indicated by the specific fluid, can be placed about the Sukkah, with cards explaining their meaning. For example, *water* (mahyim-chayyim), "Water is life — may life be vouchsafed unto you"; *oil*, prosperity, plenty; *honey*, sweetness; and *wine*, spirit. Corn stalks readily available in late September or October can serve as background for the Sukkah walls.

Select one of the corners of the Sukkah and there arrange a holiday table with a cornucopia (horn of plenty) serving as the centerpiece for fruits and vegetables. Adjoining the horn of plenty, place the Sukkos bouquet or the lulov and esrog.

Our homes, too, should be graced with the beauty of the holiday. The holiday table may have as centerpiece a miniature Sukkah or a horn of plenty — both will prove holiday reminders for the children and family.

You can generate the festive spirit by designating a place in your living room for a symbolic Sukkah. This is not intended to replace the garden or synagogue Sukkah, but to enhance the over-all celebration. It may contain miniature decorations of flowers and fruits, and have a horn of plenty also. Here are a few suggestions:

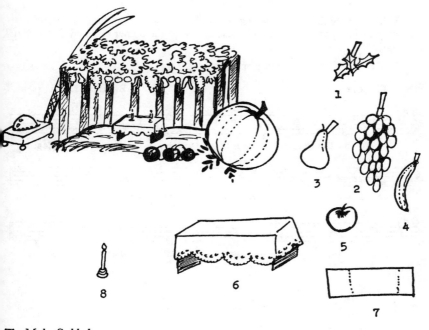

To Make Sukkah:

1. Turn a box, such as a shoebox, on its side. If box is plain, color in alternate stripes of brown and green on sides, back, and top. If there is printing or a design on the box, cut strips from crepe paper or construction paper and paste in strips to represent wooden boards of Sukkah with greenery showing through.
2. Cut out fruits and leaves (1 to 5) from colored paper, leaving a tab. Put Duco cement or paste on tab and paste fruits to ceiling and sides of Sukkah.
3. Gather leaves, twigs, acorns, and arrange on roof of Sukkah.

To Make Table:

1. Cut a rectangular strip of cardboard, score, and bend evenly at both ends. A paper napkin may be cut in a fancy pattern for a tablecloth.
2. Make candleholders and candle by building up coiled strips of clay and a cylinder of clay for candle. A bright piece of paper may be used for the flame.
3. A bowl of fruit made of clay, and a clay lulov and esrog may be placed on the table in the Sukkah.
4. Arrange fall fruits, such as pumpkins, on table with Sukkah and add leaves and twigs.

While the children are working on the Sukkah with you, here is a jolly song they may be taught to sing (you can also sing it at the dinner table on the holiday evenings):

TO THE SUKKAH

SARA C. LEVY   BEATRICE L. DEUTSCH

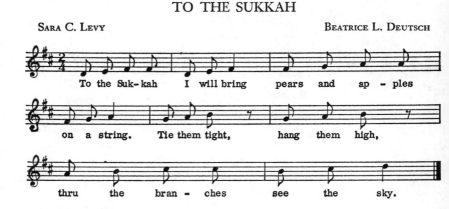

To the Suk-kah   I will bring   pears and   ap - ples

on a string.   Tie them tight,   hang them high,

thru the bran - ches   see the sky.

THE HOME CEREMONY

1. *Blessing the Holiday Candles*

As on all holidays, the dinner usually begins with blessing the holiday candles. This is mother's responsibility, and she performs it in the presence of her children.

בָּרוּךְ אַתָּה יְיָ, אֱלֹהֵינוּ מֶלֶךְ הָעוֹלָם, אֲשֶׁר קִדְּשָׁנוּ בְּמִצְוֹתָיו וְצִוָּנוּ

לְהַדְלִיק נֵר שֶׁל (On Sabbath add) שַׁבָּת וְ) יוֹם טוֹב:

בָּרוּךְ אַתָּה יְיָ, אֱלֹהֵינוּ מֶלֶךְ הָעוֹלָם, שֶׁהֶחֱיָנוּ, וְקִיְּמָנוּ, וְהִגִּיעָנוּ

לַזְּמַן הַזֶּה:

Baw-rooch ah-taw Ado-noy, Elo-hay-noo meh-lech haw-o-lawm, ah-shehr ki-d'shaw-noo b'mitz-vo-sawv, v'tzi-vaw-noo, l'hahd-leek nayr shel (*On Sabbath add:* Sha-baws v') yom tov.

Baw-rooch ah-taw Ado-noy, Elo-hay-noo meh-lech haw-o-lawm, sheh-heh-cheh-yaw-noo, v'kee-y'maw-noo, v'hi-gee-aw-noo, la-z'mahn ha-zeh.

Blessed art Thou, O Lord our God, King of the universe, who hast sanctified us by Thy commandments and granted us the privilege of kindling the (Sabbath and) holiday candles.

Blessed art Thou, O Lord our God, King of the universe, who hast granted us life, sustained us, and brought us to this festive season.

We thank Thee, O God, for the blessings of earth and air and the fruit of the earth, which, in the goodness of Thy bounty, Thou hast granted us. Bless our home and all within it with health and joy. May the glow of these holiday candles inspire us to understand deeply the meaning and the beauty of the festival of Sukkos.   Amen.

2. *The Kiddush or Blessing of Wine*

You should know that the Kiddush of Sukkos, Pesach, and Shovuos are alike excepting the name of the holiday mentioned, and a brief reference to the season's importance. These are called the Three Pilgrimage Festivals, Shawlosh R'gawleem in Hebrew; in Temple days tradition prescribed three annual visits or pilgrimages to the Temple in Jerusalem. The similarity of these holidays is apparent in the general pattern of the synagogue service.

Father rises as he leads the family in the chant or recitation of the Kiddush. Each member holds his wine cup in his right hand.

On Sabbath, add first paragraph and words in brackets:

וַיְהִי עֶרֶב וַיְהִי בֹקֶר

יוֹם הַשִּׁשִּׁי. וַיְכֻלּוּ הַשָּׁמַיִם וְהָאָרֶץ וְכָל צְבָאָם. וַיְכַל אֱלֹהִים בַּיּוֹם הַשְּׁבִיעִי מְלַאכְתּוֹ אֲשֶׁר עָשָׂה. וַיִּשְׁבֹּת בַּיּוֹם הַשְּׁבִיעִי, מִכָּל מְלַאכְתּוֹ אֲשֶׁר עָשָׂה. וַיְבָרֶךְ אֱלֹהִים אֶת יוֹם הַשְּׁבִיעִי, וַיְקַדֵּשׁ אֹתוֹ, כִּי בוֹ שָׁבַת מִכָּל מְלַאכְתּוֹ, אֲשֶׁר בָּרָא אֱלֹהִים לַעֲשׂוֹת:

When holiday occurs on weekday, begin here:

בָּרוּךְ אַתָּה יְיָ, אֱלֹהֵינוּ מֶלֶךְ הָעוֹלָם, בּוֹרֵא פְּרִי הַגָּפֶן:

בָּרוּךְ אַתָּה יְיָ, אֱלֹהֵינוּ מֶלֶךְ הָעוֹלָם, אֲשֶׁר בָּחַר בָּנוּ מִכָּל עָם,
וְרוֹמְמָנוּ מִכָּל לָשׁוֹן, וְקִדְּשָׁנוּ בְּמִצְוֹתָיו. וַתִּתֶּן לָנוּ, יְיָ אֱלֹהֵינוּ, בְּאַהֲבָה,
[שַׁבָּתוֹת לִמְנוּחָה וּ] מוֹעֲדִים לְשִׂמְחָה, חַגִּים וּזְמַנִּים לְשָׂשׂוֹן. אֶת יוֹם
[הַשַּׁבָּת הַזֶּה וְאֶת יוֹם]

חַג הַסֻּכּוֹת הַזֶּה, זְמַן שִׂמְחָתֵנוּ,

On Shemini Atzeres and Simchas Torah say:

הַשְּׁמִינִי חַג הָעֲצֶרֶת הַזֶּה, זְמַן שִׂמְחָתֵנוּ,

[בְּאַהֲבָה] מִקְרָא קֹדֶשׁ, זֵכֶר לִיצִיאַת מִצְרָיִם. כִּי בָנוּ בָחַרְתָּ, וְאוֹתָנוּ
קִדַּשְׁתָּ מִכָּל־הָעַמִּים. [וְשַׁבָּת] וּמוֹעֲדֵי קָדְשֶׁךָ [בְּאַהֲבָה וּבְרָצוֹן] בְּשִׂמְחָה
וּבְשָׂשׂוֹן הִנְחַלְתָּנוּ. בָּרוּךְ אַתָּה יְיָ, מְקַדֵּשׁ [הַשַּׁבָּת וְ] יִשְׂרָאֵל וְהַזְּמַנִּים:

On Saturday night add:

בָּרוּךְ אַתָּה יְיָ, אֱלֹהֵינוּ מֶלֶךְ הָעוֹלָם, בּוֹרֵא מְאוֹרֵי הָאֵשׁ:

בָּרוּךְ אַתָּה יְיָ, אֱלֹהֵינוּ מֶלֶךְ הָעוֹלָם, הַמַּבְדִּיל בֵּין קֹדֶשׁ לְחֹל, בֵּין אוֹר לְחֹשֶׁךְ, בֵּין
יִשְׂרָאֵל לָעַמִּים, בֵּין יוֹם הַשְּׁבִיעִי, לְשֵׁשֶׁת יְמֵי הַמַּעֲשֶׂה. בֵּין קְדֻשַּׁת שַׁבָּת לִקְדֻשַּׁת יוֹם טוֹב
הִבְדַּלְתָּ, וְאֶת יוֹם הַשְּׁבִיעִי מִשֵּׁשֶׁת יְמֵי הַמַּעֲשֶׂה קִדַּשְׁתָּ. הִבְדַּלְתָּ וְקִדַּשְׁתָּ אֶת עַמְּךָ יִשְׂרָאֵל
בִּקְדֻשָּׁתֶךָ. בָּרוּךְ אַתָּה יְיָ, הַמַּבְדִּיל בֵּין קֹדֶשׁ לְקֹדֶשׁ:

בָּרוּךְ אַתָּה יְיָ, אֱלֹהֵינוּ מֶלֶךְ הָעוֹלָם, שֶׁהֶחֱיָנוּ, וְקִיְּמָנוּ, וְהִגִּיעָנוּ
לַזְּמַן הַזֶּה:

When the Kiddush is said in the Sukkah, the following blessing is included:

בָּרוּךְ אַתָּה יְיָ, אֱלֹהֵינוּ מֶלֶךְ הָעוֹלָם, אֲשֶׁר קִדְּשָׁנוּ בְּמִצְוֹתָיו, וְצִוָּנוּ לֵישֵׁב בַּסֻּכָּה:

On Sabbath, add first paragraph and words in parentheses:

Va-y'hee eh-rehv, va-y'hee vo-kehr

Yom ha-shi-shee: Va-y'choo-loo ha-shaw-mah-yeem v'haw-aw-retz v'chawl tz'vaw-awm. Va-y'chahl Elo-heem ba-yom ha-sh'vee-ee, m'lahch-to ah-shehr aw-saw; va-yish-bos ba-yom ha-sh'vee-ee, mi-kawl m'lahch-to ah-sher aw-saw. Va-y'vaw-rech Elo-heem ehs yom ha-sh'vee-ee, va-y'ka-daysh o-so, kee vo shaw-vahs mi-kawl m'lahch-to, ah-shehr baw-raw Elo-heem la-ah-sos.

When holiday occurs on weekday, begin here:

Baw-rooch ah-taw Ado-noy, Elo-hay-noo meh-lech haw-o-lawm, bo-ray p'ree ha-gaw-fen.

Baw-rooch ah-taw Ado-noy, Elo-hay-noo meh-lech haw-o-lawm, ah-shehr baw-chahr baw-noo mi-kawl awm, v'ro-m'maw-noo mi-kawl law-shon, v'ki-d'shaw-noo b'mitz-vo-sawv. Va-ti-ten law-noo, Ado-noy Elo-hay-noo, b'ah-ha-vaw (sha-baw-sos li-m'noo-chaw oo-) mo-ah-deem l'sim-chaw, chah-geem oo-z'ma-neem l'saw-son, ehs yom (ha-sha-baws ha-zeh v'ehs yom) chahg ha-soo-kos ha-zeh, z'mahn sim-chaw-say-noo.

On Shemini Atzeres and Simchas Torah say:

Ha-sh'mee-nee chahg haw-ah-tzeh-rehs ha-zeh, z'mahn sim-chaw-say-noo

(b'ah-ha-vaw) mik-raw ko-desh, zay-chehr lee-tzee-ahs mitz-raw-yeem. Kee vaw-noo vaw-chahr-taw, v'o-saw-noo ki-dahsh-taw mi-kawl haw-ah-meem, (v'sha-baws) oo-mo-ah-day kawd-sh'chaw (b'ah-ha-vaw oo-v'raw-tzon) b'sim-chaw oo-v'saw-son hin-chahl-taw-noo. Baw-rooch a-taw Ado-noy, m'ka-daysh (ha-sha-baws v') Yis-raw-ayl v'ha-z'mah-neem.

On Saturday night add following two paragraphs:

Baw-rooch ah-taw Ado-noy, Elo-hay-noo meh-lech haw-o-lawm, bo-ray m'o-ray haw-aysh.

Baw-rooch ah-taw Ado-noy, Elo-hay-noo meh-lech haw-o-lawm, ha-mahv-deel bayn ko-desh l'chol, bayn or l'cho-shech, bayn Yis-raw-ayl law-ah-meem, bayn yom ha-sh'vee-ee l'shay-shehs y'may hah-mah-ah-seh. Bayn k'doo-shahs shah-baws li-k'doo-shahs yom tov hiv-dahl-taw, v'ehs yom ha-sh'vee-ee mi-shay-shehs y'may hah-mah-ah-seh ki-dahsh-taw, hiv-dahl-taw v'ki-dahsh-taw ehs ah-m'chaw Yis-raw-ayl bi-k'doo-shaw-seh-chaw. Baw-rooch ah-taw Ado-noy, ha-mahv-deel bayn ko-desh l'ko-desh.

Baw-rooch ah-taw Ado-noy, Elo-hay-noo meh-lech haw-o-lawm, sheh-heh-cheh-yaw-noo, v'kee-y'maw-noo, v'hi-gee-aw-noo, la-z'mahn ha-zeh.

When the Kiddush is said in the Sukkah, the following blessing is included:

Baw-rooch ah-taw Ado-noy, Elo-hay-noo meh-lech haw-o-lawm, ah-shehr ki-d'shaw-noo b'mitz-vo-sawv, v'tzi-vaw-noo lay-shayv ba-soo-kaw.

Heavenly Father:

We thank Thee for this festival of Sukkos, the festival of our rejoicing, and we offer to Thee our heartfelt gratitude for the blessings of Thy bounty. We thank Thee for the beauty of home and the love of family. May the spirit of this holiday teach us to appreciate more deeply that all that is good in life comes from Thee.

Blessed art Thou, O Lord our God, King of the universe, who createst the fruit of the vine.

Blessed art Thou, O Lord our God, King of the universe, who hast granted us life, sustained us, and brought us to this festive season. Amen.

3. *Washing the Hands*

The traditional home service suggests the washing of the hands before dinner. The custom is reminiscent of the act of preparation and consecration which priests performed before they began their functions in Temple days of old. The blessing recited is:

בָּרוּךְ אַתָּה יְיָ, אֱלֹהֵינוּ מֶלֶךְ הָעוֹלָם, אֲשֶׁר קִדְּשָׁנוּ בְּמִצְוֹתָיו, וְצִוָּנוּ
עַל נְטִילַת יָדָיִם:

Baw-rooch ah-taw Ado-noy, Elo-hay-noo meh-lech haw-o-lawm, ah-shehr ki-d'shaw-noo b'mitz-vo-sawv, v'tzi-vaw-noo, ahl n'tee-lahs yaw-daw-yeem.

Blessed art Thou, O Lord our God, King of the universe, who hast sanctified us by Thy commandments and granted us the privilege of partaking of Thy blessings of food and sustenance after the symbolic washing of the hands.

4. *Breaking Bread Together*

Father then uncovers the Challahs, and leads the family in the recitation of Hamotzee as he slices the Challah:

בָּרוּךְ אַתָּה יְיָ, אֱלֹהֵינוּ מֶלֶךְ הָעוֹלָם, הַמּוֹצִיא לֶחֶם מִן הָאָרֶץ:

Baw-rooch ah-taw Ado-noy, Elo-hay-noo meh-lech haw-o-lawm, ha-mo-tzee leh-chem min haw-aw-retz.

Blessed art Thou, O Lord our God, King of the universe, who bringest forth bread from the earth.

5. *Dinner is served*

During the course of dinner the following songs, appropriate to the holiday and the family spirit, can be sung:

LAWMAW SOOKAW ZOO

לָמָה סֻכָּה זוּ? — WHAT'S OUR SUKKAH FOR?

J. S. GOLUB

Slowly, with expression

Law-maw soo-kaw zoo, ah-baw tov sheh-lee?
What's our suk-kah for? Fa-ther pray do tell;

Law-maw soo-kaw zoo, ah-baw tov sheh-lee?
With-out roof or floor? Please ex-plain it well.

Lay-shayv bah-soo-kaw yah-kee-ree, lay-shayv bah-soo-kaw chah-vee-vee, Lay-
A re — min-der, lit-tle one, Of days of wandering, lit-tle son, In

shayv bah-soo-kaw yeh-led chayn, yeh-led chayn sheh-lee.___ Lay-
scor-ching de-sert, dear est one,___ Dear-est child of mine.___ In

shayv bah-soo-kaw yeh-led chayn, yeh-led chayn, sheh-lee.
scor-ching de-sert, dear-est one,___ Dear-est child of mine.

.1

לָמָה סֻכָּה זוּ, אַבָּא טוֹב שֶׁלִּי?
לָמָה סֻכָּה זוּ, אַבָּא טוֹב שֶׁלִּי?
לֵישֵׁב בַּסֻּכָּה יַקִּירִי, לֵישֵׁב בַּסֻּכָּה חֲבִיבִי,
לֵישֵׁב בַּסֻּכָּה יֶלֶד חֵן, יֶלֶד חֵן שֶׁלִּי.

‎.2

‎לָמָה לֵישֵׁב בָּהּ, אַבָּא טוֹב שֶׁלִּי?
‎לָמָה לֵישֵׁב בָּהּ, אַבָּא טוֹב שֶׁלִּי?
‎אֲבוֹתֵינוּ יַקִּירִי, אֲבוֹתֵינוּ חֲבִיבִי,
‎אֲבוֹתֵינוּ אַף גַּם הֵמָּה יָשְׁבוּ בַּסֻּכָּה.

‎.3

‎מַה בַּקֻּפְסָה יֵשׁ, אַבָּא טוֹב שֶׁלִּי?
‎מַה בַּקֻּפְסָה יֵשׁ, אַבָּא טוֹב שֶׁלִּי?
‎אֶתְרוֹג, אֶתְרוֹג, יַקִּירִי, אֶתְרוֹג, אֶתְרוֹג, חֲבִיבִי,
‎אֶתְרוֹג, אֶתְרוֹג, יֶלֶד חֵן, יֶלֶד חֵן שֶׁלִּי.

2.

What's in this little box?
Father, pray do tell;
What does it contain?
Please explain it well.

A yellow Esrog, little one,
From Israel, my little son,
For Sukkos blessing, dearest one,
Dearest child of mine.
For Sukkos blessing, dearest one,
Dearest child of mine.

2.

Law-maw lay-shayv baw,
  Ah-baw tov sheh-lee?
Law-maw lay-shayv baw,
  Ah-baw tov sheh-lee?
Ah-vo-say-noo, yah-kee-ree,
  Ah-vo-say-noo, chah-vee-vee,
Ah-vo-say-noo ahf gahm hay-maw
  Yawsh-voo bah-soo-kaw.
Ah-vo-say-noo ahf gahm hay-maw
  Yawsh-voo bah-soo-kaw.

3.

What's this rustling thing?
Father, pray do tell;
A stick to which leaves cling?
Please explain it well.

A Lulov green, little one,
A branch of palm, little son,
For festive beauty, dearest one,
Dearest child of mine.
For festive beauty, dearest one,
Dearest child of mine.

3.

Mah bah-koof-saw yaysh,
  Ah-baw tov sheh-lee?
Mah bah-koof-saw yaysh,
  Ah-baw tov sheh-lee?
Es-rog, es-rog yah-kee-ree,
  Es-rog, es-rog, chah-vee-vee,
Es-rog, es-rog, yeh-lehd chayn,
  Yeh-lehd chayn sheh-lee,
Es-rog, es-rog, yeh-lehd chayn,
  Yeh-lehd chayn sheh-lee.

SIMAWN TOV

סִימָן טוֹב — GOOD LUCK AND GOOD FORTUNE

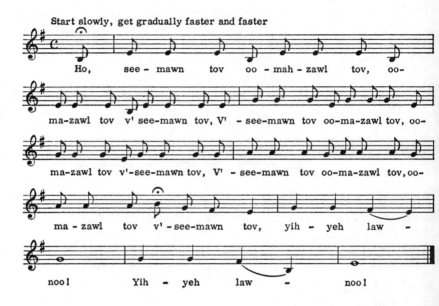

Start slowly, get gradually faster and faster

Ho, see - mawn tov oo - mah - zawl tov, oo-

ma-zawl tov v' see-mawn tov, V' - see-mawn tov oo-ma-zawl tov, oo-

ma-zawl tov v'-see-mawn tov, V' - see-mawn tov oo-ma-zawl tov, oo-

ma - zawl tov v' - see-mawn tov, yih - yeh law -

noo!   Yih - yeh law - noo!

סִימָן טוֹב וּמַזָּל טוֹב, מַזָּל טוֹב וְסִימָן טוֹב יִהְיֶה לָנוּ !

6. *Grace*

After dinner, father leads the family in grace, thanking God for His bounty.

Father: רַבּוֹתַי, נְבָרֵךְ.

Ra-bo-sai n'vaw-raych

Family: יְהִי שֵׁם יְיָ מְבֹרָךְ מֵעַתָּה וְעַד עוֹלָם.

Y'hee shaym Ado-noy m'vo-rawch may-ah-taw v'ahd
o-lawm.

Father: יְהִי שֵׁם יְיָ מְבֹרָךְ מֵעַתָּה וְעַד עוֹלָם. בִּרְשׁוּת מִשְׁפַּחְתִּי,
נְבָרֵךְ שֶׁאָכַלְנוּ מִשֶּׁלּוֹ.

Y'hee shaym Ado-noy m'vo-rawch may-ah-taw v'ahd
o-lawm. Bi-r'shoos mish-pahch-tee, n'vaw-raych sheh-aw-
chahl-noo mi-sheh-lo.

Family: בָּרוּךְ שֶׁאָכַלְנוּ מִשֶּׁלּוֹ וּבְטוּבוֹ חָיִינוּ:

Baw-rooch sheh-aw-chahl-noo mi-sheh-lo, oo-v'too-vo
chaw-yee-noo.

Father: בָּרוּךְ שֶׁאָכַלְנוּ מִשֶּׁלּוֹ וּבְטוּבוֹ חָיִינוּ:

Baw-rooch sheh-aw-chahl-noo mi-sheh-lo, oo-v'too-vo
chaw-yee-noo.

Father: Let us join in thanking God of whose bounty we have
partaken.

Family: Blessed be our God of whose bounty we have partaken
and through whose goodness we live.

Family:

בָּרוּךְ הוּא וּברוּךְ שְׁמוֹ.

בָּרוּךְ אַתָּה יְיָ, אֱלֹהֵינוּ מֶלֶךְ הָעוֹלָם, הַזָּן אֶת הָעוֹלָם כֻּלּוֹ בְּטוּבוֹ,
בְּחֵן בְּחֶסֶד וּבְרַחֲמִים. הוּא נֹתֵן לֶחֶם לְכָל בָּשָׂר, כִּי לְעוֹלָם חַסְדּוֹ.
וּבְטוּבוֹ הַגָּדוֹל תָּמִיד לֹא חָסַר לָנוּ, וְאַל יֶחְסַר לָנוּ מָזוֹן לְעוֹלָם וָעֶד.
בַּעֲבוּר שְׁמוֹ הַגָּדוֹל, כִּי הוּא אֵל זָן וּמְפַרְנֵס לַכֹּל, וּמֵטִיב לַכֹּל, וּמֵכִין
מָזוֹן לְכָל בְּרִיּוֹתָיו אֲשֶׁר בָּרָא.
בָּרוּךְ אַתָּה יְיָ, הַזָּן אֶת הַכֹּל:

Baw-rooch hoo oo-vaw-rooch sh'mo.

Baw-rooch ah-taw Ado-noy, Elo-hay-noo meh-lech haw-o-lawm, ha-zawn ehs haw-o-lawm koo-lo b'too-vo, b'chayn b'cheh-sed oo-v'rah-chah-meem. Hoo no-sayn leh-chem l'chawl baw-sawr, kee l'o-lawm chahs-do. Oo-v'too-vo ha-gaw-dol taw-meed lo chaw-sahr law-noo, v'ahl yech-sahr law-noo maw-zon l'o-lawm vaw-ed. Bah-ah-voor sh'mo ha-gaw-dol, kee hoo Ayl zawn oo-m'fahr-nays la-kol, oo-may-teev la-kol, oo-may-cheen maw-zon l'chawl b'ri-yo-sawv ah-sher baw-raw.

Baw-rooch ah-taw Ado-noy, ha-zawn ehs ha-kol.

Father:

Blessed art Thou, O Lord our God, King of the universe, who providest food for all. Through Thy goodness food has never failed us. Mayest Thou provide sustenance for all Thy children at all times for the sake of Thy great Name.

Family:

We thank Thee, O Lord our God, for our liberation from bondage, for the heritage of Eretz Yisroel, for Thy Torah which Thou didst reveal and impart unto us, and for the life of grace and blessing which Thou hast bestowed upon us.

וְעַל הַכֹּל, יְיָ אֱלֹהֵינוּ, אֲנַחְנוּ מוֹדִים לָךְ, וּמְבָרְכִים אוֹתָךְ, יִתְבָּרַךְ
שִׁמְךָ בְּפִי כָּל חַי תָּמִיד לְעוֹלָם וָעֶד: כַּכָּתוּב, וְאָכַלְתָּ וְשָׂבָעְתָּ וּבֵרַכְתָּ
אֶת יְיָ אֱלֹהֶיךָ, עַל הָאָרֶץ הַטּוֹבָה אֲשֶׁר נָתַן לָךְ.
בָּרוּךְ אַתָּה יְיָ, עַל הָאָרֶץ וְעַל הַמָּזוֹן:

V'ahl ha-kol, Ado-noy Elo-hay-noo, ah-nahch-noo mo-deem
lawch, oo-m'vawr-cheem o-sawch, yis-baw-rahch shi-m'chaw b'fee
kawl chai taw-meed l'o-lawm vaw-ed. Kah-kaw-soov, v'aw-chahl-
taw, v'saw-vaw-taw oo-vay-rahch-taw, ehs Ado-noy Elo-heh-
chaw, ahl haw-aw-retz ha-to-vaw ah-shehr naw-sahn lawch.
Baw-rooch ah-taw Ado-noy, ahl haw-aw-retz, v'ahl ha-maw-
zon.

Father:

Have mercy, O Lord our God, upon Israel, Thy people, and
upon Zion, and hasten the day of peace for all mankind.

וּבְנֵה יְרוּשָׁלַיִם עִיר הַקֹּדֶשׁ בִּמְהֵרָה בְיָמֵינוּ. בָּרוּךְ אַתָּה יְיָ, בֹּנֵה
בְרַחֲמָיו יְרוּשָׁלָיִם. אָמֵן:

Oo-v'nay Y'roo-shaw-la-yeem eer ha-ko-desh bi-m'hay-raw
v'yaw-may-noo. Baw-rooch ah-taw Ado-noy, bo-neh b'ra-cha-
mawv Y'roo-shaw-law-yeem, Aw-mayn.

בָּרוּךְ אַתָּה יְיָ, אֱלֹהֵינוּ מֶלֶךְ הָעוֹלָם, הָאֵל, אָבִינוּ, מַלְכֵּנוּ,
אַדִּירֵנוּ, בּוֹרְאֵנוּ, גּוֹאֲלֵנוּ, יוֹצְרֵנוּ, קְדוֹשֵׁנוּ, קְדוֹשׁ יַעֲקֹב, רוֹעֵנוּ, רוֹעֶה
יִשְׂרָאֵל, הַמֶּלֶךְ הַטּוֹב וְהַמֵּטִיב לַכֹּל, שֶׁבְּכָל יוֹם וָיוֹם הוּא הֵטִיב, הוּא
מֵטִיב, הוּא יֵיטִיב לָנוּ. הוּא גְמָלָנוּ, הוּא גוֹמְלֵנוּ, הוּא יִגְמְלֵנוּ לָעַד, לְחֵן
וּלְחֶסֶד וּלְרַחֲמִים וּלְרֶוַח, הַצָּלָה וְהַצְלָחָה, בְּרָכָה וִישׁוּעָה, נֶחָמָה,
פַּרְנָסָה וְכַלְכָּלָה, וְרַחֲמִים וְחַיִּים וְשָׁלוֹם, וְכָל טוֹב, וּמִכָּל טוֹב לְעוֹלָם
אַל יְחַסְּרֵנוּ:

Baw-rooch ah-taw Ado-noy, Elo-hay-noo meh-lech haw-o-
lawm, haw-ayl aw-vee-noo, mahl-kay-noo, a-dee-ray-noo, bo-
r'ay-noo, go-ah-lay-noo, yo-tz'ray-noo, k'do-shay-noo, k'dosh Yah-

ah-kov, ro-ay-noo, ro-ay Yis-raw-ayl, ha-meh-lehch ha-tov
v'ha-may-teev la-kol, sheh-b'chawl yom vaw-yom hoo hay-teev,
hoo may-teev, hoo yay-teev law-noo; hoo g'maw-law-noo, hoo
go-m'lay-noo, hoo yig-m'lay-noo law-ahd, l'chayn oo-l'cheh-sed
oo-l'ra-chah-meem oo-l'reh-vahch, ha-tzaw-law v'hahtz-law-chaw,
b'raw-chaw vee-shoo-aw, neh-chaw-maw, pahr-naw-saw v'chahl-
kaw-law, v'ra-cha-meem v'cha-yeem v'shaw-lom, v'chawl tov,
oo-mi-kawl tov l'o-lawm ahl y'chah-s'ray-noo.

Family:

Blessed art Thou, O Lord our God, King of the universe.
Thou art our God who showerest kindnesses upon all Thy creatures.
Every day dost Thou grant unto us the blessings of Thy hand.
Thou art kind and dost deal kindly with us. Thou hast bestowed
upon us Thy blessings, yielding us lovingkindness, grace, sustenance
and support, mercy, life and peace. We pray Thee, withhold not
Thy blessings from us.

Father: May God sustain us in health.

Family: Amen.

Father: May God bless all assembled at this table.

Family: Amen.

Father: May God send plentiful blessings upon this house, and
all who are near and dear to us.

Family: Amen.

(On the Sabbath)

Father: הָרַחֲמָן, הוּא יַנְחִילֵנוּ יוֹם שֶׁכֻּלוֹ שַׁבָּת וּמְנוּחָה לְחַיֵּי הָעוֹלָמִים:

Family: אָמֵן — Amen:

Father: May this Sabbath eve bring its message of rest and peace to us.

Family: Amen.

Father: הָרַחֲמָן, הוּא יַנְחִילֵנוּ יוֹם שֶׁכֻּלוֹ טוֹב:

Family: אָמֵן — Amen:

Father: May this festival eve bring its message of joy and happiness to us.

Family: Amen.

Father: הָרַחֲמָן, הוּא יָקִים לָנוּ אֶת סֻכַּת דָּוִד הַנּוֹפֶלֶת:

Family: אָמֵן — Amen:

Family:

מִגְדּוֹל יְשׁוּעוֹת מַלְכּוֹ, וְעֹשֶׂה חֶסֶד לִמְשִׁיחוֹ, לְדָוִד וּלְזַרְעוֹ עַד עוֹלָם. עֹשֶׂה שָׁלוֹם בִּמְרוֹמָיו, הוּא יַעֲשֶׂה שָׁלוֹם עָלֵינוּ וְעַל כָּל יִשְׂרָאֵל, וְאִמְרוּ, אָמֵן:

Mig-dol y'shoo-os mahl-ko, v'o-seh cheh-sed li-m'shee-cho, l'Daw-vid oo-l'zahr-o ahd o-lawm. O-seh shaw-lom bi-m'ro-mawv, hoo yah-ah-seh shaw-lom, aw-lay-noo v'ahl kawl Yis-raw-ayl, v'i-m'roo, aw-mayn.

May He who creates peace in His celestial heights, grant us peace and contentment and joy during this festival of Sukkos. Amen.

The Lulov and Esrog

We have spoken of the lulov and esrog, the meaning of its ceremonial in the synagogue, and recommended that its spirit be carried over to the home during the week of the holiday. Each family should have the use of lulov and esrog. Several families may purchase them jointly (at a Jewish book store or through the rabbi) and share them, each offering daily thanksgiving to God for the fruit of the earth.

This brief service may take the following form:

Take the lulov and the attachments in the right hand and the esrog in the left, with the stem held upward, and recite this blessing:

בָּרוּךְ אַתָּה יְיָ, אֱלֹהֵינוּ מֶלֶךְ הָעוֹלָם, אֲשֶׁר קִדְּשָׁנוּ בְּמִצְוֹתָיו, וְצִוָּנוּ עַל נְטִילַת לוּלָב:

Baw-rooch ah-taw Ado-noy, Elo-hay-noo meh-lech haw-o-lawm, ah-shehr ki-d'shaw-noo b'mitz-vo-sawv, v'tzi-vaw-noo, ahl n'tee-lahs loo-lawv.

Blessed art Thou, O Lord our God, King of the universe, who hast sanctified us by Thy commandments and granted us the privilege of raising the esrog and lulov.

(Shake the lulov and esrog pointing in turn to each of the four corners of the earth, then turn esrog over and recite:)

(On first day only)

בָּרוּךְ אַתָּה יְיָ, אֱלֹהֵינוּ מֶלֶךְ הָעוֹלָם, שֶׁהֶחֱיָנוּ, וְקִיְּמָנוּ, וְהִגִּיעָנוּ לַזְּמַן הַזֶּה:

Baw-rooch ah-taw Ado-noy, Elo-hay-noo meh-lech haw-o-lawm, sheh-heh-cheh-yaw-noo, v'ki-y'maw-noo, v'hi-gee-aw-noo, la-z'mahn ha-zeh.

Blessed art Thou, O Lord our God, King of the universe, who hast granted us life, sustained us, and brought us to this festive season.

(Shake lulov and esrog again and read the following blessing:)

We thank Thee, O God, for the gifts of nature and the blessings of life. Cause us to understand that these gifts and blessings should be used not only for our benefit alone, but for the good of others as well. May this season of the harvest, and Thy blessings unto us, inspire us to be ever grateful for the sweetness of family life and for Thy continuous protection. Make us worthy of Thy bounty and direct us to serve Thee and all our fellowmen.   Amen.

To make the service more effective, you may establish a *Charity Time* by selecting a specific charity in your community to which you and your children would contribute in honor of the holiday of plenty. By associating a charitable contribution with the blessings for plenty, our children learn that we do more than say we are grateful; we share with those who have need of the blessings we possess.

THE LAST TWO DAYS OF SUKKOS

SHEMINI ATZERES

The eighth and ninth days of Sukkos have additional names and are both synagogue days. Feast of Solemn Assembly, or Shemini Atzeres, is the name of the eighth, and while the pattern of the synagogue service is similar to the first two days, a special prayer called Geshem or Rain is included and Yizkor (Memorial) services are conducted. For the former, the cantor dons a white gown and chants strains vaguely reminiscent of the High Holy Day melody;

for Shemini Atzeres is also conceived as a Day of Judgment for water, for the much needed rain required by the arid land in Israel.

The home ceremony with the blessings and Kiddush and Grace is similar to that of the first two evenings of Sukkos.

SIMCHAS TORAH

Children, particularly, look forward with much anticipation and excitement to the jubilant second evening called Simchas Torah. (In the Reform ritual, Simchas Torah is observed on the eighth night and day.) You know that the word *simchah* means a happy occasion and Simchas Torah means Rejoicing of the Law or Joy of the Torah.

In the Home

The home ceremony is like that of the first two nights of the holiday, but one addition should be made. A symbolic Torah should be seen either as a centerpiece at the dinner table or placed on a small table surrounded by Bibles.

Here are suggestions for things to prepare before the holiday comes:

To Make Torah:

1. Colored plastic or paper drinking straws may be used for the handles.

2. Cut off a rather long strip of shelving paper about ten inches high. Draw wavy lines in columns to represent text as in 3. Attach one straw to each end of paper by either wrapping paper around straw and stapling or putting glue along each edge and wrapping around straw tightly.

3. From a piece of colored paper make the Torah cover by drawing and coloring the design and cutting fringes at bottom.

4. Torah may be tied with ribbon (2) after being rolled. Roll cover and paste sides together. Roll Torah tightly and place in cover, letting it unroll until cover does not slip off too easily.

On a bookshelf place one or two model Torahs, and the family Bibles. Use bookends of Jewish motifs if available.

Here are two simple melodies the children will love to learn and sing, and which will prepare them for the Torah processions:

SIMCHAS TORAH

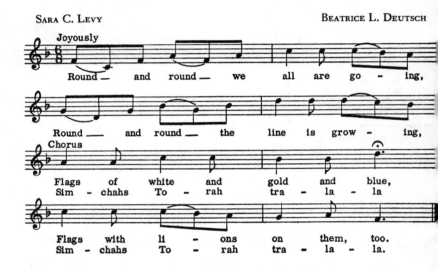

Sara C. Levy

Beatrice L. Deutsch

Joyously

Round — and round — we all are go - ing,

Round — and round — the line is grow - ing,

Chorus

Flags of white and gold and blue,
Sim - chahs To - rah tra - la - la

Flags with li - ons on them, too.
Sim - chahs To - rah tra - la - la.

YOM TOV LAWNOO
יוֹם טוֹב לָנוּ — A HOLIDAY FOR US

Translation by BEN ARONIN

Arr. HARRY COOPERSMITH

Gaily

Yom tov law - noo chag saw-may - ach Y'- law - deem naw
All the world is danc-ing, sing - ing, On this joy - ous

gee - law naw! L'soo - kaw-say - noo baw o - ray - ach
ho - li day. Hearts are mer - ry voi - ces ring - ing,

Ahvraw-hawm aw-vee-noo, bawrooch hah-baw. Yah-chad-es hah-chag naw - chog
See how the To-rah leads the way. On! On! March a - long!

B' - loo-lawv hah - daws es - rog Hoy heh - awch, nis-
All our voi - ces join in song. Hear the mel - o - dy

mach m' od Oo vah - mah - gawl nir - kod.
live - ly, gay; This is Sim - chas To - rah day.

2.

All dressed up for this occasion,
There's sparkle in each glance.
Not a soul that needs persuasion,
To step blithely in a dance.

Chorus

3.

Apples, banners bobbing gaily,
Carried high by the happy throng.
Torah must be studied daily,
That's the spirit of our song.

Chorus

.1

יוֹם טוֹב לָנוּ, חַג שָׂמֵחַ,
יְלָדִים, נָגִילָה נָא!
לְסֻכָּתֵנוּ בָּא אוֹרֵחַ:
*אַבְרָהָם אָבִינוּ, בָּרוּךְ הַבָּא.

.2

יַחַד אֶת הַחַג נָחֹג,
בְּלוּלָב, הֲדַס, אֶתְרוֹג;
הוֹי הֶאָח, נִשְׂמַח מְאֹד
וּבְמַעֲגָל נִרְקֹד.

* On second time around substitute "Yitz-chawk" for "Avrawhawm." On third time around substitute "Yah-ah-kov" for "Avrawhawm" and "Yitz-chawk."

In the Synagogue

The Torah plays the most important role during the evening as well as in the next morning's service, more than on any other day in the calendar. The reason is as follows: In the synagogue, the Torah or Pentateuch (Five Books of Moses) is read during the course of the year. Every Sabbath morning, a specific portion of the Bible is read or chanted, beginning with Genesis, or the first book. The procedure is begun on Simchas Torah, continues on every Sabbath throughout the year, until the Five Books are concluded, on the next Simchas Torah. To create the idea that Torah reading or study is a continuous, never-ending process, the Torah reading is begun anew on this day in a ceremony we shall shortly describe.

On the evening of Simchas Torah, the interest of the children is drawn to the warm gay ceremony known as Hakawfos or Torah circuits. All the Torahs are withdrawn from the Ark and the honor of carrying them accorded to congregants. Led by the cantor, while he chants melodies of the delight of the Jew in his Torah, the circuits proceed about the synagogue. Seven such processions are usually conducted; at the end of every circuit new congregants are honored by carrying the Torahs. In larger congregations, more processions are added in order to distribute the honors to all present. Children share the happy custom by following the processions, singing as they march. Some carry miniature Torahs which they proudly hold aloft; others have colorful descriptive flags, on top of which apples are placed; and still others hold both in their hands. In many communities, young men approaching Bar Mitzvah age are privileged to carry the smaller Torahs. Following the circuits, many synagogues hold a Torah reading service.

Refreshments, including honey cake and apples, are served following the services. The children, particularly, enjoy these.

The Simchas Torah morning service again conducts Torah processions. During the Torah reading service, many synagogues follow the custom of calling all the men in attendance to recite the blessings. In traditional synagogues, a ceremony known as "All the Children" or Eem Kawl Ha-N'awreem is conducted, during which all the younger children are summoned to the pulpit. Under the canopy of a large prayershawl, the children are led in reciting the blessings over the Torah. In this way, all the congregants have an opportunity to participate in the service.

Two special Torah honors are accorded which betoken the meaning of Simchas Torah, the unending course of Torah and its ending and beginning on this day.

As the reading approaches the end of the scroll, the honor called "Bridegroom of the Torah — Chahsahn Torah" is announced; and the worshiper given this privilege approaches to the words of a special chant, translated as follows:

With permission of God, great, mighty, and revered,
I will raise my voice in psalm and song
To thank Him and to praise Him who dwelleth high in light,
That He hath kept us in life and preserved us in His unfailing
    love,
And hath brought us near to be joyful in
The Rejoicing of the Torah.
The Torah that gladdens the heart and enlightens the eyes,
Prolonging the days and adding strength unto all those
Who love the Torah and heed its precepts and admonitions.
Thus may it be acceptable before the Almighty
To grant life and grace, and to crown with virtue (name)
Who has been chosen to complete the reading of the Torah.
Stand forth, stand forth, stand forth (name), Chahsahn Torah.
By the merit of this deed, may you be deemed worthy by the
    God we revere.
To behold children and children's children delighting in the
    Torah.

When the Torah is concluded the congregation rises and recites:

חֲזַק חֲזַק וְנִתְחַזֵּק

"Chah-zahk, chah-zahk, v'nis-chah-zayk. Be strong, be strong and let us strengthen each other," a phrase recited also at the completion of every book of the Bible. It is a call to the congregation to be strong in loyalty and devotion to God and to Torah. The concluded Torah is raised and rolled and set in a place of honor on the pulpit

The new scroll is then placed on the reading desk and the Baal K'riah, he who reads the Torah, prepares to begin the Torah anew

The person selected to recite the blessings over the beginning of the Torah is called "Bridegroom of the Beginning — Chahsahn Brayshees." He, too, is summoned to the pulpit with a special chant translated as follows:

> With permission of Him who is exalted above all blessing and adoration,
> Revered above all hymns of praise,
> Wise in heart and mighty in strength and power,
> Sovereign of the world and Lord of all creation,
> And with permission of all the righteous ones of this congregation,
> Gathered here this day to rejoice in the Torah,
> And assembled to complete, then reverently to begin again in joy, to read the Torah,
> Stand forth, stand forth, stand forth (name), Chahsahn Brayshees,
> Inasmuch as you are chosen to be the first to perform so perfect a command,
> How great is your privilege, exceedingly great your reward.

Thus the continuity of Torah is maintained, as it has been for hundreds of years.

Simchas Torah has also become appropriate for the conducting of consecration services. Children, new in the Hebrew or Sunday School, are welcomed into study of Torah by a modern interpretation of an old ceremony whereby parents brought their child to the rabbi for induction into Torah study. Today, in most communities, the children rise to affirm their desire and intention to become devoted students of Torah. The rabbi then blesses them and offers prayer for them in their new venture. Some communities give the children a small prayerbook or miniature Torah as token of the consecration service, and also a small jar of honey or honey cake, with the hope that the child's diligence and study prove as sweet as the honey itself.

THE BEAUTIFUL WILLOW*

Of course, everyone knows that the weeping willow is so named because it also wept by the waters of Babylon.

When the Jews were taken into captivity by Nebuchadnezzar they sat down along the riverbanks of Babylon and cried bitterly and longingly for the freedom which they lost and for the holiness and beauty of the Temple which was destroyed. Now, the willow trees near the rivers, moved by sympathy for the unfortunate souls sitting beneath their boughs, bent their heads in sorrow and joined the unhappy Jews in crying for the glories that were no more. Hence, "weeping" willow.

However, few people know that this noble act of the willows had its beginning many, many years before, when the willows were. . .

It happened in that strange and distant place which is inhabited by the souls and spirits of all living things. I am not too familiar with the geography of the place, never having been there (that I know of), but I do know that there is a special section there for the spirits of all trees and flowers and grasses — and a beautiful place it must be, too. Everyone knows that a soul is more beautiful than a body. Can you imagine, then, how much more beautiful are the souls of a rose or an orchid than the flowers themselves, or the souls of an evergreen or a fern than their earthly embodiments?

Why do you look at me so strangely? Because I said that grasses and flowers and trees have souls? Well, you needn't take *my* word for it; I'm just repeating what the Talmud says. It's written in the Talmud, black on white, that there isn't a single blade of grass in this world that doesn't have a spirit which tells it to grow! But I'm wandering from the story . . .

It seems that many, many years ago there was some trouble

---

* Reprinted by permission of Barton's Candy Corporation, New York City.

in the spirit-world of the grasses. As a matter of fact, at that time there was an air of high excitement in all parts of the spirit-world. You see, word had somehow gotten around that the Almighty, King of the universe (which, of course, includes all worlds), was planning to give the Torah to the Jewish people, with certain Mitzvos (commandments) for them to perform. As each commandment became known to the different inhabitants of the spirit-world, there was much excitement and joy and pride, as they each became involved in the performance of one or another of the commandments.

Sad to say, however, that there was one exception to the pride and joy which greeted each commandment. The exception happened with the Four Kinds. As you know, this commandment called for the Jews to take during the week of Sukkos, a lulov (palm branch), an esrog (citron), three hadasim (myrtle branches), and two arovos (willow branches). What the intent of the Almighty was, none of the four knew; all they had heard was that all four of them were to be combined in the fulfillment of this one commandment. And, at first, like all the others, they too were proud to have been chosen to play a part in the performance of the Lord's will on earth.

But after the first flush of pride had passed, three of the Four Kinds were not so pleased at all. The three — the palm branch, citron, and myrtle — were not so much displeased at having been chosen themselves, as they were at the willow's having been chosen — and, what's more, lumped together with them. As often happens in such cases, the three found themselves meeting each other more and more as they went strolling about the gardens of the greens' spirit world, and wherever the willow would approach them, they would casually walk off in another direction. And of course, they never said they had anything against the willow — after all, the Almighty had chosen her and He certainly knew best. All they said was that they failed to see why the Almighty should have chosen the willow. They just couldn't understand, really they couldn't!

Of course, they could very well understand why they were chosen. Any fool could see that. And as they strolled together, that's all they talked about.

"Now, take me, for instance," the esrog would say. "Where else could you find a fruit with a form as beautiful as mine? Not to mention my color and my delicate aroma. Why, I'm so refined that even the wood of my tree tastes exactly like me. Now that's what I call beautiful! Of course," the esrog would hasten to add, "I don't mean to boast or anything. I just mean to say that the glory of the Almighty would be enhanced by choosing me for one of His commandments."

The myrtle was also very understanding. "It's easy to see why I was chosen. Who else has such smooth and almond-shaped leaves. And my fragrance! When the Jews will be commanded to smell pleasant things when they chant the Havdalah at the close of the Sabbath, I shall be one of them. And did you know that my namesake, Hadassah, is the Hebrew name of a woman destined to be famous in history for her beauty — Queen Esther! Of course, I speak only for the glory of the Almighty."

The palm seemed to be most upset of all. "I can see why the Almighty should have chosen a tall and stately tree like myself. Not only do I wear my branches like a crown, but I also give fruit and shade. Furthermore, you don't find me just anywhere, like most other trees. Frankly, I think it's a disgrace, the way the willow droops her branches and leaves. It's not fitting."

And so, the esrog and myrtle and palm found a new friendship among themselves, and a common cause. The willow just kept her silence and minded her own ways.

Now, the Almighty moves in mysterious ways His wonders to perform, and I can't say for certain how it all came about. Even the record of it in the Midrash only hints at the full story. But I have a feeling that this is what happened. . . .

A date palm near the village of Chamson became ill. Her trunk began to flake, her branches began to dry, and she stopped bearing fruit. The owner of the palm did what anyone else would have done in such a case — he called a doctor. He was a tree doctor and he was called Diklai. When Diklai came and examined the sick palm near Chamson, he began the usual cure. He went to another palm tree, a healthy one, cut off a branch, and then grafted it onto the sick palm tree. If the sick palm was at all still curable, this would do it. It had worked in the past and there was no reason why it shouldn't work now.

But the fact was that it didn't work now. For some reason, the sick palm would not become healthy again. Diklai was very upset about this, not only because his cure had failed, but also because it had once been a beautiful palm tree and it was saddening to see it die. However, there was nothing else he could think of, so he gave up and went home.

On his way home, Diklai stopped by a stream to get a drink when he decided to sit down and rest a while. He saw a pleasant willow tree near the bank and lay down at its foot. A steady breeze rustled the willow's leaves as he dozed lazily on the soft ground. Suddenly, not quite sure whether he was dreaming or awake, Diklai heard whispered words in the leaves' rustling.

"Diklai, Diklai," he heard, "why do you give up so easily? Why don't you try to heal the sick palm tree?"

"What do you mean, why don't I try? I can't. I don't know how. I've done what I could."

"No, you haven't, Diklai. Do you feel sorry for the tree? Do you sympathize with the sick palm?"

"Of course," answered Diklai, a little angrily, "but what does that have to do with it?"

"If you would really feel with the palm," answered the willow softly, "you would know what ails her. Your heart would feel what her heart feels."

"Nonsense, "Diklai almost shouted, "sheer nonsense. If you're so smart then you tell me what ails her!"

"I'll tell you, but you must promise me that you'll do what I say. I'm almost sick myself with sympathy for that poor tree. Promise me."

"Oh, all right," said Diklai. "What is it?"

"The sick palm tree," said the willow, "has a friend, another palm tree, near Jericho, and she is sick with longing for her. If you will go to Jericho and take a branch from that palm tree and graft it onto the palm tree here at Chamson, she will become well again."

Diklai sat up. "What! Now I'm to go to Jericho for a grafting branch! All the way to Jericho just for a sick tree! Anyway, I already tried grafting and it won't work."

The willow did not become angry. She just said, quietly, "Diklai, you promised. Besides, how can you see another suffering and not suffer yourself? If you are a man, you must go! You will see that I am right."

Diklai stood up and shook his head, perhaps with disbelief. He stood thinking for a moment — and then set out for Jericho.

As things turned out, the willow was right. With a graft from the Jericho palm, the Chamson palm soon became well again, a joy and pride to all who saw her and had pleasure from her. She herself felt very grateful for her recovery and said so to Diklai, the tree doctor.

"Oh, no, no," said Diklai, modestly but honestly, "don't thank me. Thank yonder willow by the stream. She cured you, for she was sick with you. What a beautiful soul that tree must have!"

Up in the spirit world of the greens, the esrog, myrtle, and the palm all saw what had happened, and when they heard Diklai speak of the willow's beautiful soul, they looked at each other a little ashamed. They finally realized that there is another sort of beauty — a beauty of the soul, a goodness of the heart, a fitness of character. Then, they all smiled at each other and, without another word, went out together to welcome and greet their fourth and rightful partner in the Almighty's commandment — all partners in the beauty of holiness.

SEVEN TIMES ROUND
(Danny's Simchas Torah)

By SADIE ROSE WEILERSTEIN

First Time Round

Hi, for Simchas Torah night!
Isn't this a jolly sight?
Every Sefer Torah's out;
All the children march about;

Bessie, Leonard, Dave and Lou,
Saul and Judith, Ann and Sue.
Every friend I have is here.
It's the best night in the year!

Second Time Round

Don't the Torahs all look fine?
Guess there must be more than nine!
Velvet mantles, red and blue,
Silver crowns and breastplates, too!
Torah bells go tinkle, tinkle!
Paper flags go crinkle, crinkle!
Step along and keep in line!
Wave *your* flag and I'll wave *mine*!

Third Time Round

Wish that baby were here too!
She would clap her hands and coo.
We could make her carriage fine
With a paper flag like mine.

Baby in her ruffled bonnet!
Paper flag with lions on it!
How the people all would smile
When we wheeled her down the aisle!

Fourth Time Round

There! We've caught up with the men
And we're starting out again.
I see Grandma! I see Mother!
I see Uncle Harry's brother.

Look! My Daddy has a scroll
(That's another word for roll).
Grandma kisses it with awe
'Cause it holds God's Holy Law.

Fifth Time Round

Now once more we wait and stand
While again the Scrolls change hand.
All the men take turns, you know.
Seven times around we go.

Wave your flag and step along!
Seesoo V'simchoo! Join in song!
Sing away with all your might!
This is Simchas Torah night.

Sixth Time Round

Soon the boys will have *their* turn;
The Bar Mitzvah ones who learn
What the Torah bids you do
If you want to be a Jew.

My turn, too, will come some day
When I grow as big as they.
Goodness me! I'll be so proud —
To bear the Torah through the crowd!

Seventh Time Round

Take a seat and rest a while?
Mother dear, you make me smile.
Rest with Simchas Torah here!
It comes only once a year.

Wave your flag and sing your song!
Rejoice! Be merry! Step along!
Have you read the Torah through?
Roll it back and start anew!

Chanukah

CHANUKAH

Menorahs gleaming with growing light,
An added candle each passing night,
A light for Torah, for Truth, for Trust,
A light to Israel: love mercy; be just.

Recounting the tale of Judah's fight
For freedom of worship, our God-given
    right.
We listen with pride to the Maccabees'
    story
Of struggle and triumph and lasting
    glory.

With spirits high, the draydel spinning,
With eyes aglow to see who's winning,
Toys and games, and laughter sweet,
And Chanukah pancakes, a special
    treat!

Chanukah

Reflected on the canvas of snow-laden trees, eight little candle lights burn brightly, while children's gleaming faces watch intently. These tell us that Chanukah, the Feast of Lights, has come in the midst of winter to spend eight days of fun and frolic with us.

The story of Chanukah, the only holiday not recorded in our Bible, takes us back more than two thousand years to a drama of religious survival. The place is the Middle East, Syria, Palestine, and Egypt. For political and other reasons, Antiochus Epiphanes, the Syrian emperor, sought to undermine the Jewish way of life and to substitute for it the Greek culture called Hellenism. But the Jews resisted this attempt forcefully. Led by Mattathias, a priest, and later by his heroic son Judah Maccabee, Jewish bands engaged the Syrians in battle, and after years of struggle proved victorious. When they returned to the Holy Temple in Jerusalem they found the altars desecrated. The task of removing the sacrilege was undertaken, and in 165 before the Common Era, the Temple, amidst pomp and splendor, was rededicated and reconsecrated as the center of Jewish worship. In perpetual remembrance of these great events, we celebrate annually the holiday of Chanukah, Festival of Dedication.

For a period of eight days, beginning on the 25th day of the third month, Kislev, we observe this feast. The eight day celebration is derived from an account in the Talmud that when the Jews returned to the Temple, they searched widely for oil with which to light the candelabrum. Only one small cruse of oil, enough to burn for one day, was found. This little jar bore the seal of the high priest and was unbroken, proving that its contents had not been touched nor defiled. When the oil was kindled, instead of giving light for one day as anticipated, it burned for eight; long enough to permit the priests to prepare new oil for Temple use. This is the reason we use eight candles on our Menorahs today; it also explains another name for Chanukah, Feast of Lights, Chag Haw-oo-reem.

The epic of Chanukah should have profound meaning for every liberty loving person, because it was the first historical battle for religious freedom and the right to worship according to the dictates of one's conscience. That right was secured by the victorious Maccabees. This would justify our saying that Chanukah can also be called the Festival of Religious Liberty.

Chanukah is primarily a home holiday. To be sure, its observance is not omitted in the synagogue. There are special services in the daily ritual such as the Hallel prayers (Hymns of Praise, Psalms 113–118, read on all holidays), a prayer which describes the events leading to the holiday's existence, "For the miracles — Ahl Hahniseem," and a daily morning Torah reading, which is normally conducted on Mondays and Thursdays only. Blessings of the candles, too, have become part of the synagogue's evening service, because of the rabbinic desire that public pronouncement be made of the miracle of the oil, and also because of the hope to have all, even those away from home, share in the ceremony.

PREPARING AND CELEBRATING

Anticipating the holiday and preparing for its coming are perhaps as important as its celebration, because they will determine your success in instilling the spirit of joy and good feeling among the members of your family. Preparations should begin two or three weeks before Chanukah. The first step is to bring your children together, to talk of the holiday. If they attend Sunday or Hebrew School they will have heard about it, but will be anxious to know more. Read the story of the Maccabees to them, or better still, tell it on their level of comprehension, with the climaxes of the narrative, the leading characters, and those symbols of the drama which have become most familiar.

Having established this base of understanding, you can now proceed to discuss the decorations to beautify your home. Should they be made as a joint family enterprise? Should the adornments be purchased at the synagogue gift shop? Who shall have the responsibility of making and hanging them? What kinds of decorations shall we include in the house preparations? These and many others are the questions you will want to answer. Though you know the layout of your home well, a tour to point out the most suitable places will be helpful, because this is where your children can be creative and original.

Here are a few suggestions for home-made decorations, which your children will enjoy preparing: (Please note that the Judah Maccabee can be used as a guardian of Chanukah gifts or, at a safe distance from flames, a watchman of the Menorah, or as a table centerpiece at dinner.)

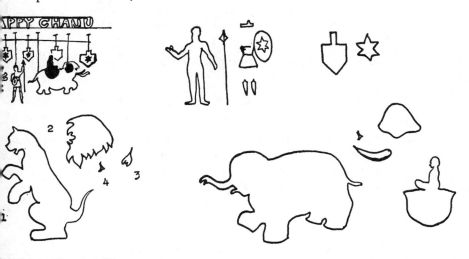

To Make Hanging Lion:

1. From one color of construction paper cut out shape 1 for body of lion in desired size.
2. From a second color cut out mane (2), eye (4), and tail tip (3), in proportion to size of lion shape. Cut two each.
3. Paste one each of mane, eye, and tail to main body. Turn over and paste other mane, eye, and tail back to back.

Judah Maccabee Guard:

1. Roll a piece of typing or heavier paper into a wide cylinder and paste ends together. On side away from seam, near top, cut out small semicircles for eyes, leaving straight side (1). Bend up uncut side and cut in fringe as for eyelashes. Cut small triangle for nose. Draw mouth.

2. From another piece of typing paper cut long arm piece and Jewish star (2 and 3).

3. Cut slits on opposite sides of cylinder a little under eye sections. Push arm piece through slits until the two arms appear of even length.

4. From a piece of colored paper cut out spear, hat, and shield. Paste Jewish star on shield. Paste hat to top of cylinder. Place spear in raised hand so that bottom of spear is even with bottom of cylinder. Fold hand around spear and paste. Paste shield to free hand.

If you have decided to purchase decorative symbols or to add to those being made, be sure to have your children join you in the venture, and permit them to select from the wide assortment of new decorations now available. Decide, too, the question as to how many Menorahs (Chanukah candelabra with places for eight candles and the Shamash) you will be using, and the kinds. The writer has been encouraging his community to acquire a Menorah for each member of the family, giving each an opportunity to light the candles. There are small, inexpensive Menorahs available for smaller children, using birthday candles. And while you are in the planning stages, think seriously about having a Chanukah party for the children. Suggestions for a party will follow.

Chanukah Customs of Interest to You

There is a vast literature on celebrating the Feast of Lights into which we cannot enter here. We have selected a few customs because of their great meaning and interest.

1. *The Place of the Menorah.*

In days gone by, the Menorah was placed at the doorway or in the window, "to publicly proclaim the miracle of the cruse of oil." It was set on the left side of the portal. With the Mezuzah on the right side of the door, the implication was that he who enters, does so flanked on either side by symbolic objects.

2. *Who Should Light the Menorah?*

According to Jewish tradition, everyone, man, woman, and child, is expected to kindle the Chanukah tapers. So important a Mitzvah (good deed) was this considered that Jewish law, at least in theory, maintained that even one completely impoverished must comply, and that he should sell his cloak or pawn it, in order to kindle the lights.

3. *When to Light.*

The candles should be kindled at sundown, if possible, as though to greet the twinkling in the heavens. When the time arrives,

declares tradition, everything else must be put aside; even one
studying Torah must desist until the commandment to kindle has
been fulfilled.

4. The Shamash — Who is He?

The Shamash, most conspicuous of the candles, is the assistant
or helper. According to tradition one is not permitted to make use
of the Chanukah lights for any purpose except the Mitzvah of
kindling. In order to avoid inadvertent use of the lights, the Shamash
was added. Thus, the light derives from the Shamash and not from
the other candles.

5. The Chanukah Dish — Potato Pancakes or Latkes.

This is one of the favorite dishes of the holiday. Its source is
the story of Judith, daughter of the High Priest Jochanan, heroine
of the Maccabean victory. Judith is credited with the capture of
the general of the Syrian army, Holofernes, while feeding him milk
and cheese. In her honor, cheese dishes are customary on the
holiday; puddings were developed from these, and eventually
pancakes.

THE HOME CEREMONY OF KINDLING LIGHTS

Instructions: Light the Shamash candle first. On the first night
place the candle on the far right of the Menorah facing you. On the
second night, an additional candle is placed to the left of the first
candle; it is the first one to be kindled by the Shamash as the blessing
is made. On the third night, the third candle is placed to the left of
the second candle, and so on each night. Thus the arrangement is
from the right, moving left, as in reading Hebrew, but the candles
are lit from left to right. (When the Sabbath coincides with
Chanukah, the Sabbath candles are lit after the Chanukah lights.)

1) The Blessings:

בָּרוּךְ אַתָּה יְיָ, אֱלֹהֵינוּ מֶלֶךְ הָעוֹלָם, אֲשֶׁר קִדְּשָׁנוּ בְּמִצְוֹתָיו,
וְצִוָּנוּ לְהַדְלִיק נֵר שֶׁל חֲנֻכָּה:

בָּרוּךְ אַתָּה יְיָ, אֱלֹהֵינוּ מֶלֶךְ הָעוֹלָם, שֶׁעָשָׂה נִסִּים לַאֲבוֹתֵינוּ,
בַּיָּמִים הָהֵם, בַּזְּמַן הַזֶּה:

(On first night only)

בָּרוּךְ אַתָּה יְיָ, אֱלֹהֵינוּ מֶלֶךְ הָעוֹלָם, שֶׁהֶחֱיָנוּ, וְקִיְּמָנוּ, וְהִגִּיעָנוּ
לַזְּמַן הַזֶּה:

Baw-rooch ah-taw Ado-noy, Elo-hay-noo meh-lech haw-o-lawm, ah-shehr ki-d'shaw-noo b'mitz-vo-sawv, v'tzi-vaw-noo, l'hahd-leek nayr shel Cha-noo-kaw.

Baw-rooch ah-taw Ado-noy, Elo-hay-noo meh-lech haw-o-lawm, sheh-aw-saw ni-seem la-ah-vo-say-noo, ba-yaw-meem haw-haym, ba-z'mahn ha-zeh.

(On first night only)

Baw-rooch ah-taw Ado-noy, Elo-hay-noo meh-lech haw-o-lawm, sheh-heh-cheh-yaw-noo, v'kee-y'maw-noo, v'hi-gee-aw-noo, la-z'mahn ha-zeh.

Blessed art Thou, O Lord our God, King of the universe, who hast sanctified us by Thy commandments and granted us the privilege of kindling the Chanukah lights.

Blessed art Thou, O Lord our God, King of the universe, who didst wondrous things for our fathers at this season, in those days.

CHANUKAH BLESSINGS

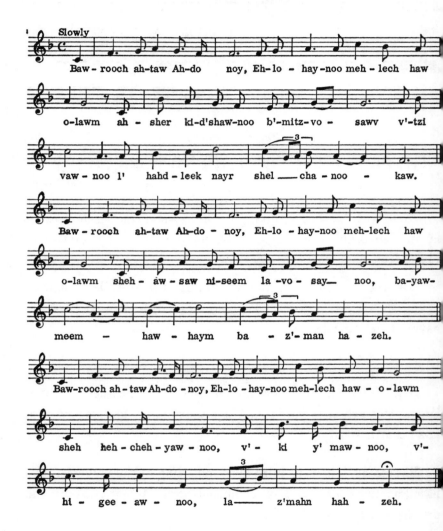

Baw-rooch ah-taw Ah-do noy, Eh-lo-hay-noo meh-lech haw

o-lawm ah-sher ki-d'shaw-noo b'-mitz-vo-sawv v'-tzi

vaw-noo l' hahd-leek nayr shel __ cha-noo-kaw.

Baw-rooch ah-taw Ah-do-noy, Eh-lo-hay-noo meh-lech haw

o-lawm sheh-aw-saw ni-seem la-vo-say__ noo, ba-yaw-

meem __ haw-haym ba-z'-man ha-zeh.

Baw-rooch ah-taw Ah-do-noy, Eh-lo-hay-noo meh-lech haw-o-lawm

sheh heh-cheh-yaw-noo, v'-ki y' maw-noo, v'-

hi-gee-aw-noo, la—— z'mahn hah-zeh.

(On first night only)

Blessed art Thou, O Lord our God, King of the universe, who hast granted us life, sustained us, and brought us to this festive season.

After you kindle the lights say:

הַנֵּרוֹת הַלָּלוּ אֲנַחְנוּ מַדְלִיקִין, עַל הַנִּסִים וְעַל הַנִּפְלָאוֹת, וְעַל
הַתְּשׁוּעוֹת וְעַל הַמִּלְחָמוֹת, שֶׁעָשִׂיתָ לַאֲבוֹתֵינוּ, בַּיָּמִים הָהֵם, בַּזְּמַן הַזֶּה,
עַל יְדֵי כֹּהֲנֶיךָ הַקְּדוֹשִׁים. וְכָל שְׁמוֹנַת יְמֵי חֲנֻכָּה, הַנֵּרוֹת הַלָּלוּ קֹדֶשׁ
הֵם, וְאֵין לָנוּ רְשׁוּת לְהִשְׁתַּמֵּשׁ בָּהֶם אֶלָּא לִרְאוֹתָם בִּלְבָד, כְּדֵי לְהוֹדוֹת
וּלְהַלֵּל לְשִׁמְךָ הַגָּדוֹל, עַל נִסֶּיךָ וְעַל יְשׁוּעָתֶךָ וְעַל נִפְלְאוֹתֶיךָ:

Hah-nay-ros hah-law-loo ah-nahch-noo mahd-lee-keen, ahl hah-ni-seem v'ahl hah-nif-law-os, v'ahl hah-t'shoo-os v'ahl hah-mil-chaw-mos, sheh-aw-see-saw lah-ah-vo-say-noo, bah-yaw-meem haw-haym, bah-z'mahn hah-zeh, ahl y'day ko-hah-neh-chaw hah-k'do-sheem. V'chawl sh'mo-nahs y'may Chah-noo-kaw, hah-nay-ros hah-law-loo ko-dehsh haym, v'ayn law-noo r'shoos l'hish-tah-maysh baw-hehm eh-law lir-o-sawm bi-l'vawd, k'day l'ho-dos oo-l'hah-layl l'shi-m'chaw hah-gaw-dol, ahl ni-seh-chaw v'ahl y'shoo-aw-seh-chaw v'ahl nif-l'o-seh-chaw.

We kindle these lights in remembrance of the miracles and deliverances which Thou didst perform for our fathers through Thy holy priests, in those days, at this season. These lights are sacred to us during the eight days of Chanukah. We are not to make any use of them except to watch them and contemplate their meaning, so that we may offer thanks unto Thee for Thy wonders and miracles and blessings of religious freedom.

2) Sing a few Chanukah songs, those which the children have learned in Hebrew or Sunday School or these:

MY DRAYDEL

(I Have a Little Draydel)

S. S. GROSSMAN   S. E. GOLDFARB

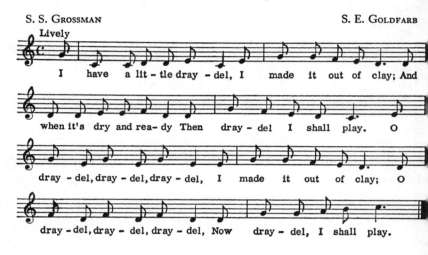

I have a lit - tle dray - del, I made it out of clay; And
when it's dry and rea - dy Then dray - del I shall play. O
dray - del, dray - del, dray - del, I made it out of clay; O
dray - del, dray - del, dray - del, Now dray - del, I shall play.

2.

It has a lovely body,
    With leg so short and thin;
And when it is all tired,
    It drops and then I win.

    O draydel, draydel, draydel,
        With leg so short and thin;
    O draydel, draydel, draydel,
        It drops and then I win.

3.

My draydel is always playful,
    It loves to dance and spin.
A happy game of draydel,
    Come play, now let's begin.

    O draydel, draydel, draydel,
        It loves to dance and spin;
    O draydel, draydel, draydel,
        Come play, now let's begin.

CHANUKAH!

Copyright by MARK DAVIS

The can-dles glow at twi-light
and the sha-maws is so up-right
Ev-'ry can-dle is a glow 'cause it's Cha-nu-kah you
know and we wish you all a yom tov ve-ry bright.

Chorus
Cha-nu-kah! Cha-nu-kah!
Joy-ous light and laugh-ter in the hall.
Cha-nu-kah Cha-nu-kah
Bless-ings of the sea-son to you all.

Y'MAY HACHANOOKAW
יְמֵי הַחֲנֻכָּה — O CHANUKAH, O CHANUKAH

A. Evronin   Translation by E. Guthmann

Y' - may ha-Cha-noo - kaw, cha-noo - kas mik-daw-
shay-noo, B' - geel oo-v'-sim-chaw m'-mah-l' eem es li - bay-noo;
Lai - law v' yom svee - vo - nay-noo yi - sov,
Soof-gaw-nee - yos no - chal bawm law - rov. -rov. Haw-
ee-roo, had - lee-koo nay - ros Cha-noo-kaw ra - beem!
Al ha-ni - seem — v' - al ha-nif-law - os — a - sher cho - l' -
loo Ma-ka beem. —   loo Ma-ka - beem. —

יְמֵי הַחֲנֻכָּה, חֲנֻכַּת מִקְדָּשֵׁנוּ,
בְּגִיל וּבְשִׂמְחָה מְמַלְאִים אֶת לִבֵּנוּ;
לַיְלָה וְיוֹם סְבִיבוֹנֵנוּ יִסֹּב,
סֻפְגָּנִיּוֹת נֹאכַל בָּם לָרֹב.

הָאִירוּ, הַדְלִיקוּ
נֵרוֹת חֲנֻכָּה רַבִּים!
עַל הַנִּסִּים וְעַל הַנִּפְלָאוֹת
אֲשֶׁר חוֹלְלוּ מַכַּבִּים.

2.

Nitz-chon hah-mah-kah-beem,
  n'sah-payr, n'zah-may-raw,
Ah-lay ha-soh-n'eem awz yaw-
  dawm kee gaw-vay-raw
Y'roo-shaw-lah-yeem shaw-vaw li-
  s'chi-yaw
Ahm Yis-raw-ayl aw-saw too-shi-
  yaw.

Haw-ee-roo, hahd-lee-koo,
Nay-ros Cha-noo-kaw rah-beem!
Ahl ha-ni-seem, v'ahl ha-nif-law-os,
Ah-shehr cho-l'loo Mah-kah-beem.

נִצְחוֹן הַמַּכַּבִּים, נְסַפֵּר, נְזַמֵּרָה:
עֲלֵי הַשּׂוֹנְאִים אָז יָדָם כִּי גָבֵרָה:
יְרוּשָׁלַיִם שָׁבָה לִתְחִיָּה;
עַם יִשְׂרָאֵל עָשָׂה תּוּשִׁיָּה.

הָאִירוּ, הַדְלִיקוּ
נֵרוֹת חֲנֻכָּה רַבִּים!
עַל הַנִּסִּים וְעַל הַנִּפְלָאוֹת
אֲשֶׁר חוֹלְלוּ מַכַּבִּים.

1.

O Chanukah, O Chanukah, a festival of joy,
A holiday, a jolly-day, for every girl and boy.
Spin the whirling trendles all week long,
Eat the sizzling "latkes," sing the happy songs!
Now light, then, tonight then, the flickering candles in a row,
Retell the wondrous story, of God in all His glory,
And dance by the candles' cheering glow.
Retell the wondrous story, of God in all His glory,
And dance by the candles' cheering glow.

2.

Brave Judah Maccabee put the enemy to rout,
And from the holy Temple he drove the tyrants out,
'Twas then in old Jerusalem that freedom was attained,
And oil of gladness filled the lamp, the Torah lamp regained.
Come sing then, and bring then
All honor to the brave Maccabees.
Let kinsmen and brethren sing praises together
And thank God for the light which is His.
Let kinsmen and brethren sing praises together
And thank God for the light which is His.

MAWOZ TZOOR

מָעוֹז צוּר — ROCK OF AGES

Maw - oz tzoor y' - shoo-aw-see, l'-chaw naw - eh l'-shah
Ti - kon bays t' - fi-law-see, v' shawm to-daw n'-zah-

bay - ach,
bay - ach,

L'ays taw-cheen mat - bay - ach

mi - tzawr ___ ha-m'nah-bay - ach, Awz eg-mor b'-

sheer miz-mor, cha - noo-kas ha - miz - bay - ach.

.2

יְוָנִים נִקְבְּצוּ עָלַי אֲזַי בִּימֵי
הַשְׁמַנִּים,
וּפָרְצוּ חוֹמוֹת מִגְדָּלַי וְטִמְּאוּ כָּל
הַשְּׁמָנִים.
וּמִנּוֹתַר קַנְקַנִּים נַעֲשָׂה נֵס
לַשּׁוֹשַׁנִּים,
בְּנֵי בִינָה יְמֵי שְׁמֹנָה קָבְעוּ שִׁיר
וּרְנָנִים.

.1

מָעוֹז צוּר יְשׁוּעָתִי לְךָ נָאֶה
לְשַׁבֵּחַ,
תִּכּוֹן בֵּית תְּפִלָּתִי וְשָׁם תּוֹדָה
נְזַבֵּחַ.
לְעֵת תָּכִין מַטְבֵּחַ מִצָּר
הַמְנַבֵּחַ,
אָז אֶגְמֹר בְּשִׁיר מִזְמוֹר, חֲנֻכַּת
הַמִּזְבֵּחַ.

2.

Y'vaw-neem nik-b'tzoo aw-lai,
Ah-zai bee-may chahsh-mah-neem,
Oo-faw-r'tzoo cho-mos mig-daw-lai,
V'ti-m'oo kawl hah-sh'maw-neem,
Oo-mi-no-sahr kahn-kah-neem,
Nah-ah-seh nays la-sho-shah-neem.
B'nay vee-naw, y'may sh'mo-naw,
Kaw-v'oo sheer oo-r'naw-neem.

Rock of Ages, let our song
Praise Thy saving power;
Thou amidst the raging foes,
Wast our shelt'ring tower.
Furious they assailed us,
But Thine arm availed us,
And Thy word
Broke their sword
When our own strength failed us.

Children of the martyr-race,
Whether free or fettered,
Wake the echoes of the songs
Where ye may be scattered.
Yours the message cheering
That the time is nearing
Which will see
All men free,
Tyrants disappearing.

חֲנֻכָּה, חֲנֻכָּה — CHANUKAH, CHANUKAH

L. KIPNIS

Cha - noo - kaw, Cha - noo - kaw, chag yaw - feh kawl kahch.

Or chaw-veev mi -saw veev, geel l'-yeh - led rahch.

Cha - noo - kaw, Cha - noo - kaw, s' - vee -von sov, sov.

Sov, sov, sov, sov, sov, sov, Ma naw-eem vaw - tov.

Chanukah is a beautiful holiday with draydels spinning, candles burning. Let us sing and dance.

.1

חֲנֻכָּה, חֲנֻכָּה, חַג יָפֶה כָּל כָּךְ,
אוֹר חָבִיב מִסָּבִיב, גִּיל לְיֶלֶד רַךְ.
חֲנֻכָּה, חֲנֻכָּה, סְבִיבוֹן סֹב, סֹב.
סֹב, סֹב, סֹב, סֹב, סֹב, סֹב,
מַה נָּעִים וָטוֹב.

2.

Chah-noo-kaw, Chah-noo-kaw,
Ayn chah-lon b'lee aysh,
L'vee-vos, soof-gaw-ni-yos,
B'chawl bah-yis yaysh.

Chah-noo-kaw, Chah-noo-kaw,
Chahg chaw-veev m'od,
Shee-roo naw, zah-m'roo naw,
Oo-tz'oo li-r'kod.

.2

חֲנֻכָּה, חֲנֻכָּה, אֵין חַלּוֹן בְּלִי אֵשׁ,
לְבִיבוֹת סֻפְגָּנִיּוֹת בְּכָל בַּיִת יֵשׁ.

חֲנֻכָּה, חֲנֻכָּה, חַג חָבִיב מְאֹד.
שִׁירוּ נָא, זַמְּרוּ נָא,
צְאוּ לִרְקֹד.

MEE Y'MAHLAYL
מִי יְמַלֵּל — WHO CAN RETELL?

Translation by B. M. Edidin

A. Ravino

Mee y'-ma-layl g'vu-ros Yis-raw-ayl O-sawn mee yim-neh? Hayn b'-chawl dor yaw-koom ha-gi-bor go-ayl haw-awm.

Sh'ma! Bah-yaw-meem haw-haym ba-z'-man hah-zeh! Mah-kah-bee mo-shee-ah oo-fo-deh Oo-v'yaw-may-noo kawl am Yis-raw-ayl Yis-ah-chayd yaw-koom l'-hi-gaw-ayl.

Who can retell
The things that befell us?
Who can count them?
In every age,
A hero or sage,
Arose to our aid!

Hark! In days of yore, in Israel's ancient land,
Brave Maccabeus led the faithful band.
But now all Israel must as one arise,
Redeem itself through deed and sacrifice.

מִי יְמַלֵּל גְּבוּרוֹת יִשְׂרָאֵל?
אוֹתָן מִי יִמְנֶה?
הֵן בְּכָל דּוֹר יָקוּם הַגִּבּוֹר,
גּוֹאֵל הָעָם.

שְׁמַע! בַּיָּמִים הָהֵם בַּזְּמַן הַזֶּה,
מַכַּבִּי מוֹשִׁיעַ וּפוֹדֶה.
וּבְיָמֵינוּ כָּל עַם יִשְׂרָאֵל
יִתְאַחֵד יָקוּם לְהִגָּאֵל.

CHANUKAH PRESENTS

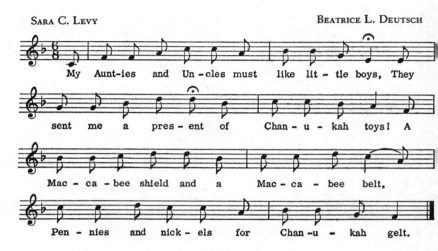

Sara C. Levy

Beatrice L. Deutsch

My Aunt-ies and Un-cles must like lit-tle boys, They
sent me a pres-ent of Chan-u-kah toys! A
Mac-ca-bee shield and a Mac-ca-bee belt,
Pen-nies and nick-els for Chan-u-kah gelt.

3) Chanukah gifts. Give your children their Chanukah gifts nightly after the blessings and songs. You will add to the spirit of the evening if, prior to the blessings, you place the gifts in places where the children can find them.

4) At the dinner table, use Chanukah napkins, home-made or purchased, and also the Judah Maccabee you have made from previous instructions. On at least one of the nights, use as centerpiece a special cake with a frosted Menorah and candles made of carrot or orange sticks.

A Chanukah Party for Your Children

With the holiday season in full swing, Chanukah is a wonderful time to have a party, a gathering which can be educational and

entertaining at the same time. The decorations are there, the spirit is evident, cheer is in the air, and all we need is to direct our attention to a few particulars. Perhaps these ideas will help you.

1. *Invitations*

Your children should make their own invitations. A Chanukah symbol such as a Draydel or cruse of oil would be an interesting introduction to the party theme.

Here are the illustrations and instructions:

1. From two pieces of the same colored paper, cut out the cruse of oil. On one side, letter such words as: *Happy Chanukah at My Home* or *My Chanukah Party*. Paste both pieces together around the sides, except across the top.

2. From a second piece of paper, white, yellow, or orange, cut out what looks like a large drop of oil and leave a long stem.

3. On this drop-shaped paper, write the details of the party, time, place, address, and other details.

4. Insert the oil drop into the cruse of oil as far as it will go.

Be sure to suggest to your guests that they bring a small gift to be used at the end of the party for a Chanukah exchange of gifts.

2. Decorations

Many of the decorations used for the holiday in other parts of the house can be brought together to the party room. Across the ceiling, you can suspend many of the holiday symbols, elephants, Maccabean soldiers, Menorahs, synagogues or temples, jars of oil. Balloons with appropriate holiday designs can be purchased; with water color, father can paint Happy Chanukah from _____ on some of the larger balloons strung across the room.

3. Table Setting

Since the Menorah is the major symbol of the season, it should occupy the place of honor in the center of the table, joined together by the Judah Maccabee (page 96), or a cake with frosted symbols. Chanukah napkins, cups, and tablecloths are available. Each child should have a crown with eight little candles, which can be cut out and pasted together. The children's names may be written on place cards in appropriate shape and design.

4. The Menu

An attractive memento of the Chanukah party, for guests to take home, should be prepared. In it may be included not only the program, but the menu as well.

The menu should have a Chanukah flavor. For example, it might include:

Fruit Cup a la Maccabee

Salade de Menorah	Potato Latkes au Judith
Hot Chocolate shel Judah	Draydeled Ice Cream

Orange Chanukah Mints

5. *The Souvenir Book*

The Souvenir Book can be called either "The Book of Chanukah" or "_____'s Book of Maccabees" or "Draydel Day." Here are directions for making them:

1. Fold two pages of equal size paper together to make four pages of book. Paper with a parchment or linen finish is desirable. Edges may be scalloped if desired.
2. Print program for party, menu, names of guests, or whatever is appropriate on these pages.
3. From a slightly larger sheet of paper make a cover as follows (use colored paper):
    Fold paper neatly in half. Punch four holes through which to thread ribbon. Tie a colorful ribbon through the holes (after punching holes on inside pages and placing them inside cover). Make a bow at the end of the ribbon. Cover may be decorated with Hebrew-style lettering, draydel, Menorah, or other Chanukah symbols.

6. *The Program*

It *is* Chanukah and, of course, the program should begin with the blessings of the candles, led by the party host or by mother or father. The blessings may be typed in transliteration in the souvenir book, or the children may listen to a Chanukah record of the blessings and follow the singing.

7. Chanukah Games

After the refreshments, the children will want to play a few games. Those suggested here are takeoffs of games and playlets which children know, and some which the parents will remember from their earlier years.

a) Pin the Shamash

You've heard of Pin the Tail on the Donkey. This game is played the same way except that a large Menorah with flames is cut out and used instead of the donkey. Each child receives a flame or candle, and is turned around and around while blindfolded and let go. He tries to pin the flame on the Shamash in the center of the Menorah, and the one who comes closest is declared the winner. (This game can be prepared by the family or purchased at the gift shop).

b) Put and Take

This is perhaps the oldest Chanukah game extant. Most of us will remember its details. Every draydel has on it, in relief or paint, four Hebrew letters. Each stands for a Hebrew word, thus: נס גדול היה שם (Nays, Gawdol, Hawyaw, Shawm), or "A Great Miracle Occurred There," in translation. In this put-and-take game, each of the letters, now used as Yiddish, means some kind of action: N (Nun) stands for nisht or do nothing; G (Gimmel) represents gahntz or all, that is, take all; H (Hay) stands for hahlb or take half; and SH (Shin) represents shtel or put up.

Begin with each child putting a specific number of items, whatever is being played with, pennies, beans, toothpicks, into the kitty. Then continue until one child has taken all, and begin all over again.

c) Musical Draydels

This is played like musical chairs. Stand the children in two lines. Take a large draydel and start passing it around when a

Chanukah song is played on the piano or on a record, or sung by one of the mothers or children. When the singing or playing stops, the child left holding the draydel is out of the game. Continue until there is only one child left, and declare him the winner.

8. *Chanukah-annah*

When the children prepare to leave the party, arrange for each to receive one of the gifts which you had asked them to bring for the Chanukah-annah or exchange.

One final suggestion. You will want to award special prizes to the children who are winners of the games. These awards, too, in the spirit of the afternoon, should be Chanukah items, such as coloring books, small Menorahs, and boxes of candles.

A NEW KIND OF DRAYDEL

By Edith B. Goldman

His name was Larry. He didn't feel like having a gay time. He just sat at the big window, looking glum. It was just before the holiday of Chanukah and it was warm and cozy in the house. He could smell the delicious cheese cake baking in the oven and hear

the whirr of the egg beaters as his mother and sisters were baking and laughing in the kitchen. Outside it threatened to snow . . . only one or two snow flakes drifted down.

His mother and sisters thought he didn't feel well because everyone liked getting ready for the best holiday of the year.

"Larry, come and join us," called his sister. "We'll let you lick the bowl. The cookies are just the best."

Larry liked the cheerfulness in the house, but he preferred to stay at the window by himself and watch the three squirrels at play in the yard. They jumped from one tree to the next and every now and then scurried about looking for hidden acorns. Larry noticed that there were three instead of two (and usually they scamper about in pairs) and suddenly one jostled up to him and seemed to talk. He *was* talking to him. Larry was so astonished, all he could do was sit there with his eyes and mouth wide open.

"Why, you're Larry Kahn, aren't you?" he asked.

Larry just nodded his head; he was too surprised to talk.

"You didn't expect a visit from a squirrel," said the animal, "did you? That's why I chose to visit you. I'm here to cheer you up. I'll tell you who I am. Do you remember the minstrels in the Purim story? They made everyone laugh with their tricks and jokes and funny faces. Well, I'm a minstrel too, but I come on Chanukah and my name is Japonica. When Japonica selects a boy or girl to visit on Chanukah, it's going to be a wonderful holiday. Come on out, I have an idea."

Larry's eyes were still filled with wonderment, but he went out into the yard. The squirrel had gathered a heap of acorns and he was busy nibbling all around them. Then, he handed them to Larry, one at a time.

"See, look at the acorn, I chewed a *Hay* and a *Gimmel* in them and there is a little hole on the top. You put these little pegs in . . . and now look what you have . . . an acorn draydel . . . acorn draydels. Try one; here, let me show you how they whirl and spin."

Larry and the squirrel Japonica worked together till they had a whole heap of acorn draydels ready for play. He got so excited that he forgot that squirrels don't usually talk and eagerly said, "Let's go in and surprise everyone."

Japonica winked and said that he must hurry off; the squirrels would miss him and would be looking for him. He did say that he would be in the yard and stay to watch the draydels hung up in the living room with the other decorations.

Larry hurried in the house with his pockets full. "Mom, Sis, look, everyone," he called, his face shining, and he showed them the draydels of acorns. They were delighted and thrilled when they tried them and they worked. He told them about Japonica and how he had chewed the Hebrew letters, *Nun, Gimmel, Hay and Shin,* on the acorns.

"Well," said his Mom, "that's my boy. That's the boy we've missed. We'll play many games with them, games like put and take, timing the draydel, guess the *Hay* and *Gimmel*.

They started stringing up the decorations. Larry sang and worked the hardest as they made the house shining bright for Chanukah. And across the wall over the fireplace, Larry made a big picture of Japonica and hung it there for all to see — Japonica making acorn draydels for Chanukah.

THE CHANUKAH LIGHTS

By Sadie Rose Weilerstein

Everybody loved the Chanukah lights. Daddy loved them. He said a *b'rawchaw*, a "thank you God for them," and Mother and Daniel said, "Amen."

The Shamash-candle — you know, the candle Daddy lights the other candles with — it loved the Chanukah lights, too. It kissed them with its flame. It sang to them.

> Rise on tip toe,
> Lift your light
> Up and up and up!
> Flicker, flicker,
> Shine and shine,
> It's Chanukah tonight.

Mother sang songs about the Chanukah lights. Baby Judith clapped her hands to show she loved them, too.

Even the wind loved the shining little flames. It crept through a crack in the window. It called to each of them.

> Sway and dance,
> Dance, little light;
> Up and up and up!
> Whirl and flicker,
> Flicker and whirl:
> It's Chanukah tonight.

And the lights rose on tiptoe and swayed and danced.

Once a light laughed too, a tiny sputtery laugh. It laughed until it cried. Big wax tears slid down its cheek, and Daniel cried, "Quick, Daddy! Shut the window tight, or the candle will cry itself away."

Then Daniel, too, sang a little song to the lights. He made it up out of his own head, but Mother and Daddy helped.

> Chanukah lights, we love you so,
> Do be careful, or out you'll go.
>> Slow and steady,
>> Steady and slow!
> We're not ready to let you go.
> Tomorrow I'll sit and watch your brother,
> And next to him there'll be another.
> Then there'll be three, four, five, six, seven.
> I wish that there might be eleven.
> Last, eight bright candles in a row.
> Chanukah lights, I love you so.

MY CHANUKAH CANDLES

By Philip M. Raskin

Eight little candles,
    All in a line;
Eight little candles
    Glitter and shine.

Eight little candles —
    Each little flame
Whispers a legend
    Of honor and fame.

Eight little candles
    Bashfully hide
The soul of a people,
    Its hope and its pride. —

Eight little candles,
    Sparklets of gold,
Stories of battles
    And heroes of old.

Heroes undaunted
    And noble, and true;
Heroes who knew
    How to dare and to do;

Heroes who taught
    The ages to be
That man can be brave,
    And that man should be free.

Eight little candles,
   Look at them well,
Floods could not quench them,
   Tempests not quell.

Modest and frail
   Is their light — yet it cheers
A people in exile
   Two thousand years.

Eight little candles —
   Their guttering gleams
Speak to my heart
   In a language of dreams.

Light to my eye
   Is their smile and their cheer,
Sweet to my ear
   Is their whisper to hear.

"Courage, but courage,
   Maccabee's brave son,
Fight for the light —
   And the battle is won."

Tu Bi-Shevat

TU BI-SHEVAT

On Arbor Day across the land,
The children go with spade in hand
To plant a sapling gleefully!
Imagine! Planting a budding tree!

How high you'll go, how strong you'll be,
And when you've grown away from me,
The birds will reach you through the air,
(But I will know who put you there!)

You'll drink the rain; be fed by sun,
You'll probably outlive everyone!
What lovelier saplings grow than these?
Born on the New Year of the Trees.

Tu Bi-Shevat

Human beings are not the only ones who have their New Year celebrations. We have spoken of Rosh Hashanah as the first day of the year, of the New Year for rain or water on the eighth day of Sukkos, and now we learn that trees, too, have their New Year. This is Tu Bi-Shevat, the semi-holiday on the fifteenth day of the month Shevat, the fifth month in the Jewish calendar. The term "tu" is a combination of two Hebrew letters, with the collective numerical value of fifteen. In many circles, Chamishaw Awsawr Bi-Shevat is the name used; "chamishaw" and "awsawr" mean five and ten respectively.

Tu Bi-Shevat marks the end of the winter season and the arrival of spring in Israel: the day when life-nourishing sap begins to flow through the veins of trunks, boughs, and branches. Thousands of Jewish children go out on the land to plant trees. What a magnificent sight it must be to see the boys and girls marching to all corners of the land to plant saplings for fruit as well as for lumber — planting for posterity in a very real sense. This now established custom has given rise to another popular name by which the day is known: Chag Ha-n'teeos, the Festival of Planting. The sowing of little seeds that will grow into great towering oaks or stately pines or fruit trees has taken on the meaning of binding together ever more closely the people and the land of Israel.

The hard, questionable delicacy known as carob-bean, *bokser*, is the mark of Tu Bi-Shevat in America. A generation of Jews has grown up knowing that then the women of the Sisterhood or Parent-Teachers' Association distribute little bags to every child. In the bags are dates, figs, apples, nuts, raisins, but the first item to reach the hand is the *bokser*. What would Tu Bi-Shevat be without it! Assemblies are held and songs sung which emphasize the importance of reforestation in desert areas.

Starting about seventy-five years ago, many American states established Arbor Days for seasonal planting of trees. Some begin with special ceremonials and festivities. This Arbor Day development in the United States is much akin to the Tu Bi-Shevat holiday, so popular as a folk-day among our people.

Of Trees and Home

Our natural love of fruit delicacies and our children's almost innate inclination to dig and plant makes Tu Bi-Shevat a day to be marked at home.

For the dinner table on this day a bowlful of specially selected fruits ought to serve as centerpiece. Around the bowl there may appear a paper forest, cut out and set up before dinner. Of course, you have to make your own trees. Here is how it can be done:

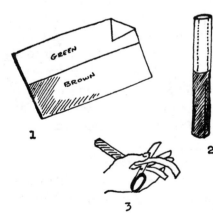

To Make Palm Tree:

1. Color a piece of typewriter or manila paper as follows: one-half of one long side, brown; the other half, green. Color green other side of paper backing the green (see 1).

2. Roll into fairly tight tube. Paste along open edge. Cut down green as far as brown but no farther. Make about four or five cuts around tube, no more.

3. Curl each strip outward as in curling ribbon (3) by holding blade of scissors against strip and placing thumb over blade and paper, gently pulling outward and curving wrist.
   Paper may also be curled by rolling each strip tightly downward and outward.

During the dinner read a poem or two on importance of trees and nature, which may be found in any children's nature book, or the poems which follow:

THE TREES' NEW YEAR

By Sadie Rose Weilerstein

Oh, Chamishaw Awsawr Bi-Shevat,
Chamishaw Awsawr Bi-Shevat:
It has a long name but I like it a lot,
'Cause we eat fruit and nuts from the loveliest spot;
Israeli oranges, almonds, and dates,
Bokser, and raisins, and figs on our plates!
And they're planting new trees in every bare spot
On Chamishaw Awsawr Bi-Shevat.

It's Chamishaw Awsawr Bi-Shevat,
Chamishaw Awsawr Bi-Shevat!
My sister is only a little tot,
But she asks more questions than goodness knows what.
"Do the trees pray today, or not?"
"What does it mean — Shevat?"
"If I swallowed a pit, would a tree grow inside?"
And a very important question beside:
"If we're supposed to plant a tree,
When, why, oh, why, oh don't we?"
Oh, it's why and where and what
On Chamishaw Awsawr Bi-Shevat.

— or the famous *Trees*, by Joyce Kilmer, which has been put to
music:

> I think that I shall never see
> A poem lovely as a tree.
> A tree whose hungry mouth is pressed
> Against the earth's sweet flowing breast.

A tree that looks at God all day
And lifts her leafy arms to pray.
A tree that may in summer wear
A nest of robins in her hair.
Upon whose bosom snow has lain;
Who intimately lives with rain.
Poems are made by fools like me,
But only God can make a tree.

You can also sing a few songs appropriate to the holiday. Here are four simple and delightful melodies:

זוּם גַּלִי גַּלִי — ZOOM GALI GALI

A round, explaining that the pioneer is meant for work and work for the pioneer.

זוּם גַּלִי, גַּלִי, גַּלִי, הֶחָלוּץ לְמַעַן עֲבוֹדָה,
עֲבוֹדָה לְמַעַן הֶחָלוּץ. זוּם גַּלִי, גַּלִי, גַּלִי.

BOKEHR

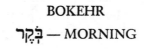

Morning is for work,	בְּקֶר בָּא לַעֲבוֹדָה.
Noon is for lunch,	צָהֳרַיִם בָּא לַאֲרוּחָה.
Evening is for rest,	עֶרֶב בָּא לִמְנוּחָה.
Night is for slumber.	לַיְלָה בָּא לְשֵׁנָה.

2.

Tzaw-haw-rah-yeem (repeat)
Tzaw-haw-rah-yeem baw lah-ah-
roo-chaw.

3.

Eh-rehv (repeat)
Eh-rehv baw li-m'noo-chaw.

4.

Lai-law (repeat)
Lai-law baw l'shay-naw.

YAW CHAI LEE LEE

יָה חַי לִי לִי —ARISE, BRETHREN

Arise, brethren, the world depends on work.

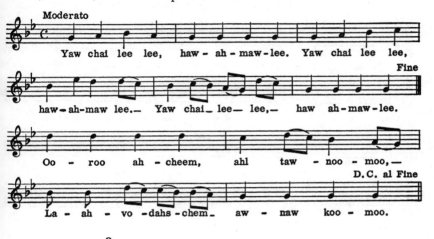

Yaw chai lee lee, haw-ah-maw-lee. Yaw chai lee lee,
haw-ah-maw lee.— Yaw chai lee lee, haw ah-maw-lee.
Oo - roo ah - cheem, ahl taw - noo - moo,—
La - ah - vo -dahs -chem aw - naw koo - moo.

.2

הָעוֹלָם עוֹמֵד עַל עֲבוֹדָה,
הָרִיעוּ שִׁירוּ בְּקוֹל תּוֹדָה.
יָה חַי מִי לִי, הָה, עֲמָלִי.

.3

הָעֲבוֹדָה הִיא חַיֵּינוּ,
מִכָּל צָרָה תּוֹצִיאֵנוּ.
יָה חַי לִי לִי, הָה, עֲמָלִי.

.1

יָה חַי לִי לִי, הָה, עֲמָלִי.

עוּרוּ, אַחִים, אַל תָּנוּמוּ,
לַעֲבוֹדַתְכֶם אָנָּא קוּמוּ.
יָה חַי לִי לִי, הָה, עֲמָלִי.

2.

Haw-o-lawm o-mayd ahl ah-vo-
daw,
Haw-ree-oo shee-roo v'kol to-daw.
Yaw chai lee lee, haw ah-maw-lee.

3.

Haw-ah-vo-daw hee chah-yay-noo,
Mi-kawl tzaw-raw so-tzee-ay-noo,
Yaw chai lee lee, haw ah-maw-lee.

KOOM BAWCHOOR AWTZAYL

קוּם בָּחוּר עָצֵל —WAKE UP, LAZY BOY, GO TO WORK

(Can be sung as a three part round)

קוּם בָּחוּר עָצֵל, וְצֵא לַעֲבוֹדָה,
קוּם קוּם וְצֵא לַעֲבוֹדָה,
קוּקוּרִיקוּ, קוּקוּרִיקוּ, הַתַּרְנְגֹל קָרָא.

When the children have learned the meaning of the day and
have seen its spirit at dinner and in the home, distribute to each a
piece of fruit and lead them in the blessing:

בָּרוּךְ אַתָּה יְיָ, אֱלֹהֵינוּ מֶלֶךְ הָעוֹלָם, בּוֹרֵא פְּרִי הָעֵץ:

Baw-rooch ah-taw Ado-noy, Elo-hay-noo meh-lech haw-o-
lawm, bo-ray p'ree haw-aytz.

Blessed art Thou, O Lord our God, King of the universe, who
createst the fruit of the tree.

We thank Thee, O God, for the blessings of earth which Thou
hast created for us. Teach us to value these blessings wisely and
to be ever grateful to Thee for Thy beneficence and goodness
to us.   Amen.

(If the fruit of which you are partaking is new to the season,
you should also recite the following prayer, which is reserved for
such special occasions.)

בָּרוּךְ אַתָּה יְיָ, אֱלֹהֵינוּ מֶלֶךְ הָעוֹלָם, שֶׁהֶחֱיָנוּ, וְקִיְּמָנוּ, וְהִגִּיעָנוּ
לַזְּמַן הַזֶּה:

Baw-rooch ah-taw Ado-noy, Elo-hay-noo meh-lech haw-o-
lawm, sheh-heh-cheh-yaw-noo, v'ki-y'maw-noo, v'hi-gee-aw-noo,
la-z'mahn ha-zeh.

Blessed art Thou, O Lord our God, King of the universe, who
hast granted us life, sustained us, and brought us to this festive
season.

We Plant Together

Children, you know, are fascinated by the planting of trees.
Contingent upon the community in which you live and weather
conditions, you might arrange a little planting party for a group of

children. Secure seeds from any nursery or feed store, being sur
to choose only those which can withstand the weather.

If cold or inclement weather precludes outdoor planting, yo
can have your party indoors. Many of the fruits we eat have seed
that can be used right at home. Some are orange, grapefruit, lim
beans, peach, or potatoes and sweet potatoes. Some of these, lik
the beans or orange or grapefruit seeds, require earth, so brin
earth into the house and have the children sow the seeds in littl

pots or glass jars. Some of these, such as sweet potatoes, need onl
water, to grow. In a few weeks, when the weather has change
the plants can be taken out for transplanting. In the meantime, yo
have provided a natural process for the children to watch daily
bring to the sun for nourishment, and see their own Tu Bi-Sheva
growing and bearing fruit.

GIFTS OF TREES

Another way of celebrating the Rosh Hashanah L'ilonos (Hebrew equivalent of New Year for Trees) is to plant a tree or two in Israel in honor of your children. This can be done through the Jewish National Fund, the agency which has planted millions of trees, at a cost of $2.50 each. A beautifully engraved certificate will be sent your children testifying that the trees were planted in their honor.

You might think of this suggestion a few weeks before Tu Bi-Shevat and have the J.N.F. offices send the certificate in time for you to present it to the children at the fruit-and-tree-dinner table on the holiday. They will be proud and happy to know that other children, their peers in Israel, are planting trees in their honor on the same day they receive the certificate.

As a concluding thought it should be noted that the Torah itself is called a tree: "It is a tree of life to them that hold fast to it, and everyone that upholds it is happy." This latter passage, from Proverbs, is chanted by the congregation every time the Torah is returned to the Ark after a reading service.

THE DATE TREE

By Judah Steinberg

In ancient Israel there once lived a pious man named Micah
Micah's house stood on the highway which led to the city of Jeru
salem. The house was built of stone, for Micah, who loved al
growing things, refused to chop down the trees of the forest.

Once, in honor of Chamishaw Awsawr Bi-Shevat, Micah plantec
a date tree beside his house. After a few years the tree grew so tal
that it cast a shade all about it. Micah put a table and benches unde
the tree. Whenever anyone passed his house going to Jerusalem
Micah would invite him to rest under the tree to eat and drink his fill

Sometimes a guest would insist on paying Micah for the meal
But when the guest was not looking, the pious man would put the
money back into the traveller's sack. When the guests departed
the birds would come down from the tree and eat the crumbs whicl
were left on the table.

One day an old man passed Micah's house. As was his custom
Micah invited him to rest and dine. When the meal was finished
the old man left money on the table for the food. Then he noticec
that his host had slipped it back into his sack when he thought he
was not looking. The old man, who was a prophet, said to Micah
"Your kindness shall be repaid. No matter where you and youl
children may be, wherever you shall live, you shall always eat the
fruit of your date tree under which the traveller enjoys youl
hospitality."

That moment the date tree silently gave its oath that its frui
would follow Micah and his children to all the lands of the world
so that the words of the prophet would come true.

The years passed peacefully and one bright day the date tree
bore its first fruits. But no sooner did Micah and his children sit at
the table to eat the dates, than the thunder of horses' hooves was
heard in the distance. Micah ran out onto the highway. A foreigr

army was speeding on its way towards Jerusalem. Micah and his children, and thousands of other Israelites, were taken captive by the conquering king.

As the monarch was returning from Jerusalem to his land, he passed Micah's house and saw the beautiful date tree. The king dismounted from his horse, plucked one of the dates, and ate it. The pit remained stuck in his throat. The soldiers quickly bore their king to their own city, where the doctors removed the pit and threw it out-of-doors. The date pit took root and grew slowly. And it happened that the house where Micah's children lived was under the date tree. Each year, on Chamishaw Awsawr Bi-Shevat, they enjoyed the fruit of the tree, as the prophet had predicted.

But Micah's grandchildren left the land of the conquering king and went to other lands to live. Each took with him fruit of the

date tree to plant beside his new home. Wherever the descendents
of Micah settled, in every land of the world, they continued to eat
the fruit of the date tree.

And as the Jewish children everywhere eat dates on Chamishaw
Awsawr Bi-Shevat, they say, "Who knows? Perhaps, I am one
of Micah's descendents."

TREE OF PEACE

Official United Nations Greeting Card design, created by Keiko Minami,
suggesting the feeling of serenity and peace — the purpose of the United
Nations. Reprinted by permission of UNICEF Greeting Card Fund.

Purim

PURIM

The carnival, the masquerade,
Means Purim and the Purim-plays.
Who'll be king? and who the jester?
What lovely lady is Queen Esther?

Hamantashen, stories told
Of happenings in days of old,
Recalling Haman's wicked scheme
Defeated by the lovely queen!

Mordecai crowned as king commands!
Let's have parties; clap our hands!
A wonderful time for everyone.
How we love the Purim fun!

Purim

No other day in the Jewish calendar boasts of as many facets as the exciting holiday of Purim. Mirth and merriment and tomfoolery are descriptive of the gladsome Feast of Lots. All came about because of the charming story of Mordecai and Esther and Haman and Ahasuerus and the deliverance of the Jewish people from Haman's plot to destroy them. Many parallel narratives of historical escapes from danger and disaster have added to the Purim celebrations of victory and the triumph of right.

THE STORY OF ESTHER

From the Scroll of Esther, known in Hebrew as *Megillas Esther*, in the third part of the Bible called Writings, we learn of the melodrama of Purim. The setting is Persia. Ahasuerus, ruler over one hundred and twenty seven domains, is making merry at a royal feast in Shushan, the capital city, with guests and friends summoned from all corners of the empire. Ostentatiously displaying his wealth and riches, the king wants to exhibit his Queen Vashti too. He sends for her, but she refuses to come. A quick consultation with his advisers yields this decision: Because of the effect such refusal might have upon the domestic relations of man and wife whereby a wife might emulate Vashti, she must be removed from her throne and replaced by a more obedient queen.

The competition to become queen is announced throughout the land and all beautiful women are invited to enter the contest. This was perhaps the most democratic selection in all human history. Many of the women of Persia vie for the honor, but Esther, lovely and graceful cousin of Mordecai, is the King's choice.

The story continues with a detailed account of two conspirators, the King's trusted guards, who seek to lay hands on Ahasuerus. Their plot is foiled by Mordecai, a master of many languages, who overhears the plans and reports them to Esther. The incident, which returns to plague Haman later, is dutifully recorded in the official Book of Remembrances.

Enter Haman — the new prime minister, a power-hungry villain who wants all the honor due his office. Mordecai, the Jew, refuses to pay him homage by bowing before him. Angered and vengeful, Haman seeks to punish Mordecai and his people. He easily convinces the king that the Jews do not respect the royal decrees. Haman receives permission to select a day for their extermination, and he does indeed cast lots or purim (*pur* means lot) to choose the day. When the news reaches Mordecai, he immediately sends word to Esther, urging her to intervene for her people in the hour of danger. He does so in a magnificent passage. "Do not think that you will escape because you are in the King's house. For if you hold your peace at this time, relief and deliverance will come to the Jews from another source, but you and your father's house will perish, and who knows whether you have not come to the royal estate for such a mission as this." Moved by her cousin's plea and her people's plight, Esther appears before the king and invites him and Haman to a party in her chambers.

On the eve of the invitation, Ahasuerus cannot sleep and orders the Book of Remembrances to be read to him. For the first time, he learns of the conspiracy against his life, and he finds that the man responsible for saving him has not been rewarded. Haman is summoned for consultation. Self-righteous and pompous, assuming that the man could not be anyone except himself, Haman suggests that the honored person be garbed in the royal garments, placed in a royal chariot, and escorted through the streets of Shushan, the Persian capital, with the proclamation, "Thus shall be done to the man whom the king desires to honor." To his utter amazement, Haman is told that Mordecai is recipient of the honor, and that he himself will be bearer of the news to the citizenry of Persia.

Humiliated and disheartened, Haman returns home. He is soon cheered as he recalls his scheduled engagement with Esther and the King. At the party, Ahasuerus is told by Esther how Haman has plotted to destroy her people. Haman is quickly removed from office. Since the King's seal had appeared on the previous decree, Ahasuerus cannot annul it, but superceding decrees are dispatched throughout Persia and Media and all the one hundred and twenty-seven provinces, granting the Jewish people the right to strike back on the 14th day of Adar — the day selected by Haman. Haman's entire family, also instigators of the plot, share with Haman the fate all would-be dictators deserve, and the triumph of justice encourages the Jewish people to celebrate Purim as a day of "feasting and gladness and of sending portions to one another and gifts to the poor."

This is the story of the original Purim. There is, however, a fascinating literature of many other Purims, particularly in the Middle Ages, marking miraculous escapes from attempts to destroy individuals, families, or entire Jewish communities. Every one of these was more than vaguely reminiscent of the original narrative. It is enough to mention some of these Purims and leave further study to the interested reader. There were a Purim De Las Bombas, Purim of Yom Tov Lipman, Bandit Purim, Purim Fettmilch, Purim Sargossa, Purim of Castile, Purim of Tripoli, Purim Shehli, and a host of others. These were always observed on days other than Purim — the only requirement for establishing an additional Purim. They were celebrated with the same hilarity and revelry as the original itself.

"On Purim one is expected to mellow himself with wine to the extent that he does not know the difference between saying 'Blessed be Mordecai' and 'Cursed be Haman,' " said Raba in Tractate Megillah (7b). It is interesting to mention that the English phrase "until he does not know" or "ahd d'lo yawdah" in Hebrew, has become the term for the masquerade on Purim. "Adloyada" means a gala Purim observance, which is gaining popularity throughout the country, as it has in Israel.

This levity, reserved only for Purim, led to merry-making without restraint, license which was carried over to community and seminary life. Worshipers and students took liberties with the Bible, Talmud, and the rabbis, although there was dignity and learning in the hilarity. Purim rabbis and Purim kings, similar to the youth programs in government like "mayor for a day" were common.

This is How We Celebrate Purim

In the Synagogue

On the night of Purim and in the morning, the Megillah is chanted after the regular evening (Maariv) service. The chant is peculiar to the Scroll of Esther and its changing tones tell the listener the story of Ahasuerus, Haman, Esther, and Mordecai, first in trouble, then in victory, and finally in peace. You will see that after every three or four columns are read, it is folded over. This is done so that the Megillah will look like a letter or dispatch similar to the one Ahasuerus sent out to his countrymen.

According to Jewish tradition we should all participate in the reading of the Megillah. Everyone in the synagogue should have a grogger or noisemaker. When the name of Haman is mentioned during the chant (it does not appear until the third chapter), the grogger is twirled and twirled and in some places feet are stamped as if to drown out the name of Haman, instigator of Purim, and prototype of oppressive dictators.

It is also customary to contribute to charity prior to reading the Megillah.

A special prayer (the first part of which is like that recited during Chanukah "Ahl Haniseem — For the Miracles") is included in the Amidah of the three daily services. It tells concisely the story of the Purim holiday and the miraculous deliverance.

On the morning of Purim in traditional synagogues, a special portion of the Torah is read.

IN THE HOME

1. *Shalach Monos — Sending Gifts*

The scroll of Esther calls Purim "a day of feasting and gladness and also a day of giving gifts." Inspired by this passage, we have the custom of exchanging gifts of fruits and delicacies between homes and families. Groups of children, on the afternoon or early evening, go from home to home visiting neighbors, bringing gifts and receiving presents, creating a spirit of neighborliness and friendship.

2. *Purim Seudah*

The Purim Seudah, Hebrew for Purim Feast, is an event requiring little preparation. No particular religious ceremony is involved, but the repast recalls the royal banquet of Esther and the King during which Esther, by her fearlessness, secured deliverance for her people. The retelling of the story, singing of songs and humorous ditties (a few are offered later), enjoying varied kinds of Hamantashen, those three-cornered cakes resembling hats of Haman's day — these lead to a delightful holiday dinner. Use the Jolly Hamantash (page 150) as centerpiece for the family dinner as well as for the party suggested below.

A Special Treat for the Children — A Purim Party

Celebrated throughout the world by carnivals, masquerades, and floats from the Esther story, Purim offers a good opportunity

for a children's party. The theme lends itself to suitable decoration. One may use the following suggestions:

1. *Invitations*

The two primary symbols of Purim are the Megillah and the grogger. Either can be used for the home-made invitation. For example: paste the edge of a piece of colored paper around a taffy stick, and roll it. You now have a scroll, or, if you have not covered the entire taffy stick, you have a symbol of the grogger. Now decorate it with Purim symbols. Draw a crown or a queen or king, and also appropriate words of invitation, such as "The Megillah at my Purim Party on _____ at _____, signed, King _____(Name)_____ or Queen _____(Name)_____. Please come dressed in costume and bring a Purimannah or Shalach Monos gift." Tie with rubber band or with the Happy Purim ribbon available in gift shops.

2. *Decorations*

Decorations are simple for this holiday, because any picture of kings or queens will be appropriate.

The table should bear a Purim theme.

The centerpiece can be either a cake with a Megillah scroll frosting or a series of jolly Hamantashen on a small box, thus:

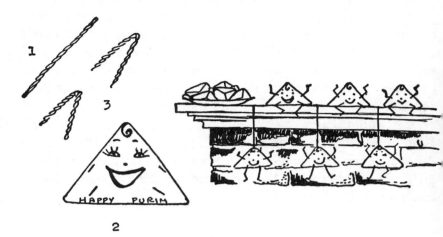

1. From a piece of any color construction paper cut a triangle. (2). Draw eyes, a nose, and a mouth. Cut a narrow slit on each side of "face."

2. Push a straight pipe cleaner through the first slit and out the other.

3. Punch or cut small holes at bottom of triangle through which to insert legs. Push straight pipe cleaners through holes until even on both sides. Bend down and twist together. Bend for knee and a little at bottom for feet.

4. Bend arms into desired position.

Individual place cards with the names of the children can be made out of plain paper, but with a pasted grogger or Megillah. Use either plain napkins folded into triangles, like the three-cornered hat of Haman, and a crayon picture of a queen or king or villain, or special Purim napkins which can be purchased in the gift shop.

See page 157 for Purim balloons which can be used as decorative pieces for the living or party room.

And naturally, since Purim is so reminiscent of royalty and all its embellishments, each guest should have a mask.

Here are instructions for making some as a family project:

To Make Mordecai Mask:

1. Cut out a face as in 1 from one color of construction paper. From a second color cut a turban.

2. Attach a small feather and sequins to turban.

3. From absorbent cotton cut and shape eyebrows, beard, and mustache.

4. Paste in appropriate places on mask.

5. Cut out eyes, a slit under nose, and a slit for mouth. Cut holes at ear level and attach string.

6. If mask is to be hung for decorative purposes, the other side should be completed as first side, so that there will be two fronts. Punch hole in top of turban and attach string.

To make crowns and coins for Esther mask:

1. Cut shapes from aluminum or gold-colored foil and paste to mask.

3. *Menu*

Now with the table properly set for Purim, the menu shoul‹
follow the holiday theme. It may be typed or written on a littl‹
Megillah, which can serve as souvenir of the day's event. Her‹
is a suggested menu:

Waldorf Salad a la Shushan

Candied Hamantashen   Persian Ice Cream with
                                     poppyseed spices

Cold Milk de Haman   Sons' (Haman's) Mints

Let us sing a few jolly Purim songs:

MAKE A HAMANTASH

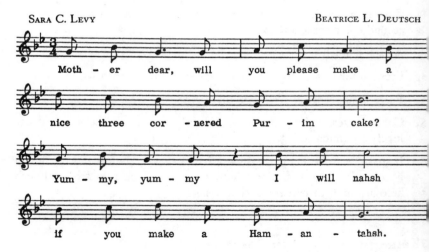

SARA C. LEVY   BEATRICE L. DEUTSCH

Moth - er dear, will you please make a
nice three cor - nered Pur - im cake?
Yum - my, yum - my I will nahsh
if you make a Ham - an - tahsh.

I LOVE THE DAY OF PURIM

S. S. Grossman   S. E. Goldfarb

Moderato

I love the day of Pu-rim so! For then, to syn-a-gogue I

go, And hear them read the sto-ry old of Es-ther brave and Ha-man

bold   O Pu-rim, O Pu-rim, O Pu-rim full of joy   For

ev-ery, for ev-ery   Jew-ish girl and boy! Have a par-ty, sing a song,

Turn the greg-er loud and long, Shlo-ach Mo-nos give and take,

Eat your Ho-men-tash - en cake! O   Pu-rim, O Pu-rim, O

Pu -rim, full of joy, For ev-ery, for ev-ery Jew - ish girl and boy.

A WICKED WICKED MAN

MIRIAM MEYERS

1. Oh! once there was a wick - ed wick - ed man, And
2. And Esth - er was the love - ly queen, _____ of

Ha - man was his name, Sir, He would have mur-dered
king A - chash - u - ay - ros, when Ha - man said he'd

all the Jews, Tho they were not to blame, Sir;
kill us all, Oh my, how he did scare us;

Oh, to-day we'll mer-ry mer-ry be Oh, to-day we'll mer-ry mer-ry be

Oh, to-day we'll mer-ry, mer-ry be And "nahsh" some Ho-men-tahsh-en.

2.

And Esther was the lovely queen,
Of King Ahasuerus,
When Haman said he'd kill us all,
Oh, my how he did scare us.
Chorus

3.

But Mordecai her cousin bold,
Said, "What a dreadful *chootz-pah*,
If guns were but invented now,
This Haman I would shoot, Sir."
Chorus

4.

When Esther speaking to the king
Of Haman's plot made mention,
"Ha, ha," said he, "Oh, no he won't!
I'll spoil his bad intention."
Chorus

5.

The guest of honor he shall be,
This clever Mr. Smarty,
And high above us he shall swing
At a little hanging party.
Chorus

6.

Of all his cruel and unkind ways
This little joke did cure him,
And don't forget we owe him thanks
For this jolly feast of Purim.
Chorus

IN SHOO SHOO SHOOSHAN LONG AGO

R. LEARSI

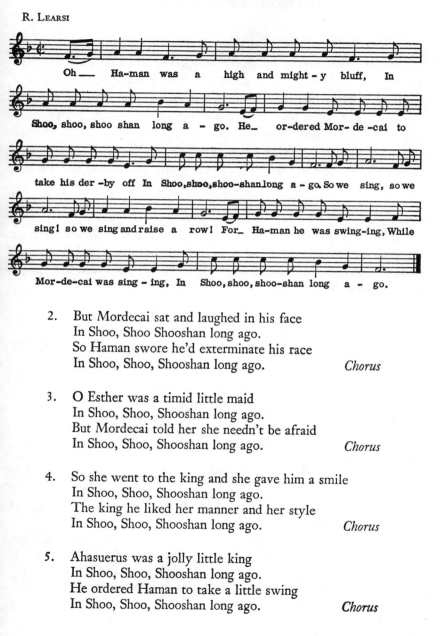

Oh— Ha-man was a high and might-y bluff, In Shoo, shoo, shoo shan long a - go. He— or-dered Mor-de-cai to take his der -by off In Shoo, shoo, shoo-shan long a - go. So we sing, so we sing! so we sing and raise a row! For— Ha-man he was swing-ing, While Mor-de-cai was sing - ing, In Shoo, shoo, shoo-shan long a - go.

2. But Mordecai sat and laughed in his face
   In Shoo, Shoo Shooshan long ago.
   So Haman swore he'd exterminate his race
   In Shoo, Shoo, Shooshan long ago.   *Chorus*

3. O Esther was a timid little maid
   In Shoo, Shoo, Shooshan long ago.
   But Mordecai told her she needn't be afraid
   In Shoo, Shoo, Shooshan long ago.   *Chorus*

4. So she went to the king and she gave him a smile
   In Shoo, Shoo, Shooshan long ago.
   The king he liked her manner and her style
   In Shoo, Shoo, Shooshan long ago.   *Chorus*

5. Ahasuerus was a jolly little king
   In Shoo, Shoo, Shooshan long ago.
   He ordered Haman to take a little swing
   In Shoo, Shoo, Shooshan long ago.   *Chorus*

Let's Play a Few Purim Games

1. *Pin the King's Horse*

This is like Pin the Shamash of Chanukah or Pin the Donkey game. You can buy the regular Pin the Donkey game, paint it over with royal colors and the word Ahasuerus. Or you can cut out your own horse and embellish it with bright regal colors. Each child is blindfolded, given a paper resembling the tail, turned around a few times, and let go toward the horse. The one who comes closest to the real king's horse's tail is declared the winner.

2. *Douse Haman*

Take a large board and cut out space enough in which to place the picture of Haman. Have Haman's mouth open and give each child three balls. See how many balls he can throw into the mouth at a distance of eight feet.

1. Use the hardest cardboard available. Cut out shape of Haman's head and paint features. Cut hole for mouth.
2. Attach sturdy bag so that ball does not get lost. Poke bag through mouth opening and staple.
3. Lean head against wall at enough of an angle so ball can go into mouth.
4. Suggestions for scoring: mouth 50 points; beard or nose, 25 points; eyes, 10 points; ears, 5 points.

3. *Break the Balloon*

Blow up regular round balloons and paint or draw pictures of the Purim characters on them. Attach them with stick pins to a large wooden sheet or board. Then, with darts, give each child three chances to puncture the balloons. Of course, most of the balloons should bear the pictures of Haman or the conspirators or Haman's sons and wife.

1. For King — use inks rather than paint for putting on features. Do the painting while balloon is not yet blown up. For crown — use construction paper. Cut and glue to balloon.
2. Cut Haman's hat, mustache, and beard from colored paper and paste to balloon.
3. Use yarn for the hair of Haman's wife, colored construction paper for headband.

4. *Purim Charades*

Before the party, prepare slips of paper equal to the number of children, each bearing the name of a Purim character, a symbol of the holiday, or an incident of the story. Distribute to the children during game time. No child should see the others' slips. Then, each acts out his charade. Time the guessing. The child whose charade takes the longest to guess is the winner.

GETTING THE MAIL

The last item of the party should be the Purimannah or the Shalach Monos ceremony, which can be a Shushan post office affair. (This is because so many letters or dispatches were involved in the Purim story.)

Have the host or hostess serve as postmaster behind a little table marked Post Office. Each child stands in line and approaches the postmaster, identifies himself, and receives his mail — the gift brought at the beginning of the party.

1. Take four cartons of the same size or two orange crates and pile into rectangle.
2. Paint the insides of the boxes and the frames facing forward. The outsides may be painted or covered with crepe paper.
3. From a large piece of cardboard cut oriental dome and color brightly.
4. Tack dome to boxes and also make sign and tack. Dome may be supported by prop in rear.
5. For postmaster have one of children dressed in oriental costume. Make official looking postmaster badge, or cut figure from large piece of cardboard and color brightly.
6. Place names of family members on each shelf, or names of guests at party. String Hamantashen and other goodies from top of shelf. Place individual presents in each shelf, or double up depending on number of presents.

And with a thank you and Happy Purim, the festivity of the afternoon is over.

HOW K'TONTON MASQUERADED ON PURIM

By Sadie Rose Weilerstein

"Father," said K'tonton, "when you were a little boy, did you dress up on Purim and wear a mask?"

"What a question!"

"And did you go to the other people's houses and sing songs?"

"Of course!"

"Could I dress up and masquerade?"

"A little fellow like you, K'tonton? You would be left behind under a doormat. But I'll make you a grogger. That will be better than masquerading." K'tonton's father took out a pen knife and a bit of wood and made him a beautiful noise-making grogger.

"Ras! Ras! Ras!" went the grogger as K'tonton whirled it about.

"It's nice to have a grogger," said K'tonton, "but not so nice as masquerading on Purim. I'd better talk to Mother."

Mother was in the kitchen rolling out Imberlach. She lifted K'tonton to the table.

"Could I masquerade on Purim?" asked K'tonton.

"You?" asked Mother. "Listen to the child! Haven't I lost you enough times already? But I'll tell you what I'll do. I'll make you a little Hamantash all for yourself. See! I've been pounding the poppy seeds." She pointed to a brass mortar on the table.

"Oh," said K'tonton, "poppy seed with honey?"

"Honey, of course," said Mother. "What else? Now sit still, K'tonton. I'll be back in a minute."

Off Mother went. K'tonton crossed his legs and waited.

"A minute is a long time," he said after a while.

He sat still again.

"I guess it must be two minutes. I guess it must be nine minutes. I guess I'll just get up and take a look at that poppy seed."

Up the side of a sack of flour he ran. Now he could see deep down into the mortar. He could see the pounder leaning against the side.

"That's a good slide," said K'tonton. He loved sliding down things. "I'll slide down and take a taste of that poppy seed. Mother wouldn't mind just a little taste."

The next moment his legs were over the top of the pestle and and he was sliding down. A thought popped into his head. "I must stop before I reach bottom. I might get stuck." But he couldn't stop. He was going too fast. Blimp! He was in poppy seed up to his waist.

And there was Mother's voice coming toward him. "Where's that K'tonton? I can't seem to keep track of him today. Well, I'll have to make the Hamantashen without him."

K'tonton felt the mortar lifted and turned over. The next moment, he was tumbling head over heels into a big bowl with poppy seed all around him. You couldn't tell which was poppy seed and which was K'tonton.

"Mother! Mother!" K'tonton began, but a stream of honey was flowing over him. The words caught in the honey and stuck fast.

And now a big wooden spoon came down into the bowl. It picked K'tonton up. It tossed him! It chased him! Round and round went K'tonton with the wooden spoon close behind. It caught him at last. It lifted him up into the air. It set him down in the middle of something soft. Dough! a flat piece of dough! K'tonton was being made into a Hamantash!

"I must speak! I must call!" thought K'tonton. "My voice! Where is my voice?" It was gone. By the time it returned, he had been slipped into a pan and was being carried off.

A Hamantash! That meant he would be put into an oven, a fiery furnace, like Abraham's and Daniel's companions. And God would not save him as He had saved Daniel's companions and Abraham. Had he not disobeyed his dear mother?

"Dear God," K'tonton prayed, "save me from the fiery oven even if I don't deserve it."

A voice was speaking. K'tonton pressed his ear to the hole in the Hamantash and listened.

"I'll leave the cakes on the shelf here to rise." The pan was lifted. Then all was still.

Then he wasn't to be put into the oven, not for a little while at least. He might yet escape. But how? He tried to move. His arms were stuck fast to the sides.

"I'll eat my way out," said K'tonton. He ate and ate and he ate. He ate so much he felt he could never look at honey or a poppy seed again. The hole grew bigger and bigger. It grew so big he could stick his head out, he could wriggle his hands loose, his arms, his legs. He was free.

Far, far below was the table. K'tonton shut his eyes tight and jumped — safe into the middle of the sack of flour.

But his troubles were not yet over.

Creak, creak, came a step across the floor.

"Mother!" thought K'tonton. "I must hide until I get this poppy seed washed off."

He slipped into a plate and hid behind a pile of Imberlach.

Mother's voice came nearer. "Father," it said, "I'm going to take this Shalach Monos to the new little boy next door. He has been sick in bed ever since they moved in. Poor little fellow! The sweets may cheer him up a bit."

She threw a napkin over the plate.

"Look after K'tonton, Father," she said. "He's somewhere about."

She lifted the plate and was off. And there was K'tonton in the Shalach Monos dish with cakes and candies and Hamentashen all about him.

"I wonder what is going to happen next?" he thought.

He was so tired he snuggled down at the bottom of the dish and shut his eyes. In another minute he was asleep.

*　　*　　*

"What has happened? Where am I?" said K'tonton when he opened his eyes a little later.

He peered cautiously over the side of a Hamantash and looked about. He was in a strange room. The dish was lying on a table near a bed, and on the bed lay a young boy propped up with pillows. Such a pale, unhappy looking fellow! He was staring soberly at the Shalach Monos, at the cakes, the Purim candies, the Hamantash, but he did not taste a thing and there wasn't a smile on his face. Something hurt inside of K'tonton.

"One oughtn't to look like that on Purim," he thought. "Purim is a good day, a day of gladness and feasting, a day of sending gifts to one another. The Megillah says it is."

K'tonton forgot that he was supposed to be hiding. He forgot he was covered with poppy seed. He forgot that he was dusted with flour. He knew only that he had to make the little boy smile. He stepped from behind the Hamantash and bowed low.

The boy's mouth opened and his eyes grew big as saucers.

"The inside of a Hamantash came alive!"

He stared hard.

"It must be a toy," he decided. "I suppose there are springs inside." He reached out his hand to feel, but K'tonton sprang back.

"I'm not a toy," he said. "I'm not the inside of a Hamantash — though I was inside one." he added truthfully. "I — I —." It was then that the great thought dawned on him. "I'm a Purim masquerader and I'm dressed up in poppy seed, and I've come to other people's houses, to your house, to sing Purim songs."

At that he lifted his shrill voice and began to sing:

> "Happy, happy Purim,
> Happy Purim day!"

For a minute the boy sat perfectly still and stared. Then he threw his head back and laughed. Such a happy, jolly, hearty, rollicking laugh, a regular Purim laugh! Ha, ha, ha, ha, ha! Ho, ho, ho, he, he!

"What could have happened?" cried the little boy's mother, who was in the next room. "I haven't heard David laugh in weeks."

She hurried into the bedroom and K'tonton's mother followed her. There was David laughing and clapping his hands; and there in the middle of the Shalach Monos dish, black with poppy seed, dusted with flour, was a wee little fellow singing and dancing away.

"K'tonton!" cried his mother. "How did you get here? What does this mean?"

"I — I'm the inside of a Hamantash," said K'tonton. "I'm in other people's houses. I'm masquerading as you did when you were a little girl."

"Please let him stay, please," begged David. "We're having such a jolly time."

So K'tonton's mother hurried home and fetched him a clean little suit and blouse and scrubbed him and dressed him in his holiday clothes.

K'tonton's father came too. He brought a Megillah with him and sang them the whole story of Purim, all about the King and Mordecai and the wicked Haman, and how good Queen Esther saved the Jews. K'tonton ran along under the words in the Megillah — to keep the place, you know — and every time he came to the name of the wicked Haman he whirled his grogger, Ras! Ras! Ras!

Then they sang songs and ate the cakes and Imberlach and Hamentashen; and everybody had such a happy time that no one thought of scolding K'tonton at all.

AN OLD-FASHIONED PURIM

By Elma Ehrlich Levinger

Now I like Chanukah a lot,
And Sukkos in the fall;
And Pesach; but I think that I
Love Purim most of all.

Maybe it's 'cause I like to watch
My mother when she bakes;
And help her pound the shiny stuff
She puts in Purim cakes.

The kitchen air smells awful sweet;
I just won't go away,
Till she gives me a Hamantash,
And sends me out to play.

We go to hear the Megillah read,
Me, mother, and the boys;
With Dad, who doesn't scold a bit,
But seems to like our noise.

At home we put on mother's clothes —
Her oldest clothes, I mean;
And cousin Rachel dresses up
And tries to act a queen.

For then we give our Purim play,
And laugh and dance and cheer; (*confidentially*)
Say, don't you wish that Purim came
'Bout twenty times a year?

ABOUT PURIM

By Miriam Myers

I love this merry Purim time;
  I know the story, too;
And if you don't mind listening,
  I'll tell it all to you.

Well, many, many years ago,
  In Persia, far away,
The King Ahasuerus lived
  And ruled with royal sway.

There was a lovely Jewish maid,
  And Esther was her name;
The king soon chose her for his wife,
  So queen she then became.

Her cousin's name was Mordecai,
  A good and pious Jew,
Who loved Queen Esther very much
  And to the king was true.

Now Haman, the king's favorite —
  A very wicked man —
Just wanted to kill all the Jews
  And formed a cruel plan.

But Mordecai let Esther know;
  At once she told the king,
Who, when he heard the wicked plot,
  Was mad as anything.

"Oh, no, the Jews shall all be saved,"
  Ahasuerus said:
And Haman and all his wicked sons
  Were hanged till they were dead.

Passover

PASSOVER

Freed from Pharaoh's heavy hand,
The Children of Israel crossed the land.
Unleavened bread they took in flight,
Led by Moses' gifted sight.

The Passover tale from days of old,
At Seder tables is retold.
Matzah, *chrayn, the bone of lamb,
Symbols to help us understand:

How precious is freedom to work and to
    pray!
How hard was the struggle to reach such
    a day.
Preserve it, deserve it, united agree:
Thank God for a life in the land of the
    free!

* Bitter herb

Passover

With the signs of Spring, birds returning after months of absence, ripeness of new green grass, buds bursting from the oaks and maples, swollen branches on azaleas, magnolias, and forsythia bushes, ready to burst at the first kiss of warm Spring sunshine, exquisite blooms of tulip, hyacinth, lilac, daffodil, and crocus, all the world blossoming in brilliant color and fragrance, comes Passover, the Festival of Spring.

Mere mention of the word Passover, or Pesach, is enough to bring happy smiles to our faces. It is the most exciting and thrilling of family experiences. It brings up visions of delightful evenings visiting our mothers' and fathers' homes; we picture grandmothers and grandfathers reclining like matriarchs and patriarchs, smiling with pride over the children and grandchildren sitting about the table — generations sprung from them and gathered for the Seder to reunite the family.

We are filled with anticipation as the holiday approaches. We talk about where to go for the first or second Seder, about last year's Seder, about the pride of watching the youngest child chant the *Feer Kashes* (Four Questions), about how many people attended, where they came from, how long the service lasted, the delicious meal which began with hard-boiled eggs in salt water, how we urged father or grandfather to hurry along or even skip a bit, how many cups of wine we drank, who managed to secure the Afikomon (the piece of Matzah hidden for use at the end of the service), what award was demanded by the culprit before he was prevailed upon to return it to close the Seder — all the magic and joy of Passover.

We are particularly happy in the knowledge that the experiences of the evenings together will mean so much to our children. Actually, Seder time and children's time are identical. The four questions, the four cups, the four sons of the Haggadah, the Afikomon, and all the rest of the ceremonials are geared to arouse the curiosity and retain the interest of the children.

While this is Passover in the setting of the Seder observance, the festival has much deeper implications and meanings. Next to the creation account in the Bible, Passover is the most important event in Jewish experience. It has influenced Jewish life strongly. Excerpts from the narrative are repeated daily in the prayer services; the first commandment emphasizes it: ("I am the Lord Thy God who brought thee out of the land of Egypt.") The Sabbath and the other two pilgrimage festivals, Sukkos and Shovuos, allude to the Exodus in their observance.

The basic concept of Passover is freedom, in every connotation. There is freedom from physical slavery, freedom from the week's stress and strain as on the Sabbath holiday, freedom from concern for sustenance as stressed by Sukkos, the harvest festival. Chanukah and Purim, too, have the ideal of freedom implicit in their stories. We see how fundamental to Jewish life freedom is, but its primary exposition is found in the story of Exodus.

PASSOVER AND AMERICA

We who are privileged to live in America can especially appreciate and understand the blessings of liberty and freedom. We remember how the founding fathers struggled for freedom in the beginnings of America as did our Jewish fathers at the beginning of our peoplehood.

And we take pride in the knowledge that the undying message of Passover — that freedom is a divine gift to be cherished and preserved — gave so much inspiration and encouragement to the creators of America as they sought independence and the great freedoms.

In the year of American independence, 1776, when Benjamin Franklin, Thomas Jefferson, and John Adams sought to portray the ideal of human freedom on the Great Seal of the United States, they recommended Moses leading the Israelites through the Red Sea. Around the rim of this seal appeared the words, "REBELLION TO TYRANTS IS OBEDIENCE TO GOD," a motto which Thomas Jefferson later made his personal seal.

When the founding fathers wanted to epitomize the American ideal, they chose from our Bible the magnificent message:

"And proclaim liberty throughout the land unto all the inhabitants thereof."

They inscribed it on the Liberty Bell enshrined in Philadelphia
cradle of American liberty.

When France presented the Statue of Liberty to our country and an appropriate inscription for its base was sought, the immortal words of Emma Lazarus were selected:

THE NEW COLOSSUS

Not like the brazen giant of Greek fame,
With conquering limbs astride from land to land,
Here at our sea-washed, sunset gates shall stand
A mighty woman with a torch, whose flame
Is the imprisoned lightning, and her name
Mother of Exiles. From her beacon-hand
Glows world-wide welcome; her mild eyes command
The air-bridged harbor that twin cities frame.

"Keep, ancient lands, your storied pomp,! " cries she,
With silent lips. "Give me your tired, your poor,
Your huddled masses yearning to breathe free,
The wretched refuse of your teeming shore.
Send these, the homeless tempest-tost to me;
I lift my lamp beside the golden door!"

For America as for all mankind, Passover is truly the Festival of Freedom.

THE PASSOVER NARRATIVE

The drama of the Passover story begins with Joseph, favorite son of Jacob, who incurred the envy and ire of his brothers by his dreams and was sold into Egyptian slavery. A chain of providential circumstances offered Joseph the opportunity to interpret the dreams of the king's royal cupbearer, baker, and finally of Pharaoh himself. So impressed was Pharaoh that he elevated Joseph to the position of prime minister. In his new role Joseph met his brothers, who had come to Egypt for food; he prevailed upon them and their aged father to move to Egypt. For many years the children of Israel lived in comparative ease and peace. But when Jacob and Joseph passed away and a new Egyptian administration assumed power, Joseph's good deeds and works for Egypt were quickly forgotten. The new Pharaoh feared the numbers of the Israelites and took oppressive steps to reduce them to slavery.

In this suddenly changed environment the Jews labored under the heavy hands of taskmasters. But Pharaoh was not sure of himself. The fear that someone would rise to overthrow him plagued Pharaoh in a dream. He ordered his people to destroy all boy babies born to Jewish women by casting them into the river.

At this point in the narrative, Moses was born to Jochebed and Amram. Fear of the king impelled Jochebed to place three-months-old Moses in a little basket, waterproofed with black pitch and tar. She set it adrift in the River Nile. That very day, Pharaoh's daughter, coming to the river to bathe, saw the floating basket, retrieved it, and decided to adopt the little occupant. She gave the baby to Miriam, Moses' sister, who had been on guard and who took her brother home to be raised. When Moses grew up, he returned to the Egyptian King's palace.

Grown to manhood, Moses went into the fields and saw at first hand how his people were suffering under the Egyptians and he determined to help them. In solemn thought one day, Moses was startled to behold a lowly thornbush burning. Out of the bush he heard a voice, "Moses, Moses!" He responded, "Hinaynee, I am here." He saw the bush burning, but not being consumed.

This was the sign of God. God told him he had been selected to lead the children of Israel out of Egypt. Moses hesitated, but it was the will of God, and he finally accepted the charge.

Two legends tell of Moses' kindly character, which impelled God to choose him for leadership. When Moses was a shepherd, he noticed one of the lambs running away and he followed. He overtook it at a brooklet where the lamb had stopped to drink.

Moses took the little animal in his arms and said, "Is this why you ran away? Had I known that you were so thirsty, I would have carried you here in my own arms." And a heavenly voice was heard to say, "Moses, Moses, you who can be so kind to animals and express such sympathy, are a fit leader to bring your people out of Egypt."

The second legend relates to the time Moses tended the flock of his father-in-law, Jethro. Moses kept the older and stronger sheep back while the younger and weaker ones fed on the tender grass. Only when the younger sheep were satisfied did he permit the older ones to feed. Again a heavenly voice came forth and was heard to say, "Let him who knows how to shepherd the flock, each according to his own strength, come forth to lead My people out of Egypt."

To continue with our story, Moses, with his brother Aaron, lay plans for Israel's redemption from slavery. Pharaoh, of course, refused to permit the valuable slaves to leave and it was only after ten dreadful plagues were visited on the Egyptians that the Israelites were given freedom to depart. On the evening of the Passover, the fourteenth day of Nisan, they baked bread in preparation for the journey. The dough had no chance to rise. The result was the flattened, unleavened cakes called Matzos.

We can imagine the great happiness, the hosannas and halleluyahs sung. They were free, no longer slaves, free to live, to think, to worship, to direct their own way of life.

Indeed, this was the "z'mahn chay-roo-say-noo — the festival of our freedom." To celebrate this festival, we call our families together annually, and retell the experiences of our forefathers. And we thank God for the freedom with which we are blessed. We do this as we sit about the table on the first two nights of Passover and comply with the biblical behest, "And thou shalt tell thy son," in the ceremony we call the Seder.

Passover is observed for a period of eight days beginning on the eve of the full moon (15th day) of Nisan. Orthodox and Conservative Jews celebrate the first two and the last two days as religious holidays, while Reform Jews recognize seven days of the holiday, with the first and the seventh, the important days. The in-between period, as in the festival of Sukkos, is called Chol Hamoed or Intermediate Days.

The synagogue service is similar to that of the other pilgrimage holidays. Yizkor (Memorial) services are recited. The Song of Songs is chanted in some traditional synagogues, and a special prayer entitled *Tal* (Dew), counterpart of the Prayer for Rain (*Geshem*) on Shemini Atzeres (see page 73), is chanted.

WE PREPARE FOR THE SEDER AT HOME

Do not think a Seder at home is too difficult to conduct. It is not. Do not deprive your family of the opportunity of building a strong tradition which will increase in depth and meaning and richness as the years go on.

The following pages are designed to detail what you will want to know about the Seder, the preparations, the items you will need for the table setting as well as the service itself, and a step by step explanatory section, with a condensed Haggadah.

In anticipation of Passover, prepare well ahead, so that the family reunion may generate excitement, warmth, and good spirit. Include your children in some of the preparations. You can do this by making a party of the Seder. For example:

a) *Invitations*

Make the Seder invitation personal. Help your children prepare their own. Since the Haggadah, the order of the service, is a book, the invitation might be a small book entitled, "My Haggadah." On the front cover you can print such phrases as "Come to My Seder Party" or "Read Your Haggadah at our Seder on _____ at _____." Pictures of Matzah or other Passover symbols can be crayoned or painted, or cut out from magazines and newspapers and pasted on the cover page.

b) *Passover Silhouette*

To add color to your table, you can arrange a silhouette to symbolize the Passover story. Here is a picture we might suggest and the directions:

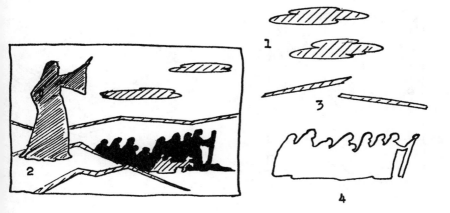

1. Select a large sheet of light colored paper for the background.

2. From a darker sheet of paper cut cloud (1) and lines for mountains (3).

3. From a still darker sheet cut the people (4). Correct detail is not as important as achieving the feeling that a crowd of people are moving forward (4).

4. From a still darker sheet or from the same sheet as 3, cut the figure of Moses.

5. Paste all figures on large sheet of paper, being careful that the figures in the foreground overlap those farther back.

6. Hang on dining room wall for Seder night.

c) *Matzah Cover*

To further add beauty to the Passover table as well as the personal touch of the family, we suggest that you prepare your own Matzah cover for the three pieces of Matzah used in the Seder service. Following is a suggested cover:

1. Use four plain white linen men's handkerchiefs or any opaque, easily stitched material cut into four equal pieces, or napkins.
2. If cut material is used, hem pieces; handkerchiefs and napkins are already hemmed.
3. Handkerchief that is used for bottom of cover is opened out and creases are pressed out. Fold second handkerchief ½ inch to 1 inch back and stitch. Third handkerchief is folded ½ to 1 inch back of second and fourth is folded in back of third, so that layers of the Matzah cover can be seen.
4. Sew all four handkerchiefs together on three sides (sides that have not been folded and stitched after embroidering design of cover).
5. Design: Three groups of Israel, Kohen, Levi, Yisroel, may be stitched one on each of the bottom layers.

The Liberty Bell, symbol of freedom, may be used for the central theme. The two Hebrew words above the bell are "Z'mahn chayroosaynoo" meaning literally "festival of our freedom."

d) *Seder Centerpiece*

To remember the flight to freedom and the hurried baking of the first Matzah in Egypt, here is a centerpiece you can help children make and which you can place at the center of the table:

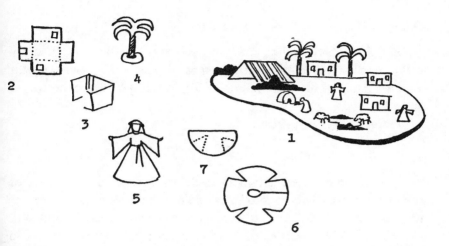

1. Cut a large piece of cardboard or plywood into a free form shape for the ground. Paint it tan or green or glue sand to it. Scatter small pebbles for rocks.
2. Houses—small boxes may be used with doors and windows cut out or they may be made from flat pieces of cardboard cut as in (2) and taped together as in (3). To fold, score with razor blade by running razor along right side of fold but not cutting through.
3. Trees are smaller version of Tu Bi-Shevat trees. Attach with putty (4).
4. Small dolls and animals may be cut from paper or may be purchased at 5 & 10 cent store. Make headgear by tying circle of fabric around head with thread or string. Robe is cut from a circle. First cut along dotted lines as in (7). Front is slit to neck and neck cut in V. May be pinned or sewn together when on doll. Tie with string at waist.
5. A small mirror may be used as a pool. To eliminate regularity of edges, border with stones, or foliage cut from cotton or sponge and dyed green.
6. Oven is made of clay. Matzos are made of thin cardboard strips.

e) *Children Help*

As the evening approaches, your children will be happy to help with preparation of the Charoses (described below) and setting the table. They will also want to make sure that each necessary item is available for the service.

f) *Activate Your Children in the Seder*

Before the Seder night you will have to think about the younger children, how to keep their attention as well as how to include them in the service. This will be especially true if you are expecting a large family.

Here are a few suggestions:

1. *Children's Recitations*

Prior to the Seder, assign to each child either a small part of the Haggadah to read or to tell, or one of the symbols or customs of the Passover to explain. At the appropriate time, each child will rise to offer his contribution to the meaning of the evening. You will find that the entire story in the Haggadah can be covered in this way, and you will also have made the younger children feel part of a great experience.

A few examples follow:

   a) "We begin the Seder with the Kiddush and thank God for the loveliness of our family."

   b) "We eat Matzah on Passover because our fathers didn't have too much time. The bread couldn't rise and it remained flat. That's Matzah."

   c) "There are four sons in the story of Passover: a good one, a bad one, a simple one, and one who doesn't know anything. I like to be like the good one, because I like Passover."

d) "We eat bitter herbs because we remember when our people were unhappy. We thank God that we are living in happiness in America."

e) "We spill drops of wine because of the plagues. We give of our gladness and think of other people's sorrows."

f) "Before dinner we make two blessings — one for bread and the second for Matzah. Both are really bread, but Matzah is unleavened."

g) "We are ready for the Afikomon. After we eat it, we're not supposed to eat any more tonight."

h) "When we open the door Elijah will come in. He brings us good wishes. We won't see him, but he takes a very tiny sip anyway."

Here is a beautiful poem one of the children might be encouraged to learn for the Seder:

THE QUESTIONS

By JESSIE E. SAMPTER

I've practiced, practiced day by day
To learn the questions I must say
   On Seder night;
Then father, like the king of kings,
Now low, now loud, the answer sings
   When I have asked aright.

To you and me the story's told,
Because 'twas we in days of old
    Whom God made free.
To Pharaoh's slave He gave His rod
And made of us a prince of God
    And dried for us the sea.

But I would ask one question more:
If we today should crowd the shore
    Of every land
With listening mind and daring heart,
Would not the oceans leap apart
    Again at God's command?

Larger portions of the Haggadah should be given the older children to recite.

2. Hiding the Afikomon

Hiding the Afikomon after father has concealed it in the early part of the service (Yahchahtz) is one of the old customs designed to retain the interest of the children and stimulate their curiosity. Tradition has it that the Seder service cannot be completed without the Afikomon, and this has led to "ransoming" the Afikomon.

(You may encourage your children to hide the Afikomon, but be sure to have a few prizes on hand to give to the children involved.)

3. Preparing the Songs

We have included the songs traditionally sung at the Seder table. They are easy to learn and require only a little preliminary practice at the piano. By going over them once or twice you will find much more delight and enjoyment in them at the Seder.

If your children are very young, try to teach them the refrains to these simple melodies, or secure the Passover children's records available in synagogue gift shops.

WHAT YOU NEED FOR THE SEDER

a) *The Table Setting*

1. Seder Plate — a special plate displaying the symbols used in the service.

2. Matzah Cover — a special cover with two dividers, allowing place for three pieces of Matzah.

3. Passover Wine — sufficient wine for four cups per person. As in all Jewish ceremonials the Kiddush or sanctification of wine introduces the service.

4. Napkin or Doily for Afikomon — a napkin or doily with which to cover the middle piece of Matzah during the service. This piece is put away for recall at the end of the dinner. Afikomon means dessert.

5. Cup of Elijah — a special goblet used following dinner to invite the spirit of Elijah to bless the home. Elijah in Jewish tradition is the messenger and harbinger of good tidings, peace, and salvation.

6. Extra Saucer — an extra saucer should be placed at each setting to be used for the ten plagues ceremony.

7. Extra Spoon — an extra spoon should be provided for each person for the Moror or bitter herbs blessing.

8. Kiddush Cups — each person should have a wine cup for the traditional four cups of wine.

9. Uniform Haggadahs — a uniform Haggadah means easier joint participation by the family and guests.

10. Pitcher and Bowl — for washing the hands during the service itself.

11. Cushioned Armchair — father or the head of the household should have a cushioned armchair to symbolize the ease and relaxation of freedom and free men.

12. Flowers — these are optional but will add beauty and freshness to the table.

b) *The Seder Service*

1. Charoses — a mixture of chopped nuts, apples, wine, and cinnamon, reminiscent of the mortar used by the Israelites in building cities for the Egyptians. The pleasant taste is designed to symbolize God's kindness to us.

2. Roasted Shankbone — symbolic of the sacrifice of the paschal lamb on the eve of departure from Egypt. A roasted chicken neck may also be used.

3. Roasted Egg — symbolizes the offering in the Temple added to the paschal sacrifice. Two other meanings are: the egg is symbolic of the continuity of life; it also signifies the beginning of Spring.

4. Karpas — watercress or parsley to remind us of the meagerness of life in Egypt and also of the greenness of the Spring season.

5. Moror — bitter herbs or horse-radish, signifying the bitterness of slavery.

6. Matzos — unleavened bread, recalling the haste in which the Israelites left Egypt. Three pieces are used. Two represent the two loaves of the Sabbath and holidays, that is, the double portion of manna which Jews received in the wilderness on the eve of the Sabbath, and the third

stands for the *"lechem oni* — bread of affliction" mentioned in the Haggadah. Another explanation of the three Matzos has it that they represent the three groupings of Israel, Kohen (priest in the Temple), Levi (assistant to the priests) and Yisroel, (Israelite).

7. Dish of Salt Water — to be used with parsley or watercress.

Place these symbols on the Seder plate in the following order:

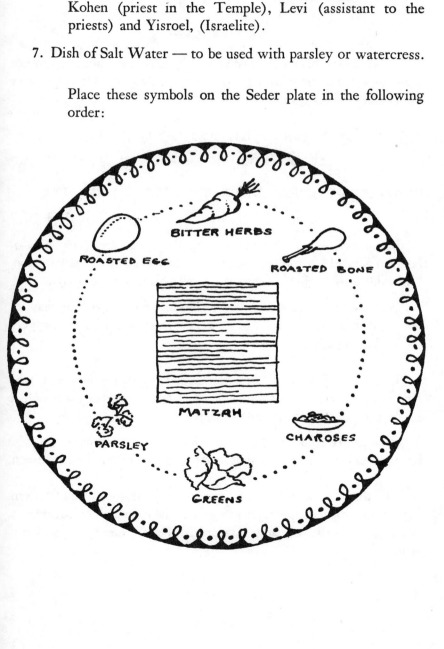

ROASTED EGG

BITTER HERBS

ROASTED BONE

MATZAH

PARSLEY

CHAROSES

GREENS

THE EVENING OF THE SEDER

The Evening Begins:

At sundown, before the Seder, as with all other holidays, mother welcomes the arrival of Passover by reciting the blessings over the candles, as follows:

בָּרוּךְ אַתָּה יְיָ, אֱלֹהֵינוּ מֶלֶךְ הָעוֹלָם, אֲשֶׁר קִדְּשָׁנוּ בְּמִצְוֹתָיו,
וְצִוָּנוּ לְהַדְלִיק נֵר שֶׁל (On Sabbath add שַׁבָּת וְ) יוֹם טוֹב:

בָּרוּךְ אַתָּה יְיָ, אֱלֹהֵינוּ מֶלֶךְ הָעוֹלָם, שֶׁהֶחֱיָנוּ, וְקִיְּמָנוּ, וְהִגִּיעָנוּ
לַזְּמַן הַזֶּה:

Baw-rooch ah-taw Ado-noy, Elo-hay-noo meh-lech haw-o-lawm, ah-shehr ki-d'shaw-noo b'mitz-vo-sawv, v'tzi-vaw-noo, l'hahd-leek nayr shel (*On Sabbath add:* Sha-baws v') yom tov.

Baw-rooch ah-taw Ado-noy, Elo-hay-noo meh-lech haw-o-lawm, sheh-heh-cheh-yaw-noo, v'kee-y'maw-noo, v'hi-gee-aw-noo, la-z'mahn ha-zeh.

Blessed art Thou, O Lord our God, King of the universe, who hast sanctified us by Thy commandments and granted us the privilege of kindling the (Sabbath and) holiday lights.

Blessed art Thou, O Lord our God, King of the universe, who hast granted us life, sustained us, and brought us to this festive season.

We thank Thee, O God, for the blessings of liberty and freedom. Grant that this most precious gift be assured us and all our dear ones. Bless, our family, we pray Thee, with health, happiness, and joy. Amen.

THE SEDER SERVICE or *Haggadah*

The family is seated around the festive table. Father begins with explanation of the significance of the holiday and the Seder.

Father:

"We are about to enjoy the beautiful Seder service and conduct it as our forefathers have done for many, many centuries. We are about to re-live the experiences our fathers had in Egypt, when they were slaves to Pharaoh, and learn from them how very fortunate we are and how appreciative we ought to be for the blessings of liberty and freedom.

"The word Seder means order. There is a set and definite order which we follow in our service. Altogether there are fifteen parts. Most are short and symbolic, that is, we take part in them because they have special meanings for us and because they teach us about slavery and freedom.

"In front of me, you will see a Seder plate on which a number of items have been placed. Most of these take us back to the days of Egyptian slavery. Let us look at each for a moment.

"Here is the Matzah, the unleavened bread, recognized as the most important symbol of the holiday. Matzah is sometimes baked square and sometimes round, but always flat and with perforations. It reminds us of the hurry in which our forefathers baked and ate the bread when they were leaving Egypt, not having time to let the bread leaven or rise. We use three Matzos in the service and we place each in a separate compartment or fold. The three represent three classes of Jewish people, Ko-hah-neem (Priests), L'vi-yeem (Levites), and Yis-r'ay-leem (Israelites). Some authorities say that the reason for the three Matzos is that two represent the two loaves of bread we use on Sabbath and holidays, and the third is the "lechem oni" or "bread of affliction," about which we will read later.

"Here is the Roasted Shankbone. We should remember that in days gone by, sacrifice was the manner of worship, and the roasted shankbone, or the chicken neck some people use, reminds us of the Paschal lamb sacrifice offered on the evening before the departure from Egypt.

"Here is the Roasted Egg. There are many reasons for having the egg on the plate. Some say it is symbolic of the continuity of life. Others tell us that it signifies the beginning of Spring. And still others say that it reminds us of the Chagigah or second and special festival offering which our fathers brought in Temple days, centuries ago.

"Here is the Moror, the horse-radish. We use the Moror, which means "bitter," because it reminds us of the bitterness of slavery in Egypt and how bitter it is to be slaves and not blessed with freedom.

"Here is the Charoses. It is a mixture of chopped nuts, apples, wine, and cinnamon, and is made to look like mortar because it reminds us of the mortar the Israelites used when they built cities for the Egyptians. The pleasant taste of the Charoses is supposed to symbolize God's kindness and grace to us.

"Here is the Karpas. Some families use watercress and others, parsley or lettuce, onions or even potatoes. This is the symbol of earth's produce and God's bounty. It also symbolizes the coming of Spring, because Pesach is also known as Chag Ha-Aviv, the Festival of Spring.

"Here is the Salt Water. It is the symbol of the bitter tears which our ancestors shed during their difficult days of slavery. We will use the salt-water together with the Karpas when we dip the Karpas into it.

"Now that we understand the symbols of the service, we are ready to begin. Every Sabbath and holiday in Jewish tradition begins with the Kiddush, the blessing over the wine. Wine is the symbol of joy and gladness, and we are joyous tonight that we are privileged to be together as a family and to observe the festival of freedom. At the Seder, we drink four cups of wine, because in the Bible there are four different expressions used by God in His redemption of our fathers. They are: I shall bring you out, I shall deliver you, I shall redeem you, and I shall take you out. We will also meet this number four when we come to the Four Sons and the Four Questions.

"We take our wine cups in our right hands and rise to begin our Seder as we recite the Kiddush, and thereby sanctify the holiday."

1. Kadaysh — קַדֵּשׁ

Adults and children who know the Kiddush should be encouraged to join in.

(When the Seder is held on Sabbath eve begin here and add all words appearing in brackets:)

וַיְהִי עֶרֶב וַיְהִי בֹקֶר

יוֹם הַשִּׁשִּׁי. וַיְכֻלּוּ הַשָּׁמַיִם וְהָאָרֶץ וְכָל צְבָאָם. וַיְכַל אֱלֹהִים בַּיּוֹם הַשְּׁבִיעִי מְלַאכְתּוֹ אֲשֶׁר עָשָׂה. וַיִּשְׁבֹּת בַּיּוֹם הַשְּׁבִיעִי, מִכָּל מְלַאכְתּוֹ אֲשֶׁר עָשָׂה. וַיְבָרֶךְ אֱלֹהִים אֶת יוֹם הַשְּׁבִיעִי, וַיְקַדֵּשׁ אֹתוֹ, כִּי בוֹ שָׁבַת מִכָּל מְלַאכְתּוֹ, אֲשֶׁר בָּרָא אֱלֹהִים לַעֲשׂוֹת:

(When the Seder is held on weekday evenings, begin here:)

בָּרוּךְ אַתָּה יְיָ, אֱלֹהֵינוּ מֶלֶךְ הָעוֹלָם, בּוֹרֵא פְּרִי הַגָּפֶן:

בָּרוּךְ אַתָּה יְיָ, אֱלֹהֵינוּ מֶלֶךְ הָעוֹלָם, אֲשֶׁר בָּחַר בָּנוּ מִכָּל עָם, וְרוֹמְמָנוּ מִכָּל לָשׁוֹן, וְקִדְּשָׁנוּ בְּמִצְוֹתָיו. וַתִּתֶּן לָנוּ, יְיָ אֱלֹהֵינוּ, בְּאַהֲבָה,

[שַׁבָּתוֹת לִמְנוּחָה וּ] מוֹעֲדִים לְשִׂמְחָה, חַגִּים וּזְמַנִּים לְשָׂשׂוֹן. אֶת יוֹם [הַשַּׁבָּת הַזֶּה וְאֶת יוֹם]

חַג הַמַּצּוֹת הַזֶּה, זְמַן חֵרוּתֵנוּ,

[בְּאַהֲבָה] מִקְרָא קֹדֶשׁ, זֵכֶר לִיצִיאַת מִצְרָיִם. כִּי בָנוּ בָחַרְתָּ, וְאוֹתָנוּ קִדַּשְׁתָּ מִכָּל־הָעַמִּים. [וְשַׁבָּת] וּמוֹעֲדֵי קָדְשֶׁךָ [בְּאַהֲבָה וּבְרָצוֹן] בְּשִׂמְחָה וּבְשָׂשׂוֹן הִנְחַלְתָּנוּ. בָּרוּךְ אַתָּה יְיָ, מְקַדֵּשׁ [הַשַּׁבָּת וְ] יִשְׂרָאֵל וְהַזְּמַנִּים:

(On Saturday night add:)

בָּרוּךְ אַתָּה יְיָ, אֱלֹהֵינוּ מֶלֶךְ הָעוֹלָם, בּוֹרֵא מְאוֹרֵי הָאֵשׁ:

בָּרוּךְ אַתָּה יְיָ, אֱלֹהֵינוּ מֶלֶךְ הָעוֹלָם, הַמַּבְדִּיל בֵּין קֹדֶשׁ לְחֹל, בֵּין אוֹר לְחֹשֶׁךְ, בֵּין יִשְׂרָאֵל לָעַמִּים, בֵּין יוֹם הַשְּׁבִיעִי, לְשֵׁשֶׁת יְמֵי הַמַּעֲשֶׂה. בֵּין קְדֻשַּׁת שַׁבָּת לִקְדֻשַּׁת יוֹם טוֹב הִבְדַּלְתָּ, וְאֶת יוֹם הַשְּׁבִיעִי מִשֵּׁשֶׁת יְמֵי הַמַּעֲשֶׂה קִדַּשְׁתָּ. הִבְדַּלְתָּ וְקִדַּשְׁתָּ אֶת עַמְּךָ יִשְׂרָאֵל בִּקְדֻשָּׁתֶךָ. בָּרוּךְ אַתָּה יְיָ, הַמַּבְדִּיל בֵּין קֹדֶשׁ לְקֹדֶשׁ:

בָּרוּךְ אַתָּה יְיָ, אֱלֹהֵינוּ מֶלֶךְ הָעוֹלָם, שֶׁהֶחֱיָנוּ, וְקִיְּמָנוּ, וְהִגִּיעָנוּ לַזְּמַן הַזֶּה:

(When the Seder is held on Sabbath eve begin here and add all words appearing in parentheses:)

Va-y'hee eh-rehv, va-y'hee vo-kehr.

Yom ha-shi-shee: Va-y'choo-loo ha-shaw-ma-yeem v'haw-aw-retz v'chawl tz'vaw-awm. Va-y'chahl Elo-heem ba-yom ha-sh'vee-ee, m'lahch-to ah-shehr aw-saw. Va-yish-bos ba-yom ha-sh'vee-ee mi-kawl m'lahch-to ah-shehr aw-saw. Va-y'vaw-rech Elo-heem, ehs yom ha-sh'vee-ee, va-y'ka-daysh o-so, kee vo shaw-vahs mi-kawl m'lahch-to, ah-shehr baw-raw Elo-heem la-ah-sos.

(When the Seder is held on weekday evenings, begin here:)

Baw-rooch ah-taw Ado-noy, Elo-hay-noo meh-lech haw-o-lawm, bo-ray p'ree ha-gaw-fen.

Baw-rooch ah-taw Ado-noy, Elo-hay-noo meh-lech haw-o-lawm, ah-shehr baw-chahr baw-noo mi-kawl awm, v'ro-m'maw-noo mi-kawl law-shon, v'ki-d'shaw-noo b'mitz-vo-sawv. Va-ti-ten law-noo, Ado-noy Elo-hay-noo, b'ah-ha-vaw, (sha-baw-sos li-m'noo-chaw oo-) mo-ah-deem l'sim-chaw, cha-geem oo-z'ma-neem l'saw-son, ehs yom (ha-sha-baws ha-zeh v'ehs yom) chahg ha-ma-tzos ha-zeh. Z'mahn chay-roo-say-noo (b'ah-ha-vaw) mik-raw ko-desh, zay-chehr lee-tzee-ahs mitz-raw-yeem. Kee vaw-noo vaw-chahr-taw, v'o-saw-noo ki-dahsh-taw, mi-kawl haw-ah-meem: (v'sha-baws) oo-mo-ah-day kawd-sh'chaw (b'ah-ha-vaw oo-v'raw-tzon) b'sim-chaw oo-v'saw-son, hin-chahl-taw-noo. Baw-rooch ah-taw Ado-noy, m'ka-daysh (ha-sha-baws v') Yis-raw-ayl, v'ha-z'ma-neem.

(On Saturday night add first two paragraphs:)

Baw-rooch ah-taw Ado-noy, Elo-hay-noo meh-lech haw-o-lawm, bo-ray m'o-ray haw-aysh.

Baw-rooch ah-taw Ado-noy, Elo-hay-noo meh-lech haw-o-lawm, ha-mahv-deel bayn ko-desh l'chol, bayn or l'cho-shech, bayn Yis-raw-ayl law-ah-meem, bayn yom ha-sh'vee-ee l'shay-shehs y'may ha-ma-ah-seh. Bayn k'doo-shahs sha-baws li-k'doo-shahs yom tov hiv-dahl-taw, v'ehs yom ha-sh'vee-ee mi-shay-shehs y'may ha-ma-ah-seh ki-dahsh-taw; hiv-dahl-taw v'ki-dahsh-taw, ehs a-m'chaw Yis-raw-ayl bi-k'doo-shaw-seh-chaw. Baw-rooch ah-taw Ado-noy, ha-mahv-deel bayn ko-desh l'ko-desh.

Baw-rooch ah-taw Ado-noy, Elo-hay-noo meh-lech haw-o-lawm, sheh-heh-cheh-yaw-noo, v'kee-y'maw-noo, v'hi-gee-aw-noo, la-z'mahn ha-zeh.

Blessed art Thou, O Lord our God, King of the universe, who createst the fruit of the vine.

Blessed art Thou, O Lord our God, King of the universe, who hast selected us from among all peoples to serve Thee and who hast sanctified us by Thy commandments. With love hast Thou given us, O Lord our God, (Sabbaths for rest) and festivals for rejoicing, holidays and festive occasions for gladness, this (Sabbath day and) Feast of Matzos, which is the festival of our freedom. Blessed art Thou, O Lord, who sanctifies (the Sabbath and) Israel and the festivals.

As we share in the sweetness of this wine, symbol of joy and gladness, we thank Thee, O God, for the beauty of home and the love of family. May the spirit of the holiday inspire us to love Thee and to follow the way of the Torah.

Blessed art Thou, O Lord our God, King of the universe, who hast granted us life, sustained us, and brought us to this festive season. Amen.

(Everyone drinks the first cup of wine.)

PASSOVER KIDDUSH

Arr. HARRY COOPERSMITH

Freely sung

Sahv - ree maw - raw - nawn v' - rah - bo - sai.   Baw-

rooch ah-taw Ah-do - noy, Eh-lo hay-noo me-lech haw - o-lawm, bo-

ray__ p'-ree ha - gaw-fehn: Baw - rooch ah-taw Ah-do-noy, Eh-lo

hay - noo   meh - lech   haw - o - lawn,   ah-

shehr baw - chahr baw - noo   mi - kawl awm __   v' - ro-

m' maw - noo   mi - kawl law - shon, __   v' - ki-d-

shaw - noo   b' mitz - vo - sawv __   Vah - tt-

tehn law - noo   Ah - do - noy   Eh - lo - hay - noo b'ah ha-

vaw __   (shah - baw - sos li - m' noo - chaw oo)   mo - ah-

deem l' sim - chaw, chah-geem oo-z'-mah - neem l' saw -   sone __ ehs

PASSOVER KIDDUSH — *Continued*

(yom ha-sha-baws ha-zeh v'es) yom chag ha-ma-tzos ha-zeh z'-

mahn chay-roo say-noo (b'ah-ha-vaw) mik-raw ko-desh,

zay-chehr li-tzi-ahs mitz-raw-yeem. Kee

vaw-noo vaw-char-taw v' o-saw-noo ki-dahsh taw mi-

kawl haw-ah-meem (v' sha-baws) oo-mo-ah-day-kawd-sheh-chaw (b'-

ah-ha-vaw oo-v' raw-tzon) b' sim-chaw oo-v'saw-sone hin-chal-taw noo. Baw-

rooch ah-taw Ah-do-noy m'kah-daysh (ha-shah baws v'Yis-raw-ayl v'ha-z'ma-neem). Baw-
Yis-raw-ayl v'ha-z'mah - - neem.

rooch ah-taw Ah-do-noy Eh-lo-hay-noo meh-lech haw-o-lawm, sheh,

heh-cheh-yaw-noo v'-ki-y' maw-noo, v'-

hi-gee-aw-noo la-z— mahn hah-zeh.

2. Oo-r'chahtz — וּרְחַץ

Father: "During our Seder we will wash our hands twice. We will wash them now, before we eat the Karpas, and we will not recite a benediction. Later, however, when we wash our hands before the meal and Hamotzee, we will recite the blessing."

(The pitcher, bowl, and towel are brought to the table and each pours water over his hands.)

3. Karpas — כַּרְפַּס

Father: "I shall give each of you a piece of parsley. We will dip the parsley into the salt-water, and recite the blessing together."

בָּרוּךְ אַתָּה יְיָ, אֱלֹהֵינוּ מֶלֶךְ הָעוֹלָם, בּוֹרֵא פְּרִי הָאֲדָמָה:

Baw-rooch ah-taw Ado-noy, Elo-hay-noo meh-lech haw-o-lawm, bo-ray p'ree haw-ah-daw-maw.

Blessed art Thou, O Lord our God, King of the universe, who createst the fruit of the earth.

4. Yah-chahtz — יַחַץ

Father: "Yah-chahtz means to divide the Matzah. We take the middle of the three in the Matzah cover and break it in half. The smaller piece we return. The larger we wrap with a napkin and hide under the pillow to bring out later in our Seder. We will eat it as part of the Afikomon, which means dessert, after we have had our dinner."

(Father hides the Matzah under the pillow. It is customary for children to try to remove the Afikomon and demand compensation or ransom for its return. This demand must be met, because the Seder cannot be completed without the Afikomon. The custom arose out of the desire to whet the curiosity of the children and to retain their interest throughout the Seder.)

5. Mah-geed — מַגִּיד

Father: "Now that we have made the necessary preparations, we are going to read the Haggadah narrative which describes the many events leading to the redemption of our ancestors from slavery in Egypt. We raise the Matzah so that everyone may see and understand the meaning of the unleavened bread, and we read together":

הָא לַחְמָא עַנְיָא דִי אֲכָלוּ אַבְהָתָנָא בְּאַרְעָא דְמִצְרָיִם.
כָּל דִּכְפִין יֵיתֵי וְיֵכָל, כָּל דִּצְרִיךְ יֵיתֵי וְיִפְסַח.
הָשַׁתָּא הָכָא, לְשָׁנָה הַבָּאָה בְּאַרְעָא דְיִשְׂרָאֵל.
הָשַׁתָּא עַבְדֵי, לְשָׁנָה הַבָּאָה בְּנֵי חוֹרִין:

Haw lahch-maw ahn-yaw dee ah-chah-loo ahv-haw-saw-naw b'ahr-aw d'Mitz-raw-yeem.

Kawl di-ch'feen yay-say v'yay-chool; kawl di-tz'reech yay-say v'yif-sahch.

Haw-sha-taw haw-chaw, l'shaw-naw ha-baw-aw, b'ahr-aw d'Yis-raw-ayl.

Haw-sha-taw ahv-day, l'shaw-naw ha-baw-aw, b'nay cho-reen.

This is the bread of affliction which our fathers ate in the land of Egypt. Let all who are hungry enter and eat. Let all who are forlorn and in want join with us in celebration of the Passover. This year we observe our people's quest for and love of freedom in our blessed land. May we also be privileged to see the land where Israel first sought freedom. This year, many of our people are enslaved; may next year find all Israel and all mankind free, and living in peace.

A. The Four Questions

Father:

"One of the main purposes of the Seder is to teach our children the story of the Exodus from Egypt so that they may understand how important freedom is for all men. We learn this from the Bible which commands, 'And thou shalt tell it to thy son.' This refers to the redemption from Egypt, and we encourage our children to take an active part in the Seder. One of the ways in which they participate is by the Four Questions, which children for two thousand years have asked of their fathers.

"We are now ready to hear these Four Questions, more popularly known as the *Feer Kashes*."

(Son or daughter rises, approaches father and recites or sings the Four Questions. All children should be urged to ask the questions. They may recite them in English or Hebrew.)

מַה נִּשְׁתַּנָּה הַלַּיְלָה הַזֶּה מִכָּל הַלֵּילוֹת.

1. שֶׁבְּכָל הַלֵּילוֹת אָנוּ אוֹכְלִין חָמֵץ וּמַצָּה, הַלַּיְלָה הַזֶּה כֻּלּוֹ מַצָּה.

2. שֶׁבְּכָל הַלֵּילוֹת אָנוּ אוֹכְלִין שְׁאָר יְרָקוֹת, הַלַּיְלָה הַזֶּה מָרוֹר.

3. שֶׁבְּכָל הַלֵּילוֹת אֵין אָנוּ מַטְבִּילִין אֲפִילוּ פַּעַם אֶחָת. הַלַּיְלָה הַזֶּה שְׁתֵּי פְעָמִים.

4. שֶׁבְּכָל הַלֵּילוֹת אָנוּ אוֹכְלִין בֵּין יוֹשְׁבִין וּבֵין מְסָבִּין, הַלַּיְלָה הַזֶּה כֻּלָּנוּ מְסָבִּין:

Mah nish-ta-naw ha-lai-law ha-zeh mi-kawl ha-lay-los?

1. Sheh-b'chawl ha-lay-los, aw-noo och-leen chaw-maytz oo-ma-tzaw, ha-lai-law ha-zeh, koo-lo ma-tzaw.

2. Sheh-b'chawl ha-lay-los, aw-noo och-leen, sh'awr y'raw-kos, ha-lai-law ha-zeh, maw-ror.

3. Sheh-b'chawl ha-lay-los, ayn aw-noo maht-bee-leen ah-fee-loo pa-ahm eh-chaws, ha-lai-law ha-zeh, sh'tay f'aw-meem.

4. Sheh-b'chawl ha-lay-los, aw-noo och-leen bayn yosh-veen oo-vayn m'soo-been, ha-lai-law ha-zeh, koo-law-noo m'soo-been.

Why is this night different from all other nights?

1. On all other nights we eat either leavened or unleavened bread. Why on this night do we eat only Matzah?

2. On all other nights we may eat any kind of herbs. Why on this night, may we eat only bitter herbs?

3. On all other nights we do not dip even once. Why on this night, do we dip twice during the service (first, parsley or watercress in salt water and second, bitter herbs in the Charoses)?

4. On all other nights we eat either in sitting or reclining position. Why on this night, are we all expected to recline?

FOUR QUESTIONS

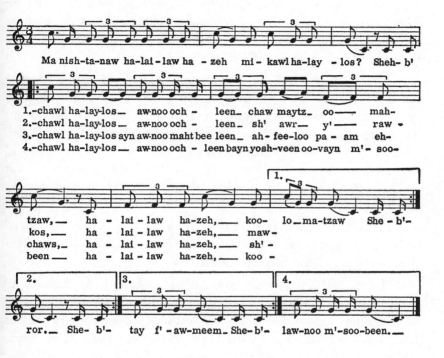

Ma nish-ta-naw ha-lai-law ha - zeh   mi - kawl ha-lay - los?   Sheh- b'

1.-chawl ha-lay-los— aw-noo och - leen— chaw maytz— oo—— mah-
2.-chawl ha-lay-los— aw-noo och - leen— sh' awr— y'—— raw •
3.-chawl ha-lay-los ayn aw-noo maht bee leen— ah- fee-loo pa - am eh-
4.-chawl ha-lay-los— aw-noo och - leen bayn yosh-veen oo-vayn m'- soo-

tzaw, — ha - lai - law ha-zeh, — koo- lo — ma-tzaw   She - b'-
kos, — ha - lai - law ha-zeh, — maw-
chaws, — ha - lai - law ha-zeh, — sh' -
been — ha - lai - law ha-zeh, — koo -

ror. — She- b'- tay f' - aw-meem — She- b'- law-noo m'-soo-been. —

B. THE RESPONSES

(There are no specific answers to the children's Four Questions. The answers are to be found in the Passover story as it unfolds for the reader of the Haggadah. However, the father may wish to make direct answer to his son, in the following suggested form:)

"Son, you have asked the questions well, as did generations of sons ask of their fathers. This night *is* different from all other nights, because tonight we and our fellow Jews all over the world celebrate one of the greatest events in Jewish history. That is the event which made us a free people, free to worship God, and free to form our own way of life.

"You have asked Four Questions! The Haggadah doesn't give direct replies. You have to listen to and participate in the reading of the Haggadah to understand. But since you have asked, let me try to give you a few brief answers.

"First, tonight we eat Matzos or unleavened bread because our fathers left Egypt in a great hurry. Naturally, they had to provide bread for their journey, and so they prepared the dough. They did not, however, have time to wait for the dough to leaven or rise. The result was that the bread was baked, but it remained flat and unleavened. And we today, as in all the generations, eat the Matzah or unleavened bread to remember this headlong eagerness for freedom.

"Second, we eat bitter herbs tonight because our fathers lived in Egypt as slaves before they were redeemed, and as slaves their lives were bitter and hard to endure.

"Third, we dip or mix twice tonight because the holiday of Passover is also the Festival of Spring, and the greens we eat remind us of the new season. We dip bitter herbs with the Charoses because both are symbolic of the hard lives our fathers endured in Egypt when they had to make bricks of mortar. Some scholars say that the Charoses stands for kindness (because it is really sweet-tasting) and means that we are grateful to God for His kindness in taking us out of Egypt, away from the bitterness of bondage.

"And fourth, we recline tonight, because in ancient times, at great feasts of free men it was the custom to recline; it was a sign, a symbol, of being free. And since this is the night our fathers were made free, we too show, by reclining, that we are now free."

"Now, let us together read parts of the Haggadah itself which give us fuller understanding of the questions and the answers."

Family:

עֲבָדִים הָיִינוּ לְפַרְעֹה בְּמִצְרַיִם, וַיּוֹצִיאֵנוּ יְיָ אֱלֹהֵינוּ מִשָּׁם, בְּיָד
חֲזָקָה וּבִזְרוֹעַ נְטוּיָה. וְאִלּוּ לֹא הוֹצִיא הַקָּדוֹשׁ בָּרוּךְ הוּא אֶת אֲבוֹתֵינוּ
מִמִּצְרַיִם, הֲרֵי אָנוּ, וּבָנֵינוּ, וּבְנֵי בָנֵינוּ, מְשֻׁעְבָּדִים הָיִינוּ לְפַרְעֹה
בְּמִצְרַיִם. וַאֲפִילוּ כֻּלָּנוּ חֲכָמִים, כֻּלָּנוּ נְבוֹנִים, כֻּלָּנוּ זְקֵנִים, כֻּלָּנוּ
יוֹדְעִים אֶת הַתּוֹרָה; מִצְוָה עָלֵינוּ לְסַפֵּר בִּיצִיאַת מִצְרָיִם. וְכָל
הַמַּרְבֶּה לְסַפֵּר בִּיצִיאַת מִצְרַיִם, הֲרֵי זֶה מְשֻׁבָּח:

We celebrate Passover tonight because we were slaves to
Pharaoh in Egypt at the beginning of our history. The Lord our
God, in His mercy and kindness, delivered us with a strong hand
and an outstretched arm. If God had not brought our forefathers
out of Egypt, we and our children and our children's children might
still be enslaved and deprived of the blessings of liberty. Therefore,
even though we are all wise and men of understanding and well
versed in the Torah, it is still our duty to tell and retell, experience
and re-experience, the story of the Exodus from Egypt. And the
more we retell this account of our liberation the more we are reminded of the blessings of freedom which we ought always to
cherish and hold dear.

Father:

"The annual retelling of the story of the Exodus, so that we
may better understand the bitterness of slavery and our need to
strive for freedom for ourselves and for all mankind, has been part
of Jewish family practice through the centuries. Not only families
who came together every year for the Seder, but our greatest sages
and scholars, great in mental stature and profound in thought —
they, too, shared in this annual experience."

Family:

מַעֲשֶׂה בְּרַבִּי אֱלִיעֶזֶר וְרַבִּי יְהוֹשֻׁעַ וְרַבִּי אֶלְעָזָר בֶּן עֲזַרְיָה וְרַבִּי
עֲקִיבָא וְרַבִּי טַרְפוֹן שֶׁהָיוּ מְסֻבִּין בִּבְנֵי בְרַק, וְהָיוּ מְסַפְּרִים בִּיצִיאַת
מִצְרַיִם כָּל אוֹתוֹ הַלַּיְלָה, עַד שֶׁבָּאוּ תַלְמִידֵיהֶם וְאָמְרוּ לָהֶם.
רַבּוֹתֵינוּ, הִגִּיעַ זְמַן קְרִיאַת שְׁמַע שֶׁל שַׁחֲרִית:

We read an example of this in the story of the five Jewish
scholars who lived in the early centuries, Rabbis Eliezer, Joshua,
Elazar ben Azaria, Akiba, and Tarfon. The account describes how
they sat around a table in the city of B'nai B'rak and discussed the
events and meanings of the Exodus. It was only when their students
came to them and said, "Our teachers! It is already morning and
time to recite the morning prayers," that they realized they had
spent the whole night talking about that great episode in Jewish
history.

C.   THE FOUR SONS

Father:

"The Rabbis tell us that we can learn the meaning of the Seder
by reading the answers to the questions asked by four kinds of
children.

בָּרוּךְ הַמָּקוֹם, בָּרוּךְ הוּא, בָּרוּךְ שֶׁנָּתַן תּוֹרָה לְעַמּוֹ יִשְׂרָאֵל,
בָּרוּךְ הוּא:

כְּנֶגֶד אַרְבָּעָה בָנִים דִּבְּרָה תוֹרָה, אֶחָד חָכָם, וְאֶחָד רָשָׁע, וְאֶחָד
תָּם, וְאֶחָד שֶׁאֵינוֹ יוֹדֵעַ לִשְׁאוֹל:

"Blessed be God, blessed be He. Blessed be He who gave the
Torah to His people Israel. The Torah speaks of four sons, —
one who is wise, one who is wicked, one who is simple, and one
who does not even know how to ask."

(Appoint children to read each of the following four sections:)

First Reader:

חָכָם מַה הוּא אוֹמֵר. מָה הָעֵדֹת וְהַחֻקִּים וְהַמִּשְׁפָּטִים אֲשֶׁר צִוָּה
יְיָ אֱלֹהֵינוּ אֶתְכֶם. וְאַף אַתָּה אֱמָר לוֹ כְּהִלְכוֹת הַפֶּסַח, אֵין מַפְטִירִין
אַחַר הַפֶּסַח אֲפִיקוֹמָן:

The wise son, what does he say? He says, "What do the laws
and traditions and customs which the Lord our God commanded
you mean?" Do you, then, in the spirit of his question, because he
is so interested in knowing, tell him precisely all the practices and
traditions of the Passover. Do you relate even the detailed laws, as
for example, the practice, "One does not go reveling after the
Afikomon is eaten," in order that the spirit of the Passover service
may linger with him.

Second Reader:

רָשָׁע מַה הוּא אוֹמֵר. מָה הָעֲבוֹדָה הַזֹּאת לָכֶם. לָכֶם וְלֹא לוֹ
וּלְפִי שֶׁהוֹצִיא אֶת עַצְמוֹ מִן הַכְּלָל כָּפַר בָּעִקָּר. וְאַף אַתָּה הַקְהֵה אֶת
שִׁנָּיו וֶאֱמָר לוֹ. בַּעֲבוּר זֶה עָשָׂה יְיָ לִי בְּצֵאתִי מִמִּצְרָיִם. לִי וְלֹא לוֹ
אִלּוּ הָיָה שָׁם. לֹא הָיָה נִגְאָל:

The wicked son, what does he say? He says, "What does this
service mean to you?" To you, he emphasizes, and not to himself.
Do you then, in the spirit of his question, answer him that because
he has excluded himself from the community, he has denied the
cardinal principle of Judaism. Set his teeth on edge, as it were, and
say to him, "All this is because of what God did for me when I
went out of Egypt." For me, and not for you. Thus imply by your
answer that if he had been there, because of his actions and his
attitude, he would not have been among those who were redeemed.

Third Reader:

תָּם מַה הוּא אוֹמֵר. מַה זֹּאת. וְאָמַרְתָּ אֵלָיו. בְּחֹזֶק יָד הוֹצִיאָנוּ

יְ מִמִּצְרַיִם, מִבֵּית עֲבָדִים:

The simple son, what does he say? He says, "What is this all about?" Do you then explain to him, "All this is because of what God did for us when He brought us out of Egypt, the house of bondage, with a mighty hand."

Fourth Reader:

וְשֶׁאֵינוֹ יוֹדֵעַ לִשְׁאוֹל אַתְּ פְּתַח לוֹ, שֶׁנֶּאֱמַר. וְהִגַּדְתָּ לְבִנְךָ בַּיּוֹם

הַהוּא לֵאמֹר. בַּעֲבוּר זֶה עָשָׂה יְיָ לִי בְּצֵאתִי מִמִּצְרָיִם:

And as for the son unable to ask, you yourself must begin by teaching him to ask, as recorded in the Bible, "And Thou shalt tell thy son on that day, saying: Because of that which God did for me when I went forth from Egypt," that is the meaning of the Passover celebration.

D. God's Promise

Father:

"We are grateful to God for having guided our destiny through out time, for His faithfulness and His ever-ready and constant protection from tyranny and evil. We cover the Matzos and raise our cups of wine in gratitude as we declare together:

וְהִיא שֶׁעָמְדָה לַאֲבוֹתֵינוּ וְלָנוּ. שֶׁלֹּא אֶחָד בִּלְבָד עָמַד עָלֵינוּ

לְכַלּוֹתֵנוּ, אֶלָּא שֶׁבְּכָל דּוֹר וָדוֹר עוֹמְדִים עָלֵינוּ לְכַלּוֹתֵנוּ. וְהַקָּדוֹשׁ

בָּרוּךְ הוּא מַצִּילֵנוּ מִיָּדָם:

V'hee sheh-awm-daw la-ah-vo-say-noo v'law-noo,
Sheh-lo eh-chawd bi-l'vawd aw-mahd aw-lay-noo l'cha-lo-say-noo.

Eh-law sheh-b'chawl dor vaw-dor o-m'deem aw-lay-noo l'cha-lo-say-noo,
V'ha-kaw-dosh baw-rooch hoo, ma-tzee-lay-noo mi-yaw-dawm.

"This promise made to our fathers holds true for us too. For not once did one arise against us to destroy our people, but in every generation they rise up against us, and the Holy One, blessed be He, delivers us from their hands and protects us."

(Set cups down and uncover the Matzos:)

E. The Events of the Exodus

Father:

"The Bible records the dramatic and moving events which led to the redemption of our forefathers from Egypt. It describes how we came down to Egypt in the hope that peace and comfort would be ours because Joseph, son of Jacob, had saved the land from economic destruction and famine. We were confident that Pharaoh would be appreciative toward Joseph and permit his people to live peacefully. But when a new king rose over Egypt and forgot Joseph's service, our people's suffering at the hands of Pharaoh began, and continued until the Lord heard our cries and sent Moses and Aaron to plead for release of our forefathers from slavery. But Pharaoh's heart was hardened and he refused to free them. And God sent ten plagues to move Pharaoh to change his heart.

"These plagues are recalled at the Seder table. We fill our cups of wine to the brim, and pour a drop to commemorate each plague as it is mentioned. We do this not to display pride or joy, but to display our regret and concern over the destruction of human lives. We show that the fullness of our joy is diminished because Israel was redeemed at the expense of much suffering. So, recalling the plagues of days gone by, we chant as each drop is released:"

Each person at the table raises his cup and participates in the ceremony, using the saucer supplied for this purpose:

שְׁחִין.	דָּם.
בָּרָד.	צְפַרְדֵּעַ.
אַרְבֶּה.	כִּנִּים.
חֹשֶׁךְ.	עָרוֹב.
מַכַּת בְּכוֹרוֹת:	דֶּבֶר.

Dawm, tz'far-day-ah, ki-neem, aw-rov, deh-vehr, sh'cheen, baw-rawd, ahr-beh, cho-shech, ma-kahs b'cho-ros.

Blood. Frogs. Gnats. Beasts. Pestilence.

Boils. Hail. Locusts. Darkness. Slaying of the First Born.

"Rabbi Judah reduced the ten words to three words by combining the first Hebrew letter of the ten words. We pour a drop of wine at the mention of each word:

רַבִּי יְהוּדָה הָיָה נוֹתֵן בָּהֶם סִמָּנִים.

דְּצַ"ךְ עַדַ"שׁ בְּאַחַ"ב:

D'tzahch, ah-dahsh. b'ah-chahv."

(Set cups down.)

F. Our Gratitude to God

Father:

"For all the blessings which God showered upon our people in days gone by and in our own days we give thanks unto Him, as we offer this hymn of gratitude:"

Day-yay-noo — It Would Have Been Enough

כַּמָּה מַעֲלוֹת טוֹבוֹת לַמָּקוֹם עָלֵינוּ:

אִלּוּ הוֹצִיאָנוּ מִמִּצְרַיִם,

דַּיֵּנוּ: וְלֹא עָשָׂה בָהֶם שְׁפָטִים,

אִלּוּ עָשָׂה בָהֶם שְׁפָטִים,

דַּיֵּנוּ: וְלֹא עָשָׂה בֵאלֹהֵיהֶם,

אִלּוּ עָשָׂה בֵאלֹהֵיהֶם,

דַּיֵּנוּ: וְלֹא הָרַג אֶת בְּכוֹרֵיהֶם,

אִלּוּ הָרַג אֶת בְּכוֹרֵיהֶם,

דַּיֵּנוּ: וְלֹא נָתַן לָנוּ אֶת מָמוֹנָם,

אִלּוּ נָתַן לָנוּ אֶת מָמוֹנָם,

דַּיֵּנוּ: וְלֹא קָרַע לָנוּ אֶת הַיָּם,

אִלּוּ קָרַע לָנוּ אֶת הַיָּם,

דַּיֵּנוּ: וְלֹא הֶעֱבִירָנוּ בְתוֹכוֹ בֶּחָרָבָה,

אִלּוּ הֶעֱבִירָנוּ בְתוֹכוֹ בֶּחָרָבָה,
וְלֹא שִׁקַּע צָרֵינוּ בְּתוֹכוֹ,   דַּיֵּנוּ:

אִלּוּ שִׁקַּע צָרֵינוּ בְּתוֹכוֹ,
וְלֹא סִפֵּק צָרְכֵּנוּ בַּמִּדְבָּר אַרְבָּעִים שָׁנָה,   דַּיֵּנוּ:

אִלּוּ סִפֵּק צָרְכֵּנוּ בַּמִּדְבָּר אַרְבָּעִים שָׁנָה,
וְלֹא הֶאֱכִילָנוּ אֶת הַמָּן,   דַּיֵּנוּ:

אִלּוּ הֶאֱכִילָנוּ אֶת הַמָּן,
וְלֹא נָתַן לָנוּ אֶת הַשַּׁבָּת,   דַּיֵּנוּ:

אִלּוּ נָתַן לָנוּ אֶת הַשַּׁבָּת,
וְלֹא קֵרְבָנוּ לִפְנֵי הַר סִינַי,   דַּיֵּנוּ:

אִלּוּ קֵרְבָנוּ לִפְנֵי הַר סִינַי,
וְלֹא נָתַן לָנוּ אֶת הַתּוֹרָה,   דַּיֵּנוּ:

אִלּוּ נָתַן לָנוּ אֶת הַתּוֹרָה,
וְלֹא הִכְנִיסָנוּ לְאֶרֶץ יִשְׂרָאֵל,   דַּיֵּנוּ:

אִלּוּ הִכְנִיסָנוּ לְאֶרֶץ יִשְׂרָאֵל,
וְלֹא בָנָה לָנוּ אֶת בֵּית הַבְּחִירָה,   דַּיֵּנוּ:

(Father reads, and family responds "Da-yay-noo.")

How many are the goodly favors which God conferred upon us.

Father: Had He brought us out of Egypt and not executed judgment upon them,

Family: Da-yay-noo, it would have been enough, and we are
grateful.

Father: Had He executed judgment upon them and not upon their idols,

Family: Da-yay-noo, it would have been enough, and we are grateful.

Father: Had He executed judgment upon their idols and not slain their first born,

Family: Da-yay-noo, it would have been enough, and we are grateful.

Father: Had He slain their first born, and not given us their treasures,

Family: Da-yay-noo, it would have been enough, and we are grateful.

Father: Had He given us their treasures, and not divided the Red Sea for us,

Family: Da-yay-noo, it would have been enough, and we are grateful.

Father: Had He divided the Red Sea for us and not led us through it on dry land,

Family: Da-yay-noo, it would have been enough, and we are grateful.

Father: Had He led us through on dry land, and not plunged our oppressors in it,

Family: Da-yay-noo, it would have been enough, and we are grateful.

Father: Had He plunged our oppressors in it, and not supplied our needs in the wilderness,

Family: Da-yay-noo, it would have been enough, and we are grateful.

Father: Had He supplied our needs in the wilderness and not brought us the gift of the manna,

Family: Da-yay-noo, it would have been enough, and we are grateful.

Father: Had He brought us the gift of the manna, and not blessed us with the Sabbath,

Family: Da-yay-noo, it would have been enough, and we are grateful.

Father: Had He blessed us with the Sabbath, and not led us to Mount Sinai,

Family: Da-yay-noo, it would have been enough, and we are grateful.

Father: Had He led us to Mount Sinai, and not given us the Torah,

Family: Da-yay-noo, it would have been enough, and we are grateful.

Father: Had He given us the Torah, and not led us into the Land of Israel,

Family: Da-yay-noo, it would have been enough, and we are grateful.

Father: Had He led us into the Land of Israel and not built for us the Sanctuary,

Family: Da-yay-noo, it would have been enough, and we are grateful.

DAYAYNOO

דַיֵּנוּ — IT WOULD HAVE BEEN ENOUGH

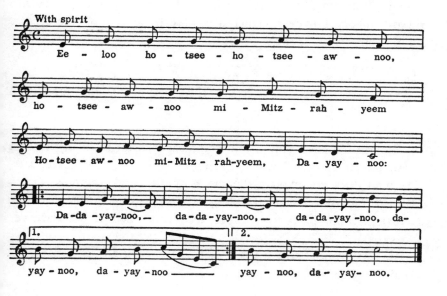

With spirit

Ee - loo ho - tsee - ho - tsee - aw - noo,

ho - tsee - aw - noo mi - Mitz - rah - yeem

Ho - tsee - aw - noo mi - Mitz - rah-yeem, Da - yay - noo:

Da-da - yay-noo, __ da - da-yay-noo, __ da - da-yay -noo, da-

1. yay - noo, da - yay - noo _____

2. yay - noo, da - yay- noo.

2.

Ee-loo naw-sahn law-noo ehs hah-shah-baws,
Naw-sahn law-noo, ehs hah-shah-baws,
Da-yay-noo.

Chorus

3.

Ee-loo naw-sahn law-noo ehs ha-To-raw,
Naw-sahn law-noo, ehs hah-To-raw,
Da-yay-noo.

Chorus

G. The Three Important Symbols of Pesach

Father:

"There are many important symbols at the Seder service which help us fully understand the meaning of this evening. There are three symbols, however, which are more basic than all the others. So important are they that —

רַבָּן גַּמְלִיאֵל הָיָה אוֹמֵר. כָּל שֶׁלֹּא אָמַר שְׁלֹשָׁה דְבָרִים אֵלוּ
בַּפֶּסַח לֹא יָצָא יְדֵי חוֹבָתוֹ, וְאֵלוּ הֵן.

פֶּסַח, מַצָּה, וּמָרוֹר:

Rabban Gamliel, one of our great sages, who lived in the first century of this era and was the religious leader of our people, said, 'He who does not explain the three fundamental symbols, *Pesach (Paschal Lamb)*, *Matzah (Unleavened Bread)*, and *Moror (Bitter Herbs)*, has not properly fulfilled the observance of the Passover festival.'

We pause now to consider each of these three and to understand the purpose and meaning of each:"

(Select three at the table to read the three sections.)

First Reader:

(Point to the symbol of the Paschal Lamb.)

פֶּסַח שֶׁהָיוּ אֲבוֹתֵינוּ אוֹכְלִים בִּזְמַן שֶׁבֵּית הַמִּקְדָּשׁ קַיָם. עַל שׁוּם
מָה. עַל שׁוּם שֶׁפָּסַח הַקָּדוֹשׁ בָּרוּךְ הוּא עַל בָּתֵּי אֲבוֹתֵינוּ בְּמִצְרַיִם,
שֶׁנֶּאֱמַר. וַאֲמַרְתֶּם זֶבַח פֶּסַח הוּא לַיָי, אֲשֶׁר פָּסַח עַל בָּתֵּי בְנֵי יִשְׂרָאֵל
בְּמִצְרַיִם, בְּנָגְפּוֹ אֶת מִצְרַיִם, וְאֶת בָּתֵּינוּ הִצִּיל; וַיִּקֹּד הָעָם וַיִּשְׁתַּחֲווּ:

The Paschal Lamb which our fathers ate while the Sanctuary was in existence — what was its purpose? It was because God passed over the houses of our forefathers in Egypt, as the Bible says, "And you shall say, this is the Passover offering unto God, who passed over the houses of our forefathers as he smote the Egyptians and spared us. And the people bowed their heads and worshiped."

Second Reader:

(Point to the Matzah.)

מַצָּה זוֹ שֶׁאָנוּ אוֹכְלִים עַל שׁוּם מָה. עַל שׁוּם שֶׁלֹּא הִסְפִּיק בְּצֵקָם
שֶׁל אֲבוֹתֵינוּ לְהַחֲמִיץ, עַד שֶׁנִּגְלָה עֲלֵיהֶם מֶלֶךְ מַלְכֵי הַמְּלָכִים,
הַקָּדוֹשׁ בָּרוּךְ הוּא. וּגְאָלָם, שֶׁנֶּאֱמַר. וַיֹּאפוּ אֶת הַבָּצֵק אֲשֶׁר הוֹצִיאוּ
מִמִּצְרַיִם, עֻגֹת מַצּוֹת, כִּי לֹא חָמֵץ; כִּי גֹרְשׁוּ מִמִּצְרַיִם, וְלֹא יָכְלוּ
לְהִתְמַהְמֵהַּ, וְגַם צֵדָה לֹא עָשׂוּ לָהֶם:

This Matzah which we eat — why do we eat it? We eat it because there was not enough time for the dough which our fathers prepared in Egypt to become leavened, when God revealed Himself to them and redeemed them. This is explained in the Bible, as follows: "And the dough which they had brought out of Egypt they baked into cakes of unleavened bread, for it had not leavened, because they were rushed out of Egypt, and they could not tarry, nor had they prepared for themselves any provisions for the journey."

Third Reader:

(Point to the Bitter Herbs.)

מָרוֹר זֶה שֶׁאָנוּ אוֹכְלִים עַל שׁוּם מָה. עַל שׁוּם שֶׁמֵּרְרוּ הַמִּצְרִים
אֶת חַיֵּי אֲבוֹתֵינוּ בְּמִצְרַיִם שֶׁנֶּאֱמַר. וַיְמָרְרוּ אֶת חַיֵּיהֶם בַּעֲבֹדָה קָשָׁה.
בְּחֹמֶר וּבִלְבֵנִים. וּבְכָל עֲבֹדָה בַּשָּׂדֶה; אֵת כָּל עֲבֹדָתָם. אֲשֶׁר עָבְדוּ
בָהֶם בְּפָרֶךְ:

These Bitter Herbs we eat — what is their significance? We eat them because we are reminded how the Egyptians embittered the lives of our fathers in Egypt, as the Bible says, "And they embittered their lives with hard work, with mortar and bricks, and with all kinds of labor in the field."

H.   Let us Praise God.

Father:

"As we think about the bitterness which our fathers endured when they were subjected to slavery, we should thank God for His redemption of our fathers to freedom, as we, each of us, experience the cherished freedom and blessings of liberty we have in this land. We ought, all of us, feel the personal experience of freedom, as if each was redeemed from Egypt. Let us express this feeling together:"

Family:

בְּכָל דּוֹר וָדֹר חַיָּב אָדָם לִרְאוֹת אֶת עַצְמוֹ כְּאִלּוּ הוּא יָצָא
מִמִּצְרַיִם, שֶׁנֶּאֱמַר. וְהִגַּדְתָּ לְבִנְךָ בַּיּוֹם הַהוּא לֵאמֹר. בַּעֲבוּר זֶה עָשָׂה
יְיָ לִי בְּצֵאתִי מִמִּצְרָיִם. לֹא אֶת אֲבוֹתֵינוּ בִּלְבָד גָּאַל הַקָּדוֹשׁ בָּרוּךְ
הוּא, אֶלָּא אַף אוֹתָנוּ גָּאַל עִמָּהֶם, שֶׁנֶּאֱמַר. וְאוֹתָנוּ הוֹצִיא מִשָּׁם, לְמַעַן
הָבִיא אֹתָנוּ לָתֶת לָנוּ אֶת הָאָרֶץ, אֲשֶׁר נִשְׁבַּע לַאֲבוֹתֵינוּ:

In every generation every one must look upon himself as if he himself had shared in the experience of the Exodus, as it is said in the Bible, "And thou shalt tell thy son on that day, saying: it is because of what the Lord did for *me* when *I* went forth from Egypt." It was not only our fathers that God redeemed, but also us did He redeem with them, as it is said, "And *us* did He bring forth from there in order to escort *us* to the Land which He promised to our forefathers."

(All raise the cups of wine.)

לְפִיכָךְ אֲנַחְנוּ חַיָּבִים לְהוֹדוֹת, לְהַלֵּל, לְשַׁבֵּחַ, לְפָאֵר, לְרוֹמֵם,
לְהַדֵּר, לְבָרֵךְ, לְעַלֵּה, וּלְקַלֵּס, לְמִי שֶׁעָשָׂה לַאֲבוֹתֵינוּ וְלָנוּ אֶת כָּל

הַנִּסִּים הָאֵלּוּ. הוֹצִיאָנוּ מֵעַבְדוּת לְחֵרוּת, מִיָּגוֹן לְשִׂמְחָה, מֵאֵבֶל לְיוֹם
טוֹב, וּמֵאֲפֵלָה לְאוֹר גָּדוֹל, וּמִשִּׁעְבּוּד לִגְאֻלָּה. וְנֹאמַר לְפָנָיו שִׁירָה
חֲדָשָׁה. הַלְלוּיָהּ:

Therefore, it is our duty to praise, extol, glorify, and thank
God who performed all these wonders for our fathers and for us,
bringing us from slavery to freedom, from anguish to joy, from
sorrow to festivity, from darkness to great light, from subjection
to redemption; and let us therefore sing unto Him a new song, in
the Hallel prayers.

(The Hallel prayers are a series of psalms, 113–118, reserved for recitation
on festivals only. Hallel means Praise. On the Seder night, the first part of Hallel
is recited before the dinner and the second part following dinner. The purpose of
this division is to show us that the meal is part of the total Seder service. It should
be noted that on the last six days of Passover, what is called Chahtzee or Half
Hallel, is chanted, for the same reason as the pouring of the drops of wine in
commemoration of the plagues, that is, that we cannot be fully happy nor full of
praise because human beings, the Egyptians, perished during the process of Israel's
redemption.)

Father:

"We continue our expressions of gratitude and thankfulness by
reading the psalms of the Hallel, which is customary on all our
festivals."

Psalm 113

הַלְלוּיָהּ

הַלְלוּ אֶת שֵׁם יְיָ.	הַלְלוּ עַבְדֵי יְיָ,
מֵעַתָּה וְעַד עוֹלָם.	יְהִי שֵׁם יְיָ מְבֹרָךְ,
מְהֻלָּל שֵׁם יְיָ.	מִמִּזְרַח שֶׁמֶשׁ עַד מְבוֹאוֹ,
עַל הַשָּׁמַיִם כְּבוֹדוֹ.	רָם עַל כָּל גּוֹיִם יְיָ,

מִי כַּיָ אֱלֹהֵינוּ   הַמַּגְבִּיהִי לָשָׁבֶת.

הַמַּשְׁפִּילִי לִרְאוֹת   בַּשָּׁמַיִם וּבָאָרֶץ.

מְקִימִי מֵעָפָר דָּל,   מֵאַשְׁפֹּת יָרִים אֶבְיוֹן.

לְהוֹשִׁיבִי עִם נְדִיבִים,   עִם נְדִיבֵי עַמּוֹ.

מוֹשִׁיבִי עֲקֶרֶת הַבַּיִת,   אֵם הַבָּנִים שְׂמֵחָה.

הַלְלוּיָהּ:

Father: Halleluyah. Praise the Lord!
Praise, O servants of the Lord,
Praise the name of the Lord!

Family: Blessed be the name of the Lord
From this time forth and forevermore!

Father: From the rising of the sun to its setting
The name of the Lord is to be praised.

Family: The Lord is high above all nations,
His glory is above the heavens.

Father: Who is like the Lord our God
Who is enthroned on high?

Family: Who looks down low
Upon the heaven and the earth?

Father: Who raises up the poor from the dust,
And lifts up the needy from the ash-heap,

Family: To make him sit with princes,
With the princes of his people.

Father: Who gives the barren woman a home
As a joyful mother of children,
Hallelluyah. Praise the Lord!

Psalm 114

בֵּית יַעֲקֹב מֵעַם לֹעֵז.   בְּצֵאת יִשְׂרָאֵל מִמִּצְרָיִם,

יִשְׂרָאֵל מַמְשְׁלוֹתָיו.   הָיְתָה יְהוּדָה לְקָדְשׁוֹ,

הַיַּרְדֵּן יִסֹּב לְאָחוֹר.   הַיָּם רָאָה וַיָּנֹס,

גְּבָעוֹת כִּבְנֵי צֹאן.   הֶהָרִים רָקְדוּ כְאֵילִים,

הַיַּרְדֵּן תִּסֹּב לְאָחוֹר.   מַה לְּךָ הַיָּם כִּי תָנוּס,

גְּבָעוֹת כִּבְנֵי צֹאן.   הֶהָרִים תִּרְקְדוּ כְאֵילִים,

מִלִּפְנֵי אֱלוֹהַּ יַעֲקֹב: מִלִּפְנֵי אָדוֹן חוּלִי אָרֶץ.

חַלָּמִישׁ לְמַעְיְנוֹ מָיִם.   הַהֹפְכִי הַצּוּר אֲגַם מָיִם,

Father: When Israel went forth from Egypt,
The house of Jacob from a people of strange language,

Family: Judah became his sanctuary,
Israel his dominion.

Father: The sea looked and fled,
The Jordan turned back.

Family: The mountains skipped like rams,
The hills like lambs.

Father: What ails you, O sea, that you flee?
O Jordan, that you turn back?

Family: You mountains, that you skip like rams?
And you hills, like lambs?

Father: Tremble, you earth, at the presence of the Lord,
At the presence of the God of Jacob.

Family: Who turns the rock into a pool of water,
The flint into a fountain of flowing waters.

(Refill the cups of wine. All raise their cups and read together.)

Blessed art Thou, O Lord our God, King of the universe, who hast redeemed our ancestors from Egypt and enabled us to reach this night, that we might share in the experiences of our forefathers and thereby become associated with them and their lives. Enable us, we pray Thee, to celebrate all our other festivals and solemn feasts. Rebuild speedily in our day Thy holy city, Jerusalem, in keeping with Thy promise, so that "From Zion shall come forth the Torah and the word of God from Jerusalem."

We thank Thee, O God, as we recite the blessing over the second of the four cups of wine we are to drink this Seder night.

בָּרוּךְ אַתָּה יְיָ, אֱלֹהֵינוּ מֶלֶךְ הָעוֹלָם, בּוֹרֵא פְּרִי הַגָּפֶן:

Baw-rooch ah-taw Ado-noy, Elo-hay-noo meh-lech haw-o-lawm, bo-ray p'ree ha-gaw-fen.

Blessed art Thou, O Lord our God, King of the universe, who createst the fruit of the vine.

(Everyone drinks the second cup of wine.)

6. Rah-chahtz — רָחַץ

Father:

"We now wash our hands again by pouring water over them; and this time, because we are preparing for the Seder dinner, we recite a blessing. We wash the hands in symbolic remembrance of the priests who raised their hands for the Levites to pour water over them as an act of purification before they began the service in the Temple."

(The pitcher, bowl, and towel are brought to the table and each pours water over his hands. As each performs this ceremony, he recites:)

בָּרוּךְ אַתָּה יְיָ, אֱלֹהֵינוּ מֶלֶךְ הָעוֹלָם, אֲשֶׁר קִדְּשָׁנוּ בְּמִצְוֹתָיו,
וְצִוָּנוּ עַל נְטִילַת יָדַיִם:

Baw-rooch ah-taw Ado-noy, Elo-hay-noo meh-lech haw-o-
lawm, ah-shehr ki-d'shaw-noo b'mitz-vo-sawv, v'tzi-vaw-noo, ahl
n'tee-lahs yaw-daw-yeem.

Blessed art Thou, O Lord our God, King of the universe, who
hast sanctified us by Thy commandments and granted us the privilege
of partaking of Thy blessings of food after the symbolic washing
of the hands.

7. Mo-tzee, Mah-tzaw — מוֹצִיא, מַצָּה

*(Father takes the broken half of the Matzah left after the larger piece
was hidden for the Afikomon and also the upper Matzah, breaks
them into smaller pieces, and gives two small pieces to everyone.)*

Father:

"Every meal begins with the blessing over bread. The bread
we eat on Pesach is the Matzah, and we, therefore, offer two
blessings, one for bread and the second for Matzah. We break bread
together as we recite:

בָּרוּךְ אַתָּה יְיָ, אֱלֹהֵינוּ מֶלֶךְ הָעוֹלָם, הַמּוֹצִיא לֶחֶם מִן הָאָרֶץ:

בָּרוּךְ אַתָּה יְיָ, אֱלֹהֵינוּ מֶלֶךְ הָעוֹלָם, אֲשֶׁר קִדְּשָׁנוּ בְּמִצְוֹתָיו,
וְצִוָּנוּ עַל אֲכִילַת מַצָּה:

Baw-rooch ah-taw Ado-noy, Elo-hay-noo meh-lech haw-o-lawm, ha-mo-tzee leh-chem min haw-aw-retz.

Baw-rooch ah-taw Ado-noy, Elo-hay-noo meh-lech haw-o-lawm, ah-shehr ki-d'shaw-noo b'mitz-vo-sawv, v'tzi-vaw-noo ahl ah-chee-lahs ma-tzaw.

Blessed art Thou, O Lord our God, King of the universe, who bringest forth bread from the earth.

Blessed art Thou, O Lord our God, King of the universe, who hast sanctified us by Thy commandments and granted us the privilege of eating the Matzah as a symbol of this festival of Pesach.

8. Moror — מָרוֹר

(Father takes a pinch of bitter herbs, dips into the Charoses, and distributes a bit to each member of the family at the table; or the bowls containing the Moror and Charoses are passed around the table for each to take with the extra spoon provided for this purpose.)

Father:

"We are now going to taste the Moror, the bitter herbs, as symbol of our better understanding of the bitterness of slavery. We add to the Moror, the Charoses, which has a sweet taste, as symbol of God's kindness to us. We recite the blessing together:"

בָּרוּךְ אַתָּה יְיָ, אֱלֹהֵינוּ מֶלֶךְ הָעוֹלָם, אֲשֶׁר קִדְּשָׁנוּ בְּמִצְוֹתָיו,
וְצִוָּנוּ עַל אֲכִילַת מָרוֹר:

Baw-rooch ah-taw Ado-noy, Elo-hay-noo meh-lech haw-o-lawm, ah-shehr ki-d'shaw-noo b'mitz-vo-sawv v'tzi-vaw-noo ahl ah-chee-lahs maw-ror.

Blessed art Thou, O Lord our God, King of the universe, who hast sanctified us by Thy commandments and granted us the privilege of tasting the Moror and by tasting it to appreciate all the more God's blessings of freedom.

9. Ko-raych — כּוֹרֵךְ

(Each member of the family takes two pieces of Matzah and places the Moror and Charoses between them to form a sandwich, uniting the important elements of the Seder into one unit. Originally, the paschal lamb meat was also included.)

Father:

"Many centuries ago, the great sage Hillel, instead of eating the symbols at the Pesach Seder individually, suggested that we combine them into one. We, too, follow this symbolic unity as we recite together:"

זֵכֶר לְמִקְדָּשׁ כְּהִלֵּל. כֵּן עָשָׂה הִלֵּל, בִּזְמַן שֶׁבֵּית הַמִּקְדָּשׁ הָיָה
קַיָּם. הָיָה כּוֹרֵךְ מַצָּה וּמָרוֹר וְאוֹכֵל בְּיַחַד; לְקַיֵּם מַה שֶׁנֶּאֱמַר. עַל
מַצּוֹת וּמְרוֹרִים יֹאכְלֻהוּ:

Zay-chehr l'mik-dawsh k'Hi-layl. Kayn aw-saw Hi-layl, bi-z'mahn sheh-bays ha-mik-dawsh haw-yaw ka-yawm. Haw-yaw ko-raych ma-tzaw oo-maw-ror, v'o-chayl b'yah-chahd; l'ka-yaym mah sheh-neh-eh-mahr: Ahl ma-tzos oo-m'ro-reem yoch-loo-hoo.

This is in commemoration of the practice of Hillel, one of our eminent sages of old. He would join together a piece of the Paschal Lamb, Matzah, and Bitter Herbs, and eat them as a unit, following the suggestion of the Bible, 'Upon leavened bread and bitter herbs shall they eat it,' meaning the meat of the Paschal Lamb.

10. Shool-chawn O-raych — שֻׁלְחָן עוֹרֵךְ

The Passover dinner is served.

11. Tzaw-foon — צָפוּן

(The Afikomon. The word "tzawfoon" means hidden, and refers to the middle piece of Matzah divided at the beginning of the service and hidden for the Afikomon. Father now takes it from its hiding place (unless it has been removed by the children who are holding it for ransom, in which case the ransom is either given or promised) and distributes it to each member at the table. No blessing is recited because Hamotzee, the blessing for bread, recited before the meal, includes this Matzah, which is viewed as the dessert and therefore part of the dinner.)

Father:

"I am now going to distribute a piece of the Afikomon to each of you. We eat it without reciting a special blessing because when we said Hamotzee, the blessing over bread, before dinner, the entire meal was included in the blessing, and the Afikomon is part of our dinner, because it is looked upon as dessert. Jewish tradition suggests that nothing be eaten after the Afikomon, because we should have the taste of the Matzah and its significance linger with us even after the Seder."

12. Baw-raych — בָּרֵךְ

Father:

"Now that we have had our dinner, we are ready to offer our thanks to God for His bounty and the blessings of food and plenty."

Psalm 126

שִׁיר הַמַּעֲלוֹת.

בְּשׁוּב יְיָ אֶת שִׁיבַת צִיּוֹן, הָיִינוּ כְּחֹלְמִים. אָז יִמָּלֵא שְׂחֹק פִּינוּ,
וּלְשׁוֹנֵנוּ רִנָּה; אָז יֹאמְרוּ בַגּוֹיִם, הִגְדִּיל יְיָ לַעֲשׂוֹת עִם אֵלֶּה. הִגְדִּיל
יְיָ לַעֲשׂוֹת עִמָּנוּ, הָיִינוּ שְׂמֵחִים:
שׁוּבָה יְיָ אֶת שְׁבִיתֵנוּ, כַּאֲפִיקִים בַּנֶּגֶב. הַזֹּרְעִים בְּדִמְעָה, בְּרִנָּה
יִקְצֹרוּ. הָלוֹךְ יֵלֵךְ וּבָכֹה נֹשֵׂא מֶשֶׁךְ הַזָּרַע. בֹּא יָבֹא בְרִנָּה נֹשֵׂא אֲלֻמֹּתָיו:

Sheer ha-ma-ah-los.

B'shoov Ado-noy, ehs shee-vahs tzi-yon, haw-yee-noo k'cho-
l'meem. Awz yi-maw-lay s'chok pee-noo, oo-l'sho-nay-noo ri-naw.
Awz yo-m'roo va-go-yeem, hig-deel Ado-noy, la-ah-sos im ay-leh.
Hig-deel Ado-noy, la-ah-sos ee-maw-noo, haw-yee-noo s'may-
cheem.

Shoo-vaw Ado-noy ehs sh'vee-say-noo, ka-ah-fee-keem ba-neh-
gev. Ha-zo-r'eem b'dim-aw, b'ri-naw yik-tzo-roo. Haw-loch yay-
laych oo-vaw-cho, no-say meh-shech ha-zaw-ra. Bo yaw-vo v'ri-
naw, no-say ah-loo-mo-sawv.

Father: רַבּוֹתַי, נְבָרֵךְ.
                    Ra-bo-sai, n'vaw-raych.

Family: יְהִי שֵׁם יְיָ מְבֹרָךְ מֵעַתָּה וְעַד עוֹלָם.
                    Y'hee shaym Ado-noy m'vo-rawch may-ah-taw v'ahd
                    o-lawm.

Father: יְהִי שֵׁם יְיָ מְבֹרָךְ מֵעַתָּה וְעַד עוֹלָם. בִּרְשׁוּת מִשְׁפַּחְתִּי,
נְבָרֵךְ שֶׁאָכַלְנוּ מִשֶּׁלּוֹ.

Y'hee shaym Ado-noy m'vo-rawch may-ah-taw v'ahd
o-lawm. Bi-r'shoos mish-pahch-tee, n'vaw-raych sheh-aw-
chahl-noo mi-sheh-lo.

Family: בָּרוּךְ שֶׁאָכַלְנוּ מִשֶּׁלּוֹ וּבְטוּבוֹ חָיִינוּ:

Baw-rooch   sheh-aw-chahl-noo   mi-sheh-lo   oo-v'too-vo
chaw-yee-noo.

Father: בָּרוּךְ שֶׁאָכַלְנוּ מִשֶּׁלּוֹ וּבְטוּבוֹ חָיִינוּ:

Baw-rooch   sheh-aw-chahl-noo   mi-sheh-lo   oo-v'too-vo
chaw-yee-noo.

Father: Let us join in thanking God, of whose bounty we have
partaken.

Family: Blessed be our God, of whose bounty we have partaken
and through whose goodness we are blessed.

Family:

בָּרוּךְ הוּא וּבָרוּךְ שְׁמוֹ.

בָּרוּךְ אַתָּה יְיָ, אֱלֹהֵינוּ מֶלֶךְ הָעוֹלָם, הַזָּן אֶת הָעוֹלָם כֻּלּוֹ בְּטוּבוֹ,
בְּחֵן בְּחֶסֶד וּבְרַחֲמִים. הוּא נֹתֵן לֶחֶם לְכָל בָּשָׂר, כִּי לְעוֹלָם חַסְדּוֹ.
וּבְטוּבוֹ הַגָּדוֹל תָּמִיד לֹא חָסַר לָנוּ, וְאַל יֶחְסַר לָנוּ מָזוֹן לְעוֹלָם וָעֶד.
בַּעֲבוּר שְׁמוֹ הַגָּדוֹל, כִּי הוּא אֵל זָן וּמְפַרְנֵס לַכֹּל, וּמֵטִיב לַכֹּל, וּמֵכִין
מָזוֹן לְכָל בְּרִיּוֹתָיו אֲשֶׁר בָּרָא.
בָּרוּךְ אַתָּה יְיָ, הַזָּן אֶת הַכֹּל:

Baw-rooch hoo oo-vaw-rooch sh'mo.

Baw-rooch ah-taw Ado-noy, Elo-hay-noo meh-lech haw-o-lawm, ha-zawn ehs haw-o-lawm koo-lo b'too-vo, b'chayn b'cheh-sed oo-v'rah-chah-meem. Hoo no-sayn leh-chem l'chawl baw-sawr, kee l'o-lawm chahs-do. Oo-v'too-vo ha-gaw-dol taw-meed lo chaw-sahr law-noo, v'ahl yech-sahr law-noo maw-zon l'o-lawm vaw-ed. Bah-ah-voor sh'mo ha-gaw-dol, kee hoo Ayl zawn oo-m'far-nays la-kol, oo-may-teev la-kol, oo-may-cheen maw-zon l'chawl b'ri-yo-sawv ah-shehr baw-raw.

Baw-rooch ah-taw Ado-noy, ha-zawn ehs ha-kol.

Blessed art Thou, O Lord our God, King of the universe, who providest food for all. Through Thy goodness food has never failed us. Mayest Thou provide sustenance for all Thy children everywhere and at all times.

Father:

We thank Thee, O Lord our God, for our liberation from bondage, for the heritage of Eretz Yisroel, for Thy Torah which Thou didst reveal and impart to us, and for the life of grace and blessing which Thou hast bestowed upon us.

וְעַל הַכֹּל, יְיָ אֱלֹהֵינוּ, אֲנַחְנוּ מוֹדִים לָךְ, וּמְבָרְכִים אוֹתָךְ, יִתְבָּרַךְ שִׁמְךָ בְּפִי כָל חַי תָּמִיד לְעוֹלָם וָעֶד: כַּכָּתוּב, וְאָכַלְתָּ וְשָׂבָעְתָּ וּבֵרַכְתָּ אֶת יְיָ אֱלֹהֶיךָ, עַל הָאָרֶץ הַטּוֹבָה אֲשֶׁר נָתַן לָךְ.

בָּרוּךְ אַתָּה יְיָ, עַל הָאָרֶץ וְעַל הַמָּזוֹן:

V'ahl ha-kol, Ado-noy Elo-hay-noo, ah-nahch-noo mo-deem lawch, oo-m'vawr-cheem o-sawch, yis-baw-rahch shi-m'chaw b'fee kawl chai taw-meed l'o-lawm vaw-ed: Kah-kaw-soov, v'aw-chahl-taw, v'saw-vaw-taw, oo-vay-rahch-taw, ehs Ado-noy Elo-heh-chaw, ahl haw-aw-retz ha-to-vaw, ah-shehr naw-sahn lawch.

Baw-rooch ah-taw Ado-noy, ahl haw-aw-retz v'ahl ha-maw-zon.

Have mercy, O Lord our God, upon Israel Thy people, and
upon Zion, and hasten the day of peace for all mankind.

וּבְנֵה יְרוּשָׁלַיִם עִיר הַקֹּדֶשׁ בִּמְהֵרָה בְיָמֵינוּ. בָּרוּךְ אַתָּה יְיָ, בֹּנֵה
בְרַחֲמָיו יְרוּשָׁלָיִם. אָמֵן:

Oo-v'nay Y'roo-shaw-la-yeem eer ha-ko-desh bi-m'hay-raw
v'yaw-may-noo.

Baw-rooch ah-taw Ado-noy, bo-neh v'ra-cha-mawv Y'roo-
shaw-law-yeem. Aw-mayn.

Family:

בָּרוּךְ אַתָּה יְיָ, אֱלֹהֵינוּ מֶלֶךְ הָעוֹלָם, הָאֵל, אָבִינוּ, מַלְכֵּנוּ,
אַדִּירֵנוּ, בּוֹרְאֵנוּ, גּוֹאֲלֵנוּ, יוֹצְרֵנוּ, קְדוֹשֵׁנוּ, קְדוֹשׁ יַעֲקֹב, רוֹעֵנוּ רוֹעֵה
יִשְׂרָאֵל, הַמֶּלֶךְ הַטּוֹב וְהַמֵּטִיב לַכֹּל, שֶׁבְּכָל יוֹם וָיוֹם הוּא הֵטִיב, הוּא
מֵטִיב, הוּא יֵיטִיב לָנוּ. הוּא גְמָלָנוּ, הוּא גוֹמְלֵנוּ, הוּא יִגְמְלֵנוּ לָעַד, לְחֵן
וּלְחֶסֶד וּלְרַחֲמִים וּלְרֶוַח, הַצָּלָה וְהַצְלָחָה, בְּרָכָה וִישׁוּעָה, נֶחָמָה,
פַּרְנָסָה וְכַלְכָּלָה, וְרַחֲמִים וְחַיִּים וְשָׁלוֹם, וְכָל טוֹב, וּמִכָּל טוֹב
לְעוֹלָם אַל יְחַסְּרֵנוּ:

Baw-rooch ah-taw Ado-noy, Elo-hay-noo meh-lech haw-o-
lawm, haw-ayl, aw-vee-noo, mahl-kay-noo, a-dee-ray-noo, bo-
r'ay-noo, go-ah-lay-noo, yo-tz'ray-noo, k'do-shay-noo, k'dosh Ya-
ah-kov: ro-ay-noo, ro-ay Yis-raw-ayl, ha-meh-lech ha-tov
v'ha-may-teev la-kol, sheh-b'chawl yom vaw-yom, hoo hay-teev,
hoo may-teev, hoo yay-teev law-noo; hoo g'maw-law-noo, hoo
go-m'lay-noo, hoo yig-m'lay-noo law-ahd, l'chayn oo-l'cheh-sed
oo-l'ra-chah-meem oo-l'reh-vahch, ha-tzaw-law v'ha-tz'law-chaw,
b'raw-chaw vee-shoo-aw, neh-chaw-maw, pahr-naw-saw v'chahl-
kaw-law, v'ra-chah-meem, v'chah-yeem v'shaw-lom, v'chawl tov
oo-mi-kawl tov, l'o-lawm ahl y'chah-s'ray-noo.

Blessed art Thou, O Lord our God, King of the universe.
Thou art our God who showerest kindnesses upon all Thy creatures.
Every day dost Thou grant to us the blessings of Thy hand. Thou
art kind and dost deal kindly with us. Thou hast bestowed upon
us Thy blessings, yielding us sustenance and support, life and peace.
We pray Thee, withhold not Thy blessings from us.

Father: May God sustain us all in health.

Family: Amen.

Father: May God bless all who are assembled at our Seder table.

Family: Amen.

Father: May God send plentiful blessings upon this house, and
to all who are near and dear to us.

Family: Amen.

On Sabbath add:

Father: הָרַחֲמָן, הוּא יַנְחִילֵנוּ יוֹם שֶׁכֻּלּוֹ שַׁבָּת וּמְנוּחָה לְחַיֵּי הָעוֹלָמִים:

Family: אָמֵן: — Amen

Father: May this Sabbath eve bring its message of rest and peace
to us.

Family: Amen.

Father: הָרַחֲמָן, הוּא יַנְחִילֵנוּ יוֹם שֶׁכֻּלּוֹ טוֹב:

Family: אָמֵן: — Amen

Father: May this festival of Pesach bring its message of joy and
happiness to us.

Family: Amen.

Family:

מִגְדוֹל יְשׁוּעוֹת מַלְכּוֹ וְעֹשֶׂה חֶסֶד לִמְשִׁיחוֹ, לְדָוִד וּלְזַרְעוֹ עַד עוֹלָם.
עֹשֶׂה שָׁלוֹם בִּמְרוֹמָיו, הוּא יַעֲשֶׂה שָׁלוֹם עָלֵינוּ וְעַל כָּל יִשְׂרָאֵל,
וְאִמְרוּ, אָמֵן:

Mig-dol y'shoo-os mahl-ko, v'o-seh cheh-sed li-m'shee-cho,
l'Daw-vid oo-l'zahr-o ahd o-lawm. O-seh shaw-lom bi-m'ro-mawv,
hoo yah-ah-seh shaw-lom, aw-lay-noo v'ahl kawl Yis-raw-ayl,
v'i-m'roo, aw-mayn.

May He who creates peace in His celestial heights, grant peace
and contentment and freedom to us, to all Israel, and to all mankind.
Amen.

(Refill the cups of wine.)

Father:

"In gratitude to God for His bounty to us, we raise our third
cup of wine on this Seder night, as we recite the blessing together:"

בָּרוּךְ אַתָּה יְיָ, אֱלֹהֵינוּ מֶלֶךְ הָעוֹלָם, בּוֹרֵא פְּרִי הַגָּפֶן:

Baw-rooch ah-taw Ado-noy, Elo-hay-noo meh-lech haw-o-
lawm, bo-ray p'ree ha-gaw-fen.

Blessed art Thou, O Lord our God, King of the universe, who
createst the fruit of the vine.

(Everyone drinks the third cup of wine.)

13. Elijah, the Prophet, is Welcomed.

(The fourth cup of wine is filled as is the special goblet for Elijah. One of
the children is asked to open the door to symbolically welcome the prophet of good
tidings, peace, and world redemption. Some authorities say that the reason for
the cup of Elijah is a fifth expression in the Bible concerning the way in which
God brought the Israelites out of Egypt, the phrase, "And I shall bring you." In
order to compromise with these authorities who insisted on a fifth cup of wine,
the four cups were retained, and the fifth became the cup of Elijah. See page 189.)

Father:

"The special cup we have filled, which stands in the middle of our table, is called the cup of Elijah. In Jewish tradition, the prophet Elijah is the harbinger, the messenger of good tidings, and he who will, in the end of days, announce the era of peace and perfect happiness. As we rise, we open the door, to indicate that we eagerly welcome Elijah into our homes, and pray that he inspire us to work for the day when peace and happiness will reign throughout the world for all mankind:"

(The door is opened and the family rises and recites:)

שְׁפֹךְ חֲמָתְךָ אֶל הַגּוֹיִם אֲשֶׁר לֹא יְדָעוּךָ,

וְעַל מַמְלָכוֹת אֲשֶׁר בְּשִׁמְךָ לֹא קָרָאוּ.

כִּי אָכַל אֶת יַעֲקֹב, וְאֶת נָוֵהוּ הֵשַׁמּוּ.

שְׁפָךְ עֲלֵיהֶם זַעְמֶךָ, וַחֲרוֹן אַפְּךָ יַשִּׂיגֵם.

תִּרְדֹּף בְּאַף וְתַשְׁמִידֵם, מִתַּחַת שְׁמֵי יְיָ:

Sh'foch cha-maws-chaw ahl ha-go-yeem, ah-shehr lo y'daw-oo-chaw,

V'ahl mahm-law-chos ah-shehr b'shi-m'chaw lo kaw-raw-oo;

Kee aw-chahl ehs Ya-ah-kov, v'ehs naw-vay-hoo hay-shah-moo:

Sh'fawch ah-lay-hem zah-meh-chaw, va-cha-ron ah-p'chaw ya-see-gaym;

Tir-dof b'ahf v'sahsh-mee-daym, mi-ta-chahs sh'may Ado-noy.

We pray Thee, O God, cause evil to disappear from the world, and imbue us with the spirit of love and kindness. May we, and all Thy children, inspired by the love of Thee, be privileged to behold the day when all peoples will "beat their swords into plowshares and their spears into pruninghooks; nation shall not lift up sword against nation, neither shall they learn war any more."   Amen.

(Family is seated and sings the song Ay-li-yaw-hoo Ha-naw-vee.)

AYLIYAWHOO HANAWVEE
אֵלִיָּהוּ הַנָּבִיא — ELIJAH, THE PROPHET

Ay-li-yaw-hoo ha-naw-vee,   אֵלִיָּהוּ הַנָּבִיא

Ay-li-yaw-hoo ha-tish-bee,   אֵלִיָּהוּ הַתִּשְׁבִּי

Ay-li-yaw-hoo, Ay-li-yaw-hoo,   אֵלִיָּהוּ, אֵלִיָּהוּ,

Ay-li-yaw-hoo ha-gil-aw-dee.   אֵלִיָּהוּ הַגִּלְעָדִי.

Bi-m'hay-raw v'yaw-may-noo,   בִּמְהֵרָה בְיָמֵינוּ

Yaw-vo ay-lay-noo,   יָבֹא אֵלֵינוּ

Im maw-shee-ach, ben Daw-vid,   עִם מָשִׁיחַ בֶּן דָּוִד

Im maw-shee-ach, ben Daw-vid.   עִם מָשִׁיחַ בֶּן דָּוִד.

Ay-li-yaw-hoo ha-naw-vee,

Ay-li-yaw-hoo ha-tish-bee,

Ay-li-yaw-hoo, Ay-li-yaw-hoo,

Ay-li-yaw-hoo ha-gil-aw-dee.

14. Hallel — הַלֵּל

Father:

"We recited the first part of the Hallel, the psalms of praise, before our Seder dinner. We are now continuing with the Hallel psalms and will read a few of the selections:"

Psalm 115

לֹא לָנוּ יְיָ לֹא לָנוּ,   כִּי לְשִׁמְךָ תֵּן כָּבוֹד

עַל חַסְדְּךָ   עַל אֲמִתֶּךָ.

לָמָּה יֹאמְרוּ הַגּוֹיִם,   אַיֵּה נָא אֱלֹהֵיהֶם.

וֵאלֹהֵינוּ בַשָּׁמָיִם,   כֹּל אֲשֶׁר חָפֵץ עָשָׂה.

עֲצַבֵּיהֶם כֶּסֶף וְזָהָב,   מַעֲשֵׂה יְדֵי אָדָם.

פֶּה לָהֶם וְלֹא יְדַבֵּרוּ,   עֵינַיִם לָהֶם וְלֹא יִרְאוּ.

אָזְנַיִם לָהֶם וְלֹא יִשְׁמָעוּ,   אַף לָהֶם וְלֹא יְרִיחוּן.

יְדֵיהֶם וְלֹא יְמִישׁוּן,   רַגְלֵיהֶם וְלֹא יְהַלֵּכוּ,

לֹא יֶהְגּוּ בִּגְרוֹנָם.

כְּמוֹהֶם יִהְיוּ עֹשֵׂיהֶם,   כֹּל אֲשֶׁר בֹּטֵחַ בָּהֶם.

יִשְׂרָאֵל בְּטַח בַּיְיָ,   עֶזְרָם וּמָגִנָּם הוּא.

בֵּית אַהֲרֹן בִּטְחוּ בַיְיָ,   עֶזְרָם וּמָגִנָּם הוּא.

יִרְאֵי יְיָ בִּטְחוּ בַיְיָ,   עֶזְרָם וּמָגִנָּם הוּא:

Father: O Israel, trust in the Lord!
He is your help and your shield.

Family: You who revere the Lord, trust in the Lord,
He is your help and your shield.

Father: The Lord has been mindful of us,
He will bless us;

Family: He will bless the house of Israel,
He will bless the house of Aaron;

Father: He will bless those who revere Him,
Both small and great.

Family: May the Lord give you more increase,
You and your children,

Father: May you be blessed by the Lord,
Who made heaven and earth.

Family: We will bless the Lord
From this time forth and forever more.   Halleluyah.

Selected from Psalms 117–118

הַלְלוּ אֶת יְיָ כָּל גּוֹיִם,
שַׁבְּחוּהוּ כָּל הָאֻמִּים:
כִּי גָבַר עָלֵינוּ חַסְדּוֹ,
וֶאֱמֶת יְיָ לְעוֹלָם, הַלְלוּיָה:

Ha-l'loo ehs Ado-noy kawl go-yeem,
Shahb-choo-hoo kawl haw-oo-meem,
Kee gaw-vhar aw-lay-noo chahs-do,
Veh-eh-mehs Ado-noy l'o-lawm, ha-l'loo-yaw.

Father: Praise the Lord all ye nations,
Extol Him, all ye peoples.

Family: For great is His mercy to us,
And His truth endures forever, Halleluyah.

Father: O give thanks to the Lord, for He is good,
For His mercy endures forever.

Family: Let Israel say,
For His mercy endures forever.

Father: Let the house of Aaron say,
          For His mercy endures forever.

Family: Let those who revere the Lord say,
          For His mercy endures forever.

Father: It is better to take refuge in the Lord,
          Than to trust in man.

Family: It is better to take refuge in the Lord,
          Than to trust in princes.

Father: This is the Lord's doing;
          It is marvelous in our eyes.

Family: This is the day which the Lord has made,
          We will rejoice and be glad in it.

Father: Blessed be he who comes in the name of the Lord,
          We will bless you from the house of the Lord.

Family: O give thanks to the Lord, for He is good,
          For His mercy endures forever.

(Refill the cups of wine.)

Father:

"We now prepare to drink the fourth of the four cups we are enjoined to have on this Seder night. We raise our cups and together recite the blessing over the wine:

בָּרוּךְ אַתָּה יְיָ, אֱלֹהֵינוּ מֶלֶךְ הָעוֹלָם, בּוֹרֵא פְּרִי הַגָּפֶן:

Baw-rooch ah-taw Ado-noy, Elo-hay-noo meh-lech haw-o-lawm, bo-ray p'ree ha-gaw-fen.

Blessed art Thou, O Lord our God, King of the universe, who createst the fruit of the vine.

(Everyone drinks the fourth cup of wine.)

15. Nirtzaw — נִרְצָה

Father:

"We have now reached the end of our service, conducting it in the spirit of tradition and family union and harmony. We recite the words which in the traditional Haggadah bring the Seder to a close. (The three larger letters which you see form an acrostic of the word חֲזַק — cha-zahk, meaning "Be Strong.")

חֲסַל סִדּוּר פֶּסַח כְּהִלְכָתוֹ,   כְּכָל מִשְׁפָּטוֹ וְחֻקָּתוֹ.

כַּאֲשֶׁר זָכִינוּ לְסַדֵּר אוֹתוֹ,   כֵּן נִזְכֶּה לַעֲשׂוֹתוֹ.

זָךְ שׁוֹכֵן מְעוֹנָה,   קוֹמֵם קְהַל עֲדַת מִי מָנָה.

קָרֵב נַהֵל נִטְעֵי כַנָּה,   פְּדוּיִם לְצִיּוֹן בְּרִנָּה:

לְשָׁנָה הַבָּאָה בִּירוּשָׁלָיִם:

CHah-sahl si-door peh-sahch k'hil-chaw-so,
K'chawl mish-paw-to v'choo-kaw-so.
Ka-ah-shehr zaw-chee-noo l'sah-dayr o-so,
Kayn niz-keh la-ah-so-so.
Zawch sho-chayn m'o-naw,
Ko-maym k'hahl ah-dahs mee maw-naw.
Kaw-rayv na-hayl nit-ay cha-naw,
P'doo-yeem l'tzi-yon b'ri-naw.

L'shaw-naw ha-baw-aw bee-roo-shaw-law-yeem.

"The Seder of Passover is concluded in accordance with our hallowed tradition. As we were privileged to perform it, so may we annually re-experience its ceremonials. O Thou who dwelleth on high, raise up Thy people, and may they and we learn to appreciate ever more deeply the lesson of the Exodus and its message of freedom. May we celebrate again in peace and liberty. May the year ahead bring redemption to Israel and Jerusalem and to all mankind. Amen."

16. Passover Songs

*(While the Seder service is officially ended, it is customary to sing
the traditional songs which follow.)*

כִּי לוֹ נָאֶה — KEE LO NAW-EH — PRAISE TO HIM

This is a song of eight stanzas which explain and describe the
greatness of God. Each begins with a different adjective referring
to God, but all end with the same phrase, "Kee lo naw-eh — To
Him praise is proper and becoming." The translation of the refrain
is: "To Thee, to Thee indeed, surely to Thee, to Thee alone,
belong all crowns of song."

כִּי לוֹ נָאֶה, כִּי לוֹ יָאֶה

אַדִּיר בִּמְלוּכָה, בָּחוּר כַּהֲלָכָה, גְּדוּדָיו יֹאמְרוּ לוֹ. לְךָ וּלְךָ, לְךָ
כִּי לְךָ, לְךָ אַף לְךָ, לְךָ יְיָ הַמַּמְלָכָה, כִּי לוֹ נָאֶה, כִּי לוֹ יָאֶה.

דָּגוּל בִּמְלוּכָה, הָדוּר כַּהֲלָכָה, וְתִיקָיו יֹאמְרוּ לוֹ. לְךָ וּלְךָ, לְךָ
כִּי לְךָ, לְךָ אַף לְךָ, לְךָ יְיָ הַמַּמְלָכָה, כִּי לוֹ נָאֶה, כִּי לוֹ יָאֶה.

זַכַּאי בִּמְלוּכָה, חָסִין כַּהֲלָכָה, טַפְסְרָיו יֹאמְרוּ לוֹ. לְךָ וּלְךָ, לְךָ
כִּי לְךָ, לְךָ אַף לְךָ, לְךָ יְיָ הַמַּמְלָכָה, כִּי לוֹ נָאֶה, כִּי לוֹ יָאֶה.

יָחִיד בִּמְלוּכָה, כַּבִּיר כַּהֲלָכָה, לִמּוּדָיו יֹאמְרוּ לוֹ. לְךָ וּלְךָ, לְךָ
כִּי לְךָ, לְךָ אַף לְךָ, לְךָ יְיָ הַמַּמְלָכָה, כִּי לוֹ נָאֶה, כִּי לוֹ יָאֶה.

מוֹשֵׁל בִּמְלוּכָה, נוֹרָא כַּהֲלָכָה, סְבִיבָיו יֹאמְרוּ לוֹ. לְךָ וּלְךָ, לְךָ
כִּי לְךָ, לְךָ אַף לְךָ, לְךָ יְיָ הַמַּמְלָכָה, כִּי לוֹ נָאֶה, כִּי לוֹ יָאֶה.

עָנָיו בִּמְלוּכָה, פּוֹדֶה כַּהֲלָכָה, צַדִּיקָיו יֹאמְרוּ לוֹ. לְךָ וּלְךָ, לְךָ
כִּי לְךָ, לְךָ אַף לְךָ, לְךָ יְיָ הַמַּמְלָכָה, כִּי לוֹ נָאֶה, כִּי לוֹ יָאֶה.

קָדוֹשׁ בִּמְלוּכָה, רַחוּם כַּהֲלָכָה, שִׁנְאַנָּיו יֹאמְרוּ לוֹ. לְךָ וּלְךָ, לְךָ
כִּי לְךָ, לְךָ אַף לְךָ, לְךָ יְיָ הַמַּמְלָכָה, כִּי לוֹ נָאֶה, כִּי לוֹ יָאֶה.

תַּקִּיף בִּמְלוּכָה, תּוֹמֵךְ כַּהֲלָכָה, תְּמִימָיו יֹאמְרוּ לוֹ. לְךָ וּלְךָ, לְךָ
כִּי לְךָ, לְךָ אַף לְךָ, לְךָ יְיָ הַמַּמְלָכָה. כִּי לוֹ נָאֶה, כִּי לוֹ יָאֶה:

1. Ah-deer bi-m'loo-chaw, baw-choor ka-ha-law-chaw, g'doo
   dawv yo-m'roo lo,
   > *Refrain:* l'chaw oo-l'chaw, l'chaw kee l'chaw, l'chaw ah
   > l'chaw, l'chaw Ado-noy ha-ma-m'law-chaw, kee lo
   > naw-eh, kee lo yaw-eh.

2. Daw-gool bim'loo-chaw, haw-door ka-ha-law-chaw, v'see-kaw
   yo-m'roo lo, l'chaw oo-l'chaw, l'chaw kee l'chaw, l'chaw ah
   l'chaw, l'chaw Ado-noy ha-ma-m'law-chaw, kee lo naw-eh
   kee lo yaw-eh.

3. Za-kai bi-m'loo-chaw, chah-seen ka-ha-law-chaw, tahf-s'raw
   yo-m'roo lo, l'chaw oo-l'chaw, l'chaw kee l'chaw, l'chaw ah
   l'chaw, l'chaw Ado-noy ha-ma-m'law-chaw, kee lo naw-eh
   kee lo yaw-eh.

4. Yaw-cheed bi-m'loo-chaw, ka-beer ka-ha-law-chaw, li-moo
   dawv yo-m'roo lo, l'chaw oo-l'chaw, l'chaw kee l'chaw
   l'chaw ahf l'chaw, l'chaw Ado-noy ha-ma-m'law-chaw, kee lo
   naw-eh, kee lo yaw-eh.

5. Mo-shayl bi-m'loo-chaw, no-raw cha-ha-law-chaw, s'vee-vaw
   yo-m'roo lo, l'chaw oo-l'chaw, l'chaw kee l'chaw, l'chaw
   ahf l'chaw, l'chaw Ado-noy ha-ma-m'law-chaw, kee lo
   naw-eh, kee lo yaw-eh.

6. Aw-nawv bi-m'loo-chaw, po-deh cha-ha-law-chaw, tzah-dee
   kawv yo-m'roo lo, l'chaw oo-l'chaw, l'chaw kee l'chaw
   l'chaw ahf l'chaw, l'chaw Ado-noy ha-ma-m'law-chaw, ke
   lo naw-eh, kee lo yaw-eh.

7. Kaw-dosh bi-m'loo-chaw, ra-choom ka-ha-law-chaw, shin-ah-
   nawv yo-m'roo lo, l'chaw oo-l'chaw, l'chaw kee l'chaw,
   l'chaw ahf l'chaw, l'chaw Ado-noy ha-ma-m'law-chaw, kee
   lo naw-eh, kee lo yaw-eh.

8. Tah-keef bi-m'loo-chaw, to-maych ka-ha-law-chaw, t'mee-
   mawv yo-m'roo lo, l'chaw oo-l'chaw, l'chaw kee l'chaw,
   l'chaw ahf l'chaw, l'chaw Ado-noy ha-ma-m'law-chaw, kee
   lo naw-eh, kee lo yaw-eh.

KEE LO NAWEH

אַדִּיר הוּא   AHDEER Hoo — MIGHTY IS HE

In the eight stanzas which comprise this song, the singer praises
God for His greatness, utilizing synonyms of praise and descriptive
adjectives and adding them to the chorus, which begins with the
words, "Yiv-neh vay-so b'kaw-rov."

These descriptive adjectives of God follow the order of the Hebrew alphabet,
indicated by larger type.

אַדִּיר הוּא,

יִבְנֶה בֵיתוֹ בְּקָרוֹב. בִּמְהֵרָה, בִּמְהֵרָה, בְּיָמֵינוּ בְּקָרוֹב.
אֵל בְּנֵה, אֵל בְּנֵה, בְּנֵה בֵיתְךָ בְּקָרוֹב.

בָּחוּר הוּא, גָּדוֹל הוּא, דָּגוּל הוּא,
יִבְנֶה בֵיתוֹ בְּקָרוֹב. בִּמְהֵרָה, בִּמְהֵרָה, בְּיָמֵינוּ בְּקָרוֹב.
אֵל בְּנֵה, אֵל בְּנֵה, בְּנֵה בֵיתְךָ בְּקָרוֹב.

הָדוּר הוּא, וָתִיק הוּא, זַכַּאי הוּא,
יִבְנֶה בֵיתוֹ בְּקָרוֹב. בִּמְהֵרָה, בִּמְהֵרָה, בְּיָמֵינוּ בְּקָרוֹב.
אֵל בְּנֵה, אֵל בְּנֵה, בְּנֵה בֵיתְךָ בְּקָרוֹב.

חָסִיד הוּא, טָהוֹר הוּא, יָחִיד הוּא,
יִבְנֶה בֵיתוֹ בְּקָרוֹב. בִּמְהֵרָה, בִּמְהֵרָה, בְּיָמֵינוּ בְּקָרוֹב.
אֵל בְּנֵה, אֵל בְּנֵה, בְּנֵה בֵיתְךָ בְּקָרוֹב.

כַּבִּיר הוּא, לָמוּד הוּא, מֶלֶךְ הוּא,
יִבְנֶה בֵיתוֹ בְּקָרוֹב. בִּמְהֵרָה, בִּמְהֵרָה, בְּיָמֵינוּ בְּקָרוֹב.
אֵל בְּנֵה, אֵל בְּנֵה, בְּנֵה בֵיתְךָ בְּקָרוֹב.

נָאוֹר הוּא, סַגִּיב הוּא, עִזּוּז הוּא,
יִבְנֶה בֵיתוֹ בְּקָרוֹב. בִּמְהֵרָה, בִּמְהֵרָה, בְּיָמֵינוּ בְּקָרוֹב.
אֵל בְּנֵה, אֵל בְּנֵה, בְּנֵה בֵיתְךָ בְּקָרוֹב.

פּוֹדֶה הוּא, צַדִּיק הוּא, קָדוֹשׁ הוּא,
יִבְנֶה בֵיתוֹ בְּקָרוֹב. בִּמְהֵרָה, בִּמְהֵרָה, בְּיָמֵינוּ בְּקָרוֹב.
אֵל בְּנֵה, אֵל בְּנֵה, בְּנֵה בֵיתְךָ בְּקָרוֹב.

רַחוּם הוּא, שַׁדַּי הוּא, תַּקִּיף הוּא,
יִבְנֶה בֵיתוֹ בְּקָרוֹב. בִּמְהֵרָה, בִּמְהֵרָה, בְּיָמֵינוּ בְּקָרוֹב.
אֵל בְּנֵה, אֵל בְּנֵה, בְּנֵה בֵיתְךָ בְּקָרוֹב.

1. Ah-deer hoo, Ah-deer hoo, yiv-neh vay-so b'kaw-rov,
   Bi-m'hay-raw, Bi-m'hay-raw, b'yaw-may-noo b'kaw-rov,
   Ayl b'nay, Ayl b'nay, b'nay vays-chaw b'kaw-rov.

2. Baw-choor hoo, gaw-dol hoo, daw-gool hoo, yiv-neh vay-so
   b'kaw-rov, Bi-m'hay-raw, Bi-m'hay-raw, b'yaw-may-noo
   b'kaw-rov, Ayl b'nay, Ayl b'nay, b'nay vays-chaw
   b'kaw-rov.

3. Haw-door hoo, vaw-seek hoo, zah-kai hoo, yiv-neh vay-so
   b'kaw-rov, Bi-m'hay-raw, Bi-m'hay-raw, b'yaw-may-noo
   b'kaw-rov, Ayl b'nay, Ayl b'nay, b'nay vays-chaw
   b'kaw-rov.

4. Chaw-seed hoo, taw-hor hoo, yaw-cheed hoo, yiv-neh vay-so
   b'kaw-rov, Bi-m'hay-raw, Bi-m'hay-raw, b'yaw-may-noo
   b'kaw-rov, Ayl b'nay, Ayl b'nay, b'nay vays-chaw
   b'kaw-rov.

5. Ka-beer hoo, law-mood hoo, meh-lech hoo, yiv-neh vay-so
   b'kaw-rov, Bi-m'hay-raw, Bi-m'hay-raw, b'yaw-may-noo
   b'kaw-rov, Ayl b'nay, Ayl b'nay, b'nay vays-chaw
   b'kaw-rov.

6. Naw-or hoo, sah-geev hoo, ee-zooz hoo, yiv-neh vay-so b'kaw-rov, Bi-m'hay-raw, Bi-m'hay-raw, b'yaw-may-noo b'kaw-rov, Ayl b'nay, Ayl b'nay, b'nay vays-chaw b'kaw-rov.

7. Po-deh hoo, tzah-deek hoo, kaw-dosh hoo, yiv-neh vay-so b'kaw-rov, Bi-m'hay-raw, Bi-m'hay-raw, b'yaw-may-noo b'kaw-rov, Ayl b'nay, Ayl b'nay, b'nay vays-chaw b'kaw-rov.

8. Ra-choom hoo, sha-dai hoo, ta-keef hoo, yiv-neh vay-so b'kaw-rov, Bi-m'hay-raw, Bi-m'hay-raw, b'yaw-may-noo b'kaw-rov, Ayl b'nay, Ayl b'nay, b'nay vays-chaw b'kaw-rov.

ADEER HOO

Arr. SHALOM ALTMAN

אֶחָד מִי יוֹדֵעַ

Eh-chawd Mee Yo-day-ah — Who Knows One?

אֶחָד מִי יוֹדֵעַ, אֶחָד אֲנִי יוֹדֵעַ. אֶחָד אֱלֹהֵינוּ שֶׁבַּשָּׁמַיִם וּבָאָרֶץ.

שְׁנַיִם מִי יוֹדֵעַ, שְׁנַיִם אֲנִי יוֹדֵעַ. שְׁנֵי לֻחוֹת הַבְּרִית, אֶחָד אֱלֹהֵינוּ שֶׁבַּשָּׁמַיִם וּבָאָרֶץ.

שְׁלֹשָׁה מִי יוֹדֵעַ, שְׁלֹשָׁה אֲנִי יוֹדֵעַ. שְׁלֹשָׁה אָבוֹת, שְׁנֵי לֻחוֹת הַבְּרִית, אֶחָד אֱלֹהֵינוּ שֶׁבַּשָּׁמַיִם וּבָאָרֶץ.

אַרְבַּע מִי יוֹדֵעַ, אַרְבַּע אֲנִי יוֹדֵעַ. אַרְבַּע אִמָּהוֹת, שְׁלֹשָׁה אָבוֹת, שְׁנֵי לֻחוֹת הַבְּרִית, אֶחָד אֱלֹהֵינוּ שֶׁבַּשָּׁמַיִם וּבָאָרֶץ.

חֲמִשָּׁה מִי יוֹדֵעַ, חֲמִשָּׁה אֲנִי יוֹדֵעַ. חֲמִשָּׁה חוּמְשֵׁי תוֹרָה, אַרְבַּע אִמָּהוֹת, שְׁלֹשָׁה אָבוֹת, שְׁנֵי לֻחוֹת הַבְּרִית, אֶחָד אֱלֹהֵינוּ שֶׁבַּשָּׁמַיִם וּבָאָרֶץ.

שִׁשָּׁה מִי יוֹדֵעַ, שִׁשָּׁה אֲנִי יוֹדֵעַ. שִׁשָּׁה סִדְרֵי מִשְׁנָה, חֲמִשָּׁה חוּמְשֵׁי תוֹרָה, אַרְבַּע אִמָּהוֹת, שְׁלֹשָׁה אָבוֹת, שְׁנֵי לֻחוֹת הַבְּרִית, אֶחָד אֱלֹהֵינוּ שֶׁבַּשָּׁמַיִם וּבָאָרֶץ.

שִׁבְעָה מִי יוֹדֵעַ, שִׁבְעָה אֲנִי יוֹדֵעַ. שִׁבְעָה יְמֵי שַׁבַּתָּא, שִׁשָּׁה סִדְרֵי מִשְׁנָה, חֲמִשָּׁה חוּמְשֵׁי תוֹרָה, אַרְבַּע אִמָּהוֹת, שְׁלֹשָׁה אָבוֹת, שְׁנֵי לֻחוֹת הַבְּרִית, אֶחָד אֱלֹהֵינוּ שֶׁבַּשָּׁמַיִם וּבָאָרֶץ.

שְׁמוֹנָה מִי יוֹדֵעַ, שְׁמוֹנָה אֲנִי יוֹדֵעַ. שְׁמוֹנָה יְמֵי מִילָה, שִׁבְעָה יְמֵי שַׁבַּתָּא, שִׁשָּׁה סִדְרֵי מִשְׁנָה, חֲמִשָּׁה חוּמְשֵׁי תוֹרָה, אַרְבַּע אִמָּהוֹת, שְׁלֹשָׁה אָבוֹת, שְׁנֵי לֻחוֹת הַבְּרִית, אֶחָד אֱלֹהֵינוּ שֶׁבַּשָּׁמַיִם וּבָאָרֶץ.

תִּשְׁעָה מִי יוֹדֵעַ, תִּשְׁעָה אֲנִי יוֹדֵעַ. תִּשְׁעָה יַרְחֵי לֵדָה, שְׁמוֹנָה יְמֵי מִילָה, שִׁבְעָה יְמֵי שַׁבַּתָּא, שִׁשָּׁה סִדְרֵי מִשְׁנָה, חֲמִשָּׁה חוּמְשֵׁי תוֹרָה, אַרְבַּע אִמָּהוֹת, שְׁלֹשָׁה אָבוֹת, שְׁנֵי לֻחוֹת הַבְּרִית, אֶחָד אֱלֹהֵינוּ שֶׁבַּשָּׁמַיִם וּבָאָרֶץ.

עֲשָׂרָה מִי יוֹדֵעַ, עֲשָׂרָה אֲנִי יוֹדֵעַ. עֲשָׂרָה דִבְּרַיָּא, תִּשְׁעָה יַרְחֵי לֵדָה, שְׁמוֹנָה יְמֵי מִילָה, שִׁבְעָה יְמֵי שַׁבַּתָּא, שִׁשָּׁה סִדְרֵי מִשְׁנָה, חֲמִשָּׁה חוּמְשֵׁי תוֹרָה, אַרְבַּע אִמָּהוֹת, שְׁלֹשָׁה אָבוֹת, שְׁנֵי לֻחוֹת הַבְּרִית, אֶחָד אֱלֹהֵינוּ שֶׁבַּשָּׁמַיִם וּבָאָרֶץ.

אַחַד עָשָׂר מִי יוֹדֵעַ, אַחַד עָשָׂר אֲנִי יוֹדֵעַ. אַחַד עָשָׂר כּוֹכְבַיָּא, עֲשָׂרָה דִבְּרַיָּא, תִּשְׁעָה יַרְחֵי לֵדָה, שְׁמוֹנָה יְמֵי מִילָה, שִׁבְעָה יְמֵי שַׁבַּתָּא, שִׁשָּׁה סִדְרֵי מִשְׁנָה, חֲמִשָּׁה חוּמְשֵׁי תוֹרָה, אַרְבַּע אִמָּהוֹת, שְׁלֹשָׁה אָבוֹת, שְׁנֵי לֻחוֹת הַבְּרִית, אֶחָד אֱלֹהֵינוּ שֶׁבַּשָּׁמַיִם וּבָאָרֶץ.

שְׁנֵים עָשָׂר מִי יוֹדֵעַ, שְׁנֵים עָשָׂר אֲנִי יוֹדֵעַ. שְׁנֵים עָשָׂר שִׁבְטַיָּא, אַחַד עָשָׂר כּוֹכְבַיָּא, עֲשָׂרָה דִבְּרַיָּא, תִּשְׁעָה יַרְחֵי לֵדָה, שְׁמוֹנָה יְמֵי מִילָה, שִׁבְעָה יְמֵי שַׁבַּתָּא, שִׁשָּׁה סִדְרֵי מִשְׁנָה, חֲמִשָּׁה חוּמְשֵׁי תוֹרָה, אַרְבַּע אִמָּהוֹת, שְׁלֹשָׁה אָבוֹת, שְׁנֵי לֻחוֹת הַבְּרִית, אֶחָד אֱלֹהֵינוּ שֶׁבַּשָּׁמַיִם וּבָאָרֶץ.

שְׁלֹשָׁה עָשָׂר מִי יוֹדֵעַ, שְׁלֹשָׁה עָשָׂר אֲנִי יוֹדֵעַ: שְׁלֹשָׁה עָשָׂר מִדַּיָּא, שְׁנֵים עָשָׂר שִׁבְטַיָּא, אַחַד עָשָׂר כּוֹכְבַיָּא, עֲשָׂרָה דִבְּרַיָּא, תִּשְׁעָה יַרְחֵי לֵדָה, שְׁמוֹנָה יְמֵי מִילָה, שִׁבְעָה יְמֵי שַׁבַּתָּא, שִׁשָּׁה סִדְרֵי מִשְׁנָה, חֲמִשָּׁה חוּמְשֵׁי תוֹרָה, אַרְבַּע אִמָּהוֹת, שְׁלֹשָׁה אָבוֹת, שְׁנֵי לֻחוֹת הַבְּרִית, אֶחָד אֱלֹהֵינוּ שֶׁבַּשָּׁמַיִם וּבָאָרֶץ.

1. Eh-chawd mee yo-day-ah? Eh-chawd ah-nee yo-day-ah!
   Eh-chawd Elo-hay-noo, sheh-ba-shaw-ma-yeem oo-vaw-
   aw-retz.

2. Sh'nah-yeem mee yo-day-ah? Sh'nah-yeem ah-nee yo-day-ah!
   Sh'nay loo-chos ha-b'rees, eh-chawd Elo-hay-noo, sheh-
   ba-shaw-ma-yeem oo-vaw-aw-retz.

3. Sh'lo-shaw mee yo-day-ah? Sh'lo-shaw ah-nee yo-day-ah.
   Sh'lo-shaw aw-vos, sh'nay loo-chos ha-b'rees, eh-chawd
   Elo-hay-noo, sheh-ba-shaw-ma-yeem oo-vaw-aw-retz.

4. Ahr-bah mee yo-day-ah? Ahr-bah ah-nee yo-day-ah!
   Ahr-bah ee-maw-hos, sh'lo-shaw aw-vos, sh'nay loo-
   chos ha-b'rees, eh-chawd Elo-hay-noo, sheh-ba-shaw-
   ma-yeem oo-vaw-aw-retz.

5. Chah-mi-shaw mee yo-day-ah? Chah-mi-shaw ah-nee yo-
   day-ah!
   Chah-mi-shaw choom-shay so-raw, ahr-bah ee-maw-hos,
   sh'lo-shaw aw-vos, sh'nay loo-chos ha-b'rees, eh-
   chawd Elo-hay-noo, sheh-ba-shaw-ma-yeem oo-vaw-
   aw-retz.

6. Shi-shaw mee yo-day-ah? Shi-shaw ah-nee yo-day-ah!
   Shi-shaw sid-ray mish-naw, chah-mi-shaw choom-shay
   so-raw, ahr-bah ee-maw-hos, sh'lo-shaw aw-vos, sh'nay
   loo-chos ha-b'rees, eh-chawd Elo-hay-noo, sheh-ba-
   shaw-ma-yeem oo-vaw-aw-retz.

7. Shiv-aw mee yo-day-ah? Shiv-aw ah-nee yo-day-ah!
   Shiv-aw y'may shah-ba-taw shi-shaw sid-ray mish-naw,
   chah-mi-shaw choom-shay so-raw, ahr-bah ee-maw-
   hos, sh'lo-shaw aw-vos, sh'nay loo-chos ha-b'rees,
   eh-chawd Elo-hay-noo, sheh-ba-shaw-ma-yeem oo-vaw-
   aw-retz.

8. Sh'mo-naw mee yo-day-ah? Sh'mo-naw ah-nee yo-day-ah!
    Sh'mo-naw y'may mee-law, shiv-aw y'may shah-ba-taw,
    shi-shaw sid-ray mish-naw, cha-mi-shaw choom-shay
    so-raw, ahr-bah ee-maw-hos, sh'lo-shaw aw-vos, sh'nay
    loo-chos ha-b'rees, eh-chawd Elo-hay-noo, sheh-ba-
    shaw-ma-yeem oo-vaw-aw-retz.

9. Tish-aw mee yo-day-ah? Tish-aw ah-nee yo-day-ah!
    Tish-aw yahr-chay lay-daw, sh'mo-naw y'may mee-law,
    shiv-aw y'may sha-ba-taw, shi-shaw sid-ray mish-naw,
    chah-mi-shaw choom-shay so-raw, ahr-bah ee-maw-hos,
    sh'lo-shaw aw-vos, sh'nay loo-chos ha-b'rees, eh-
    chawd Elo-hay-noo, sheh-ba-shaw-ma-yeem oo-vaw-
    aw-retz.

10. Ah-saw-raw mee yo-day-ah? Ah-saw-raw ah-nee yo-day-ah!
    Ah-saw-raw dib-ra-yaw, tish-aw yahr-chay lay-daw,
    sh'mo-naw y'may mee-law, shiv-aw y'may shah-ba-
    taw, shi-shaw sid-ray mish-naw, cha-mi-shaw choom-
    shay so-raw, ahr-bah ee-maw-hos, sh'lo-shaw aw-vos,
    sh'nay loo-chos ha-b'rees, eh-chawd Elo-hay-noo, sheh-
    ba-shaw-ma-yeem, oo-vaw-aw-retz.

11. Ah-chahd aw-sawr mee yo-day-ah? Ah-chahd aw-sawr ah-nee
    yo-day-ah!
    Ah-chahd aw-sawr koch-va-yaw, ah-saw-raw dib-ra-yaw,
    ʻtish-aw yahr-chay lay-daw, sh'mo-naw y'may mee-
    law, shiv-aw y'may shah-ba-taw, shi-shaw sid-ray
    mish-naw, chah-mi-shaw choom-shay so-raw, ahr-bah
    ee-maw-hos, sh'lo-shaw aw-vos, sh'nay loo-chos ha-
    b'rees, eh-chawd Elo-hay-noo, sheh-ba-shaw-ma-yeem
    oo-vaw-aw-retz.

12: Sh'naym aw-sawr mee yo-day-ah? Sh'naym aw-sawr ah-nee yo-day-ah!

Sh'naym aw-sawr shiv-ta-yaw, ah-chahd aw-sawr koch-va-yaw, ah-saw-raw dib-ra-yaw, tish-aw yahr-chay lay-daw, sh'mo-naw y'may mee-law, shiv-aw y'may shah-ba-taw, shi-shaw sid-ray mish-naw, chah-mi-shaw choom-shay so-raw, ahr-bah ee-maw-hos, sh'lo-shaw aw-vos, sh'nay loo-chos ha-b'rees, eh-chawd Elo-hay-noo, sheh-ba-shaw-ma-yeem oo-vaw-aw-retz.

13. Sh'lo-shaw aw-sawr mee yo-day-ah? Sh'lo-shaw aw-sawr ah-nee yo-day-ah!

Sh'lo-shaw aw-sawr mi-da-yaw, sh'naym aw-sawr shiv-ta-yaw, ah-chahd aw-sawr koch-va-yaw, ah-saw-raw dib-ra-yaw, tish-aw yahr-chay lay-daw, sh'mo-naw y'may mee-law, shiv-aw y'may shah-ba-taw, shi-shaw sid-ray mish-naw, chah-mi-shaw choom-shay so-raw, ahr-bah ee-maw-hos, sh'lo-shaw aw-vos, sh'nay loo-chos ha-b'rees, eh-chawd Elo-hay-noo, sheh-ba-shaw-ma-yeem oo-vaw-aw-retz.

(If you read the melody, you can ask the questions and have the children, one after another, read the answers.)

Who knows the meaning of One?

I know one!   One is our God, in heaven and on earth.

Who knows the meaning of Two?

I know Two!   Two are the Tables of the Covenant (Ten Commandments). One is our God, in heaven and on earth.

Who knows the meaning of Three?

I know Three!   Three are the Patriarchs, Abraham, Isaac, and Jacob. Two are the Tables of the Covenant. One is our God, in heaven and on earth.

Who knows the meaning of Four?

> I know Four! Four are the Matriarchs, Sarah, Rebecca, Rachel, and Leah. Three are the Patriarchs. Two are the Tables of the Covenant. One is our God, in heaven and on earth.

Who knows the meaning of Five?

> I know Five! Five are the books of the Bible (the Pentateuch — Genesis, Exodus, Leviticus, Numbers, Deuteronomy). Four are the Matriarchs. Three are the Patriarchs. Two are the Tables of the Covenant. One is our God, in heaven and on earth.

Who knows the meaning of Six?

> I know Six! Six are the books of the Mishnah (part of the Talmud). Five are the books of the Bible. Four are the Matriarchs. Three are the Patriarchs. Two are the Tables of the Covenant. One is our God, in heaven and on earth.

Who knows the meaning of Seven?

> I know Seven! Seven are the days of the week. Six are the books of the Mishnah. Five are the books of the Bible. Four are the Matriarchs. Three are the Patriarchs. Two are the Tables of the Covenant. One is our God, in heaven and on earth.

Who knows the meaning of Eight?

> I know Eight! Eight are the days of the Covenant (The Covenant of Abraham). Seven are the days of the week. Six are the books of the Mishnah. Five are the books of the Bible. Four are the Matriarchs. Three are the Patriarchs. Two are the Tables of the Covenant. One is our God, in heaven and on earth.

Who knows the meaning of Nine?

I know Nine! Nine are the months of childbirth. Eight are the days of the Covenant. Seven are the days of the week. Six are the books of the Mishnah. Five are the books of the Bible. Four are the Matriarchs. Three are the Patriarchs. Two are the Tables of the Covenant. One is our God, in heaven and on earth.

Who knows the meaning of Ten?

I know Ten! Ten are the Commandments. Nine are the months of childbirth. Eight are the days of the Covenant. Seven are the days of the week. Six are the books of the Mishnah. Five are the books of the Bible. Four are the Matriarchs. Three are the Patriarchs. Two are the Tables of the Covenant. One is our God, in heaven and on earth.

Who knows the meaning of Eleven?

I know Eleven! Eleven are the stars (in the dream of Joseph, they bowed down to him.) Ten are the Commandments. Nine are the months of childbirth. Eight are the days of the Covenant. Seven are the days of the week. Six are the books of the Mishnah. Five are the books of the Bible. Four are the Matriarchs. Three are the Patriarchs. Two are the Tables of the Covenant. One is our God, in heaven and on earth.

Who knows the meaning of Twelve?

I know Twelve! Twelve are the tribes of Israel. Eleven are the stars of Joseph's dream. Ten are the Commandments. Nine are the months of childbirth. Eight are the days of the Covenant. Seven are the days of the week. Six are the books of the Mishnah. Five are the books of the Bible. Four are the Matriarchs. Three are the Patriarchs. Two are the Tables of the Covenant. One is our God, in heaven and on earth.

Who knows the meaning of Thirteen?

I know Thirteen! Thirteen are the attributes of God (descriptions of God's greatness mentioned in Exodus 34:6). Twelve are the tribes of Israel. Eleven are the stars of Joseph's dream. Ten are the Commandments. Nine are the months of childbirth. Eight are the days of the Covenant. Seven are the days of the week. Six are the books of the Mishnah. Five are the books of the Bible. Four are the Matriarchs. Three are the Patriarchs. Two are the Tables of the Covenant. One is our God, in heaven and on earth.

ECHAWD MEE YODAYAH

Arr. Shalom Altman

חַד גַּדְיָא CHAHD GAHD-YAW — AN ONLY KID

The melody and words of Chahd Gahdyaw have captivated the imaginations of many generations of children. The story, and it is a story in verse, tells of the father who bought an only kid for two zuzim, how it was eaten by the cat, the cat by a dog, the dog beaten by a stick, the stick burned by the fire, the fire doused by the water, the water drunk by the ox, the ox slaughtered by the slaughterer, the slaughterer taken by the angel of death, and finally the angel of death erased by the Holy One, by God. It is God who comes to solve this continuing problem and is triumphant. Symbolically, it marks the time when the kingdom of the Almighty will be established on earth; then, all will live in perfect peace and happiness.

חַד גַּדְיָא, חַד גַּדְיָא,

דְּזַבִּין אַבָּא בִּתְרֵי זוּזֵי, חַד גַּדְיָא, חַד גַּדְיָא.

וְאָתָא שׁוּנְרָא, וְאָכַל לְגַדְיָא, דְּזַבִּין אַבָּא בִּתְרֵי זוּזֵי, חַד גַּדְיָא, חַד גַּדְיָא.

וְאָתָא כַלְבָּא, וְנָשַׁךְ לְשׁוּנְרָא, דְּאָכַל לְגַדְיָא, דְּזַבִּין אַבָּא בִּתְרֵי זוּזֵי, חַד גַּדְיָא, חַד גַּדְיָא.

וְאָתָא חוּטְרָא, וְהִכָּה לְכַלְבָּא, דְּנָשַׁךְ לְשׁוּנְרָא, דְּאָכַל לְגַדְיָא, דְּזַבִּין אַבָּא בִּתְרֵי זוּזֵי, חַד גַּדְיָא, חַד גַּדְיָא.

וְאָתָא נוּרָא, וְשָׂרַף לְחוּטְרָא, דְּהִכָּה לְכַלְבָּא, דְּנָשַׁךְ לְשׁוּנְרָא, דְּאָכַל לְגַדְיָא, דְּזַבִּין אַבָּא בִּתְרֵי זוּזֵי, חַד גַּדְיָא, חַד גַּדְיָא.

וְאָתָא מַיָּא, וְכָבָה לְנוּרָא, דְּשָׂרַף לְחוּטְרָא, דְּהִכָּה לְכַלְבָּא, דְּנָשַׁךְ לְשׁוּנְרָא, דְּאָכַל לְגַדְיָא, דְּזַבִּין אַבָּא בִּתְרֵי זוּזֵי, חַד גַּדְיָא, חַד גַּדְיָא.

וְאָתָא תוֹרָא, וְשָׁתָה לְמַיָּא, דְּכָבָה לְנוּרָא, דְּשָׂרַף לְחוּטְרָא,
דְּהִכָּה לְכַלְבָּא, דְּנָשַׁךְ לְשׁוּנְרָא, דְּאָכַל לְגַדְיָא, דְּזַבִּין אַבָּא בִּתְרֵי זוּזֵי,
חַד גַּדְיָא, חַד גַּדְיָא.

וְאָתָא הַשּׁוֹחֵט, וְשָׁחַט לְתוֹרָא, דְּשָׁתָה לְמַיָּא, דְּכָבָה לְנוּרָא,
דְּשָׂרַף לְחוּטְרָא, דְּהִכָּה לְכַלְבָּא, דְּנָשַׁךְ לְשׁוּנְרָא, דְּאָכַל לְגַדְיָא,
דְּזַבִּין אַבָּא בִּתְרֵי זוּזֵי, חַד גַּדְיָא, חַד גַּדְיָא.

וְאָתָא מַלְאַךְ הַמָּוֶת, וְשָׁחַט לְשׁוֹחֵט, דְּשָׁחַט לְתוֹרָא, דְּשָׁתָה לְמַיָּא,
דְּכָבָה לְנוּרָא, דְּשָׂרַף לְחוּטְרָא, דְּהִכָּה לְכַלְבָּא, דְּנָשַׁךְ לְשׁוּנְרָא,
דְּאָכַל לְגַדְיָא, דְּזַבִּין אַבָּא בִּתְרֵי זוּזֵי, חַד גַּדְיָא, חַד גַּדְיָא.

וְאָתָא הַקָּדוֹשׁ בָּרוּךְ הוּא, וְשָׁחַט לְמַלְאַךְ הַמָּוֶת, דְּשָׁחַט לְשׁוֹחֵט,
דְּשָׁחַט לְתוֹרָא, דְּשָׁתָה לְמַיָּא, דְּכָבָה לְנוּרָא, דְּשָׂרַף לְחוּטְרָא, דְּהִכָּה
לְכַלְבָּא, דְּנָשַׁךְ לְשׁוּנְרָא, דְּאָכַל לְגַדְיָא, דְּזַבִּין אַבָּא בִּתְרֵי זוּזֵי, חַד
גַּדְיָא, חַד גַּדְיָא:

Chahd gahd-yaw, chahd gahd-yaw.

1. D'zah-been ah-baw bi-s'ray zoo-zay, chahd gahd-yaw, chahd
gahd-yaw.

2. V'aw-saw shoon-raw, v'aw-chahl l'gahd-yaw, d'zah-been ah-
baw bi-s'ray zoo-zay, chahd gahd-yaw, chahd gahd-yaw.

3. V'aw-saw chahl-baw, v'naw-shahch l'shoon-raw, d'aw-chahl
l'gahd-yaw, d'zah-been ah-baw bi-s'ray zoo-zay, chahd
gahd-yaw, chahd gahd-yaw.

4. V'aw-saw choot-raw, v'hi-kaw l'chahl-baw, d'naw-shahch
l'shoon-raw, d'aw-chahl l'gahd-yaw, d'zah-been ah-baw
bi-s'ray zoo-say, chahd gahd-yaw, chahd gahd-yaw.

5. V'aw-saw noo-raw, v'saw-rahf l'choot-raw, d'hi-kaw l'chahl-baw, d'naw-shahch l'shoon-raw, d'aw-chahl l'gahd-yaw, d'zah-been ah-baw bi-s'ray zoo-zay, chahd gahd-yaw, chahd gahd-yaw.

6. V'aw-saw ma-yaw, v'chaw-vaw l'noo-raw, d'saw-rahf l'choot-raw, d'hi-kaw l'chahl-baw, d'naw-shahch l'shoon-raw, d'aw-chahl l'gahd-yaw, d'zah-been ah-baw bi-s'ray zoo-zay, chahd gahd-yaw, chahd gahd-yaw.

7. V'aw-saw so-raw, v'shaw-saw l'ma-yaw, d'chaw-vaw l'noo-raw, d'saw-rahf l'choot-raw, d'hi-kaw l'chahl-baw, d'naw-shahch l'shoon-raw, d'aw-chahl l'gahd-yaw, d'zah-been ah-baw bi-s'ray zoo-zay, chahd gahd-yaw, chahd gad-yaw.

8. V'aw-saw ha-sho-chayt v'shaw-chaht l'so-raw, d'shaw-saw l'ma-yaw, d'chaw-vaw l'noo-raw, d'saw-rahf l'choot-raw, d'hi-kaw l'chahl-baw, d'naw-shahch l'shoon-raw, d'aw-chahl l'gahd-yaw, d'zah-been ah-baw bi-s'ray zoo-zay, chahd gahd-yaw, chahd gahd-yaw.

9. V'aw-saw mahl-ahch ha-maw-vehs, v'shaw-chaht l'sho-chayt, d'shaw-chaht l'so-raw, d'shaw-saw l'ma-yaw, d'chaw-vaw l'noo-raw, d'saw-rahf l'choot-raw, d'hi-kaw l'chahl-baw, d'naw-shahch l'shoon-raw, d'aw-chahl l'gahd-yaw, d'zah-been ah-baw bi-s'ray zoo-zay, chahd gahd-yaw, chahd gahd-yaw.

10. V'aw-saw ha-Kaw-dosh baw-rooch hoo, v'shaw-chaht l'mahl-ahch ha-maw-vehs, d'shaw-chaht l'sho-chayt, d'shaw-chaht l'so-raw, d'shaw-saw l'ma-yaw, d'chaw-vaw l'noo-raw, d'saw-rahf l'choot-raw, d'hi-kaw l'chahl-baw, d'naw-shahch l'shoon-raw, d'aw-chahl l'gahd-yaw, d'zah-been ah-baw bi-s'ray zoo-zay, chahd gahd-yaw, chahd gahd-yaw.

CHAHD GAHDYAW

Arr. Shalom Altman

Lively

Refrain

Chahd gahd yaw___ Chahd gahd-yaw. D'- zah-bin ah-baw

Fine

bi-s'ray zoo-zay. Chahd gahd-yaw___ chahd gahd-yaw.

1st Verse

V'-aw-saw shoon-raw v'aw-chahl l'-gahd-yaw, D'-

2nd Verse

V'-aw-saw kahl-baw v'naw-shach l' shoon-raw d'-aw-chawl l'gahd-

3rd Verse

yaw D'-V'-aw-saw choot-raw v'hi-kaw l'-kahl baw d'-

naw-shach l'-shoon-raw, D'-aw-chal l'-gad-

4th Verse

yaw, D'-V'-aw-saw noo-raw v'saw-raf l' choot-raw D'-

hi-kaw l' chal-baw, d'-naw-shach l'-shoon-raw, D'-
aw-chal l'-gad-yaw, D'-

AMERICA

My country, 'tis of thee,
Sweet land of liberty,
 Of thee I sing;
Land where my fathers died,
Land of the pilgrims' pride,
From every mountain side
 Let freedom ring.

My native country, thee,
Land of the noble free,
 Thy name I love;
I love thy rocks and rills,
Thy woods and templed hills;
My heart with rapture thrills,
 Like that above.

Let music swell the breeze,
And ring from all the trees
 Sweet freedom's song;
Let mortal tongues awake,
Let all that breathe partake,
Let rocks their silence break,
 The sound prolong.

Our fathers' God, to Thee,
Author of liberty,
 To Thee we sing;
Long may our land be bright,
With freedom's holy light,
Protect us by Thy might,
 Great God, our King!

A PASSOVER DREAM

By David Einhorn

The Seder table was decked in gleaming white and the flickering candles drew rainbow sparks from the crystal winecups.

Little Joel, however, saw only the large goblet of the Prophet Elijah that stood brimful of ruby-red wine in the center of the table on a silver tray.

"I must see him today," little Joel said to himself. "I've just got to stay up."

He knew very well that before the fourth cup, the door would be opened and a tiny bit of wine would disappear from the large goblet — a sign that the Prophet Elijah had been a guest in the house.

But at every Seder, right after the third cup, he would fall fast asleep and not wake up until the next morning.

"I *won't* fall asleep! I *won't* fall asleep!" little Joel repeated over and over to himself even though his eyes seemed full of sand and glued tighter and tighter together. Joel yawned and stretched and yawned again.

At last Mother rose and opened the front door. Everyone stood up solemnly and raised his cup in welcome. Suddenly Joel saw an old man with a white beard enter the room. He wore a spotless white robe tied with a leather belt and was leading a small white Goat with large brown eyes. The old man slowly raised the crystal goblet and barely brushed the rim with his lips.

Little Joel was beside himself with excitement. He slid off his chair, ran over to the Goat and patted it.

"Would you like to come with us?" The little Goat spoke suddenly in a very human voice.

"Of course!" Joel bubbled.

Quick as a wink the whole house vanished and Joel found himself walking with Elijah and the Goat on a wide road in the moonlight.

"Are you the Goat of the Haggadah that was bought by the father for two zuzim and then was eaten up by the Cat?" asked Joel.

"Me-e-eow! Did you ever hear of a nice, tame Cat eating a Goat?" said a voice from the side of the road. And suddenly a big fat Cat scrambled out from under a nearby fence, its tail high in the air. It padded over to the Goat and, purring softly, rubbed heads in a neighborly fashion.

"But that's what it says in the Haggadah," Joel reminded him.

"That's a big fib my enemy the Dog has been spreading about me."

"Don't call me a fibber!" a voice broke in. And there was a Dog, his mouth open and his tongue hanging out, running towards them across the fields.

"Woof! Let me tell you what gr-r-really happened. My master went out of the house and left me in charge of the little Goat. Woof! No one else was home but the Cat. While I was making my rounds the Goat disappeared. Naturally, I barked at the Cat because she hadn't watched the Goat. That's why everyone thought that the Cat had eaten up the Goat. I just barked, that's all. Woof!"

"Oh, yes, you were very polite," the Cat said sarcastically. "If I hadn't run up the apple tree you would have torn me to bits-s-s-s."

"You're not so gentle yourself!"

"Meow! I'm just as good as you are!" the Cat sniffed.

"Is that so!" growled the Dog. "Do you know what the Torah says about me? It says that on the night the Jews left Egypt my ancestors did not bark at them even once. Not even once!"

"That *was* quite a surprise," said the Cat. "After they were so friendly with Pharaoh's hangman and all, and always barking at the Jews and never letting a single one rest from his hard labor. Me-e-eow!"

"Well, anyway," grumbled the Dog, "you're not even mentioned once in the Bible, and I am. So there!"

"Please don't quarrel," the Goat waggled his little beard gently. "You seem to have forgotten that this is Layl Shimooreem, the night of Freedom and Peace, when God watches over the whole world."

"Gr-r-r-r-r . . ." growled the Dog, lowering his tail between his legs.

"Me-e-eow!" replied the Cat, arching his back.

Walking along, they soon met a Stick.

"Gr-r-r-r-r . . . lie down or go away. I hate a lifted Stick," said the Dog angrily.

"I'm not harming anyone," stated the Stick drily. "It all depends on who holds me. Why, look here. Wasn't it with me that Moses performed all his miracles? With whom did he split the sea so that the Jews might pass through on dry land? And with whom did he strike the rock in the desert? With his rod, of course. Everyone knows that."

"That is very true," the little Goat agreed. "An evil shepherd beats his sheep and a kind one uses his Stick to chase away the bad wolves."

"Oh, very well," the Dog shrugged and walked over to sniff at the Stick.

Suddenly they spied a little Flame dancing on the road. It grew closer and closer.

"I'd better run away," said the Stick uneasily.

"Are you afraid of me?" crackled the Flame.

"Yes, yes, you burn everything."

"I don't harm anyone who knows how to watch himself. Don't you know the story in the Bible about Moses and the burning bush that was never consumed? Why, I am the Spirit of Life. I give warmth, and all living things are warm. Without the light of the sun the world would be dark and nothing would live or grow. It all depends on who uses me. Wise people use me to light up the dark of night, to drive away the cold of winter, and to cook delicious meals. Evil people wage war with me and destroy cities and forests. Oh, I could tell you many more things, but I've got to leave now. I see a Water coming."

And, lo and behold, a little Water was seen slinking along the road, as pretty as a silver necklace.

"Don't be afraid of me," the little Water trilled. "I only put out bad fires. I leave the good ones alone. Have you ever seen water douse the rays of the sun? Or a tear drown the flame of love or the spark of mercy in someone's eye? Oh-oh. Isn't that an Ox coming? I am afraid that he will drink me all up."

"A-a-ah, it's always that way. When one is small, one is very foolish," the Ox bellowed. "Never fear, I have just come from a broad stream where I stilled my thirst and left the stream as full as ever. There is so much water on this earth and yet you are stingy about a few drops for a poor thirsty Ox."

The Water was about to answer but just then everyone began to cry: "Save yourself! The slaughterer is coming and behind him walks the Angel of Death."

Little Joel saw a tall man holding a long broadsword in his hand. Behind him strode the Angel of Death, a thousand eyes peering angrily out of his head. Suddenly the Prophet Elijah spread his robe over the little group and sternly ordered the two newcomers to remember that this was the night of Freedom and Peace on which no one could be harmed.

"Elijah," Joel tugged at the Prophet's sleeve. "Couldn't you make peace last forever, so that these two wicked people would never come back?"

"Someday that will happen," Elijah smiled. "In the days of the Messiah all nations will live in peace. They will break their swords and make plows of them. A wolf will lie down with a sheep, and a lion will eat grass like a cow, and little boys like yourself will lead them to pasture."

"When will that be?" Joel insisted.

"When the time will come, I shall blow a loud blast on a great Shofar and all the world will hear it."

"I want to hear it! . . . I want to hear it! . . . I want to. . ."

"What do you want to hear, dear?" This was mother's voice. Joel opened his eyes and saw that he was in his own room and his own bed.

"The Shofar, Mother."

"What Shofar, my child?"

"The Shofar of the Messiah."

"Perhaps you *will* hear it, my child," his mother said softly. "We pray each day that he may come soon." A quiet tear rolled down her cheek.

"The Water told the truth, Mother. I see — something glowing in your eyes and the tear does not put it out. . . . Does not put it out. . . . Does not — put — it — out. . . Does — not — put. . ."

And Joel, still holding his mother's hand, went back to sleep.

ONE HAPPY PASSOVER

By EDITH B. GOLDMAN

Around and around went the jump rope —

> "Buster Brown, turn around,
> Buster Brown, touch the ground,
> Buster Brown, show your shoe,
> Buster Brown, will you please skidoo."

Thus chorused the group of girls as each hopped into the rope, jumping, turning, bending, kicking, and hopping out in turn.

"Kim, Kim," Mother called, "it's time to come in and wash and change before dinner."

"Oh, dear. So soon? Right after this next turn, please," begged Kim.

The next time they played it was "O'Leary."

"You missed, it's my turn," called Bea, as the ball rolled down the walk. Kim dashed to get it and passed it to Beatrice.

"One, two, three, O'Leary," sang Bea as she bounced the ball, turning her foot over the ball at each O'Leary, "Four, five, six, O'Leary, seven, eight, nine, O'Leary, ten O'Leary, postman."

"You're on twosers now," said Kim. "You turn your foot over twice on each O'Leary."

Beatrice began twosers. "One, two, three, O'Leary, O'Leary," they sang and played.

"Girls, girls, Kim, Bea, it's time for dinner." And again the girls protested, "So, soon? Just a little longer, please."

It made no difference how long they had been at play, whether it was jump rope or bounce ball, or peg and stick, or tag, or button button guess which hand has the button, or any of the outdoor games. They always resented being called in for dinner.

There was one very special time when Bea didn't mind at all.
I'll tell you about it. It was even more exciting than playing the
games she so loved. It was preparing for the Seder. Oh! the joy of
everyone working together for the big day, the hustle and bustle
of spring cleaning, the delight of shopping for new spring outfits,
the exchange of letters and plans to meet cousins coming to visit
for the holiday, making Passover candy, mahndlen with honey
and nuts. The one she liked best had a very long name, aingemahchtz;
she never could remember the name, but she remembered to visit
the tin very often to nibble the candy. They would pack it in pretty
paper doilies, and in tins to send as gifts. It seemed the whole
world sang with the vibrancy of expectation of the coming Seder.

There was one Seder in particular she loved best. It was the year
Seder was planned at Grandpa's house. The whole family gathered
from far and near. Everyone had house guests. Uncle Sam and Aunt
Ann came from Wisconsin with cousins Bobby and Verna. Aunt
Rose and Aunt Sarah came from California with cousin Ruth. Uncle
Aaron and Aunt Ida came with cousins Melvin and Bernice, and
Kim was one of four. Her brother Stuart had been industriously
studying the Four Questions he was to recite at the Seder. He was
the oldest of the grandsons and he wanted to make his family proud.
Their Dad had told them many times, "You may play and visit all
day. Dinner is going to be delicious, and after dinner we'll have
games with nuts, and there will be prizes. But during the service,
while the grownups read from the Haggadah, you will have to set
an example for the other children and show how well you can listen
and learn to participate."

Well, that didn't seem like such a hard thing to do, especially
with so many treats in store for them. The big day finally came.
They were dressed in their new finery, surrounded by the joviality
of the visiting family, and set out for Grandpa's house.

When they arrived they were first greeted by the drifting odors
from Grandpa's pipe; their uncles were chatting in the living
room. The savory cooking odors filled the house. Kim felt hungry
just thinking about the glazed fish, golden soup, roast chicken,

crisp salad, bright green vegetables. She thought to herself, "I'll bet tonight even the egg and water will taste good."

The table looked beautiful, and wine glasses were placed at each setting, even the children's. When Kim entered the living room, she saw the large bowls of nuts and thought of the fun she would have trying to win at the games with her brothers and sisters and cousins.

Grandpa announced the Seder was about to begin. It was pretty neat having all the family about the table. Grandpa looked at his sons and daughters and grandchildren and, with a happy smile on his face made the blessing over the wine. They then began to recite from the Haggadah, taking turns to read aloud.

Kim was too young to keep up with the grownups' speed, and this is what she remembered most. . . .

It feels so nice and cozy to be here . . . the table is beautiful . . . the herbs are bitter . . . do I have to taste them? I like the wine . . . it makes me drowsy, it makes me want to giggle. I must remember Daddy said we should act grown-up. Stuart is standing up now to read the Four Questions and he's doing very well. Even my little sister Joy is being good. I mustn't look at Bea . . . she winks across the table and it makes me giggle. The Charoses is being passed now . . . mmmm . . . mmmm . . . good. We had more fun sampling it when we made it. Mommy said there wouldn't be enough. Daddy is showing us how to let the drops of wine fall. I'd better be careful not to spill on the lovely cloth. . . We don't have to be quiet any more and everyone is talking.

I would like to talk to Stuart across the table, but I can't see him . . . the centerpiece is in the way. Dinner is being served. Everything seems especially elegant . . . even better than I had imagined. . . Stuart is signalling to me to talk with Grandpa so that he can get the Afikomon. I'll tell Grandpa what fun we had making the Charoses. . . . Oh! Grandpa is talking to me . . . perfect!

Grandpa says, "Kim, how do you like having all this compan
for the Seder?"

"Oh, Grandpa, it's wonderful. This is the best time we'v
ever had. We all love it. I'd like it to be like this ever
year. . . ."

Stuart is signalling again. He has it. He has the Afikomon. . .
I wonder what he will ask for a reward. . . . I hope he'll shar
with me. . . . It will be fun when Grandpa tries to find it. He'
look everywhere and then have to give up, because he can'
finish the Seder without it.

Dessert is being served, and I feel too stuffed to eat an
more. . . . Everyone is still laughing and talking, but I fee
awfully drowsy . . . I'm not used to having so much wine. . .
The glasses are being filled again for the third cup . . . . Grandp
is looking for the Afikomon. . . . I don't want to miss th
games with nuts and prizes, and I, and I . . . zzzzz . .
Shh . . . sh . . . sh . . . Kim is fast asleep.

P.S.   I want to tell you she was carried to bed, and after a naj
she did get to play the games, and she won a prize, too.

Lag Bo-Omer

LAG BO-OMER

Count the Omer to thirty-three,
Remember a town in Galilee,
Bar Kochba, Akiba, Bar Yochai the names
We honor today in our prayers and games.

This is a field day filled with fun,
Outings planned by everyone.
Hikes and races, games of skill,
Picnics spread upon a hill.

And when the light of day retires,
Join hands and dance around bonfires,
And render a prayerful thought to those
Upon whose courage our joys repose.

Lag Bo-Omer

Forests, wide open spaces, stadia, and parks are the places, and field games and athletics are the activities played on Lag Bo-Omer, the only outdoor holiday in the Jewish calendar. Hebrew and Sunday School teachers take the children and athletic equipment to the fields for a day of general outdoor fun. Families, too, make Lag Bo-Omer a picnic day.

Lag Bo-Omer comes between Passover and Shovuos, between Spring and Summer. It is the thirty-third day of the Omer. The word *Lag* means thirty-three; *l* (ל) has the numerical value of thirty, in Hebrew, and *g* (ג) three, hence, thirty-three. The word *omer* is an agricultural measure (a sheaf of the first fruit of the fields) which the Israelites were expected to bring to God on the second day of Passover, as a thanksgiving offering. From this day, forty-nine days, seven full weeks, were to be counted until Shovuos, the Feast of Weeks. This period is, therefore, called Sefirah or Counting.

Why the thirty-third day should be set aside as a day of sporting and celebration we shall see after we have retold the enchanting story of Rabbi Akiba and Rachel, and the drama of Bar Kochba and the Romans.

RABBI AKIBA AND RACHEL

Back in the second century of the common era, there lived in Jerusalem a wealthy man by the name of Kalba Sabua who, when the capital was besieged by the Romans, pledged to support the entire Jewish population even if the siege lasted twenty years. Now this man had a beautiful daughter, Rachel, whose hand was sought by many.

Among Kalba Sabua's helpers was a handsome shepherd named

Akiba who did not attract much attention because of his poverty and ignorance. As a matter of fact, he scorned education and knowledge. When Rachel heard of this, she came to rebuke Akiba; but as they talked longer and oftener, they fell in love. He did not, however, dare ask her to marry him because of his lowly status and fear of her father. Rachel, on the other hand, was so much in love that she approached Akiba one day and told him she wanted him to marry her, on one condition: after they were married, he must leave for a seminary, and there study Torah. Akiba hesitated; he was too old to begin studying. Legend tells that as they sat and talked, Akiba saw the grooves worn in a stone by the constant stream of water and said, "If a stone can be softened by drops of water, then I, too, can still learn." He gave Rachel his solemn word that he would study.

When Kalba Sabua heard of his daughter's elopement, he was so enraged that he disinherited Rachel; he was sure she had brought disgrace upon him and his family.

As he had promised, Akiba left his beloved Rachel, and went to the great seminary (Yeshivah) to study. Rachel was very poor, worked hard, but she felt confident that one day Akiba would be a great man.

For twelve long years, Akiba devoted all his time to his studies, and acquired a wealth of knowledge. One day he decided to return home for a visit. When he came to the house where Rachel was living, he overheard an old woman reprimanding her, "Why do you waste your time on Akiba? You're a foolish woman to wait so long for a man so unworthy of your love." But Rachel was still in love with Akiba and she responded, "I would gladly wait another twelve years, if need be, as long as Akiba becomes a great rabbi and scholar." When Akiba heard Rachel's answer, he returned to the seminary and studied for another twelve years. During this time, his name became renowned, and many thousands came to hear his words of wisdom and to study under his tutelage. Akiba had become the recognized leader of the Jewish people.

He now felt that the time had come to return to Jerusalem.

Word spread quickly that the great Akiba was coming. Hundreds and thousands pressed close to catch a glimpse of the distinguished rabbi. Rachel, too, shabbily clothed, was in the crowd. When she saw Akiba, she began to push forward to reach him, but the disciples ordered her away. Akiba, however, had already seen her and called to his students, "Stop, let her pass. *Shelee v'shelawchem, shelaw vee;* what is mine and what is yours, come from her. The Torah I learned and the Torah you learned from me, came because of her."

Akiba and Rachel were reunited after twenty-four years and Rachel was the proudest woman in the land. There was only one emptiness in her heart: her longing to see her father. But fate played its role at this point.

Rachel's father had heard about the great Akiba, but had not the faintest idea that he was really the ignorant shepherd who had married his beautiful Rachel. One day, at the time Akiba and Rachel were reunited, Kalba Sabua decided to seek the advice of his renowned rabbi. He came to Akiba and said, "Great rabbi, I have a grave problem. Many years ago, I had a beautiful daughter, Rachel. She married a poor ignorant shepherd and in my rage I sent her out of my home. Now, after all these years, I am sorry. What can I do? What should I do?"

Akiba looked into Kalba Sabua's eyes and said, "I am Akiba, father-in-law. I am the ignorant shepherd whom Rachel married against your will. Never fear. All is forgiven. Let us be reunited again."

Kalba Sabua was most happy to hear this news. He gave Akiba and Rachel a beautiful home, where they lived happily while Akiba continued to teach Torah to his followers and to guide the destiny of his people.

RABBI AKIBA AND BAR KOCHBA

Akiba lived during the time of the Roman oppression. As leader of his people he had to help them live in freedom so that they might pursue their studies and enjoy other blessings of life. He sought many means to alleviate their difficulties. While Akiba was consulting with his advisers, a leader came forth called Bar Kochba (Son of a Star). Bar Kochba was a mighty man of valor, reminiscent of the great Samson. He undertook to lead a Jewish army against the Romans. Many rallied to his banner. Akiba was among those who supported him.

When the revolt came, the Jews, inspired by Bar Kochba's courage, fought with all their might. For a while it appeared that they would triumph, but Rome's army was so well trained and equipped, that the heroic band was defeated. In 132 C. E. the Son of a Star fell, and with his death, the Jewish army disintegrated.

The Romans became more oppressive. They sought out the leaders of the revolt. One of Akiba's distinguished disciples was Simeon ben Yochai. When the Romans sentenced him to death, he took his son Eleazar, and hid in a cave in Galilee, at Meron, taking with them the Torahs and other scrolls. For thirteen years they hid there, and one day each year Simeon's students brought food to the cave. They disguised themselves as hunters, with bows and arrows, in order to deceive the Roman soldiers.

When the Romans eventually were defeated, it was on the thirty-third day of the Omer, Lag Bo-Omer. A heavenly voice was heard to say to Simeon and Eleazar, "Go forth from your cave." Father and son departed after thirteen years of study and concealment.

For this reason Lag Bo-Omer is called the Scholars' Festival. In Israel, it is celebrated by children going into the fields and woods and caves dressed like hunters and woodsmen, and playing outdoor games. Another explanation of Lag Bo-Omer is that, on this day, a plague which had struck Rabbi Akiba's students came to an end.

Many sad events occurred during the period between Passover and Shovuos, called Sefirah, and particularly during the month of Iyar. Weddings, especially with music, are not celebrated among Orthodox and Conservative Jews during this time, with exception of Rosh Chodesh (New Moon Days), Yom Ha-Atzmaut (Israel Independence Day), and Lag Bo-Omer.

We Observe the Day

You can observe this outdoor festival by telling your children the fascinating stories of Akiba and Bar Kochba.

At home, you can help your child with a few cutouts of personalities of the period, such as Akiba, Simeon bar Yochai, Bar Kochba, or with finger painting these people on scenes of woods and caves.

Here are directions for making an archer and also a Rabbi Akiba:

To Make Archer:

1. Twist end of a pipe cleaner to form head and body.

2. Twist one pipe cleaner around neck area to form arms.

3. Twist one long pipe cleaner around bottom of body to form legs.

4. Make bow by twisting and curving pipe cleaner. An arrow may also be made. Bend feet out and balance.

To Make Rabbi Akiba:

1. Start with cylinder and cut-out eyes and nose as for Judah Maccabee. (See page 96).

2. Cut yarmulke and arms from a dark piece of paper and attach.

3. Draw Torah as in (8), on lighter paper, and also mustache. Cut out and attach to cylinder in proper places.

All children love picnics. Make Lag Bo-Omer a family picnic day in some beautiful spot where you can enjoy games and feel that you are together commemorating the great past. Be sure to plan the kind of outing which will include bows and arrows, rifle-shooting, archery, and other sports symbolic of Lag Bo-Omer.

HAWVAW NAWGEELAW
הָבָה נָגִילָה — COME, LET US SING AND BE HAPPY

הָבָה נָגִילָה וְנִשְׂמְחָה.
הָבָה נְרַנְּנָה וְנִשְׂמְחָה.
עוּרוּ, אַחִים, בְּלֵב שָׂמֵחַ.

בום דַלִי דַה — BOOM DA LI DA

SHALOM CHAVAYREEM
שָׁלוֹם חַבֵרִים — FAREWELL, FRIENDS

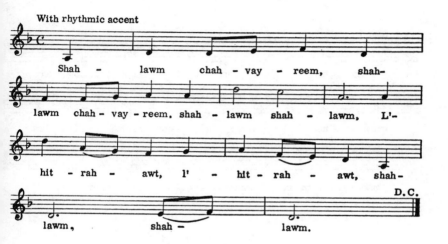

Farewell, friends,
Till we meet again.

שָׁלוֹם חַבֵרִים, שָׁלוֹם חַבֵרִים, שָׁלוֹם, שָׁלוֹם,
לְהִתְרָאוֹת, לְהִתְרָאוֹת, לְהִתְרָאוֹת, שָׁלוֹם.

If your outing lasts until nightfall, you can sing Taps in Hebrew.

RAHD HAYOM
רַד הַיּוֹם — DAY IS DONE

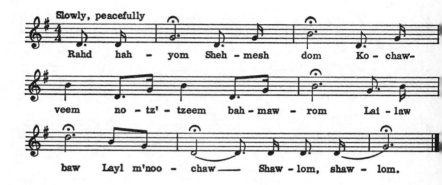

רַד הַיּוֹם, שֶׁמֶשׁ דּוֹם,

כּוֹכָבִים נוֹצְצִים בַּמָּרוֹם.

לַיְלָה בָּא, לֵיל מְנוּחָה,

שָׁלוֹם, שָׁלוֹם.

Day is done, the sun has set,
Stars sparkle on high.
Night has come, restful night,
Peace to all.

THE HERMIT OF LAG BO-OMER HILL

By Morris Epstein

Danny had made his mind up. This year he would track down the Hermit of Lag Bo-Omer Hill.

Of course Danny knew that no one in the village had ever seen the Hermit, but everyone said that he lived in a cave on the little hill where the boys would go on their Lag Bo-Omer hikes.

Danny had been sitting in the wooden schoolroom studying the Bible, while the Rabbi nodded over the table, his beard gently caressing the pages of an open book. The Rabbi was a kindly man, but he always wore a mournful look, and he was fond of making boys stay after school. But now he was dozing, and Danny slid his hand along the bench and pinched his friend Saul.

"Saul, you know what tomorrow is?" he whispered.

"Sure. Tuesday!" Saul answered crossly.

"No-o-o! It's Lag Bo-Omer. That means no lessons. And a hike!"

Danny moved closer. "Suppose we try to find the Hermit of Lag Bo-Omer Hill tomorrow, Saul."

Saul opened his big eyes. Danny shrugged his shoulders, and Saul nodded:

"Very well, I'll go with you."

Danny felt someone hovering behind him.

"Whispering, Daniel? When you should be studying?"

Danny's heart bumped. "Please, Rabbi. I won't whisper again."

"A little encouragement will help you remember. One half-hour after school, Daniel. Fifteen minutes for you, and fifteen minutes for the Hermit."

The Rabbi had heard every word, Daniel thought. But he didn't care. He winked at Saul, who smiled back bravely. Perhaps the Rabbi was only guessing, the wink said. It seemed that way, too, when the Rabbi made his little speech to the class, for he didn't mention the episode at all.

"Tomorrow is Lag Bo-Omer, boys," the Rabbi said. "We will celebrate as usual by going on a picnic."

The next morning the class met at the schoolroom, carrying lunches and bows and arrows made of branches of young saplings cut in the nearby woods. The Rabbi was waiting. He wore a broad-brimmed hat and his usual sad expression. Into the woods tramped the little group pausing occasionally to rest. While the boys sat in the deep shade of the trees, the Rabbi told them tales of long ago.

"Did you know, lads," he said, "that to join Bar Kochba's army in the fight against the Roman invaders of Judea, each soldier had to prove his strength by pulling a young tree from the ground while riding by on horseback at full speed?"

The day passed quickly. It was late afternoon when Danny and Saul were finally able to slip away into the dense thicket covering the peak of the hill. The voices of their classmates faded into the distance. Once it seemed to Danny that someone was following them, but when he looked back, he saw nothing but low-hanging branches and swaying bushes. The brambly undergrowth made the going slow and after a while Saul began to grow nervous.

"Let's go back, Danny. I — I think I heard thundering."

"We're practically there!" Danny panted. And it's not —"
C-R-A-ACK! !

A booming peal of heavy thunder rolled from the lowering skies.

Then, before you could say Bar Kochba, it began to rain. Danny felt a small wet hand grasp his own.

"I'm f-frightened, Danny."

Danny squeezed back. "It's all right, Saul. We should be near the cave now. We'll get dry up there. . . . Oh — I see it!"

"What?" squeaked Saul.

"The cave! Quick, let's duck in!"

The dripping pair sloshed into the cave. Swallowed by the

yawning entrance, they stood huddled together in the darkness, two soggy statues in an unfriendly emptiness.

"Ah-choo!" sneezed Saul. "Say . . . Danny, did you feel anything swish by you?"

"No-o-o. There's no one in this old cave. That Hermit story is just a big . . ."

That was exactly when it happened. Somewhere in the darkness a strange, uncanny, throbbing guffaw swept through the cavernous depths. Then an eerie voice spoke.

"Did you say *no one* was here? Do I sound like *no one*? Step closer, boys. Surely you know who I am?"

Danny's throat felt like grainy sandpaper.

"You're the . . . the Hermit. . ."

The voice finished the sentence " — of Lag Bo-Omer Hill. I'm a friendly old Hermit, too. I never hurt good little boys."

Danny took a step backwards.

"Just a moment boys," the Hermit ordered sternly. "Don't rush away. After all, this is Lag Bo-Omer. And no one leaves here . . . unless he answers a question or two about my favorite holiday. Are you ready, boys? Very well. Number one: What does Bar Kochba mean?"

"Son of a star," said two quavering voices.

"That's right," said the Hermit. "And now the second question: How did Jewish soldiers prove themselves worthy of Bar Kochba's army?"

Danny's mind raced. Surely he knew the answer to that one. Of course! "I know," he said. "To join Bar Kochba's army, soldiers had to tear out a young tree while riding full speed on horseback."

"PER-FECT!" boomed the Hermit. "And now you may go, my friends. Don't forget how fortunate you have been. You are the only ones ever to have visited the Hermit of Lag Bo-Omer Hill — and returned. . . . One word of caution: As you leave this cave, do — not — LOOK BACK!"

Saul jerked his friend's hand and veered towards the entrance.

But little Danny was full of spunk. He couldn't help turning his head. He strained his eyes and peered this way and that. The darkness seemed thicker than ever before, and he was about to give up, when — z-z-z-C-R-A-ASH!

A blinding blue-white flash of lightning split the sky and filled the area with dazzling light.

Danny's scalp tingled. For there, way back in the cave, holding his sides and bent double in silent laughter, was the — Rabbi!

The two boys were the heroes of the village for weeks afterward. *They* had spoken to the Hermit. But whenever the Rabbi would point a bony finger at Danny and say:

"Thirty minutes after class, Daniel."

The mighty hunter would answer:

"The Hermit wouldn't like you to punish me, Rabbi."

The old Rabbi would grin, scratch his ear, and then laugh, right out loud.

And nobody could ever understand why little Danny was the only one who could make the Rabbi laugh.

A POEM FOR LAG BO-OMER

By Sadie Rose Weilerstein

Shut the Hebrew School up tight!
Shut it up and lock it!
A bow and arrow's in my hand,
A lunch is in my pocket!
    It's Lag Bo-Omer in May
    And we're off to the woods to stay all day.
So shut the Hebrew School up tight!
Shut it up and lock it!

Today's a scholar's holiday!
That's what our teachers say;
It's good to be a scholar,
When it's Lag Bo-Omer day.
    Games and races, open spaces,
    Colored eggs in grassy places,
Happy smiles on all our faces,
Lag Bo-Omer day!

Shovuos

SHOVUOS

How beautiful is this holiday,
Confirming Israel in her way.
Through Moses came the Holy Law
Commandments, Ten: our trials
    foresaw.

We read the tender Book of Ruth,
And view her insight to the truth.
"Thy God, my God," and Ruth accept
The way of life that is the best.

"Keep My Commandments," said the
    Lord,
Love and peace is your reward.
Shovuos has this tale to tell
To all the world, through Israel.

Shovuos

In the late Spring or early Summer, when you see the synagogue elaborately decorated with flowers and foliage and fruits, or if you see young men and women in holiday attire, the girls carrying white flowers and small silk or mohair Bibles, and going gaily to the synagogue in company of their parents, you will know that fifty days have passed since Passover and that Shovuos, the Feast of Weeks, has arrived.

The ornamentation of the house of God tells us that Shovuos commemorates Chag Ha-Katzir, Festival of the Harvest of wheat, grain, and barley. The fruits indicate that Shovuos is also Chag Ha-Bikkurim, Festival of First Fruits. This celebrates the offering to God of the first products of the earth. The happy faces of the young people and their proud parents tell us that they are participants in the confirmation ceremony. They have pursued a prescribed course of study for a number of years and now, at fifteen or sixteen, in the presence of families, friends, and congregation, they confirm their faith in God and in Israel. Shovuos has been selected for this ceremony because it celebrates Z'man Mattan Torosaynu — the Festival of the Giving of our Torah — on which Moses ascended to Sinai to receive the Ten Commandments.

Shovuos is the third of the three pilgrimage holidays, but differs from Pesach and Sukkos in that it does not have intermediate days. It lasts for two days in the traditional observance and is celebrated for one day in the Reform ritual. While the synagogue service is similar to that of the other holidays, two distinct features are added.

One is the reading of the book of Ruth, which describes the devotion of a woman embracing Judaism as the Jews embraced the Torah; and the second is the chant Akdomus, a liturgical poem recited on the first day, before the Torah reading, which exalts Israel's attachment to the Torah. The book of Ruth is read on the second day of Shovuos, before the reading of the Torah.

As is established practice for all holidays, Yizkor or memorial services are also conducted on Shovuos. In traditional observance, this takes place on the second day.

Not too many generations ago, Shovuos was considered the appropriate holiday for the consecration of children into the study of Torah; a ceremony which in our day is generally reserved for Simchas Torah.

THE STORY OF SHOVUOS

Shovuos is the climax of Pesach. The dramatic exodus from Egypt and the release from bondage, retold in the Seder service, were hardly enough to sustain a people which had been enslaved for hundreds of years. A large population accustomed to one pattern of living could not be expected to change its ways overnight. Education and guidance were the needs of the hour, and Shovuos supplied them.

Safely across the Red Sea, though pursued by the vengeful Egyptians, the Israelites were not led directly to the Promised Land as they had anticipated. True, Eretz Yisroel was the goal, but not the immediate goal. They had to unlearn the habits of slave existence, and learn to live as free men. This was the process of education Moses had to carry out.

Moses led them to Mount Sinai. In a magnificent, moving scene, the Bible (Exodus 19) records the elaborate preparations for Moses' ascent to the top of the mountain, his acceptance of the *Aseres Ha-D'vorim* (Decalogue or Ten Commandments), and his return to the Israelites below.

LEGENDS

Many are the fanciful interpretations of the scene at Sinai. They are beautiful, these legends, refreshing to the reader. Here are a few of these flights into fancy:

One deals with the quarrel of the mountains. Each one in the area of Sinai, the legend has it, clamored for the privilege of being the honored peak on which Moses was to receive the Decalogue. Mounts Tabor, Hermon, Carmel, Ararat, were among the contestants. Each felt that her own beauty, stateliness, or magnitude would impel her choice. But the only one who remained silent was Sinai, a

mountain of medium height. Sinai was stirred by the drama of hundreds of thousands of Israelites preparing for the great event. When God saw the modesty and humility of Sinai, He sent forth a heavenly voice, "Moses will receive the Torah from Sinai."

A second legend tells of the conference between God and Israel immediately preceding. "I will give you the Torah," said God to

Israel, "but you must first present me with sufficient insurance that it will be observed and heeded." The children of Israel offered Abraham, Isaac, and Jacob as security, but God deemed them an insufficient guarantee. Finally, after much consultation, the Israelites approached God and said, "O God, we offer our children to You as security that the Torah will be maintained." When God heard this offer, He accepted, and gladly gave the Torah to our fathers.

A third story comes to us, saying that God was still not completely convinced about the future of the Torah, and wanted the women of Israel, too, to have a share in the drama. They were summoned, and presented themselves, holding tots in their arms. God asked them if they would offer solemn pledges that as custodians and guardians of the home they would keep the Torah and teach their children the good way of life. The women gave their word, for themselves and for posterity. Shovuos, Festival of the Giving of the Torah, was born.

THE STORY OF RUTH

A beautiful maiden gleaning grain in the fields of Moab is the first picture which comes to mind at the mention of Ruth, whose story has captured the imaginations of many generations of Jews and non-Jews. Many have been the translations, as well as its retelling, in novels, plays, and films.

The opening scene is laid in the city of Bethlehem where Elimelech and his wife Naomi reside with their two sons. Mahlon and Chilion, their only children, take wives from the land of Moab — Orpah and Ruth. They live peacefully for ten years, until at one time the father and sons pass away. Naomi, widowed and grief-stricken, looks upon her daughters-in-law, and weeps. She plans to return to her home where food is simpler to obtain and where she would find life easier among her family.

The decision reached, all three women depart. At the crossroads, Naomi speaks to the younger ones, pleads with them to leave her, to return to their own homeland where they can begin life over again, but both refuse to go. However, after more persuasion, Orpah submits, receives Naomi's blessings, and turns back. Naomi now turns to Ruth, but Ruth replies, "Entreat me not to leave thee. For whither thou goest, I will go, and where thou lodgest I will lodge; thy people shall be my people, and thy God my God."

Together they travel to Naomi's early home. Naomi has aged and is hardly recognized. Among the members of her family there is Boaz, relative of her husband, a man of valor, and owner of many fields. Naomi urges Ruth to go to his fields and there glean the ears of corn after the reapers have passed. Ruth heeds her mother-in-law. Boaz notices Ruth, inquires about her, and learning who she is, leaves instructions that not only is she to be permitted to glean but that more gleanings are to be left for her.

In time Boaz meets Ruth, falls in love with her, and with the blessings of a happier Naomi, they are married.

The selflessness of love which Ruth displayed for Naomi is rewarded in kind by the love of Boaz. From this union sprang David, King and sweet singer of Israel.

THE TORAH HOLIDAY AT HOME

Adornment of the synagogue should be emulated in the home, the miniature sanctuary. From your garden, gather flowers and foliage for the house. Encourage your children to draw or paint scenes of fields, pictures of the Torah and of Moses holding it up on the mountain, and place them on the walls and amid the flowers and plants.

For your dinner table, set a miniature Torah among flowers and fruits, which serve as centerpiece. You may also, with your children, contrive a Moses uplifting the Decalogue and station him along the centerpiece. Here are the directions:

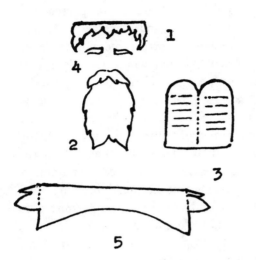

1. Start as for Judah Maccabee and Akiba. See page 96.

2. Cut hair (1) from white paper and paste at top of cylinder, or shape absorbent cotton and glue.

3. Cut beard and mustache (2) and paste under cut-out nose. These may also be made of cotton.

4. Cut eyebrows (4) of paper or cotton and paste.

5. Cut arms of same paper as cylinder and pass through slits at sides of cylinder (5).

6. Cut Ten Commandments stone of heavy white paper (3) and paste hands over it.

THE HOME CEREMONY

1. *Blessing of Holiday Candles*

Dinner begins with blessing of the holiday candles. This is mother's responsibility, performed in the presence of her family.

בָּרוּךְ אַתָּה יְיָ, אֱלֹהֵינוּ מֶלֶךְ הָעוֹלָם, אֲשֶׁר קִדְּשָׁנוּ בְּמִצְוֹתָיו, וְצִוָּנוּ

לְהַדְלִיק נֵר שֶׁל (On Sabbath add וְ) שַׁבָּת וְ) יוֹם טוֹב:

בָּרוּךְ אַתָּה יְיָ, אֱלֹהֵינוּ מֶלֶךְ הָעוֹלָם, שֶׁהֶחֱיָנוּ, וְקִיְּמָנוּ, וְהִגִּיעָנוּ

לַזְּמַן הַזֶּה:

Baw-rooch ah-taw Ado-noy, Elo-hay-noo meh-lech haw-o-lawm, ah-shehr ki-d'shaw-noo b'mitz-vo-sawv, v'tzi-vaw-noo, l'hahd-leek nayr shel (*On Sabbath add:* sha-baws v') yom tov.

Baw-rooch ah-taw Ado-noy, Elo-hay-noo meh-lech haw-o-lawm, sheh-heh-cheh-yaw-noo, v'kee-y'maw-noo, v'hi-gee-aw-noo, la-z'mahn ha-zeh.

Blessed art Thou, O Lord our God, King of the universe, who hast sanctified us by Thy commandments and granted us the privilege of kindling the (Sabbath and) holiday lights.

Blessed art Thou, O Lord our God, King of the universe, who hast granted us life, sustained us, and brought us to this festive season.

We thank Thee, O God, for the Torah, our priceless heritage, and for its teachings. May the spirit of the Torah inspire us to live always in peace and harmony and with love abiding in our home and family. May these holiday candles radiate warmth and understanding of the deeper meaning of this beautiful festival. Amen.

2. *The Kiddush or Blessing of Wine*

Father rises as he leads the family in recitation of the Kiddush. Each member holds his wine cup in his right hand.

On Sabbath, add first paragraph and words in brackets:

וַיְהִי עֶרֶב וַיְהִי בֹקֶר

יוֹם הַשִּׁשִּׁי. וַיְכֻלּוּ הַשָּׁמַיִם וְהָאָרֶץ וְכָל צְבָאָם. וַיְכַל אֱלֹהִים בַּיּוֹם הַשְּׁבִיעִי מְלַאכְתּוֹ אֲשֶׁר עָשָׂה. וַיִּשְׁבֹּת בַּיּוֹם הַשְּׁבִיעִי, מִכָּל מְלַאכְתּוֹ אֲשֶׁר עָשָׂה. וַיְבָרֶךְ אֱלֹהִים אֶת יוֹם הַשְּׁבִיעִי, וַיְקַדֵּשׁ אֹתוֹ, כִּי בוֹ שָׁבַת מִכָּל מְלַאכְתּוֹ, אֲשֶׁר בָּרָא אֱלֹהִים לַעֲשׂוֹת:

When holiday occurs on weekday, begin here:

בָּרוּךְ אַתָּה יְיָ, אֱלֹהֵינוּ מֶלֶךְ הָעוֹלָם, בּוֹרֵא פְּרִי הַגָּפֶן:

בָּרוּךְ אַתָּה יְיָ, אֱלֹהֵינוּ מֶלֶךְ הָעוֹלָם, אֲשֶׁר בָּחַר בָּנוּ מִכָּל עָם, וְרוֹמְמָנוּ מִכָּל לָשׁוֹן, וְקִדְּשָׁנוּ בְּמִצְוֹתָיו. וַתִּתֶּן לָנוּ, יְיָ אֱלֹהֵינוּ, בְּאַהֲבָה, [שַׁבָּתוֹת לִמְנוּחָה וּ] מוֹעֲדִים לְשִׂמְחָה, חַגִּים וּזְמַנִּים לְשָׂשׂוֹן. אֶת יוֹם [הַשַּׁבָּת הַזֶּה וְאֶת יוֹם] חַג הַשָּׁבוּעוֹת הַזֶּה, זְמַן מַתַּן תּוֹרָתֵנוּ, [בְּאַהֲבָה] מִקְרָא קֹדֶשׁ, זֵכֶר לִיצִיאַת מִצְרָיִם. כִּי בָנוּ בָחַרְתָּ, וְאוֹתָנוּ קִדַּשְׁתָּ מִכָּל הָעַמִּים. [וְשַׁבָּת] וּמוֹעֲדֵי קָדְשֶׁךָ [בְּאַהֲבָה וּבְרָצוֹן] בְּשִׂמְחָה וּבְשָׂשׂוֹן הִנְחַלְתָּנוּ. בָּרוּךְ אַתָּה יְיָ, מְקַדֵּשׁ [הַשַּׁבָּת וְ] יִשְׂרָאֵל וְהַזְּמַנִּים:

On Saturday night add:

בָּרוּךְ אַתָּה יְיָ, אֱלֹהֵינוּ מֶלֶךְ הָעוֹלָם, בּוֹרֵא מְאוֹרֵי הָאֵשׁ:

בָּרוּךְ אַתָּה יְיָ, אֱלֹהֵינוּ מֶלֶךְ הָעוֹלָם, הַמַּבְדִּיל בֵּין קֹדֶשׁ לְחֹל, בֵּין אוֹר לְחֹשֶׁךְ, בֵּין יִשְׂרָאֵל לָעַמִּים, בֵּין יוֹם הַשְּׁבִיעִי לְשֵׁשֶׁת יְמֵי הַמַּעֲשֶׂה. בֵּין קְדֻשַּׁת שַׁבָּת לִקְדֻשַּׁת יוֹם טוֹב הִבְדַּלְתָּ, וְאֶת יוֹם הַשְּׁבִיעִי מִשֵּׁשֶׁת יְמֵי הַמַּעֲשֶׂה קִדַּשְׁתָּ. הִבְדַּלְתָּ וְקִדַּשְׁתָּ אֶת עַמְּךָ יִשְׂרָאֵל בִּקְדֻשָּׁתֶךָ. בָּרוּךְ אַתָּה יְיָ, הַמַּבְדִּיל בֵּין קֹדֶשׁ לְקֹדֶשׁ:

בָּרוּךְ אַתָּה יְיָ, אֱלֹהֵינוּ מֶלֶךְ הָעוֹלָם, שֶׁהֶחֱיָנוּ, וְקִיְּמָנוּ, וְהִגִּיעָנוּ לַזְּמַן הַזֶּה.

On Sabbath, add first paragraph and words in parentheses:

Va-y'hee eh-rehv, va-y'hee vo-kehr

Yom ha-shi-shee: Va-y'choo-loo ha-shaw-ma-yeem v'haw-aw-retz v'chawl tz'vaw-awm. Va-y'chahl Elo-heem ba-yom ha-sh'vee-ee, m'lahch-to ah-shehr aw-saw; va-yish-bos ba-yom ha-sh'vee-ee, mi-kawl m'lahch-to ah-shehr aw-saw. Va-y'vaw-rech Elo-heem ehs yom ha-sh'vee-ee, va-y'ka-daysh o-so, kee vo shaw-vahs mi-kawl m'lahch-to, ah-sher baw-raw Elo-heem la-ah-sos.

When holiday occurs on weekday, begin here:

Baw-rooch ah-taw Ado-noy, Elo-hay-noo meh-lech haw-o-lawm, bo-ray p'ree ha-gaw-fen.

Baw-rooch ah-taw Ado-noy, Elo-hay-noo meh-lech haw-o-lawm, ah-shehr baw-chahr baw-noo mi-kawl awm, v'ro-m'maw-noo mi-kawl law-shon, v'ki-d'shaw-noo b'mitz-vo-sawv, va-ti-ten law-noo, Ado-noy Elo-hay-noo, b'ah-ha-vaw (sha-baw-sos li-m'noo-chaw oo-) mo-ah-deem l'sim-chaw, cha-geem oo-z'mah-neem l'saw-son, ehs yom (ha-sha-baws ha-zeh v'ehs yom) chahg ha-shaw-voo-os ha-zeh, z'mahn ma-tahn to-raw-say-noo, (b'ah-ha-vaw) mik-raw ko-desh, zay-chehr lee-tzee-ahs mitz-raw-yeem. Kee vaw-noo vaw-chahr-taw, v'o-saw-noo ki-dahsh-taw mi-kawl haw-ah-meem, (v'sha-baws) oo-mo-ah-day kawd-sh'chaw (b'ah-ha-vaw oo-v'raw-tzon) b'sim-chaw oo-v'saw-son hin-chahl-taw-noo. Baw-rooch ah-taw Ado-noy, m'ka-daysh (ha-sha-baws v') Yis-raw-ayl v'ha-z'ma-neem.

On Saturday night add first two paragraphs:

Baw-rooch ah-taw Ado-noy, Elo-hay-noo meh-lech haw-o-lawm, bo-ray m'o-ray haw-aysh.

Baw-rooch ah-taw Ado-noy, Elo-hay-noo meh-lech haw-o-lawm, ha-mahv-deel bayn ko-desh l'chol, bayn or l'cho-shech, bayn Yis-raw-ayl law-ah-meem, bayn yom ha-sh'vee-ee l'shay-shehs y'may ha-ma-ah-seh. Bayn k'doo-shahs sha-baws li-k'doo-

shahs yom tov hiv-dahl-taw, v'ehs yom ha-sh'vee-ee mi-shay-shehs
y'may ha-ma-ah-seh ki-dahsh-taw; hiv-dahl-taw v'ki-dahsh-taw
ehs a-m'chaw Yis-raw-ayl bi-k'doo-shaw-seh-chaw. Baw-rooch
ah-taw Ado-noy, ha-mahv-deel bayn ko-desh l'ko-desh.

Baw-rooch ah-taw Ado-noy, Elo-hay-noo meh-lech haw-o-
lawm, sheh-heh-cheh-yaw-noo, v'kee-y'maw-noo, v'hi-gee-aw-noo,
la-z'mahn ha-zeh.

Heavenly Father:

For this festival of Shovuos, season of the giving of our Torah,
we thank Thee, and pray that the spirit of the Torah be ever with
us, in all our thoughts and deeds. We pray Thee that the Torah
continue to be a beacon light for us, for our people, and for all
mankind. In gratitude for the glorious heritage of Torah and for
the blessings of life and joy and gladness, we thank Thee with the
blessing over wine:

Blessed art Thou, O Lord our God, King of the universe, who
createst the fruit of the vine.

Blessed art Thou, O Lord our God, King of the universe, who
hast granted us life, sustained us, and brought us to this festive
season. Amen.

3. *Washing the Hands*

The traditional home service suggests the washing of the hands before dinner
The custom is reminiscent of the act of preparation and consecration which priests
performed before they began their functions in Temple days of old. The blessing
recited is:

בָּרוּךְ אַתָּה יְיָ, אֱלֹהֵינוּ מֶלֶךְ הָעוֹלָם, אֲשֶׁר קִדְּשָׁנוּ בְּמִצְוֹתָיו, וְצִוָּנוּ
עַל נְטִילַת יָדֶיִם:

Baw-rooch ah-taw Ado-noy, Elo-hay-noo meh-lech haw-o-
lawm, ah-shehr ki-d'shaw-noo b'mitz-vo-sawv, v'tzi-vaw-noo, ahl
n'tee-lahs yaw-daw-yeem.

Blessed art Thou, O Lord our God, King of the universe, who hast sanctified us by Thy commandments and granted us the privilege of partaking of Thy blessings of food and sustenance after the symbolic washing of the hands.

4. *Hamotzee — Breaking Bread Together*

Father uncovers the Challahs or bread and leads the family in recitation of Hamotzee as he slices the Challah.

בָּרוּךְ אַתָּה יְיָ, אֱלֹהֵינוּ מֶלֶךְ הָעוֹלָם, הַמּוֹצִיא לֶחֶם מִן הָאָרֶץ:

Baw-rooch ah-taw Ado-noy, Elo-hay-noo meh-lech haw-o-lawm, ha-mo-tzee leh-chem min haw-aw-retz.

Blessed art Thou, O Lord our God, King of the universe, who bringest forth bread from the earth.

5. *Dinner is served*

It is the custom to partake of dairy foods and honey on this holiday. The tradition derives from the passage in the Bible, "Milk and honey shall be under your tongue." The Torah is compared to milk and honey; so should its study prove as pleasant as milk and honey.

6. *Story Time*

During the meal you have a wonderful opportunity for emphasizing the holiday and its meaning. You may do this by reading the story of Ruth or of how the holiday began, and also the Ten Commandments, which you will find on page 309.

7. *Song Time*

Holiday songs can be sung between courses to further create the festival spirit.

YISRAWAYL V'ORAISAW

יִשְׂרָאֵל וְאוֹרַיְתָא — THE PEOPLE ISRAEL AND THE TORAH
ARE ONE

יִשְׂרָאֵל, יִשְׂרָאֵל וְאוֹרַיְתָא חַד הוּא.

תּוֹרָה אוֹרָה, תּוֹרָה אוֹרָה, הַלְלוּיָהּ.

YISMAHCH MOSHEH
יִשְׂמַח מֹשֶׁה — MOSES REJOICED

Yis-mahch Mo-sheh b'maht - nahs Yis mahch Mo-sheh b'maht - nahs

Yis-mahch Mo-sheh b'maht - nahs b' - maht-nahs chel - ko.

Kay-tzahd kaw-raw-saw lo, Kay-tzahd kaw-raw-saw lo? Kee eh-ved neh-mawn

kaw raw-saw lo. Kay-tzahd kaw-raw-saw lo, Kay-tzahd kaw-raw-saw lo,

Kee eh - ved neh - mawn — kaw- raw - saw - lo.

Moses rejoiced in his portion, for Thou didst call him a faithful servant, and set a crown of glory upon his head.

יִשְׂמַח מֹשֶׁה בְּמַתְּנַת,
בְּמַתְּנַת חֶלְקוֹ.

.1

כֵּיצַד קָרָאתָ לוֹ, כֵּיצַד קָרָאתָ לוֹ?
כִּי עֶבֶד נֶאֱמָן קָרָאתָ לוֹ.
יִשְׂמַח מֹשֶׁה בְּמַתְּנַת,
בְּמַתְּנַת חֶלְקוֹ.

2.

Oo-mah naw-sah-taw lo, oo-mah naw-sah-taw lo,
K'leel tif-eh-rehs b'ro-sho naw-sah-taw,
Yis-mahch Mo-she b'maht-nahs, b'maht-nahs chehl-ko.

.2

וּמַה נָּתַתָּ לוֹ, וּמַה נָּתַתָּ לוֹ?
כְּלִיל תִּפְאֶרֶת בְּרֹאשׁוֹ נָתָתָּ.
יִשְׂמַח מֹשֶׁה בְּמַתְּנַת,
בְּמַתְּנַת חֶלְקוֹ.

BAWROOCH ELOHAYNOO

בָּרוּךְ אֱלֹהֵינוּ—BLESSED BE OUR GOD

.1

Blessed be our God who created us for His glory, who distinguished us from those who err, who gave us the Torah, and everlasting life.

בָּרוּךְ אֱלֹהֵינוּ שֶׁבְּרָאָנוּ לִכְבוֹדוֹ
עוֹד הַפַּעַם, עוֹד הַפַּעַם, לִכְבוֹדוֹ.

2.

V'hiv-dee-law-noo min hah-to-eem (3).

Od ha-pah-ahm, min hah-to-eem (3).

.2

וְהִבְדִּילָנוּ מִן הַתּוֹעִים . . .
עוֹד הַפַּעַם מִן הַתּוֹעִים . . .

3.

V'naw-sahn law-noo To-rahs eh-mehs (3).

Od ha-pah-ahm, To-rahs eh-mehs (3).

.3

וְנָתַן לָנוּ תּוֹרַת אֱמֶת . . .
עוֹד הַפַּעַם תּוֹרַת אֱמֶת . . .

4.

V'chah-yay o-lawm naw-tah b'so-chay-noo (3)

Od ha-pah-ahm, b'so-chay-noo (3).

.4

וְחַיֵּי עוֹלָם נָטַע בְּתוֹכֵנוּ . . .
עוֹד הַפַּעַם בְּתוֹכֵנוּ . . .

DUNDAI

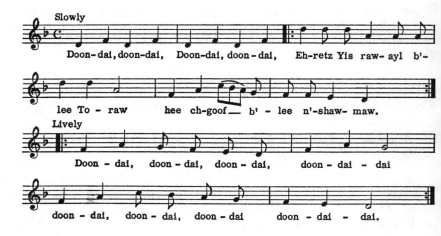

Israel without a Torah is like a
body without a soul.

אֶרֶץ יִשְׂרָאֵל בְּלִי תוֹרָה
הִיא כְגוּף בְּלִי נְשָׁמָה.

8. *Grace*

After dinner, father leads his family in the recitation of the
grace, thanking God for His bounty.

Father: רַבּוֹתַי, נְבָרֵךְ.

Ra-bo-sai, n'vaw-raych

Family: יְהִי שֵׁם יְיָ מְבֹרָךְ מֵעַתָּה וְעַד עוֹלָם.

Y'hee shaym Ado-noy m'vo-rawch may-ah-taw v'ahd
o-lawm.

Father: יְהִי שֵׁם יְיָ מְבֹרָךְ מֵעַתָּה וְעַד עוֹלָם. בִּרְשׁוּת מִשְׁפַּחְתִּי,

נְבָרֵךְ שֶׁאָכַלְנוּ מִשֶּׁלּוֹ.

Y'hee shaym Ado-noy m'vo-rawch may-ah-taw v'ahd
o-lawm. Bi-r'shoos mish-pach-tee, n'vaw-raych sheh-
aw-chahl-noo mi-sheh-lo.

Family: בָּרוּךְ שֶׁאָכַלְנוּ מִשֶּׁלּוֹ וּבְטוּבוֹ חָיִינוּ:

Baw-rooch sheh-aw-chahl-noo mi-sheh-lo, oo-v'too-vo
chaw-yee-noo.

Father: בָּרוּךְ שֶׁאָכַלְנוּ מִשֶּׁלּוֹ וּבְטוּבוֹ חָיִינוּ:

Baw-rooch sheh-aw-chahl-noo mi-sheh-lo, oo-v'too-vo
chaw-yee-noo.

Father: Let us join in thanking God, of whose bounty we have
partaken.

Family: Blessed be our God, of whose bounty we have partaken
and through whose goodness we live.

Family:

בָּרוּךְ הוּא וּבָרוּךְ שְׁמוֹ.

בָּרוּךְ אַתָּה יְיָ, אֱלֹהֵינוּ מֶלֶךְ הָעוֹלָם, הַזָּן אֶת הָעוֹלָם כֻּלּוֹ בְּטוּבוֹ,
בְּחֵן בְּחֶסֶד וּבְרַחֲמִים. הוּא נוֹתֵן לֶחֶם לְכָל בָּשָׂר, כִּי לְעוֹלָם חַסְדּוֹ.
וּבְטוּבוֹ הַגָּדוֹל תָּמִיד לֹא חָסַר לָנוּ, וְאַל יֶחְסַר לָנוּ מָזוֹן לְעוֹלָם וָעֶד.
בַּעֲבוּר שְׁמוֹ הַגָּדוֹל, כִּי הוּא אֵל זָן וּמְפַרְנֵס לַכֹּל, וּמֵטִיב לַכֹּל, וּמֵכִין
מָזוֹן לְכָל בְּרִיּוֹתָיו אֲשֶׁר בָּרָא.
בָּרוּךְ אַתָּה יְיָ, הַזָּן אֶת הַכֹּל:

Baw-rooch hoo oo-vaw-rooch sh'mo.

Baw-rooch ah-taw Ado-noy, Elo-hay-noo meh-lech haw-o-lawm, ha-zawn ehs haw-o-lawm koo-lo b'too-vo, b'chayn b'cheh-sed oo-v'rah-chah-meem. Hoo no-sayn leh-chem l'chawl baw-sawr, kee l'o-lawm chahs-do. Oo-v'too-vo ha-gaw-dol taw-meed lo chaw-sahr law-noo, v'ahl yech-sahr law-noo maw-zon l'o-lawm vaw-ed. Bah-ah-voor sh'mo ha-gaw-dol, kee hoo Ayl zawn oo-m'far-nays la-kol, oo-may-teev la-kol, oo-may-cheen maw-zon l'chawl b'ri-yo-sawv ah-sher baw-raw.
Baw-rooch ah-taw Ado-noy, ha-zawn ehs ha-kol.

Blessed art Thou, O Lord our God, King of the Universe, who providest food for all. Through Thy goodness food has never failed us. Mayest Thou provide sustenance for all Thy children, at all times, for the sake of Thy great Name.

Father:

We thank Thee, O Lord our God, for our liberation from bondage, for the heritage of Eretz Yisroel, for Thy Torah which Thou didst reveal and impart unto us, and for the life of grace and blessing which Thou hast bestowed upon us.

וְעַל הַכֹּל, יְיָ אֱלֹהֵינוּ, אֲנַחְנוּ מוֹדִים לָךְ, וּמְבָרְכִים אוֹתָךְ, יִתְבָּרַךְ

שִׁמְךָ בְּפִי כָּל חַי תָּמִיד לְעוֹלָם וָעֶד: כַּכָּתוּב, וְאָכַלְתָּ וְשָׂבָעְתָּ וּבֵרַכְתָּ

אֶת יְיָ אֱלֹהֶיךָ, עַל הָאָרֶץ הַטּוֹבָה אֲשֶׁר נָתַן לָךְ.

בָּרוּךְ אַתָּה יְיָ, עַל הָאָרֶץ וְעַל הַמָּזוֹן:

V'ahl ha-kol, Ado-noy Elo-hay-noo, ah-nahch-noo mo-deem lawch, oo-m'vawr-cheem o-sawch, yis-baw-rach shi-m'chaw b'fee kawl chai taw-meed l'o-lawm vaw-ed. Ka-kaw-soov, v'aw-chahl-taw, v'saw-vaw-taw oo-vay-rahch-taw, ehs Ado-noy Elo-heh-chaw, ahl haw-aw-retz ha-to-vaw ah-shehr naw-sahn lawch.
Baw-rooch ah-taw Ado-noy, ahl haw-aw-retz, v'ahl ha-maw-zon.

Have mercy, O Lord our God, upon Israel Thy people, and upon Zion, and hasten the day of peace for all mankind.

וּבְנֵה יְרוּשָׁלַיִם עִיר הַקֹּדֶשׁ בִּמְהֵרָה בְיָמֵינוּ. בָּרוּךְ אַתָּה יְיָ, בֹּנֵה בְרַחֲמָיו יְרוּשָׁלָיִם. אָמֵן:

Oo-v'nay Y'roo-shaw-la-yeem eer ha-ko-desh bi-m'hay-raw v'yaw-may-noo.

Baw-rooch ah-taw Ado-noy, bo-neh v'ra-cha-mawv Y'roo-shaw-law-yeem, Aw-mayn.

Family:

בָּרוּךְ אַתָּה יְיָ, אֱלֹהֵינוּ מֶלֶךְ הָעוֹלָם, הָאֵל, אָבִינוּ, מַלְכֵּנוּ, אַדִּירֵנוּ, בּוֹרְאֵנוּ, גּוֹאֲלֵנוּ, יוֹצְרֵנוּ, קְדוֹשֵׁנוּ, קְדוֹשׁ יַעֲקֹב, רוֹעֵנוּ, רוֹעֵה יִשְׂרָאֵל, הַמֶּלֶךְ הַטּוֹב וְהַמֵּטִיב לַכֹּל, שֶׁבְּכָל יוֹם וָיוֹם הוּא הֵטִיב, הוּא מֵטִיב, הוּא יֵיטִיב לָנוּ. הוּא גְמָלָנוּ, הוּא גוֹמְלֵנוּ, הוּא יִגְמְלֵנוּ לָעַד, לְחֵן וּלְחֶסֶד וּלְרַחֲמִים וּלְרֶוַח, הַצָּלָה וְהַצְלָחָה, בְּרָכָה וִישׁוּעָה, נֶחָמָה, פַּרְנָסָה וְכַלְכָּלָה, וְרַחֲמִים וְחַיִּים וְשָׁלוֹם, וְכָל טוֹב, וּמִכָּל טוֹב לְעוֹלָם אַל יְחַסְּרֵנוּ:

Baw-rooch ah-taw Ado-noy, Elo-hay-noo meh-lech haw-o-lawm, haw-ayl aw-vee-noo, mahl-kay-noo, a-dee-ray-noo, bo-r'ay-noo, go-ah-lay-noo, yo-tz'ray-noo, k'do-shay-noo, k'dosh Ya-ah-kov, ro-ay-noo, ro-ay Yis-raw-ayl, ha-meh-lehch ha-tov v'ha-may-teev la-kol, sheh-b'chawl yom vaw-yom hoo hay-teev, hoo may-teev, hoo yay-teev law-noo, hoo g'maw-law-noo, hoo go-m'lay-noo, hoo yig-m'lay-noo law-ahd, l'chayn oo-l'cheh-sed oo-l'ra-cha-meem oo-l'reh-vahch, ha-tzaw-law v'hahtz-law-chaw, b'raw-chaw vee-shoo-aw, neh-chaw-maw, par-naw-saw v'chahl-kaw-law, v'ra-cha-meem v'cha-yeem v'shaw-lom, v'chawl tov, oo-mi-kawl tov l'o-lawm ahl y'chah-s'ray-noo.

Blessed art Thou, O Lord our God, King of the universe. Thou art our God who showerest kindnesses upon all Thy creatures. Every day dost Thou grant unto us the blessings of Thy hand. Thou art kind and dost deal kindly with us. Thou hast bestowed upon us Thy blessings, yielding us lovingkindness, grace, sustenance and support, mercy, life and peace. We pray Thee, withhold not Thy blessings from us.

Father: May God sustain us in health.

Family: Amen.

Father: May God bless all assembled at this table.

Family: Amen.

Father: May God send plentiful blessings upon this house, and all who are near and dear to us.

Family: Amen.

(On the Sabbath)

Father: הָרַחֲמָן, הוּא יַנְחִילֵנוּ יוֹם שֶׁכֻּלוֹ שַׁבָּת וּמְנוּחָה לְחַיֵּי הָעוֹלָמִים:

Family: אָמֵן: — Amen

Father: May this Sabbath eve bring its message of rest and peace to us.

Family: Amen.

Father: הָרַחֲמָן, הוּא יַנְחִילֵנוּ יוֹם שֶׁכֻּלוֹ טוֹב:

Family: אָמֵן: — Amen

Father: May this Festival eve bring its message of joy and happiness to us.

Family: Amen.

Family:

מִגְדוֹל יְשׁוּעוֹת מַלְכּוֹ וְעֹשֶׂה חֶסֶד לִמְשִׁיחוֹ, לְדָוִד וּלְזַרְעוֹ עַד עוֹלָם.
עֹשֶׂה שָׁלוֹם בִּמְרוֹמָיו, הוּא יַעֲשֶׂה שָׁלוֹם עָלֵינוּ וְעַל כָּל יִשְׂרָאֵל, וְאִמְרוּ,
אָמֵן:

Mig-dol y'shoo-os mahl-ko, v'o-seh cheh-sed li-m'shee-cho,
l'Daw-vid oo-l'zar-o ahd o-lawm. O-seh shaw-lom bi-m'ro-mawv,
hoo ya-ah-seh shaw-lom, aw-lay-noo v'ahl kawl Yis-raw-ayl,
v'i-m'roo, aw-mayn.

May He who creates peace in His celestial heights, grant
peace and contentment and joy to us, to all Israel, and to all mankind. Amen.

CONFIRMATION DAY

By EDITH B. GOLDMAN

"I'm sorry, Naomi," said Sharol, "I'm sorry I can't come to lunch tomorrow." Sharol had been talking on the telephone to her friend. "We're invited to my cousin's confirmation. It's next week, on the holiday of Shovuos. Mom and I are going shopping tomorrow for a gift for Miriam, and new white gloves and a summer hat for me. Oh, fine, then I'll come for lunch one day soon and I'll tell you all about it. Goodby." She hung up the phone; she could hardly wait for the time to pass.

The next afternoon she dashed home from school and arrived quite breathless.

"My goodness," laughed her mother, "why such a hurry?"

"Oh, Mommy," she cried, "you didn't forget, did you?"

"Of course not," smiled her mother. "But you've quite lost your breath for hurrying. I think you'll have to go back out and bring it back before you have your lunch."

"Don't tease," laughed Sharol. "I have my breath now. You *are* ready, aren't you?"

"Of course. Your lunch is on the table. Now wash your hands. We have plenty of time."

Sharol hurried anyhow. She loved to go shopping with her mother. There was so much to see and do. She loved selecting gifts, and it was delightful trying on new summer hats. She chose a cool lime-colored pique hat and gloves to match. It would go very well with her white crisp dress.

It was quite a warm day and Sharol was also flushed with pleasure. Her Mom looked down at the rosy little girl and suggested, "I think an ice cream soda would be refreshing, don't you?"

"Oh yes," beamed Sharol, and she led the way, carrying her packages. She knew just where the snack bar was.

As she perched on the high stool she said to her mother, "I can hardly wait for Confirmation on Shovuos," and then she scanned the menu.

The important day arrived. The entire family and all friends had been invited. Sharol was awake at the crack of dawn. She took out her new outfit, and sat looking at it until the family awakened. Everyone was ready early and they were quite happy when they arrived at the synagogue. It seemed everyone was coming early so that all could be seated close to the pulpit. When they entered, Sharol's eyes opened wide with delight. It was beautiful, as beautiful as springtime. The synagogue was sprinkled with fresh flower arrangements and the bright sun shining through the stained glass windows gave the synagogue a warm and delicate splendor.

Everyone was seated, and the services began in an air of expectancy. The Rabbi and Cantor were dressed in white gowns. The melodies from the choir floated through the synagogue. Sharol glanced at her mother and dad as they followed the service in the Prayerbook and they smiled back at her. She thought, "I'm glad I'll be old enough to begin learning Hebrew next year. I would like to read along with everyone."

Then the choir began singing a hymn, "Blessed are you who come in the name of the Lord." The confirmands entered and walked down the aisle strewn with flower petals. All turned to watch the processional. Sharol, seeing her cousin in the march, felt the thrill of pride. Miriam was now sixteen years old and had been studying at Hebrew School for six years. She had worked hard on her part in the ceremony. And now they were being confirmed. They wore white gowns, and carried bouquets. Their faces shone with a special radiance.

When they reached the front of the synagogue just below the pulpit they were seated. Two of the confirmands were called up to the pulpit to read from the Torah. Sharol always liked to see the open ark and the tall, stately Torahs looking very beautiful in their white satin and silver ornaments.

She watched how they carefully bore one Torah to the pulpit and unrolled it for the reading. The boys were proud as they each read in a clear voice in Hebrew. It was the portion that celebrates the giving of the Torah on Mount Sinai.

After reading the Torah the choir sang, "*Vzos ha-Toraw*, And this is the Torah," and the Rabbi and Cantor circled the pulpit with the Torah before returning it to the ark. The ark was closed. It was very quiet now and there was a beauty of holiness everywhere evident.

The confirmands delivered their addresses. One by one they came to the pulpit and told of the great teachers and prophets of our people. The girls, with a gracefulness beyond the reaches of art, made their floral offerings, mindful of the first fruits and flowers of the season. The choir sang as the parents of the confirmands rose to bless their children, and they returned to their seats for the rest of the service.

When the service was over, Sharol jumped up to wish everyone a "Goot Yom Tov" (Happy Holiday) and tried to reach her cousin to congratulate her. She could feel the rejoicing and festivity as Mazal Tov (congratulations) was heard from everyone's lips. Sharol felt like a football player running interference as she managed her way to the confirmands. She was so full of affection and pride she had to hug Miriam before telling her how beautiful the service was and how captivating the confirmands looked.

"Oh, Mim, she said, "I'm going to study so hard. If my confirmation is half as lovely as yours, I'll be so very happy."

Mim, overjoyed herself, laughed, and said, "Thank you, Sharol, I know yours will be just as beautiful and even more so. Let's go down to the reception together." Mim clasped her hand, and together they went down into the Reception Hall where the Rabbi and Cantor and all the parents and friends of the confirmands had gathered for the Kiddush and to wish each other a happy holiday.

It was such a beautiful holiday and Sharol was just as happy as if she were being confirmed herself.

THE MODEST MOUNTAIN

By Edith B. Goldman

It was a sunny afternoon just before the holiday of Shovuos. Danny, Kinery, and Wendy were sitting on the stone steps in front of their house.

"What shall we play?" asked Kinery. "How about a game of jacks and ball?"

"No!" said Danny. "That's a girls' game. Let's play cowboys."

"Oh, no!" chorused the girls. "That's a boys' game."

"I have it," popped Wendy. "Yesterday, our teacher at Sunday School, Miss Gordon, told us the story of the Torah and the mountains. Let's get big sheets and put it over our heads and pretend we're the mountains."

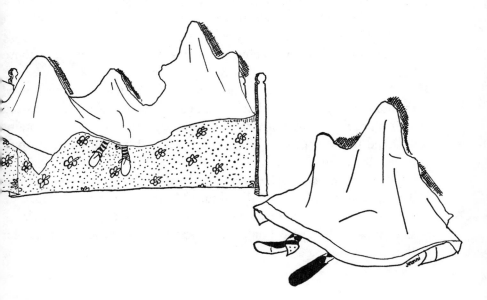

"That's a great idea," answered the others, and they ran to get the sheets. They fixed them over their heads and squatted down, laughing at the funny shapes they made. One mountain was crooked because his arm was sticking out. Another mountain was bent because the head was tilted over on the side. And the third mountain was lopsided because he was reaching over and down.

"Danny, you're the tallest, so you be Mount Tabor. Kinery, you're next tallest, so you be Mount Hermon. I'm the youngest, so I'll be Mount Sinai."

"Oh, no," protested the other two. "Why should you be Sinai?"

"Well now, that's the play," answered Wendy. "Don't forget. Danny, you're not Danny, you're Mount Tabor. You're not Kinery, Kinery, you're Mount Hermon."

The little mountains nestled down and the play was on.

"I heard that God is going to give the Jewish people the Torah," said Mount Tabor. "And I heard, too, that He will choose a mountain on which Moses will go to receive the Torah. If that is so, then *I* will be chosen because I am the tallest of all the mountains. Look at me, so stately, so handsome. God will certainly choose me!"

"No," said Mount Hermon. "God will choose *me*."

And each of the mountains gave reasons why God would choose her.

Now, all this time, Mount Sinai, which was a mountain of medium size, listened and said nothing. Suddenly, a cloud appeared over all of them, and when the cloud disappeared, the two mountains saw and were surprised. They saw the Torah resting on the top of little Mount Sinai.

"Mount Sinai," asked Mount Tabor. "how did you get the Torah? I was to be chosen!" Mount Hermon complained, too.

"You two mountains were so busy quarreling and boasting," said Sinai, "that you didn't hear God call to Moses to come for the Torah."

The two mountains bent their peaks and said, "That's a lesson for us that boasting and bragging is not very good. Next time we won't quarrel. We'll listen very carefully."

The play was over and they took a bow.
"I pretended so hard that I thought I was really a mountain," said Wendy. "Let's surprise everyone and play it again at Sunday School, shall we?"
And they did.

The Ten Commandments

(Exodus 20:1–14)

1. I am the Lord Thy God, who brought thee out of the land of Egypt, out of the house of bondage.

2. Thou shalt have no other gods before Me. Thou shalt not make unto thee a graven image, nor any manner of likeness, of anything that is in heaven above, or that is in the earth beneath, or that is in the water under the earth; thou shalt not bow down unto them, nor serve them; for I the Lord thy God am a jealous God, visiting the iniquity of the fathers upon the children unto the third and fourth generation of them that hate Me; and showing mercy unto the thousandth generation of them that love Me and keep My commandments.

3. Thou shalt not take the name of the Lord thy God in vain; for the Lord will not hold him guiltless that taketh His name in vain.

4. Remember the Sabbath day to keep it holy. Six days shalt thou labor, and do all thy work; but the seventh day is a Sabbath unto the Lord thy God, in it thou shalt not do any manner of work, thou, nor thy son, nor thy daughter, nor thy man-servant, nor thy maid-servant, nor thy cattle, nor thy stranger that is within thy gates; for in six days the Lord made heaven and earth, the sea, and all that in them is, and rested on the seventh day; wherefore the Lord blessed the Sabbath day, and hallowed it.

5. Honor thy father and thy mother, that thy days may be long upon the land which the Lord thy God giveth thee.

6. Thou shalt not murder.

7. Thou shalt not commit adultery.

8. Thou shalt not steal.

9. Thou shalt not bear false witness against thy neighbor.

10. Thou shalt not covet thy neighbor's house; thou shalt not covet thy neighbor's wife, nor his man-servant, nor his maid-servant, nor his ox, nor his ass, nor anything that is thy neighbor's.

Sabbath

SABBATH

The holy Sabbath, Queen of days,
Brings pious rest, we sing God's praise
With song and prayer. Our candles shine,
We bless the Challah; bless the wine.

Then love and friendship fills the air
In temple, where we meet in prayer
To thank God for His loving hands
O'er everyone — in all the lands.

This day each week we set aside
All work, and with our faith as guide
We worship God in all these ways
On this, our Sabbath, Queen of days.

Sabbath

Monday, Tuesday, Wednesday, Thursday, and Friday, the days of the week, have similar import to most families. Father goes to work or to the office, mother is involved with her housekeeping duties and club responsibilities, and children attend public and Hebrew schools, and engage in activities that round out their personalities. But week-day functions, with each member traveling on his own road of interest, are relaxed with the refreshing spirit of the Sabbath. Friday eve draws the divergent paths together and reunites family ties. The Sabbath is the weekly opportunity for renewing intimacy, for becoming reacquainted with family at home and with our people at the synagogue.

Perhaps this is the reason that in Jewish legendry the Jewish family on the Sabbath is portrayed as a royal family, the home converted to a palace, father a king, mother a queen, and the children princes and princesses. The increased warmth and attachment on what the prophet Isaiah calls "a day of delight" tell us that there may be something to the rabbinic dictum that on the Sabbath each of us has a *"neshomoh yesayroh* — an added soul." We are more than our weekly selves on the Sabbath.

As the Sabbath is the heart of Jewish family union, so is it the heart of Judaism. "More than Israel has kept the Sabbath, the Sabbath has kept Israel," are the words of Achad Ha-Am, the famous writer. This means simply that they are intertwined; they are of equal significance, like two sides of one coin.

Two traditional reasons are given for the Sabbath — the only holiday mentioned in the Ten Commandments. One is that it commemorates the creation of the world and God's rest on the seventh day. Just as God rested after six days of labor, so are we expected to sanctify the day by emulating divinity. The second is that the Sabbath recalls the exodus of our forefathers from Egyptian bondage. In other words, our fathers were released unto freedom in ancient days; on the Sabbath we are released from the labor and concerns of the week's toil and can come closer to our family and our people. From these basic reasons, the genius of our forebears has glorified the Sabbath day with songs and stories and legends, making it one of refreshment of soul, spiritual joy, and relaxation of mind.

IN THE SYNAGOGUE

A bride dressed in white, accompanied by ministering angels, spiritual delight, rest and peace, are terms used in Jewish folklore to describe the spirit of the Sabbath. Like a bride warmly and gladly welcomed, the Sabbath is received with joy and enthusiasm.

"Kabbolas Shabbos — Welcoming the Sabbath," is the name of the early Sabbath eve service; a series of psalms climaxed by the well known refrain, "L'chaw do-dee li-k'rahs kah-law, p'nay sha-baws n'kah-b'law — Come, my friend, to meet the bride; let us welcome the presence of the Sabbath." The regular evening, or Maariv service, follows immediately, but with additional prayers and excerpts from the Bible relating to the theme of the Sabbath. The Kiddush or blessing over the wine is sung in a special Sabbath chant from the pulpit, so that the entire congregation may share in the benediction.

The Sabbath morning service contains three parts: Shachahris (morning), Torah reading, and Musaf (additional) services. The first includes psalms recited in the daily service, to which are added special Sabbath prayers, and a specific Amidah. This prayer, for which the entire congregation rises, is recited silently and is also known as Shemoneh Esray or Eighteen Benedictions, from the number of blessings recited in the daily Amidah.

The Torah reading is the central feature of the service, and the prayers revolve about it. Special melodies are sung as the Torah* is withdrawn from the Ark and the responses to the Sh'ma (confession of faith of the Jew, which in its entirety reads: Sh'ma Yis-raw-ayl Ado-noy Elo-hay-noo Ado-noy Eh-chawd — Hear O Israel, the Lord our God, the Lord is One), are recited aloud. A brief Torah procession about the pulpit precedes the Torah reading.

The Pentateuch (Five Books of Moses) is divided into sections. Each Sabbath, one section, called Sidra, is read. The reader, called Baal K'riah, uses the special cantillation marks which appear in the printed Hebrew texts of the Bible. The readings for the year begin and are completed on Simchas Torah (see page 78).

Usually seven men are called to the Torah to recite the blessings, although in many cases more honors are added. The call begins with the word "ya-a-mod — let him rise," and the specific honor follows. For example, the first is called Kohayn (Kohen); the second, Layvee (Levi); the third, sh'lee-shee; the fourth, r'vee-ee; the fifth, chah-mee-shee; the sixth, shee-shee, and the seventh, sh'vee-ee. Each one called is shown his place of the reading with the pointer or *yahd* and recites the blessing:

---

* Generally, one Torah is read, unless a special Sabbath is observed, in which case two and sometimes three Torahs are read.

בָּרְכוּ אֶת יְיָ הַמְבֹרָךְ.

בָּרוּךְ יְיָ הַמְבֹרָךְ לְעוֹלָם וָעֶד.

בָּרוּךְ אַתָּה יְיָ, אֱלֹהֵינוּ מֶלֶךְ הָעוֹלָם, אֲשֶׁר בָּחַר בָּנוּ מִכָּל

הָעַמִּים, וְנָתַן לָנוּ אֶת תּוֹרָתוֹ. בָּרוּךְ אַתָּה יְיָ נוֹתֵן הַתּוֹרָה:

Bawr-choo ehs Ado-noy ha-m'vo-rawch

Baw-rooch Ado-noy ha-m'vo-rawch l'o-lawm vaw-ed.

Baw-rooch ah-taw Ado-noy, Elo-hay-noo meh-lech haw-o-lawm, ah-shehr baw-chahr baw-noo mi-kawl haw-ah-meem, v'naw-sahn law-noo ehs to-raw-so. Baw-rooch ah-taw Ado-noy, no-sayn ha-to-raw.

After Torah portion is chanted, the second blessing is recited:

בָּרוּךְ אַתָּה יְיָ, אֱלֹהֵינוּ מֶלֶךְ הָעוֹלָם, אֲשֶׁר נָתַן לָנוּ תּוֹרַת אֱמֶת,

וְחַיֵּי עוֹלָם נָטַע בְּתוֹכֵנוּ. בָּרוּךְ אַתָּה יְיָ, נוֹתֵן הַתּוֹרָה:

Baw-rooch ah-taw Ado-noy, Elo-hay-noo meh-lech haw-o-lawm, ah-shehr naw-sahn law-noo to-rahs eh-mes, v'chah-yay o-lawm naw-tah b'so-chay-noo. Baw-rooch ah-taw Ado-noy, no-sayn ha-to-raw.

The last honor is called Maftir or "closing," and when there is a young man to be called to the Torah for the first time as a Bar Mitzvah, the honor is reserved for him. He, too, recites the above blessings.

After his recitation, two more honors are accorded, one to elevate the Torah (Hagbohoh) and one to roll up and bind the Torah (Geliloh). The congregation rises to join in the chant, "And this is the Torah which was proclaimed by Moses to the children of Israel at the behest of the Lord."

The Maftir or last honoree sings the blessings which precede the chanting of the Haftorah, that portion of the Prophets selected for the specific Sabbath because of themes which relate to the Torah reading. Five blessings conclude the prophetic portion, and with that, the reading service.

The Torah or Torahs are then returned to the Ark, following a procession either about the pulpit or through the synagogue. The congregation sings the appropriate words: "It (Torah) is a tree of life to them that hold fast to it, and everyone that upholds it is happy. Its ways are ways of pleasantness, and all its paths are peace. Turn us unto Thee, O Lord, and we shall return; renew our days as of old."

The Musaf or additional service is then conducted with its own Amidah, underscoring the Sabbath as a day of rest.

In the Home

As Jewish parents, you will want to provide impressive Sabbath experiences for your children. The Sabbath eve is the most appropriate time for your children to be imbued with the spirit of the day. You should take the lead and draw the children into the arrangements. Let them help set the table, bring the candlesticks, place the candles in them, shine the silver pieces to be used, and similar tasks.

The family can select the flowers for the centerpiece together. In season, this may be done from one's own garden. In any case, the flowers are a happy portent of the arriving Sabbath. Alongside this centerpiece, your children can make a Sabbath angel; the combination will symbolize Sabbath sweetness and fragrance.

Here are the directions for a Sabbath Angel:

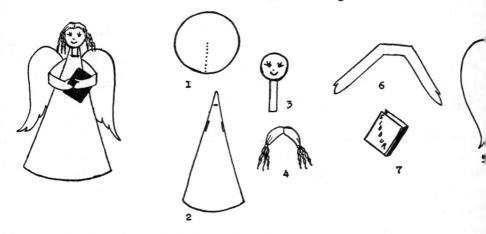

1. Cut a large circle from plain white paper and cut a slit at one point to the center (1).
2. Roll into cone and paste cone together. Cut slits as in cylinder figures for armholes (2).
3. Cut head from heavy paper and draw and color features. Leave long tab at neck to fit into slit in cone (3). Make hair from colored paper, yarn, or absorbent cotton, and attach to head (4).
4. Cut two wings (5) with tabs. Put glue on tabs and fold wings out at dotted line. Paste to back or cone, or cone may be sliced and wings inserted.
5. Cut arms from same paper as cone and pass through slits.
6. Push head through neck slit in cone.
7. You may cut out small Siddur (7), place in hands of figure, and paste.

WHAT YOU NEED FOR THE SABBATH TABLE AND CEREMONY

1. Candlesticks — It is customary to have two candlesticks for the Sabbath blessings, although many families have an additional candlestick for each member of the family. Father, if he comes home earlier on the Sabbath eve, or the children, should have the responsibility of readying the candlesticks.

2. White Tablecloth — A white tablecloth symbolizes the purity or whiteness of the Sabbath. Specially prepared Sabbath tablecloths are now available in synagogue gift shops as are tablecloths into which the Sabbath blessing and Kiddush are woven.

3. Two Sabbath Challahs — Two bread loaves or specially braided Challahs are used on the Sabbath. The number two is commemorative of the double portion of manna gathered by our forefathers on Friday following the departure from Egypt.

4. Sabbath Challah Cover — The Challahs or loaves are covered prior to the Hamotzee, the blessing over bread. Special Challah covers with Sabbath inscriptions can be secured from gift shops. Your children can help make a Challah cover by following these simple instructions:

1. Use a plain white, large size, man's handkerchief. Design may be crayoned, embroidered, or painted with textile paint.
2. If crayoned—when all colors have been put on, iron on reverse side to set wax in crayons.
3. Design may be as elaborate or simple as desired.

5. Sabbath Challah Knife — This is not required, although the Challah knives have appropriate Sabbath inscriptions.

6. Salt — Salt is sprinkled on the Challah after the blessing.

7. Wine — Wine is used for the Kiddush, which opens the Sabbath dinner ceremony.

8. Wine Cups and Decanter — Each member of the family should have his own cup of wine.

THE HOME CEREMONY

1. *Kindling the Sabbath Lights*

With the mellowing of day into twilight, mother has the children watch her welcome the Sabbath as she recites: (Traditionally, the candles are kindled at least twenty minutes before sundown.)

בָּרוּךְ אַתָּה יְיָ, אֱלֹהֵינוּ מֶלֶךְ הָעוֹלָם, אֲשֶׁר קִדְּשָׁנוּ בְּמִצְוֹתָיו,
וְצִוָּנוּ לְהַדְלִיק נֵר שֶׁל שַׁבָּת:

Baw-rooch ah-taw Ado-noy, Elo-hay-noo meh-lech haw-o-lawm, ah-shehr ki-d'shaw-noo b'mitz-vo-sawv, v'tzi-vaw-noo, l'hahd-leek nayr shel sha-baws.

Blessed art Thou, O Lord our God, King of the universe, who hast sanctified us by Thy commandments and granted us the privilege of kindling the Sabbath lights.

(Mother may offer a silent prayer for her family.)

As we light the Sabbath candles, may they fill our hearts with love for one another. May they serve to unite our family in devotion and faithfulness, bring harmony into our lives, and the spirit of Sabbath joy and peace into our home.   Amen.

(Mother then wishes the family "Shabbat Shalom Oo'mvorach — a peaceful and blessed Sabbath" or simply "Goot Sha-baws — Good Sabbath." The children can sing this simple melody:)

SHABBAT SHALOM

SABBATH BLESSING

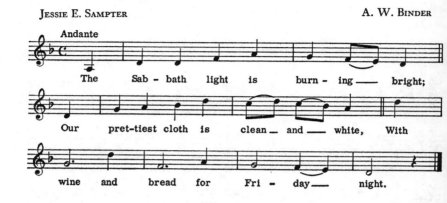

JESSIE E. SAMPTER   A. W. BINDER

Andante

The Sab - bath light is burn - ing —— bright;

Our pret-tiest cloth is clean — and —— white, With

wine and bread for Fri - day —— night.

2.

At set of sun our work is done,
The happy Sabbath has begun,
Now bless us, Father, ev'ry one.

3.

O Sabbath guest, dear Sabbath guest,
Come, share the blessing with the rest,
For all our house tonight is blest.

2. *Singing of Shaw-lom Ah-lay-chem*

The entire family can sing this song (Peace be Unto You),
the traditional melody which introduces the Sabbath.

SHAWLOM ALAYCHEM

Israel Goldfarb

1. Shaw - lom ah-lay - chem   mahl- ah-chay ha-shaw - rays, mahl-
4. Tzays-chem l' shaw - lom   mahl- ah-chay ha-shaw- lom, mahl-

ah- chay el - yon; _____ mi - meh- lech
ah- chay el - yon; _____ mi - meh- lech

mahl - chay ha- m' law-cheem ha - kaw-dosh baw- rooch_ hoo.
mahl - chay ha- m' law-cheem ha - kaw-dosh baw- rooch_ hoo.

2. Bo-ah-chem l' shaw - lom   mahl-ah-chay ha-shaw - lom,
3. Bawr-choo-nee l' shaw - lom   mahl-ah-chay ha-shaw - lom,

mahl-ah-chay__ el - yon,   mi - meh- lech,
mahl-ah-chay__ el - yon,

mahl- chay ha-m' law-cheem, ha-kaw-dosh baw-rooch hoo. Bawr- hoo.

שָׁלוֹם עֲלֵיכֶם. מַלְאֲכֵי הַשָּׁרֵת. מַלְאֲכֵי עֶלְיוֹן.
מִמֶּלֶךְ מַלְכֵי הַמְּלָכִים. הַקָּדוֹשׁ בָּרוּךְ הוּא:

בּוֹאֲכֶם לְשָׁלוֹם. מַלְאֲכֵי הַשָּׁלוֹם. מַלְאֲכֵי עֶלְיוֹן.
מִמֶּלֶךְ מַלְכֵי הַמְּלָכִים. הַקָּדוֹשׁ בָּרוּךְ הוּא:

בָּרְכוּנִי לְשָׁלוֹם. מַלְאֲכֵי הַשָּׁלוֹם. מַלְאֲכֵי עֶלְיוֹן.
מִמֶּלֶךְ מַלְכֵי הַמְּלָכִים. הַקָּדוֹשׁ בָּרוּךְ הוּא:

צֵאתְכֶם לְשָׁלוֹם. מַלְאֲכֵי הַשָּׁלוֹם. מַלְאֲכֵי עֶלְיוֹן.
מִמֶּלֶךְ מַלְכֵי הַמְּלָכִים. הַקָּדוֹשׁ בָּרוּךְ הוּא:

3. *Family Blessings*

One of the old traditions of the Sabbath eve at home is the blessings offered by father for mother and over the children.

The mother is blessed by the father as he reads the thirty-first chapter of Proverbs. Here are selections from this beautiful chapter:

> A good wife, who can find?
> For she is far more precious than jewels.
> The heart of her husband trusts her completely,
> And he has no lack of gain.
> She does him good and not harm,
> All the days of her life.
> She opens her hand to the poor,
> She reaches forth her hands to the needy.
> Strength and dignity are her clothing,
> And she laughs at the time to come.
> She opens her mouth with wisdom,
> And the law of kindness is on her tongue.
> She looks well to the ways of her household,
> And does not eat the bread of idleness.
> Her children rise up and call her blessed;
> Her husband also, and he praises her, saying:
> "Many women have done excellently,
> But you surpass them all."
> Grace is deceitful and beauty is vain,
> But a woman who reveres the Lord is to be praised.
> Give her of the fruit of her hands,
> And let her works praise her in the gates.

The children are blessed with the words of Jacob and the Priestly Benediction by the father as he places his hands on his child's head.

To sons say:

יְשִׂמְךָ אֱלֹהִים כְּאֶפְרַיִם וְכִמְנַשֶּׁה:

Y'si-m'chaw Elo-heem k'Eph-ra-yeem v'chi-M'na-sheh.

May God make you like Ephraim and Menassah, the sons of Joseph.

To daughters say:

יְשִׂמֵךְ אֱלֹהִים כְּשָׂרָה, רִבְקָה, רָחֵל וְלֵאָה:

Y'si-maych Elo-heem k'Saw-raw, Riv-kaw, Raw-chayl, v'Lay-aw.

May God make you like our mothers, Sarah, Rebecca, Rachel, and Leah.

To sons and daughters say:

יְבָרֶכְךָ יְיָ וְיִשְׁמְרֶךָ.
יָאֵר יְיָ פָּנָיו אֵלֶיךָ וִיחֻנֶּךָּ.
יִשָּׂא יְיָ פָּנָיו אֵלֶיךָ, וְיָשֵׂם לְךָ שָׁלוֹם:

Y'vaw-reh-ch'chaw Ado-noy v'yish-m'reh-chaw.
Yaw-ayr Ado-noy paw-nawv ay-leh-chaw vee-choo-neh-kaw.
Yi-saw Ado-noy paw-nawv ay-leh-chaw, v'yaw-saym l'chaw shaw-lom.

May the Lord bless you and keep you.

May the Lord make His face to shine upon you and be gracious unto you.

May the Lord lift up His countenance upon you and give you peace.

* * *

One may introduce the custom of pausing at the dinner table, to ask each member of the family, adult and child, to mention the event of the week for which he is particularly grateful on the Sabbath eve.

4. Kiddush (Blessing of Wine)

All rise while father chants the Sabbath Kiddush, holding the goblet in his right hand.

וַיְהִי עֶרֶב וַיְהִי בֹקֶר

יוֹם הַשִּׁשִּׁי. וַיְכֻלּוּ הַשָּׁמַיִם וְהָאָרֶץ וְכָל צְבָאָם. וַיְכַל אֱלֹהִים בַּיּוֹם הַשְּׁבִיעִי מְלַאכְתּוֹ אֲשֶׁר עָשָׂה. וַיִּשְׁבֹּת בַּיּוֹם הַשְּׁבִיעִי, מִכָּל מְלַאכְתּוֹ אֲשֶׁר עָשָׂה. וַיְבָרֶךְ אֱלֹהִים אֶת יוֹם הַשְּׁבִיעִי, וַיְקַדֵּשׁ אֹתוֹ, כִּי בוֹ שָׁבַת מִכָּל מְלַאכְתּוֹ, אֲשֶׁר בָּרָא אֱלֹהִים לַעֲשׂוֹת:

בָּרוּךְ אַתָּה יְיָ, אֱלֹהֵינוּ מֶלֶךְ הָעוֹלָם, בּוֹרֵא פְּרִי הַגָּפֶן.

בָּרוּךְ אַתָּה יְיָ, אֱלֹהֵינוּ מֶלֶךְ הָעוֹלָם, אֲשֶׁר קִדְּשָׁנוּ בְּמִצְוֹתָיו וְרָצָה בָנוּ. וְשַׁבַּת קָדְשׁוֹ, בְּאַהֲבָה וּבְרָצוֹן הִנְחִילָנוּ, זִכָּרוֹן לְמַעֲשֵׂה בְרֵאשִׁית. כִּי הוּא יוֹם, תְּחִלָּה לְמִקְרָאֵי קֹדֶשׁ, זֵכֶר לִיצִיאַת מִצְרָיִם, כִּי בָנוּ בָחַרְתָּ, וְאוֹתָנוּ קִדַּשְׁתָּ מִכָּל הָעַמִּים, וְשַׁבַּת קָדְשְׁךָ, בְּאַהֲבָה וּבְרָצוֹן הִנְחַלְתָּנוּ. בָּרוּךְ אַתָּה יְיָ, מְקַדֵּשׁ הַשַּׁבָּת.

Va-y'hee eh-rehv, va-y'hee vo-kehr

Yom ha-shi-shee. Va-y'choo-loo ha-shaw-ma-yeem v'haw-aw-retz v'chawl tz'vaw-awm. Va-y'chahl Elo-heem ba-yom ha-sh'vee-ee m'lahch-to ah-shehr aw-saw. Va-y'vaw-rech Elo-heem ehs yom ha-sh'vee-ee, va-y'ka-daysh o-so, kee vo shaw-vahs mi-kawl m'lahch-to, ah-shehr baw-raw Elo-heem la-ah-sos.

Baw-rooch ah-taw Ado-noy, Elo-hay-noo meh-lech haw-o-lawm, bo-ray p'ree ha-gaw-fen.

Baw-rooch ah-taw Ado-noy, Elo-hay-noo meh-lech haw-o-lawm, ah-shehr ki-d'shaw-noo b'mitz-vo-sawv v'raw-tzaw vaw-noo. V'sha-bahs kawd-sho, b'ah-ha-vaw oo-v'raw-tzon hin-chee-law-noo, zi-kaw-ron l'ma-ah-say v'ray-shees. Kee hoo yom, t'chi-law l'mik-raw-ay ko-desh, zay-chehr lee-tzee-ahs mitz-raw-yeem. Kee vaw-noo vaw-chahr-taw, v'o-saw-noo ki-dahsh-taw mi-kawl haw-ah-meem, v'sha-bahs kawd-sh'chaw, b'ah-ha-vaw oo-v'raw-tzon hin-chahl-taw-noo. Baw-rooch ah-taw Ado-noy, m'ka-daysh ha-sha-baws.

Heavenly Father:

As we share in the sweetness of this wine, we thank Thee, for the sanctity of home and family. May this coming week bring happiness to us and pleasant associations with our family and fellows. In gratitude to Thee for Thy goodness and for the Sabbath rest, we thank Thee as we recite the blessing over wine, the symbol of joy and gladness:

Blessed art Thou, O Lord our God, King of the universe, who createst the fruit of the vine.

SABBATH KIDDUSH

ISRAEL GOLDFARB

5. Washing the Hands

The traditional home service suggests the washing of the hands before dinner. The custom is reminiscent of the preparation and consecration of the priests before they began their functions in Temple days. The blessing recited is:

בָּרוּךְ אַתָּה יְיָ, אֱלֹהֵינוּ מֶלֶךְ הָעוֹלָם, אֲשֶׁר קִדְּשָׁנוּ בְּמִצְוֹתָיו, וְצִוָּנוּ עַל נְטִילַת יָדָיִם.

Baw-rooch ah-taw Ado-noy, Elo-hay-noo meh-lech haw-o-lawm, ah-shehr ki-d'shaw-noo b'mitz-vo-sawv, v'tzi-vaw-noo, ahl n'tee-lahs yaw-daw-yeem.

Blessed art Thou, O Lord our God, King of the universe, who hast sanctified us by Thy commandments and granted us the privilege of partaking of Thy blessings of food and sustenance after the symbolic washing of the hands.

6. Hamotzee — Breaking Bread Together

Uncover the Challahs or breads and recite in unison:

בָּרוּךְ אַתָּה יְיָ, אֱלֹהֵינוּ מֶלֶךְ הָעוֹלָם, הַמּוֹצִיא לֶחֶם מִן הָאָרֶץ:

Baw-rooch ah-taw Ado-noy, Elo-hay-noo meh-lech haw-o-lawm, ha-mo-tzee leh-chem min haw-aw-retz.

Blessed art Thou, O Lord our God, King of the universe, who bringest forth bread from the earth.

Slice one of the Challahs, sprinkle with a pinch of salt, and distribute to the family.

7. The Sabbath Dinner is Served

8. Sabbath Songs

Sabbath songs are called Z'miros, and they are customarily sung during the course of dinner. Here are a few of the songs which will help cultivate the Sabbath spirit. Others may be found in any Jewish music book which can be secured from your synagogue gift shop.

SABBATH QUEEN

שַׁבָּת הַמַּלְכָּה — SHABAWS HAMAHLKAW

CHAIM NACHMAN BIALIK
Translation by A. I. COHON

P. MINKOWSKY

Ha - chah-maw may-rosh haw-ee - law-nos nis - tahl-kaw, Bo-
The sun on the tree-tops no long - er is seen, Come,

oo v'-nay-tzay lik - rahs sha-baws ha - mahl-kaw. Hi - nay hee yo-
gath-er to wel-come the Sab - bath, our queen. Be - hold her de-

reh dehs ha - k'do-shaw ha -b'roo - chaw, V' - i - maw mahl-
scend- ing, the ho - ly the—blest, And with her the

aw-cheem tz'vaw shaw-lom oo-m'noo-chaw. Bo - ee, bo - ee ha-
an-gels of peace and of— rest. Draw near, O Queen and

mahl - kaw, Bo - ee, bo - ee, ha - kah -
here a - bide Draw near, draw near, O Sab - bath

law. Shaw - lom ah- lay- chem mahl-ah -chay ha - shaw - lom.
bride. Peace al - so to you, ye an -gels of peace.

.1

הַחַמָּה מֵרֹאשׁ הָאִילָנוֹת נִסְתַּלְּקָה—
בֹּאוּ וְנֵצֵא לִקְרַאת שַׁבָּת הַמַּלְכָּה,
הִנֵּה הִיא יוֹרֶדֶת, הַקְּדוֹשָׁה, הַבְּרוּכָה,
וְעִמָּהּ מַלְאָכִים, צְבָא שָׁלוֹם וּמְנוּחָה.
בֹּאִי בֹּאִי, הַמַּלְכָּה!
בֹּאִי בֹּאִי, הַמַּלְכָּה!—
שָׁלוֹם עֲלֵיכֶם, מַלְאֲכֵי הַשָּׁלוֹם!

.2

קִבַּלְנוּ פְּנֵי שַׁבָּת בִּרְנָנָה וּתְפִלָּה,
הַבַּיְתָה נָשׁוּבָה בְּלֵב מָלֵא גִילָה;
שָׁם עָרוּךְ הַשֻּׁלְחָן, הַנֵּרוֹת יָאִירוּ,
כָּל פִּנּוֹת הַבַּיִת יִזְרָחוּ, יַזְהִירוּ.

שַׁבָּת שָׁלוֹם וּבְרָכָה,
שַׁבָּת שָׁלוֹם וּמְנוּחָה—
בּוֹאֲכֶם לְשָׁלוֹם, מַלְאֲכֵי הַשָּׁלוֹם!

2.

Ki-bahl-noo f'nay Sha-baws, bi-r'naw-naw oo-s'fi-law,
Ha-bai-saw naw-shoo-vaw b'layv maw-lay gee-law;
Shawm aw-rooch hah-shool-chawn, hah-nay-ros yaw-ee-roo,
Kawl pi-nos hah-bah-yis yiz-r'choo, yahz-hee-roo.
Shah-baws shaw-lom oo-v'raw-chaw,
Shah-baws shaw-lom oo-m'noo-chaw —
Bo-ah-chehm l'shaw-lom, mahl-a-chay hah-shaw-lom.

2.

We've welcomed the Sabbath with song and with prayer;
And home we return, our heart's gladness to share.
The table is set and the candles are lit,
The tiniest corner for Sabbath made fit.
O day of blessing, day of rest!
Sweet day of peace be ever blest!
Bring ye also peace, ye angels of peace!

COME, O SABBATH DAY

GUSTAV GOTTHEIL   A. W. BINDER

Come, O Sab - bath day, and — bring
Peace and heal - ing on thy— wing; And to ev - 'ry
troub - led breast Speak of the di - vine be - hest:
Thou — shalt — rest, — Thou shalt rest!

2.

Earthly longings bid retire,
Quench the passions' hurtful fire;
To the wayward, sin oppressed,
Bring Thou Thy divine behest:
Thou shalt rest,
Thou shalt rest!

3.

Wipe from ev'ry cheek the tear,
Banish care and silence fear;
All things working for the best,
Teach us the divine behest:
Thou shalt rest,
Thou shalt rest!

AYN KAYLOHAYNOO

אֵין כֵּאלֹהֵינוּ — THERE IS NONE LIKE OUR GOD

Louis Lewandowski

Andante con moto

1. Ayn   kay-lo - hay - noo,   Ayn   kah-do - nay - noo,
3. No-deh lay-lo - hay - noo,   No-deh lah-do - nay - noo,

Ayn   k'-mahl - kay - noo,   Ayn   k'mo - shee - ay - noo,
No-deh l'-mahl - kay - noo,   No-deh l'mo-shee - ay - noo,

2. Mee   chay-lo - hay - noo,   Mee   cha-do - nay - noo,
4. Baw-rooch Eh-lo - hay - noo,   Baw-rooch A - do - nay - noo, D.C.

Mee   ch'mahl - kay - noo,   Mee ch'mo - shee - ay - noo.
Baw - rooch Mahl - kay - noo,   Baw-rooch Mo-shee - ay - noo.

5. Ah - taw hoo Eh-lo - hay noo, Ah - taw hoo Ah-do - nay - noo, Ah-

taw hoo Mahl -   kay - noo, ah - taw hoo Mo-shee - ay - noo.

אֵין כֵּאלֹהֵינוּ. אֵין כֵּאדוֹנֵינוּ. אֵין כְּמַלְכֵּנוּ. אֵין כְּמוֹשִׁיעֵנוּ:

מִי כֵאלֹהֵינוּ. מִי כַאדוֹנֵינוּ. מִי כְמַלְכֵּנוּ. מִי כְמוֹשִׁיעֵנוּ:

נוֹדֶה לֵאלֹהֵינוּ. נוֹדֶה לַאדוֹנֵינוּ. נוֹדֶה לְמַלְכֵּנוּ. נוֹדֶה לְמוֹשִׁיעֵנוּ:

בָּרוּךְ אֱלֹהֵינוּ. בָּרוּךְ אֲדוֹנֵינוּ. בָּרוּךְ מַלְכֵּנוּ. בָּרוּךְ מוֹשִׁיעֵנוּ:

אַתָּה הוּא אֱלֹהֵינוּ. אַתָּה הוּא אֲדוֹנֵינוּ. אַתָּה הוּא מַלְכֵּנוּ. אַתָּה הוּא מוֹשִׁיעֵנוּ:

אַתָּה הוּא שֶׁהִקְטִירוּ אֲבוֹתֵינוּ לְפָנֶיךָ אֶת קְטֹרֶת הַסַּמִּים:

ADON OLAWM

אֲדוֹן עוֹלָם — LORD OF THE UNIVERSE

The hymn, *Adon Olawm*, which treats of God's existence, sovereignty, and providence, has been attributed to Solomon Ibn Gabirol, who lived in Spain in the eleventh century.

ELIEZER GEROVITCH

Ah - don o - lawm ah - shehr maw-lahch, b'

teh-rehm_kawl y' tseer_niv-raw, l' ays nah-ah-saw v'

chef - tso kol, ah - zai Meh - lech sh' mo nik - raw.

אֲדוֹן עוֹלָם אֲשֶׁר מָלַךְ   בְּטֶרֶם כָּל יְצִיר נִבְרָא:

לְעֵת נַעֲשָׂה בְחֶפְצוֹ כֹּל   אֲזַי מֶלֶךְ שְׁמוֹ נִקְרָא:

וְאַחֲרֵי כִּכְלוֹת הַכֹּל   לְבַדּוֹ יִמְלוֹךְ נוֹרָא:

וְהוּא הָיָה וְהוּא הֹוֶה   וְהוּא יִהְיֶה בְּתִפְאָרָה:

וְהוּא אֶחָד וְאֵין שֵׁנִי   לְהַמְשִׁיל לוֹ לְהַחְבִּירָה:

בְּלִי רֵאשִׁית בְּלִי תַכְלִית   וְלוֹ הָעֹז וְהַמִּשְׂרָה:

וְהוּא אֵלִי וְחַי גּוֹאֲלִי   וְצוּר חֶבְלִי בְּעֵת צָרָה:

וְהוּא נִסִּי וּמָנוֹס לִי   מְנָת כּוֹסִי בְּיוֹם אֶקְרָא:

בְּיָדוֹ אַפְקִיד רוּחִי   בְּעֵת אִישַׁן וְאָעִירָה:

וְעִם רוּחִי גְּוִיָּתִי   יְיָ לִי וְלֹא אִירָא:

Ah-don o-lawm ah-shehr maw-lahch,
B'teh-rehm kawl y'tzeer niv-raw.

L'ays nah-ah-saw, v'chef-tzo kol,
Ah-zai meh-lehch sh'mo nik-raw.

V'ah-cha-ray ki-ch'los hah-kol,
L'vah-do yim-loch no-raw.

V'hoo haw-yaw, v'hoo ho-veh,
V'hoo yih-yeh b'sif-aw-raw.

V'hoo eh-chawd v'ayn shay-nee,
L'hahm-sheel lo l'hahch-bee-raw.

B'lee ray-shees, b'lee sahch-lees,
V'lo haw-oz v'ha-mis-raw.

V'hoo Ay-lee v'chai go-ah-lee,
V'tzoor chehv-lee b'ays tzaw-raw.

V'hoo ni-see oo-maw-nos lee,
M'naws ko-see b'yom ehk-raw.

B'yaw-do ahf-keed roo-chee,
B'ays ee-shahn v'aw-ee-raw.

V'im roo-chee g'vee-yaw-see,
Ado-noy lee, v'lo ee-raw.

יִגְדַּל — YIGDAHL

The hymn, *Yigdahl*, is a summary, in verse, of the Thirteen Principles of Faith formulated by Moses Maimonides in the twelfth century.

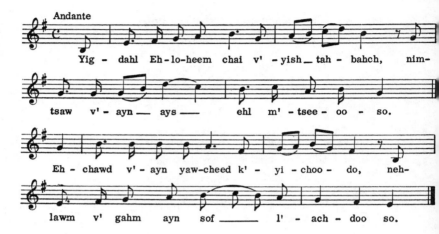

Yig - dahl Eh-lo-heem chai v' - yish—tah - bahch, nim-
tsaw v' - ayn — ays — ehl m' - tsee - oo - so.
Eh - chawd v' - ayn yaw-cheed k' - yi - choo - do, neh-
lawm v' gahm ayn sof — l' - ach - doo so.

נִמְצָא וְאֵין עֵת אֶל מְצִיאוּתוֹ:	יִגְדַּל אֱלֹהִים חַי וְיִשְׁתַּבַּח
נֶעְלָם וְגַם אֵין סוֹף לְאַחְדּוּתוֹ:	אֶחָד וְאֵין יָחִיד כְּיִחוּדוֹ
לֹא נַעֲרוֹךְ אֵלָיו קְדֻשָּׁתוֹ:	אֵין לוֹ דְּמוּת הַגּוּף וְאֵינוֹ גוּף
רִאשׁוֹן וְאֵין רֵאשִׁית לְרֵאשִׁיתוֹ:	קַדְמוֹן לְכָל דָּבָר אֲשֶׁר נִבְרָא
יוֹרֶה גְדֻלָּתוֹ וּמַלְכוּתוֹ:	הִנּוֹ אֲדוֹן עוֹלָם לְכָל נוֹצָר
אֶל אַנְשֵׁי סְגֻלָּתוֹ וְתִפְאַרְתּוֹ:	שֶׁפַע נְבוּאָתוֹ נְתָנוֹ
נָבִיא. וּמַבִּיט אֶת תְּמוּנָתוֹ:	לֹא קָם בְּיִשְׂרָאֵל כְּמֹשֶׁה עוֹד
עַל יַד נְבִיאוֹ נֶאֱמַן בֵּיתוֹ:	תּוֹרַת אֱמֶת נָתַן לְעַמּוֹ אֵל
לְעוֹלָמִים לְזוּלָתוֹ:	לֹא יַחֲלִיף הָאֵל וְלֹא יָמִיר דָּתוֹ
מַבִּיט לְסוֹף דָּבָר בְּקַדְמָתוֹ:	צוֹפֶה וְיוֹדֵעַ סְתָרֵינוּ
נוֹתֵן לְרָשָׁע רַע כְּרִשְׁעָתוֹ:	גּוֹמֵל לְאִישׁ חֶסֶד כְּמִפְעָלוֹ
לִפְדּוֹת מְחַכֵּי קֵץ יְשׁוּעָתוֹ:	יִשְׁלַח לְקֵץ יָמִין מְשִׁיחֵנוּ
בָּרוּךְ עֲדֵי עַד שֵׁם תְּהִלָּתוֹ:	מֵתִים יְחַיֶּה אֵל בְּרֹב חַסְדּוֹ

Yig-dahl Elo-heem chai, v'yis-tah-bahch,
Nim-tzaw v'ayn ays ehl m'tzee-oo-so.

Eh-chawd v'ayn yaw-cheed k'yi-choo-do,
Neh-lawm v'gahm ayn sof l'ach-doo-so.

Ayn lo d'moos ha-goof, v'ay-no goof,
Lo nah-ah-roch ay-lawv k'doo-shaw-so.

Kahd-mon l'chawl daw-vawr ah-shehr niv-raw,
Ri-shon v'ayn ray-shees l'ray-shee-so.

Hi-no ah-don o-lawm l'chawl no-tsawr,
Yo-reh g'doo-law-so, oo-mahl-choo-so.

Sheh-fah n'voo-aw-so, n'saw-no,
Ehl ahn-shay s'goo-law-so v'sif-ahr-to.

Lo kawm b'yis-raw-ayl k'Mo-sheh od
Naw-vee, oo-mah-beet ehs t'moo-naw-so.

To-rahs eh-mehs naw-sahn l'ah-mo Ayl,
Ahl yahd n'vee-o neh-eh-mahn bay-so.

Lo yah-chah-leef haw-Ayl, v'lo yaw-meer daw-so,
L'o-law-meem l'zoo-law-so.

Tzo-feh v'yo-day-ah s'saw-ray-noo,
Mah-beet l'sof daw-vawr b'kahd-maw-so.

Go-mayl l'eesh cheh-sehd k'mif-aw-lo,
No-sayn l'raw-shaw rah k'rish-aw-so.

Yish-lahch l'kaytz yaw-meen m'shee-chay-noo,
Lif-dos m'chah-kay kaytz y'shoo-aw-so.

May-seem y'chah-yeh Ayl, b'rov chahs-do,
Baw-rooch ah-day ahd, shaym t'hi-law-so.

9. *Recitation of Grace or Birkas Hamozon*

The family now recites the grace, thanking God for the blessings of food and plenty. On Sabbath eve, Psalm 126 is sung, as follows:

שִׁיר הַמַּעֲלוֹת.

בְּשׁוּב יְיָ אֶת שִׁיבַת צִיּוֹן, הָיִינוּ כְּחֹלְמִים. אָז יִמָּלֵא שְׂחֹק פִּינוּ,
וּלְשׁוֹנֵנוּ רִנָּה; אָז יֹאמְרוּ בַגּוֹיִם, הִגְדִּיל יְיָ לַעֲשׂוֹת עִם אֵלֶּה. הִגְדִּיל
יְיָ לַעֲשׂוֹת עִמָּנוּ, הָיִינוּ שְׂמֵחִים:

שׁוּבָה יְיָ אֶת שְׁבִיתֵנוּ, כַּאֲפִיקִים בַּנֶּגֶב. הַזֹּרְעִים בְּדִמְעָה, בְּרִנָּה
יִקְצֹרוּ. הָלוֹךְ יֵלֵךְ וּבָכֹה נֹשֵׂא מֶשֶׁךְ הַזָּרַע. בֹּא יָבֹא בְרִנָּה נֹשֵׂא אֲלֻמֹּתָיו:

Sheer ha-ma-ah-los.

B'shoov Ado-noy ehs shee-vahs tzi-yon, haw-yee-noo k'chol-meem. Awz yi-maw-lay s'chok pee-noo, oo-l'sho-nay-noo ri-naw. Awz yo-m'roo va-go-yeem, hig-deel Ado-noy la-ah-sos im ay-leh. Hig-deel Ado-noy la-ah-sos ee-maw-noo, haw-yee-noo s'may-cheem.

Shoo-vaw Ado-noy ehs sh'vee-say-noo, ka-ah-fee-keem ba-neh-gev. Ha-zo-r'eem b'dim-aw, b'ri-naw yik-tzo-roo. Haw-loch yay-laych oo-vaw-cho, no-say meh-shech ha-zaw-rah. Bo yaw-vo v'ri-naw, no-say ah-loo-mo-sawv.

Father: רַבּוֹתַי, נְבָרֵךְ.

Ra-bo-sai, n'vaw-raych.

Family: יְהִי שֵׁם יְיָ מְבֹרָךְ מֵעַתָּה וְעַד עוֹלָם.

Y'hee shaym Ado-noy m'vo-rawch may-ah-taw v'ahd o-lawm.

Father: יְהִי שֵׁם יְיָ מְבֹרָךְ מֵעַתָּה וְעַד עוֹלָם. בִּרְשׁוּת מִשְׁפַּחְתִּי,
נְבָרֵךְ שֶׁאָכַלְנוּ מִשֶּׁלּוֹ.

Y'hee shaym Ado-noy m'vo-rawch may-ah-taw v'ahd
o-lawm. Bi-r'shoos mish-pahch-tee, n'vaw-raych sheh-
aw-chahl-noo mi-sheh-lo.

Family: בָּרוּךְ שֶׁאָכַלְנוּ מִשֶּׁלּוֹ וּבְטוּבוֹ חָיִינוּ:

Baw-rooch sheh-aw-chahl-noo mi-sheh-lo, oo-v'too-vo
chaw-yee-noo.

Father: בָּרוּךְ שֶׁאָכַלְנוּ מִשֶּׁלּוֹ וּבְטוּבוֹ חָיִינוּ:

Baw-rooch sheh-aw-chahl-noo mi-sheh-lo, oo-v'too-vo
chaw-yee-noo.

Father: Let us join in thanking God of whose bounty we have
partaken.

Family: Blessed be our God of whose bounty we have partaken
and through whose goodness we live.

Family:

בָּרוּךְ הוּא וּבָרוּךְ שְׁמוֹ.

בָּרוּךְ אַתָּה יְיָ, אֱלֹהֵינוּ מֶלֶךְ הָעוֹלָם, הַזָּן אֶת הָעוֹלָם כֻּלּוֹ בְּטוּבוֹ,
בְּחֵן בְּחֶסֶד וּבְרַחֲמִים. הוּא נֹתֵן לֶחֶם לְכָל בָּשָׂר, כִּי לְעוֹלָם חַסְדּוֹ.
וּבְטוּבוֹ הַגָּדוֹל תָּמִיד לֹא חָסַר לָנוּ, וְאַל יֶחְסַר לָנוּ מָזוֹן לְעוֹלָם וָעֶד.
בַּעֲבוּר שְׁמוֹ הַגָּדוֹל, כִּי הוּא אֵל זָן וּמְפַרְנֵס לַכֹּל, וּמֵטִיב לַכֹּל, וּמֵכִין
מָזוֹן לְכָל בְּרִיּוֹתָיו אֲשֶׁר בָּרָא.
בָּרוּךְ אַתָּה יְיָ, הַזָּן אֶת הַכֹּל:

Baw-rooch hoo oo-vaw-rooch sh'mo.

Baw-rooch ah-taw Ado-noy, Elo-hay-noo meh-lech haw-o-lawm, ha-zawn ehs haw-o-lawm koo-lo b'too-vo, b'chayn b'cheh-sed oo-v'ra-cha-meem. Hoo no-sayn leh-chem l'chawl baw-sawr, kee l'o-lawm chahs-do. Oo-v'too-vo ha-gaw-dol taw-meed lo chaw-sahr law-noo, v'ahl yech-sahr law-noo maw-zon l'o-lawm vaw-ed. Ba-ah-voor sh'mo ha-gaw-dol, kee hoo Ayl zawn oo-m'far-nays la-kol, oo-may-teev la-kol, oo-may-cheen maw-zon l'chawl b'ri-yo-sawv ah-shehr baw-raw.

Baw-rooch ah-taw Ado-noy, ha-zawn ehs ha-kol.

Blessed art Thou, O Lord our God, King of the universe, who providest food for all. Through Thy goodness food has never failed us. Mayest Thou provide sustenance for all Thy children at all times, for the sake of Thy great Name.

Father:

We thank Thee, O Lord our God, for our liberation from bondage, for the heritage of Eretz Yisroel, for Thy Torah which Thou didst reveal and impart unto us, and for the life of grace and blessing which Thou hast bestowed upon us.

וְעַל הַכֹּל, יְיָ אֱלֹהֵינוּ, אֲנַחְנוּ מוֹדִים לָךְ, וּמְבָרְכִים אוֹתָךְ, יִתְבָּרַךְ
שִׁמְךָ בְּפִי כָּל חַי תָּמִיד לְעוֹלָם וָעֶד. כַּכָּתוּב, וְאָכַלְתָּ וְשָׂבָעְתָּ וּבֵרַכְתָּ
אֶת יְיָ אֱלֹהֶיךָ, עַל הָאָרֶץ הַטּוֹבָה אֲשֶׁר נָתַן לָךְ.
בָּרוּךְ אַתָּה יְיָ, עַל הָאָרֶץ וְעַל הַמָּזוֹן:

V'ahl ha-kol, Ado-noy Elo-hay-noo, ah-nahch-noo mo-deem lawch, oo-m'vawr-cheem o-sawch, yis-baw-rahch shi-m'chaw b'fee kawl chai taw-meed l'o-lawm vaw-ed. Kah-kaw-soov, v'aw-chahl-taw, v'saw-vaw-taw oo-vay-rahch-taw, ehs Ado-noy Elo-heh-chaw, ahl haw-aw-retz ha-to-vaw ah-shehr naw-sahn lawch.

Baw-rooch ah-taw Ado-noy, ahl haw-aw-retz, v'ahl ha-maw-zon.

Have mercy, O Lord our God, upon Israel Thy people, and upon Zion, and hasten the day of peace for all mankind.

וּבְנֵה יְרוּשָׁלַיִם עִיר הַקֹּדֶשׁ בִּמְהֵרָה בְיָמֵינוּ. בָּרוּךְ אַתָּה יְיָ, בֹּנֵה בְרַחֲמָיו יְרוּשָׁלָיִם. אָמֵן:

Oo-v'nay Y'roo-shaw-la-yeem eer ha-ko-desh bi-m'hay-raw v'yaw-may-noo. Baw-rooch ah-taw Ado-noy, bo-neh v'ra-cha-mawv Y'roo-shaw-law-yeem, Aw-mayn.

Family:

בָּרוּךְ אַתָּה יְיָ, אֱלֹהֵינוּ מֶלֶךְ הָעוֹלָם, הָאֵל אָבִינוּ, מַלְכֵּנוּ, אַדִּירֵנוּ, בּוֹרְאֵנוּ, גּוֹאֲלֵנוּ, יוֹצְרֵנוּ, קְדוֹשֵׁנוּ, קְדוֹשׁ יַעֲקֹב, רוֹעֵנוּ, רוֹעֵה יִשְׂרָאֵל, הַמֶּלֶךְ הַטּוֹב וְהַמֵּטִיב לַכֹּל, שֶׁבְּכָל יוֹם וָיוֹם הוּא הֵטִיב, הוּא מֵטִיב, הוּא יֵיטִיב לָנוּ. הוּא גְמָלָנוּ, הוּא גוֹמְלֵנוּ, הוּא יִגְמְלֵנוּ לָעַד, לְחֵן וּלְחֶסֶד וּלְרַחֲמִים וּלְרֶוַח, הַצָּלָה וְהַצְלָחָה, בְּרָכָה וִישׁוּעָה, נֶחָמָה, פַּרְנָסָה וְכַלְכָּלָה, וְרַחֲמִים וְחַיִּים וְשָׁלוֹם, וְכָל טוֹב, וּמִכָּל טוֹב לְעוֹלָם אַל יְחַסְּרֵנוּ:

Baw-rooch ah-taw Ado-noy, Elo-hay-noo meh-lech haw-o-lawm, haw-ayl aw-vee-noo, mahl-kay-noo, ah-dee-ray-noo, bo-r'ay-noo, go-ah-lay-noo, yo-tz'ray-noo, k'do-shay-noo, k'dosh Ya-ah-kov, ro-ay-noo, ro-ay Yis-raw-ayl, ha-meh-lech ha-tov v'ha-may-teev la-kol, sheh-b'chawl yom vaw-yom hoo hay-teev, hoo may-teev, hoo yay-teev law-noo, hoo g'maw-law-noo, hoo go-m'lay-noo, hoo yig-m'lay-noo law-ahd, l'chayn oo-l'cheh-sed oo-l'ra-cha-meem oo-l'reh-vahch, ha-tzaw-law v'hahtz-law-chaw, b'raw-chaw vee-shoo-aw, neh-chaw-maw, pahr-naw-saw v'chal-kaw-law, v'ra-cha-meem v'cha-yeem v'shaw-lom, v'chawl tov, oo-mi-kawl tov l'o-lawm ahl y'chah-s'raynoo.

Blessed art Thou, O Lord our God, King of the universe. Thou art our God who showerest kindnesses upon all Thy creatures. Every day dost Thou grant unto us the blessings of Thy hand. Thou art kind and dost deal kindly with us. Thou hast bestowed upon us Thy blessings, yielding us lovingkindness, grace, sustenance and support, mercy, life and peace. We pray Thee, withhold not Thy blessings from us.

Father: May God sustain us in health.

Family: Amen.

Father: May God bless all assembled at this table.

Family: Amen.

Father: May God send plentiful blessings upon this house, and all who are near and dear to us.

Family: Amen.

Father: הָרַחֲמָן, הוּא יַנְחִילֵנוּ יוֹם שֶׁכֻּלּוֹ שַׁבָּת וּמְנוּחָה לְחַיֵּי הָעוֹלָמִים:

Family: אָמֵן: — Amen

Father: May this Sabbath eve bring its message of rest and peace to us.

Family: Amen.

(*On the New Moon*)

Father: הָרַחֲמָן, הוּא יְחַדֵּשׁ עָלֵינוּ אֶת הַחֹדֶשׁ הַזֶּה לְטוֹבָה וְלִבְרָכָה:

Family: אָמֵן: — Amen

Father: May God grant us only good and blessing this coming month.

Family: Amen.

(*On Chanukah*)

Father: On this festival of Chanukah, we thank Thee, O Lord our God, for the miracle of liberation wrought for our fathers in the days of Mattathias, the high priest, and his sons.

Family: Amen.

Family:

מִגְדּוֹל יְשׁוּעוֹת מַלְכּוֹ וְעֹשֶׂה חֶסֶד לִמְשִׁיחוֹ, לְדָוִד וּלְזַרְעוֹ עַד עוֹלָם. עֹשֶׂה שָׁלוֹם בִּמְרוֹמָיו, הוּא יַעֲשֶׂה שָׁלוֹם, עָלֵינוּ וְעַל כָּל יִשְׂרָאֵל, וְאִמְרוּ, אָמֵן:

Mig-dol y'shoo-os mahl-ko, v'o-seh cheh-sed li-m'shee-cho, l'Daw-vid oo-l'zahr-o ahd o-lawm. O-seh shaw-lom bi-m'ro-mawv, hoo ya-ah-seh shaw-lom, aw-lay-noo v'ahl kawl Yis-raw-ayl, v'i-m'roo, aw-mayn.

May He who creates peace in His celestial heights, grant peace and contentment to us, to all Israel, and to all mankind. Amen.

THE SPECIAL FIREFLY

By Edith B. Goldman

It wiggled and it pushed and it wriggled and it shook. It huffed and it puffed, it spread out, and it stood. "Why, why, I'm here. I'm out, after waiting so long in my cocoon. I'm no longer a grub;

I'm a firefly. A light-up and light-out, dance-about firefly. I can spread my wings and fly, and I feel *very* special. Not just because this is my first birthday; it is a *very very* special feeling. I'll have to do some exploring around, now that I can get about on wing, and find out why I feel so special.

Oh! they work, my wings, they flitter-flutter so easily. I can fly as high as the shrubs. I'm as high as the branches. I'm as high as the treetops. It's a wonderful world, and I feel so special. I must find out why!

"Well, hello there! You're a firefly, too! This is my first day, and I'm just getting acquainted with everything. It's very exciting to look at the flowers, the trees, the farms, and the roof tops. And I feel very special."

"Well, I guess you do," said the other firefly with a chuckle. "You're just an infant and have much to see. Look about and find the other fireflies. Have you lit up yet?"

"No," said the new firefly. "I'm waiting for dusk, then I'll shine. Oh! I feel so special." And away he flew. He lighted on a corral fence and watched a farmer milk a cow. Then he flew about till he came to a small schoolhouse and zoomed down to buzz about the children at play in the yard. Oh, the fun of flying about and exploring. He flew till he came to a small group of homes. He perched on a branch, where he heard two children's voices coming through the window. He flew to a lower branch so he could look into the house.

"Let's surprise Mom, 'cause it's Friday and get everything ready for the Sabbath. When she comes home she'll be pleased as Punch to see we are being so helpful," said Robert.

"Oh! good!" said Pam. "We'll be so grown up. I'll get the

things that won't break. You can get those other things because you're bigger. I'll get the pretty white cloth and the silver goblets for the wine, and napkins, and silver, forks and knives and spoons. You get the china and stemware. We'll also need two Challahs and the pretty Challah cover. I'm glad now that we made our own in Sunday School. And we'll need candlesticks and candles."

"That's fair enough," said Robert, and they both set about their tasks.

Little firefly was interested. "Such busy little children. What can this Sabbath be?" he said to himself. "It must be something special, too, if their Mom will be pleased as they expect. I'll just watch."

By this time the children were arranging everything on the table.

"It is lovely, isn't it Rob?" said Pam. "Sabbath dinner is the best. Everything is so pretty. Let's go and cut flowers for the table. Mom likes roses best of all." They scampered out to the yard.

Little firefly watched while Rob cut and Pam carried the flowers. They took three white roses, three tea roses, a few miniature yellow roses and some bright green leaves.

"Quick, let's see how they look on the table. We'll arrange them together." Rob surveyed the table when it was all finished. "Pretty neat," he said and winked at Pam. "I can hardly wait for Mom to come home and see it. All we need now are the matches to light the candles."

Little firefly had been admiring how pretty the table looked. He perked up his ears at the word LIGHT and began to dance about, "I know now why I feel sooooooo special. I want to help for the Sabbath, too."

"I have a light," he called. "I have a light," he called again.

But the children didn't hear the teeny voice. They were busily looking in cabinets and drawers.

"I don't think we have any matches," said Rob. Pam looked disappointed. "I want it to be perfect," she said. "Dad will probably have some," said Rob, walking to the window screen to see what it was that sounded like a miniature battle.

All this time, little firefly had been trying almost in a frenzy to attract their attention. Rob saw the firefly through the screen and called to Pam. "Come and see who's calling on us. As soon as dusk comes, he'll light up with the other fireflies."

At hearing this, little firefly couldn't contain himself. "Listen to me, listen," he chirped, "I want to help for the Sabbath too. I can help light your candles. I've had a very special feeling ever since I was born this morning. I think it's because I'll light for a very special reason."

Pam looked with wonder from the astonished Robert to the impish firefly. "Can he? Can he really?"

"I don't know," said Rob, "but if we wanted to surprise Mom, this is it."

"Little firefly," said Pam, "if Daddy doesn't bring matches home, you'll have your chance." And little firefly danced merrily about, happy because the children had heard him and would let him help light the Sabbath candles.

The other fireflies had gathered about in awe. "I guess he is a special firefly," said one to another. An older firefly flew to where little firefly was buzzing around a flower and asked, "How can we be special, too?"

"Well," said little firefly, "You'll have to light for a special reason. I am a Sabbath firefly and I'll light only when the Sabbath comes at dusk on Friday and when the Sabbath goes out at night on Saturday. Then I'll light at the Havdalah candle lighting time. But if the children's daddy brings home matches, then I'll lead the parade. We'll all light up and fly about in shining formation:

When mother came home she was even more delighted than they had anticipated. A smile spread over her face as she looked at the lovely table. And when she saw her two delighted children, she stooped to hug them in turn and laughed, "My, but you're both growing up." Then she said more seriously, "It's a beautiful surprise. It makes me very happy that you wanted to help our being together for Sabbath dinner."

Pam couldn't wait any longer and blurted out about the matches and the little firefly. They walked to the window and saw a group of fireflies buzzing about a shrub.

It seemed they were flying in formation. Why, yes, it looked like:

One little firefly said to the leader, "How can I be a Sabbath firefly, too, and be a leader?"

"Well," said the special firefly, "you have to find a home where little Jewish children live and where they are getting ready for the Sabbath. Then, at dusk on Friday and Saturday, you lead your parade of flickering fireflies, singing:

> Sabbath candles, flicker brightly,
> Show us how to dance so lightly,
> Teach us how to shine so brightly,
> For a HAPPY SABBATH."

And that's how little Sabbath firefly learned he was sooooooooo special.

The Sabbath Lunch

To retain the Sabbath spirit of Friday eve, the Sabbath lunch is preceded by a brief ceremony which includes a shortened version of the Kiddush, the Hamotzee, and the Grace.

1. Kiddush (Blessing of the Wine)

עַל כֵּן בֵּרַךְ יְיָ אֶת יוֹם הַשַּׁבָּת וַיְקַדְּשֵׁהוּ:

בָּרוּךְ אַתָּה יְיָ, אֱלֹהֵינוּ מֶלֶךְ הָעוֹלָם, בּוֹרֵא פְּרִי הַגָּפֶן:

Ahl kayn bay-rahch Ado-noy ehs yom ha-sha-baws, va-y'kad'shay-hoo:

Baw-rooch ah-taw Ado-noy, Elo-hay-noo meh-lech haw-o-lawm, bo-ray p'ree ha-gaw-fen.

God blessed the Sabbath day and made it holy. Blessed art Thou, O Lord our God, King of the universe, who createst the fruit of the vine.

2. Hamotzee (Breaking of Bread)

בָּרוּךְ אַתָּה יְיָ, אֱלֹהֵינוּ מֶלֶךְ הָעוֹלָם, הַמּוֹצִיא לֶחֶם מִן הָאָרֶץ:

Baw-rooch ah-taw Ado-noy, Elo-hay-noo meh-lech haw-o-lawm, ha-mo-tzee leh-chem min haw-aw-retz.

Blessed art Thou, O Lord our God, King of the universe, who bringest forth bread from the earth.

3. Lunch

4. Sabbath songs

5. Grace

THE SABBATH AFTERNOON PARTY

Oneg Shabbat, a term which has gained popularity in recent years, means literally Delight of the Sabbath, and refers to a social gathering on the day. The afternoon of the Sabbath is usually a good time for a children's party, and suggestions for such an affair are offered here:

Prepare a week or so before the party date by sending out invitations indicative of the Sabbath. Candlesticks or Kiddush cups can be the shape of the cut-out invitations. On them such words as "Enjoy Sabbath joy at my home on _____ at _____" or "Kiddush at my home on _____ at _____" may be printed or typed.

The Sabbath Table

The party table should simulate the Sabbath dinner table as much as possible, with candlesticks, Kiddush cups, wine (or grape juice), individual miniature Challahs covered with little napkins.

Favors for the Children

You remember the legendary portrayal of the home on the Sabbath which pictures the father as a king, mother a queen, and the children princes and princesses. The favors for the party should include king crowns for the boys, queen crowns for the girls, while some children can wear crowns of princes and princesses.

Delicacies

The refreshments ought to include cookies made by cutters showing Jewish symbols. If such cookie cutters are not available, you can take regular cookies and frost them with Jewish symbols such as a Kiddush cup, or candlestick, or the Hebrew word for Sabbath, שַׁבָּת.

Kiddush and Hamotzee

This being the Sabbath, your Oneg Shabbat party should begin with the Kiddush and the Hamotzee. Here is a wonderful opportunity to teach the children the elementary blessings of the Sabbath.

Games for the Sabbath

The games may be similar to those played at any party, with Sabbath terminology and theme added. For example:

a) Singing Sabbath Chairs

While one or two children sing a Sabbath song, the children march around chairs lined in two rows, back to back, with one chair less than the number of children playing. When the singer stops, the child who does not have a chair is out of the game. Another chair is then removed, and singing is resumed. This continues until there is only one child left. He is declared the winner.

b) *Story of Creation*

This game is educational as well as entertaining. Have one of the older children or an adult tell the story of creation. Then, have the children try to guess what day a certain thing was created. For example: adult says "fish," and the correct answer is "sixth day." or "man," and the correct answer is, again, "sixth day."

Sabbath Songs

A few of the more simple Sabbath songs (pages 322, 330, 332), in addition to children's favorites, can be sung.

SATURDAY NIGHT AND HAVDALAH

Over twenty-four hours ago, we kindled the Sabbath lights as the day mellowed into night, and now, one day later, we escort the Sabbath from our homes, confident that it has been the sign of God's presence in our homes and in our hearts. We usher the Sabbath out in a ceremony called Havdalah which means separation or division, until its reappearance six days later. The Sabbath is thus separated from the other working days of the week.

When we see three stars in the darkened sky, we take up the symbols used in this ceremony. They are:

a) *Cup of Wine*

The wine cup is filled to overflowing, to express our hopes for a week brimful of divine blessings.

b) *Havdalah Candle*

A candle, specially woven or braided, usually of two colors, suggesting a flame or torch and symbolizing light and guidance on our paths of life.

c) *Spice Box*

B'saw-meem is the Hebrew word meaning spices. On Saturday night we partake of sweet smelling spices, hoping to sweeten the days of the coming week. The Havdalah candle and spice box can be secured from your synagogue gift shop.

THE CEREMONY

Your children can share in the ceremony by holding the candle and the spice box.

After nightfall, father recites the Havdalah:

a) *Take cup in right hand and recite:*

הִנֵּה אֵל יְשׁוּעָתִי אֶבְטַח וְלֹא אֶפְחָד, כִּי עָזִּי וְזִמְרָת יָהּ יְיָ וַיְהִי לִי
לִישׁוּעָה; וּשְׁאַבְתֶּם מַיִם בְּשָׂשׂוֹן מִמַּעַיְנֵי הַיְשׁוּעָה. לַיְיָ הַיְשׁוּעָה עַל
עַמְּךָ בִרְכָתֶךָ סֶּלָה. יְיָ צְבָאוֹת עִמָּנוּ מִשְׂגָּב לָנוּ אֱלֹהֵי יַעֲקֹב סֶלָה.
לַיְהוּדִים הָיְתָה אוֹרָה וְשִׂמְחָה וְשָׂשׂוֹן וִיקָר. כֵּן תִּהְיֶה לָּנוּ. כּוֹס יְשׁוּעוֹת
אֶשָּׂא וּבְשֵׁם יְיָ אֶקְרָא:

בָּרוּךְ אַתָּה יְיָ, אֱלֹהֵינוּ מֶלֶךְ הָעוֹלָם, בּוֹרֵא פְּרִי הַגָּפֶן:

Hi-nay Ayl y'shoo-aw-see ehv-tahch, v'lo ehf-chawd,

Kee aw-zee v'zim-raws yaw, Ado-noy, va-y'hee lee lee-shoo-aw.

Oo-sh'ahv-tem ma-yeem b'saw-son mi-ma-ah-y'nay ha-y'shoo-aw.

La-do-noy ha-y'shoo-aw ahl ah-m'chaw bir-chaw-seh-chaw, seh-law.

Ado-noy tz'vaw-os ee-maw-noo mis-gahv law-noo Elo-hay
Ya-ah-kov, seh-law.

La-y'hoo-deem haw-y'saw o-raw v'sim-chaw, v'saw-son vee-
kawr;

Kayn tih-yeh law-noo, kos y'shoo-os eh-saw, oo-v'shaym
Ado-noy ehk-raw.

Baw-rooch ah-taw Ado-noy, Elo-hay-noo meh-lech haw-o-
lawm, bo-ray p'ree ha-gaw-fen.

Heavenly Father:

As the Sabbath begins to depart, we pray Thee that its spirit
of rest and joy abide with us during the coming week. Blessed art
Thou, O Lord our God, King of the universe, who createst the
fruit of the vine.

b) *Take the spice box and say:*

בָּרוּךְ אַתָּה יְיָ, אֱלֹהֵינוּ מֶלֶךְ הָעוֹלָם, בּוֹרֵא מִינֵי בְשָׂמִים:

Baw-rooch ah-taw Ado-noy, Elo-hay-noo meh-lech haw-o-
lawm, bo-ray mee-nay v'saw-meem.

Blessed art Thou, O Lord our God, King of the universe, who
createst many kinds of fragrant spices.

(Enjoy the fragrance of the spices in the box)

c) *Spread hands toward light and say:*

בָּרוּךְ אַתָּה יְיָ, אֱלֹהֵינוּ מֶלֶךְ הָעוֹלָם, בּוֹרֵא מְאוֹרֵי הָאֵשׁ:

Baw-rooch ah-taw Ado-noy, Elo-hay-noo meh-lech haw-o-
lawm, bo-ray m'o-ray haw-aysh.

Blessed art Thou, O Lord our God, King of the universe, who
createst the light of the fire.

d) *Take cup again, and read the following blessings:*

בָּרוּךְ אַתָּה יְיָ, אֱלֹהֵינוּ מֶלֶךְ הָעוֹלָם. הַמַּבְדִּיל בֵּין קֹדֶשׁ לְחוֹל,
בֵּין אוֹר לְחְשֶׁךְ, בֵּין יִשְׂרָאֵל לָעַמִּים, בֵּין יוֹם הַשְּׁבִיעִי לְשֵׁשֶׁת יְמֵי
הַמַּעֲשֶׂה. בָּרוּךְ אַתָּה יְיָ, הַמַּבְדִּיל בֵּין קֹדֶשׁ לְחוֹל:

Baw-rooch ah-taw Ado-noy, Elo-hay-noo meh-lech haw-o-
lawm, ha-mahv-deel bayn ko-desh l'chol, bayn or l'cho-shech,
bayn Yis-raw-ayl law-ah-meem, bayn yom ha-sh'vee-ee l'shay-
shehs y'may ha-ma-ah-seh. Baw-rooch ah-taw Ado-noy, ha-mahv-
deel bayn ko-desh l'chol.

We thank Thee, O God, for the distinction Thou hast made
between the Sabbath day and the ordinary days of the week, so
that we may rest and enjoy the spirit of Thy Torah. We pray
Thee, may the Sabbath spirit stay with us every day of the week
ahead. May the work of our hands be blessed, and may we again,
together, be privileged to welcome the joy of the Sabbath. Amen

(*Now drink the cup of wine*)

e) *Sing the following melody:*

You will note that the melody is followed by the refrain Shaw-
vooah Tov, which means, Good Week, a good week to you.

HAMAHVDEEL
הַמַּבְדִּיל — HE WHO SEPARATES

Ha-mahv-deel bayn ko - desh bayn ko - desh l'
chol, Cha-to - say - noo hoo yim - chol, Zahr - ay - noo v'-chahs-
pay -noo yar-beh ka - chol V' cha-ko-chaw - veem bah-loy -
law— shaw - voo-ah tov, shaw-voo - ah tov, shaw - voo - ah
tov, shaw - voo - ah tov, shaw - voo - ah tov, shaw-voo - ah
tov, shaw - voo - ah tov, shaw - voo - ah tov.

May He who separates the Sabbath from the week days, bless us with prosperity, health, and good children.

הַמַּבְדִּיל בֵּין קֹדֶשׁ לְחוֹל,
חַטֹּאתֵינוּ הוּא יִמְחוֹל,
זַרְעֵנוּ וְכַסְפֵּנוּ יַרְבֶּה כַּחוֹל
וְכַכּוֹכָבִים בַּלַּיְלָה.
שָׁבוּעַ טוֹב ...

2.

Yom paw-naw ch'tzayl to-mehr,
Ehk-raw law-Ayl aw-lai go-mayr,
Aw-mahr sho-mayr, aw-saw vo-kehr,
Aw-saw vo-kehr, v'gahm loy-law,
Shaw-voo-ah tov ...

יוֹם פָּנָה כְּצֵל תֹּמֶר,
אֶקְרָא לָאֵל עָלַי גֹּמֵר.
אָמַר שׁוֹמֵר אָתָא בֹקֶר,
אָתָא בֹקֶר וְגַם לָיְלָה.
שָׁבוּעַ טוֹב ...

f) Sing "Ayleeyawhoo Hanawvee" together:

AYLEEYAWHOO HANAWVEE

אֵלִיָּהוּ הַנָּבִיא,
אֵלִיָּהוּ הַתִּשְׁבִּי,
אֵלִיָּהוּ, אֵלִיָּהוּ,
אֵלִיָּהוּ הַגִּלְעָדִי.

בִּמְהֵרָה בְיָמֵינוּ,
יָבֹא אֵלֵינוּ,
עִם מָשִׁיחַ בֶּן דָּוִד,
עִם מָשִׁיחַ בֶּן דָּוִד.

g) *Concluding Prayer*

O God, as the Sabbath Day leaves us, may the spirit of delight which we have enjoyed, remain with us during the week ahead. May the rest we have gained imbue us with strength to meet the challenges of the week. May love for each other, in family union and sanctity, abide with us always. Amen.

A Good Week to all.

Other Feasts and Fasts

BRIEFLY NOTED

There are other days in the year regarded as semi-holidays, and a number of fast days. These feasts and fasts are here briefly noted:

Rosh Chodesh or New Moon

The Jewish calendar follows the lunar system. All the holidays are reckoned by the revolution of the moon. However, in order to harmonize with the solar system in use throughout the world, we add an extra month to the calendar, seven times in nineteen years. This month is added immediately preceding the month of Nisan, usually in late March or April. Thus, our calendar is called lunisolar.

The coming of the new month is announced in the synagogue on the previous Sabbath through a special blessing. Birkas Hachodesh is the name of this service, or Blessing of the New Moon. The Hallel, reserved for all holidays, is included in the service of Rosh Chodesh, and there is a special Torah reading.

Where Rosh Chodesh is observed for two days, depending upon whether the month consists of twenty-nine or thirty days, the first is always the last day of the passing month, and the second is the first day of the new month.

Hoshana Rabba

The name of this holiday means "The Great Hosannah," so named because the prayers begin with the words *Ho-shah Naw,*

Save, we pray Thee. Observed on the seventh day of Sukkos, it is reminiscent of the last celebration of Sukkos in the Temple of old and is traditionally observed by seven processions around the pulpit with esrog and lulov, and willow branches called "Hoshanos."

Tishah B'Av

The words Tishah B'Av mean the ninth day in the month of Av, usually in August but sometimes in late July. It is the day of national mourning over the destruction of the First Temple in 586 B. C. E., the Second Temple, 70 C. E., the fall of Bethar, 135 C. E., and many other catastrophes in Jewish history.

As a fast day, it is similar to Yom Kippur. That is, Yom Kippur and Tishah B'Av are the two fast days which begin on the eve before and extend through the day. The others, to be noted below, begin in the morning and end in the evening.

Tishah B'Av marks the end of a period known as the Three Weeks, which begins with Shivah Asar B'Tammuz, the seventeenth day of the month of Tammuz, the month which precedes the month of Av. It also marks the end of the nine days of the month, popularly known as the *Nine Tehg — Nine Days*, and considered the more intensive mourning period of the Three Weeks.

Shivah Asar B'Tammuz

This fast day also bears the name of the day and month when it is observed. It commemorates the day on which the Babylonians, during First Temple days, broke through the fortifications of Jerusalem's wall. Three weeks later, on Tishah B'Av, the Temple was destroyed; hence the three week period of mourning. Weddings are customarily not performed during this time.

Two other fast days are related to this event. Asarah B'Tevet or the tenth of Tevet (fourth month from Tishri), is the day when Nebuchadnezzar began the siege of Jerusalem. Tzom Gedaliah or Fast of Gedaliah, which is observed on the third of Tishri, the day after Rosh Hashanah, commemorates the assassination of Gedaliah, governor of Jerusalem during the siege.

Taanit Esther

The day before Purim is known as Taanit Esther, Fast of Esther. You will recall that in the Esther story, the queen asked all the Jews of Persia and Media to pray and fast while she went to speak to the king about Haman's plot. In memory of this event, the fast was instituted.

When Purim does not occur on a Sunday, this fastday is always observed on the day before it; however, if Purim falls on a Sunday, the fastday is observed on the preceding Thursday.

Yom Ha-Atzmaut

Israel Independence Day. On the 29th of November 1947, the United Nations General Assembly passed a resolution calling for the founding of a Jewish State in Palestine and on Friday, the 5th of Iyar, 5708, May 14, 1948, the Provisional Council "on the soil of the homeland, in the city of Tel Aviv, on this Sabbath Eve," declared the establishment of a Jewish State to be known as Israel.

On October 28, 1948, the Provisional Government adopted the blue and white colors with the Shield of David as the flag of Israel and the flag was first unfurled on May 11, 1949, at Lake Success in New York, when Israel became the 59th member of the United Nations.

The 5th of Iyar has become a recognized holiday in the Jewish calendar. Special services are conducted in synagogues and special prayers, including the Hallel psalms which are reserved for festivals, are recited.

While the day occurs in the Sephira period (between Pesach and Shovuos), during which weddings are not generally celebrated, the 5th of Iyar has been acknowledged as equal in significance to

Lag Bo-Omer and Rosh Chodesh (New Moon Days) and weddings are now being performed.

Home ceremonies include a festive dinner, blessing of candles, Kiddush with Israeli wine, and a cake decorated with the symbols of the State of Israel (Magen David, Menorah, Israeli flag). Literature may be obtained at the Department of Education and Culture of the Jewish Agency, 515 Park Avenue, New York, New York. 10022

Your Home Consecration Ceremony

Affixing A Mezuzah to Your Door

A Mezuzah (literally, doorpost) placed on the door of a house symbolizes that it is a Jewish home consecrated to God, and carries with it the implicit prayer that the spirit of Godliness permeate the home and the hearts of all who reside in it.

Contained on the parchment scroll is the inscription, done in Torah script by hand, of two paragraphs from the Bible. Both are part of the Sh'ma and are found in the last book of the Bible, Deuteronomy 6:4–9 and 11:13–21. You will remember it by the beginning of the paragraph "Hear, O Israel: the Lord our God, the Lord is One. And thou shalt love the Lord thy God with all thy heart, with all thy soul, and with all thy might." Both paragraphs include the words, "And thou shalt write them upon the doorposts of thy house and upon thy gates."

On the back of the parchment scroll, as well as on the front of the container, be it metal or wood, the word Shaddai, Almighty, appears. In some Mezuzahs this word or the Hebrew letter "ש" — "SH" is visible through a small opening.

The ceremony of consecrating the home or affixing the Mezuzah is a family event and should be conducted with all present. Dinner time is an excellent hour.

The Ceremony

1. *The family stands together at the entrance of the home as father and mother read together:*

אֱלֹהֵינוּ וֵאלֹהֵי אֲבוֹתֵינוּ

Elo-hay-noo vay-lo-hay avo-say-noo.

Our God and God of our fathers.

Thou who hast joined us together in family union, we turn to Thee at this hour of our joy as we consecrate our home. Thou hast guided us throughout life, blessed us with dear ones, and richly sent happiness our way. We sanctify this home unto our family and pray Thee for continued guidance, that love and peace and kindness abide here always, and that contentment and mutual confidence be our portion. As we affix the Mezuzah to our door, we pray Thee, may its meaning sink into our hearts and bind us ever closer unto Thee and unto those whom we love. Guard our going out and our coming in unto life and health from this time forth and forevermore. Amen.

2. *Children recite the following prayer:*

O Lord our God, we turn in prayer unto Thee on behalf of our home, our parents, and all who live here. Be pleased, O God, to bless this house, and sanctify it by Thy love. Bless our parents and give them the strength and health to shelter us in the beauty of home and family, and let sweetness and love and trust always be with us. Amen.

3. *Mother places Mezuzah on right doorpost (right of entrance) about two thirds of the way up, the top slanted toward the house, and father recites the following blessings:*

בָּרוּךְ אַתָּה יְיָ, אֱלֹהֵינוּ מֶלֶךְ הָעוֹלָם, אֲשֶׁר קִדְּשָׁנוּ בְּמִצְוֹתָיו, וְצִוָּנוּ לִקְבּוֹעַ מְזוּזָה:

בָּרוּךְ אַתָּה יְיָ, אֱלֹהֵינוּ מֶלֶךְ הָעוֹלָם, שֶׁהֶחֱיָנוּ, וְקִיְּמָנוּ, וְהִגִּיעָנוּ לַזְּמַן הַזֶּה:

Baw-rooch ah-taw Ado-noy, Elo-hay-noo meh-lech haw-o-lawm, ah-shehr ki-d'shaw-noo b'mitz-vo-sawv v'tzi-vaw-noo, lik-bo-ah m'zoo-zaw.

Baw-rooch ah-taw Ado-noy, Elo-hay-noo meh-lech haw-o-lawm, sheh-heh-cheh-yaw-noo, v'ki-y'maw-noo, v'hi-gee-aw-noo, la-z'mahn ha-zeh.

Blessed art Thou, O Lord our God, King of the universe, who hast sanctified us by Thy commandments and granted us the privilege of placing the Mezuzah on the doorposts of our home.

Blessed art Thou, O Lord our God, King of the universe, who hast granted us life, sustained us, and brought us to this happy day.

4. Father then nails the Mezuzah to the door and all the family express their affection and joy.

5. At the dinner table, begin with the blessing over wine:

בָּרוּךְ אַתָּה יְיָ, אֱלֹהֵינוּ מֶלֶךְ הָעוֹלָם, בּוֹרֵא פְּרִי הַגָּפֶן:

Baw-rooch ah-taw Ado-noy, Elo-hay-noo meh-lech haw-o-lawm, bo-ray p'ree ha-gaw-fen.

Blessed art Thou, O Lord our God, King of the universe, who createst the fruit of the vine.

This is followed by wishing each other "L'chah-yim — For life," after which a festive dinner is served.

6. Here is a melody the children can sing in honor of the occasion:

OUR MEZUZAH

Sara C. Levy   Beatrice L. Deutsch

We have a tin me - zuz - ah, it has a sec - ret slide. I op - ened it and there I found a tin - y scroll in - side.

Prayers for Your Children

EVENING PRAYERS

For the younger children as they go to bed, the following are a few suggested prayers:

I

Sh'ma Yis-raw-ayl, Ado-noy Elo-hay-noo, Ado-noy Eh-chawd.

Hear, O Israel: the Lord our God, the Lord is One.

Thank you for the world so sweet;
Thank you for the food we eat;
Thank you for the birds that sing,
Thank you, God, for everything.

II

Baw-rooch ah-taw Ado-noy, Elo-hay-noo meh-lech haw-o-lawm, ha-ma-peel chev-lay shay-naw ahl ay-noy, oo-s'noo-maw ahl ahf-ah-poy.

Heavenly Father, for this day
And Thy kind, protecting care,
For the joy of work and play,
Before I sleep, accept my prayer.

Thou who givest me slumber sweet
Close mine eyelids till the morn.
May I wake the dawn to greet,
Full of strength and cheer new-born.

Bless my parents kind and dear;
Keep my loved ones in Thy care;
To all lonely hearts be near;
Bless Thy children everywhere.

Sh'ma Yis-raw-ayl, Ado-noy Elo-hay-noo, Ado-noy Eh-chawd.

Hear, O Israel: the Lord our God, the Lord is One.

And you shall love the Lord your God with all your heart, with all your soul, and with all your might.   Amen.

III

We thank You, God, for food and drink,
We thank You, God, for the power to think.
We thank You, God, for each happy day,
We thank You, God, for long hours of play.
We thank You, God, for bright butterflies,
We thank You, God, for our two eyes.
We thank You, God, for the birds that sing,
We thank You, God, for just everything.

Sh'ma Yis-raw-ayl, Ado-noy Elo-hay-noo, Ado-noy Eh-chawd.

Hear, O Israel: the Lord our God, the Lord is One.

IV

Elohai, my God:

Now that the day is over and the quiet night has come, I ask Thee once more to bless me before I sleep. Forgive me if I have done anything wrong during the day and help me to be better tomorrow.

Take care of my parents and all whom I love. Watch over us while we sleep that we may wake again in the light of Thy love.

Sh'ma Yis-raw-ayl, Ado-noy Elo-hay-noo, Ado-noy Eh-chawd.

Hear, O Israel: the Lord our God, the Lord is One.

And you shall love the Lord your God with all your heart, with all your soul, and with all your might. Amen.

V

For older children, the previous prayer can be used, and the complete first paragraph of the Sh'ma added:

שְׁמַע יִשְׂרָאֵל, יְיָ אֱלֹהֵינוּ, יְיָ אֶחָד:

בָּרוּךְ שֵׁם כְּבוֹד מַלְכוּתוֹ לְעוֹלָם וָעֶד:

וְאָהַבְתָּ אֵת יְיָ אֱלֹהֶיךָ, בְּכָל לְבָבְךָ, וּבְכָל נַפְשְׁךָ, וּבְכָל מְאֹדֶךָ. וְהָיוּ הַדְּבָרִים הָאֵלֶּה, אֲשֶׁר אָנֹכִי מְצַוְּךָ הַיּוֹם עַל לְבָבֶךָ. וְשִׁנַּנְתָּם לְבָנֶיךָ, וְדִבַּרְתָּ בָּם, בְּשִׁבְתְּךָ בְּבֵיתֶךָ, וּבְלֶכְתְּךָ בַדֶּרֶךְ, וּבְשָׁכְבְּךָ וּבְקוּמֶךָ, וּקְשַׁרְתָּם לְאוֹת עַל יָדֶךָ, וְהָיוּ לְטֹטָפֹת בֵּין עֵינֶיךָ. וּכְתַבְתָּם עַל מְזֻזוֹת בֵּיתֶךָ וּבִשְׁעָרֶיךָ.

Hear, O Israel: the Lord our God, the Lord is One.

Blessed be His glorious kingdom for ever and ever.

And thou shalt love the Lord thy God with all thy heart, and with all thy soul, and with all thy might. And these words, which I command thee this day, shall be in thy heart; and thou shalt teach them diligently unto thy children, and shalt talk of them when thou sittest in thy house, and when thou walkest by the way, and when thou liest down, and when thou risest up. And thou shalt bind them for a sign upon thine hand, and they shall be for frontlets between thine eyes. And thou shalt write them upon the doorposts of thy house, and upon thy gates.

MORNING PRAYERS

מוֹדֶה אֲנִי לְפָנֶיךָ, מֶלֶךְ חַי וְקַיָּם, שֶׁהֶחֱזַרְתָּ בִּי נִשְׁמָתִי בְּחֶמְלָה.
רַבָּה אֱמוּנָתֶךָ:

Mo-deh ah-nee l'faw-neh-chaw, meh-lech chai v'ka-yawm,
sheh-heh-cheh-zahr-taw bee nish-maw-see b'chem-law, ra-baw
eh-moo-naw-seh-chaw.

I give thanks unto Thee, O God, who lives forever, and who
has caused me to sleep peacefully and awakened me to this wonderful
world of Thy creation.

שְׁמַע יִשְׂרָאֵל, יְיָ אֱלֹהֵינוּ, יְיָ אֶחָד:

Sh'ma Yis-raw-ayl, Ado-noy Elo-hay-noo, Ado-noy Eh-chawd

בָּרוּךְ שֵׁם כְּבוֹד מַלְכוּתוֹ לְעוֹלָם וָעֶד:

Baw-rooch shaym k'vod mahl-choo-so l'o-lawm vaw-ed.

(Older children can recite entire Sh'ma)

וְאָהַבְתָּ אֵת יְיָ אֱלֹהֶיךָ, בְּכָל לְבָבְךָ, וּבְכָל נַפְשְׁךָ, וּבְכָל מְאֹדֶךָ.
וְהָיוּ הַדְּבָרִים הָאֵלֶּה, אֲשֶׁר אָנֹכִי מְצַוְּךָ הַיּוֹם עַל לְבָבֶךָ. וְשִׁנַּנְתָּם
לְבָנֶיךָ, וְדִבַּרְתָּ בָּם, בְּשִׁבְתְּךָ בְּבֵיתֶךָ, וּבְלֶכְתְּךָ בַדֶּרֶךְ, וּבְשָׁכְבְּךָ
וּבְקוּמֶךָ. וּקְשַׁרְתָּם לְאוֹת עַל יָדֶךָ, וְהָיוּ לְטֹטָפֹת בֵּין עֵינֶיךָ. וּכְתַבְתָּם
עַל מְזֻזוֹת בֵּיתֶךָ וּבִשְׁעָרֶיךָ:

Hear, O Israel: the Lord our God, the Lord is One.

Blessed be His glorious kingdom for ever and ever.

And thou shalt love the Lord thy God with all thy heart, and with all thy soul, and with all thy might. And these words, which I command thee this day, shall be in thy heart; and thou shalt teach them diligently unto thy children, and shalt talk of them when thou sittest in thy house, and when thou walkest by the way, and when thou liest down, and when thou risest up. And thou shalt bind them for a sign upon thine hand, and they shall be for frontlets between thine eyes. And thou shalt write them upon the doorposts of thy house, and upon thy gates.

GRACE AFTER MEALS

I

בָּרוּךְ אַתָּה יְיָ, אֱלֹהֵינוּ מֶלֶךְ הָעוֹלָם, הַזָּן אֶת הָעוֹלָם כֻּלּוֹ בְּטוּבוֹ.
בָּרוּךְ אַתָּה יְיָ, הַזָּן אֶת הַכֹּל:

Baw-rooch ah-taw Ado-noy, Elo-hay-noo meh-lech haw-o-lawm, ha-zawn ehs haw-o-lawm koo-lo b'too-vo. Baw-rooch ah-taw Ado-noy, ha-zawn ehs ha-kol.

Blessed art Thou, O Lord our God, King of the universe, who feeds the whole world with Thy goodness. Blessed art Thou, who gives food to all.

II

בְּרִיךְ רַחֲמָנָא מַלְכָּא דְעָלְמָא, מָרֵיהּ דְּהַאי פִּתָּא:

B'reech ra-cha-maw-naw mahl-kaw d'aw-l'maw, maw-ray d'hai pi-taw.

Blessed be the Lord, King of the universe, who gives us this bread.

III

בָּרוּךְ שֶׁאָכַלְנוּ מִשֶּׁלּוֹ, וּבְטוּבוֹ חָיִינוּ:

Baw-rooch sheh-aw-chahl-noo mi-sheh-lo, oo-v'too-vo chaw-yee-noo.

Blessed be He of whose bounty we have partaken, and through whose goodness we live.

OTHER PRAYERS FOR CHILDREN

Blessing over Bread (Hamotzee)

בָּרוּךְ אַתָּה יְיָ, אֱלֹהֵינוּ מֶלֶךְ הָעוֹלָם, הַמּוֹצִיא לֶחֶם מִן הָאָרֶץ:

Baw-rooch ah-taw Ado-noy, Elo-hay-noo meh-lech haw-o-lawm, ha-mo-tzee leh-chem min haw-aw-retz.

Blessed art Thou, O Lord our God, King of the universe, who bringest forth bread from the earth.

Blessing over Wine

בָּרוּךְ אַתָּה יְיָ, אֱלֹהֵינוּ מֶלֶךְ הָעוֹלָם, בּוֹרֵא פְּרִי הַגָּפֶן:

Baw-rooch ah-taw Ado-noy, Elo-hay-noo meh-lech haw-o-lawm, bo-ray p'ree ha-gaw-fen.

Blessed art Thou, O Lord our God, King of the universe, who createst the fruit of the vine.

Blessing over Delicacies

בָּרוּךְ אַתָּה יְיָ, אֱלֹהֵינוּ מֶלֶךְ הָעוֹלָם, בּוֹרֵא מִינֵי מְזוֹנוֹת:

Baw-rooch ah-taw Ado-noy, Elo-hay-noo meh-lech haw-o-lawm, bo-ray mee-nay m'zo-nos.

Blessed art Thou, O Lord our God, King of the universe, who createst many kinds of delicacies.

Blessing over Fruit

בָּרוּךְ אַתָּה יְיָ, אֱלֹהֵינוּ מֶלֶךְ הָעוֹלָם, בּוֹרֵא פְּרִי הָעֵץ:

Baw-rooch ah-taw Ado-noy, Elo-hay-noo meh-lech haw-o-lawm, bo-ray p'ree haw-aytz.

Blessed art Thou, O Lord our God, King of the universe, who createst the fruit of the tree.

Blessing over Vegetables

בָּרוּךְ אַתָּה יְיָ, אֱלֹהֵינוּ מֶלֶךְ הָעוֹלָם, בּוֹרֵא פְּרִי הָאֲדָמָה:

Baw-rooch ah-taw Ado-noy, Elo-hay-noo meh-lech haw-o-lawm, bo-ray p'ree haw-ah-daw-maw.

Blessed art Thou, O Lord our God, King of the universe, who createst the fruit of the earth.

Blessing over Foods and Drinks other than above

בָּרוּךְ אַתָּה יְיָ, אֱלֹהֵינוּ מֶלֶךְ הָעוֹלָם, שֶׁהַכֹּל נִהְיֶה בִּדְבָרוֹ:

Baw-rooch ah-taw Ado-noy, Elo-hay-noo meh-lech haw-o-lawm, sheh-ha-kol nih-yeh bi-d'vaw-ro.

Blessed art Thou, O Lord our God, King of the universe, by whose word all things exist.

Books of the Bible

We are always speaking or hearing about the Bible. Rabbis and ministers select passages to prove points or indicate important lessons. But there are many people who do not know what books comprise the Bible or how many parts there are. For them we list the sections of the Bible, in the hope that familiarity with them will develop.

The Hebrew Bible is divided into three general categories and is known to us by the term TeNaCH (תְּנַ"ךְ), a three letter symbol in which each letter stands for one division of the Bible.

I. PENTATEUCH

The ת (T) stands for Torah (תּוֹרָה) which here includes only the Choomawsh (חֻמָשׁ) or Five Books of Moses. These are:

A. Genesis   —   בְּרֵאשִׁית
B. Exodus   —   שְׁמוֹת
C. Leviticus   —   וַיִּקְרָא
D. Numbers   —   בְּמִדְבָּר
E. Deuteronomy —   דְּבָרִים

II. PROPHETS

The נ (N) which is the second letter in the symbol TeNaCH (תְּנַ"ךְ) stands for Prophets (נְבִיאִים). This division is divided into two parts, Early Prophets (נְבִיאִים רִאשׁוֹנִים) and Latter Prophets (נְבִיאִים אַחֲרוֹנִים).

A. Early Prophets

The Early Prophets (נְבִיאִים רִאשׁוֹנִים), are primarily historical books containing the records of the Jewish people from the death of Moses until the Babylonian exile in 586 B. C. E. The books which comprise this section are:

1. Joshua   —   יְהוֹשֻׁעַ
2. Judges   —   שׁוֹפְטִים
3. Samuel I   —   שְׁמוּאֵל א׳
4. Samuel II   —   שְׁמוּאֵל ב׳
5. Kings I   —   מְלָכִים א׳
6. Kings II   —   מְלָכִים ב׳

B. Latter Prophets

The Latter Prophets (נְבִיאִים אַחֲרוֹנִים), on the other hand, contain prophetic messages. The first three of these books are usually referred to as the Major Prophets. They are:

1. Isaiah   —   יְשַׁעְיָה
2. Jeremiah   —   יִרְמְיָה
3. Ezekiel   —   יְחֶזְקֵאל

C. Twelve Minor Prophets

These are called תְּרֵי עָשָׂר (Twelve) Minor Prophets only because their books are much smaller in size than are the larger compilations of the Major Prophets. They are:

1. Hosea — הוֹשֵׁעַ
2. Joel — יוֹאֵל
3. Amos — עָמוֹס

4. Obadiah — עֹבַדְיָה
5. Jonah — יוֹנָה
6. Micah — מִיכָה
7. Nahum — נַחוּם
8. Habakkuk — חֲבַקּוּק
9. Zephaniah — צְפַנְיָה
10. Haggai — חַגַּי
11. Zechariah — זְכַרְיָה
12. Malachi — מַלְאָכִי

III. The Writings

The third and last letter of the three-lettered symbol of תָּנַ״ךְ (TeNaCH), the כ (CH), stands for Writings (כְּתוּבִים). Five of the books in this section, known as חָמֵשׁ מְגִלּוֹת (Five Scrolls), are associated with and read in the Synagogue on various days. For example: Song of Songs, Passover; Ruth, Shovuos; Lamentations, Tisha B'Av; Ecclesiastes, Sukkos; and Esther, Purim. The books of this division are:

1. Psalms — תְּהִלִּים
2. Proverbs — מִשְׁלֵי
3. Job — אִיּוֹב
4. Song of Songs — שִׁיר הַשִּׁירִים
5. Ruth — רוּת
6. Lamentations — אֵיכָה
7. Ecclesiastes — קֹהֶלֶת
8. Esther — אֶסְתֵּר
9. Daniel — דָּנִיֵּאל
10. Ezra — עֶזְרָא
11. Nehemiah — נְחֶמְיָה
12. Chronicles I — דִּבְרֵי הַיָּמִים א׳
13. Chronicles II — דִּבְרֵי הַיָּמִים ב׳

Grace after Meals – סֵדֶר בִּרְכַּת הַמָּזוֹן

Psalm 126 is recited on Sabbaths and Festivals, before the Grace.

שִׁיר הַמַּעֲלוֹת.

בְּשׁוּב יְיָ אֶת שִׁיבַת צִיּוֹן הָיִינוּ כְּחֹלְמִים. אָז יִמָּלֵא שְׂחוֹק פִּינוּ,
וּלְשׁוֹנֵנוּ רִנָּה; אָז יֹאמְרוּ בַגּוֹיִם הִגְדִּיל יְיָ לַעֲשׂוֹת עִם אֵלֶּה. הִגְדִּיל יְיָ
לַעֲשׂוֹת עִמָּנוּ, הָיִינוּ שְׂמֵחִים.

שׁוּבָה יְיָ אֶת שְׁבִיתֵנוּ כַּאֲפִיקִים בַּנֶּגֶב. הַזֹּרְעִים בְּדִמְעָה בְּרִנָּה
יִקְצֹרוּ. הָלוֹךְ יֵלֵךְ וּבָכֹה נֹשֵׂא מֶשֶׁךְ הַזָּרַע. בֹּא יָבֹא בְרִנָּה נֹשֵׂא
אֲלֻמֹּתָיו:

Psalm 137 is recited on weekdays before the Grace.

עַל נַהֲרוֹת בָּבֶל, שָׁם יָשַׁבְנוּ גַּם בָּכִינוּ בְּזָכְרֵנוּ אֶת צִיּוֹן. עַל עֲרָבִים
בְּתוֹכָהּ תָּלִינוּ כִּנֹּרוֹתֵינוּ. כִּי שָׁם שְׁאֵלוּנוּ שׁוֹבֵינוּ דִּבְרֵי שִׁיר, וְתוֹלָלֵינוּ
שִׂמְחָה; שִׁירוּ לָנוּ מִשִּׁיר צִיּוֹן. אֵיךְ נָשִׁיר אֶת שִׁיר יְיָ עַל אַדְמַת נֵכָר.
אִם אֶשְׁכָּחֵךְ יְרוּשָׁלָיִם, תִּשְׁכַּח יְמִינִי. תִּדְבַּק לְשׁוֹנִי לְחִכִּי, אִם לֹא
אֶזְכְּרֵכִי, אִם לֹא אַעֲלֶה אֶת יְרוּשָׁלַיִם עַל רֹאשׁ שִׂמְחָתִי:

זְכֹר יְיָ לִבְנֵי אֱדוֹם אֵת יוֹם יְרוּשָׁלָיִם, הָאוֹמְרִים עָרוּ עָרוּ עַד
הַיְסוֹד בָּהּ. בַּת בָּבֶל הַשְּׁדוּדָה, אַשְׁרֵי שֶׁיְשַׁלֶּם לָךְ אֶת גְּמוּלֵךְ שֶׁגָּמַלְתְּ
לָנוּ. אַשְׁרֵי שֶׁיֹּאחֵז וְנִפֵּץ אֶת עֹלָלַיִךְ אֶל הַסָּלַע:

The leader begins by saying:

רַבּוֹתַי, נְבָרֵךְ.*

The others respond:

יְהִי שֵׁם יְיָ מְבֹרָךְ מֵעַתָּה וְעַד עוֹלָם.

The leader continues:

(at father's house)	אָבִי מוֹרִי
(as guest)	בִּרְשׁוּת רַב בַּעַל הַבַּיִת
(on other occasions)	מָרָנָן וְרַבָּנָן וְרַבּוֹתַי

(If a minyan, that is, ten men, is present, add: נְבָרֵךְ (אֱלֹהֵינוּ)
שֶׁאָכַלְנוּ מִשֶּׁלּוֹ.

The others respond:

בָּרוּךְ (אֱלֹהֵינוּ) שֶׁאָכַלְנוּ מִשֶּׁלּוֹ וּבְטוּבוֹ חָיִינוּ.

The leader repeats:

בָּרוּךְ (אֱלֹהֵינוּ) שֶׁאָכַלְנוּ מִשֶּׁלּוֹ וּבְטוּבוֹ חָיִינוּ.

בָּרוּךְ הוּא וּבָרוּךְ שְׁמוֹ.

בָּרוּךְ אַתָּה יְיָ, אֱלֹהֵינוּ מֶלֶךְ הָעוֹלָם, הַזָּן אֶת הָעוֹלָם כֻּלּוֹ בְּטוּבוֹ,
בְּחֵן בְּחֶסֶד וּבְרַחֲמִים. הוּא נוֹתֵן לֶחֶם לְכָל בָּשָׂר, כִּי לְעוֹלָם חַסְדּוֹ.
וּבְטוּבוֹ הַגָּדוֹל תָּמִיד לֹא חָסַר לָנוּ, וְאַל יֶחְסַר לָנוּ מָזוֹן לְעוֹלָם וָעֶד.
בַּעֲבוּר שְׁמוֹ הַגָּדוֹל, כִּי הוּא אֵל זָן וּמְפַרְנֵס לַכֹּל, וּמֵטִיב לַכֹּל, וּמֵכִין
מָזוֹן לְכָל בְּרִיּוֹתָיו אֲשֶׁר בָּרָא. בָּרוּךְ אַתָּה יְיָ, הַזָּן אֶת הַכֹּל:

---

* In traditional Jewish practice, three adults above Bar Mitzvah age, constitute a required quorum (m'zoo-mawn) to recite the preliminary prayers.

נוֹדֶה לְךָ, יְיָ אֱלֹהֵינוּ, עַל שֶׁהִנְחַלְתָּ לַאֲבוֹתֵינוּ אֶרֶץ חֶמְדָּה טוֹבָה
וּרְחָבָה, וְעַל שֶׁהוֹצֵאתָנוּ, יְיָ אֱלֹהֵינוּ, מֵאֶרֶץ מִצְרַיִם, וּפְדִיתָנוּ מִבֵּית
עֲבָדִים, וְעַל בְּרִיתְךָ שֶׁחָתַמְתָּ בִּבְשָׂרֵנוּ וְעַל תּוֹרָתְךָ שֶׁלִּמַּדְתָּנוּ, וְעַל
חֻקֶּיךָ שֶׁהוֹדַעְתָּנוּ, וְעַל חַיִּים חֵן וָחֶסֶד שֶׁחוֹנַנְתָּנוּ, וְעַל אֲכִילַת מָזוֹן
שָׁאַתָּה זָן וּמְפַרְנֵס אוֹתָנוּ תָּמִיד, בְּכָל יוֹם וּבְכָל עֵת וּבְכָל שָׁעָה*:

On Chanukah and Purim the following is added:

עַל הַנִּסִּים, וְעַל הַפֻּרְקָן, וְעַל הַגְּבוּרוֹת, וְעַל הַתְּשׁוּעוֹת, וְעַל
הַמִּלְחָמוֹת, שֶׁעָשִׂיתָ לַאֲבוֹתֵינוּ, בַּיָּמִים הָהֵם בַּזְּמַן הַזֶּה:

On Chanukah:

בִּימֵי מַתִּתְיָהוּ בֶּן יוֹחָנָן כֹּהֵן גָּדוֹל, חַשְׁמוֹנַי וּבָנָיו, כְּשֶׁעָמְדָה
מַלְכוּת יָוָן הָרְשָׁעָה עַל עַמְּךָ יִשְׂרָאֵל לְהַשְׁכִּיחָם תּוֹרָתֶךָ, וּלְהַעֲבִירָם
מֵחֻקֵּי רְצוֹנֶךָ. וְאַתָּה בְּרַחֲמֶיךָ הָרַבִּים עָמַדְתָּ לָהֶם בְּעֵת צָרָתָם, רַבְתָּ
אֶת רִיבָם, דַּנְתָּ אֶת דִּינָם, נָקַמְתָּ אֶת נִקְמָתָם, מָסַרְתָּ גִּבּוֹרִים בְּיַד
חַלָּשִׁים, וְרַבִּים בְּיַד מְעַטִּים, וּטְמֵאִים בְּיַד טְהוֹרִים, וּרְשָׁעִים בְּיַד
צַדִּיקִים, וְזֵדִים בְּיַד עוֹסְקֵי תוֹרָתֶךָ, וּלְךָ עָשִׂיתָ שֵׁם גָּדוֹל וְקָדוֹשׁ
בְּעוֹלָמֶךָ, וּלְעַמְּךָ יִשְׂרָאֵל עָשִׂיתָ תְּשׁוּעָה גְדוֹלָה וּפֻרְקָן כְּהַיּוֹם הַזֶּה.
וְאַחַר כֵּן בָּאוּ בָנֶיךָ לִדְבִיר בֵּיתֶךָ, וּפִנּוּ אֶת הֵיכָלֶךָ, וְטִהֲרוּ אֶת
מִקְדָּשֶׁךָ, וְהִדְלִיקוּ נֵרוֹת בְּחַצְרוֹת קָדְשֶׁךָ. וְקָבְעוּ שְׁמוֹנַת יְמֵי חֲנֻכָּה
אֵלּוּ, לְהוֹדוֹת וּלְהַלֵּל לְשִׁמְךָ הַגָּדוֹל:

On Purim:

בִּימֵי מָרְדְּכַי וְאֶסְתֵּר בְּשׁוּשַׁן הַבִּירָה, כְּשֶׁעָמַד עֲלֵיהֶם הָמָן
הָרְשָׁע. בִּקֵּשׁ לְהַשְׁמִיד, לַהֲרוֹג וּלְאַבֵּד אֶת כָּל הַיְּהוּדִים, מִנַּעַר וְעַד
זָקֵן, טַף וְנָשִׁים, בְּיוֹם אֶחָד, בִּשְׁלוֹשָׁה עָשָׂר לְחֹדֶשׁ שְׁנֵים עָשָׂר, הוּא

חֹדֶשׁ אֲדָר, וּשְׁלָלָם לָבוֹז. וְאַתָּה בְּרַחֲמֶיךָ הָרַבִּים הֵפַרְתָּ אֶת עֲצָתוֹ
וְקִלְקַלְתָּ אֶת מַחֲשַׁבְתּוֹ, וַהֲשֵׁבוֹתָ לּוֹ גְּמוּלוֹ בְּרֹאשׁוֹ, וְתָלוּ אוֹתוֹ וְאֶת
בָּנָיו עַל הָעֵץ:

וְעַל הַכֹּל, יְיָ אֱלֹהֵינוּ, אֲנַחְנוּ מוֹדִים לָךְ וּמְבָרְכִים אוֹתָךְ, יִתְבָּרַךְ
שִׁמְךָ בְּפִי כָּל חַי תָּמִיד לְעוֹלָם וָעֶד, כַּכָּתוּב, וְאָכַלְתָּ וְשָׂבָעְתָּ וּבֵרַכְתָּ
אֶת יְיָ אֱלֹהֶיךָ עַל הָאָרֶץ הַטּוֹבָה אֲשֶׁר נָתַן לָךְ.
בָּרוּךְ אַתָּה יְיָ, עַל הָאָרֶץ וְעַל הַמָּזוֹן:

רַחֵם, יְיָ אֱלֹהֵינוּ, עַל יִשְׂרָאֵל עַמֶּךָ, וְעַל יְרוּשָׁלַיִם עִירֶךָ, וְעַל
צִיּוֹן מִשְׁכַּן כְּבוֹדֶךָ, וְעַל מַלְכוּת בֵּית דָּוִד מְשִׁיחֶךָ, וְעַל הַבַּיִת הַגָּדוֹל
וְהַקָּדוֹשׁ שֶׁנִּקְרָא שִׁמְךָ עָלָיו. אֱלֹהֵינוּ, אָבִינוּ, רְעֵנוּ, זוּנֵנוּ, פַּרְנְסֵנוּ,
וְכַלְכְּלֵנוּ, וְהַרְוִיחֵנוּ, וְהַרְוַח לָנוּ, יְיָ אֱלֹהֵינוּ, מְהֵרָה מִכָּל צָרוֹתֵינוּ,
וְנָא אַל תַּצְרִיכֵנוּ, יְיָ אֱלֹהֵינוּ, לֹא לִידֵי מַתְּנַת בָּשָׂר וָדָם וְלֹא לִידֵי
הַלְוָאָתָם, כִּי אִם לְיָדְךָ הַמְּלֵאָה, הַפְּתוּחָה, הַקְּדוֹשָׁה וְהָרְחָבָה, שֶׁלֹּא
נֵבוֹשׁ וְלֹא נִכָּלֵם לְעוֹלָם וָעֶד:

On Sabbath say:

רְצֵה וְהַחֲלִיצֵנוּ, יְיָ אֱלֹהֵינוּ, בְּמִצְוֹתֶיךָ, וּבְמִצְוַת יוֹם הַשְּׁבִיעִי, הַשַּׁבָּת הַגָּדוֹל
וְהַקָּדוֹשׁ הַזֶּה. כִּי יוֹם זֶה גָּדוֹל וְקָדוֹשׁ הוּא לְפָנֶיךָ, לִשְׁבָּת בּוֹ וְלָנוּחַ בּוֹ בְּאַהֲבָה, כְּמִצְוַת
רְצוֹנֶךָ, וּבִרְצוֹנְךָ הָנִיחַ לָנוּ יְיָ אֱלֹהֵינוּ, שֶׁלֹּא תְהֵא צָרָה, וְיָגוֹן וַאֲנָחָה, בְּיוֹם מְנוּחָתֵנוּ.
וְהַרְאֵנוּ יְיָ אֱלֹהֵינוּ בְּנֶחָמַת צִיּוֹן עִירֶךָ, וּבְבִנְיַן יְרוּשָׁלַיִם עִיר קָדְשֶׁךָ. כִּי אַתָּה הוּא בַּעַל
הַיְשׁוּעוֹת וּבַעַל הַנֶּחָמוֹת:

On Rosh Chodesh and Festivals add:

אֱלֹהֵינוּ וֵאלֹהֵי אֲבוֹתֵינוּ, יַעֲלֶה, וְיָבֹא, וְיַגִּיעַ, וְיֵרָאֶה, וְיֵרָצֶה, וְיִשָּׁמַע, וְיִפָּקֵד, וְיִזָּכֵר
זִכְרוֹנֵנוּ וּפִקְדוֹנֵנוּ וְזִכְרוֹן אֲבוֹתֵינוּ, וְזִכְרוֹן מָשִׁיחַ בֶּן דָּוִד עַבְדֶּךָ, וְזִכְרוֹן יְרוּשָׁלַיִם עִיר

קָדְשֶׁךָ, וְזִכְרוֹן כָּל עַמְּךָ בֵּית יִשְׂרָאֵל לְפָנֶיךָ, לִפְלֵיטָה וּלְטוֹבָה, לְחֵן וּלְחֶסֶד וּלְרַחֲמִים, לְחַיִּים וּלְשָׁלוֹם, בְּיוֹם

On Rosh Chodesh say:

רֹאשׁ הַחֹדֶשׁ הַזֶּה.

On Pesach say:

חַג הַמַּצּוֹת הַזֶּה.

On Shovuos say:

חַג הַשָּׁבוּעוֹת הַזֶּה.

On Rosh Hashanah say:

הַזִּכָּרוֹן הַזֶּה.

On Sukkos say:

חַג הַסֻּכּוֹת הַזֶּה.

On Shemini Atzeres and Simchas Torah say:

הַשְּׁמִינִי חַג הָעֲצֶרֶת הַזֶּה.

זָכְרֵנוּ, יְיָ אֱלֹהֵינוּ, בּוֹ לְטוֹבָה, וּפָקְדֵנוּ בּוֹ לִבְרָכָה, וְהוֹשִׁיעֵנוּ בּוֹ לְחַיִּים. וּבִדְבַר יְשׁוּעָה וְרַחֲמִים חוּס וְחָנֵּנוּ, וְרַחֵם עָלֵינוּ וְהוֹשִׁיעֵנוּ, כִּי אֵלֶיךָ עֵינֵינוּ, כִּי אֵל מֶלֶךְ חַנּוּן וְרַחוּם אָתָּה:

וּבְנֵה יְרוּשָׁלַיִם עִיר הַקֹּדֶשׁ בִּמְהֵרָה בְיָמֵינוּ. בָּרוּךְ אַתָּה יְיָ, בּוֹנֵה בְרַחֲמָיו יְרוּשָׁלָיִם. אָמֵן:

בָּרוּךְ אַתָּה יְיָ, אֱלֹהֵינוּ מֶלֶךְ הָעוֹלָם, הָאֵל, אָבִינוּ, מַלְכֵּנוּ, אַדִּירֵנוּ, בּוֹרְאֵנוּ, גּוֹאֲלֵנוּ, יוֹצְרֵנוּ, קְדוֹשֵׁנוּ, קְדוֹשׁ יַעֲקֹב, רוֹעֵנוּ רוֹעֵה יִשְׂרָאֵל, הַמֶּלֶךְ הַטּוֹב וְהַמֵּטִיב לַכֹּל, שֶׁבְּכָל יוֹם וָיוֹם הוּא הֵטִיב, הוּא מֵטִיב, הוּא יֵיטִיב לָנוּ. הוּא גְמָלָנוּ, הוּא גוֹמְלֵנוּ, הוּא יִגְמְלֵנוּ לָעַד לְחֵן וּלְחֶסֶד וּלְרַחֲמִים וּלְרֶוַח, הַצָּלָה וְהַצְלָחָה, בְּרָכָה וִישׁוּעָה, נֶחָמָה, פַּרְנָסָה וְכַלְכָּלָה, וְרַחֲמִים וְחַיִּים וְשָׁלוֹם, וְכָל טוֹב, וּמִכָּל טוּב לְעוֹלָם אַל יְחַסְּרֵנוּ:

הָרַחֲמָן, הוּא יִמְלֹךְ עָלֵינוּ לְעוֹלָם וָעֶד.

הָרַחֲמָן, הוּא יִתְבָּרַךְ בַּשָּׁמַיִם וּבָאָרֶץ.

הָרַחֲמָן, הוּא יִשְׁתַּבַּח לְדוֹר דּוֹרִים, וְיִתְפָּאַר בָּנוּ לָעַד וּלְנֶצַח נְצָחִים, וְיִתְהַדַּר בָּנוּ לָעַד וּלְעוֹלְמֵי עוֹלָמִים.

הָרַחֲמָן, הוּא יְפַרְנְסֵנוּ בְּכָבוֹד.

הָרַחֲמָן, הוּא יִשְׁבּוֹר עֻלֵּנוּ מֵעַל צַוָּארֵנוּ, וְהוּא יוֹלִיכֵנוּ קוֹמְמִיּוּת לְאַרְצֵנוּ.

הָרַחֲמָן, הוּא יִשְׁלַח לָנוּ בְּרָכָה מְרֻבָּה בַּבַּיִת הַזֶּה וְעַל שֻׁלְחָן זֶה שֶׁאָכַלְנוּ עָלָיו.

הָרַחֲמָן, הוּא יִשְׁלַח לָנוּ אֶת אֵלִיָּהוּ הַנָּבִיא, זָכוּר לַטּוֹב, וִיבַשֶּׂר לָנוּ בְּשׂוֹרוֹת טוֹבוֹת יְשׁוּעוֹת וְנֶחָמוֹת:

At parents' home, say:

הָרַחֲמָן, הוּא יְבָרַךְ אֶת אָבִי מוֹרִי בַּעַל הַבַּיִת הַזֶּה וְאֶת אִמִּי מוֹרָתִי בַּעֲלַת הַבַּיִת הַזֶּה, אוֹתָם וְאֶת בֵּיתָם וְאֶת זַרְעָם וְאֶת כָּל אֲשֶׁר לָהֶם —

At own home, say:

הָרַחֲמָן, הוּא יְבָרַךְ אוֹתִי (וְאָבִי וְאִמִּי) וְאִשְׁתִּי וְזַרְעִי וְאֶת כָּל אֲשֶׁר לִי —

As guests of others, say:

הָרַחֲמָן, הוּא יְבָרַךְ אֶת בַּעַל הַבַּיִת הַזֶּה וְאֶת אִשְׁתּוֹ בַּעֲלַת הַבַּיִת הַזֶּה, אוֹתָם וְאֶת בֵּיתָם וְאֶת זַרְעָם וְאֶת כָּל אֲשֶׁר לָהֶם —

אוֹתָנוּ וְאֶת כָּל אֲשֶׁר לָנוּ. כְּמוֹ שֶׁנִּתְבָּרְכוּ אֲבוֹתֵינוּ, אַבְרָהָם יִצְחָק וְיַעֲקֹב, בַּכֹּל, מִכֹּל, כֹּל; כֵּן יְבָרֵךְ אוֹתָנוּ, כֻּלָּנוּ יַחַד, בִּבְרָכָה שְׁלֵמָה. וְנֹאמַר, אָמֵן:

בַּמָּרוֹם יְלַמְּדוּ עָלָיו וְעָלֵינוּ זְכוּת, שֶׁתְּהֵא לְמִשְׁמֶרֶת שָׁלוֹם. וְנִשָּׂא בְרָכָה מֵאֵת יְיָ וּצְדָקָה מֵאֱלֹהֵי יִשְׁעֵנוּ, וְנִמְצָא חֵן וְשֵׂכֶל טוֹב בְּעֵינֵי אֱלֹהִים וְאָדָם:

On Sabbath say:

הָרַחֲמָן, הוּא יַנְחִילֵנוּ יוֹם שֶׁכֻּלּוֹ שַׁבָּת וּמְנוּחָה לְחַיֵּי הָעוֹלָמִים:

On Rosh Chodesh say:

הָרַחֲמָן, הוּא יְחַדֵּשׁ עָלֵינוּ אֶת הַחְדֶשׁ הַזֶּה לְטוֹבָה וְלִבְרָכָה:

On Festivals say:

הָרַחֲמָן, הוּא יַנְחִילֵנוּ יוֹם שֶׁכֻּלּוֹ טוֹב:

On Rosh Hashanah say:

הָרַחֲמָן, הוּא יְחַדֵּשׁ עָלֵינוּ אֶת הַשָּׁנָה הַזֹּאת לְטוֹבָה וְלִבְרָכָה:

On Sukkos say:

הָרַחֲמָן, הוּא יָקִים לָנוּ אֶת סֻכַּת דָּוִיד הַנּוֹפֶלֶת:

הָרַחֲמָן, הוּא יְזַכֵּנוּ לִימוֹת הַמָּשִׁיחַ וּלְחַיֵּי הָעוֹלָם הַבָּא. מַגְדִּיל (מִגְדּוֹל *On Sabbath, Festivals and Rosh Chodesh*) יְשׁוּעוֹת מַלְכּוֹ וְעֹשֶׂה חֶסֶד לִמְשִׁיחוֹ, לְדָוִד וּלְזַרְעוֹ עַד עוֹלָם. עֹשֶׂה שָׁלוֹם בִּמְרוֹמָיו, הוּא יַעֲשֶׂה שָׁלוֹם עָלֵינוּ וְעַל כָּל יִשְׂרָאֵל, וְאִמְרוּ, אָמֵן:

יְראוּ אֶת יְיָ קְדֹשָׁיו, כִּי אֵין מַחְסוֹר לִירֵאָיו. כְּפִירִים רָשׁוּ וְרָעֵבוּ, וְדֹרְשֵׁי יְיָ לֹא יַחְסְרוּ כָל טוֹב. הוֹדוּ לַיְיָ כִּי טוֹב, כִּי לְעוֹלָם חַסְדּוֹ. פּוֹתֵחַ אֶת יָדֶךָ, וּמַשְׂבִּיעַ לְכָל חַי רָצוֹן. בָּרוּךְ הַגֶּבֶר אֲשֶׁר יִבְטַח בַּיְיָ, וְהָיָה יְיָ מִבְטַחוֹ. נַעַר הָיִיתִי, גַּם זָקַנְתִּי, וְלֹא רָאִיתִי צַדִּיק נֶעֱזָב, וְזַרְעוֹ מְבַקֶּשׁ לָחֶם. יְיָ עֹז לְעַמּוֹ יִתֵּן, יְיָ יְבָרֵךְ אֶת עַמּוֹ בַשָּׁלוֹם:

Glossary of Terms and Explanations

Either at a social affair at home, or in your daily conversations, or in the synagogue, you have probably heard many Hebrew words which you did not fully understand. Some of these express important ideas or feelings, or they may be related to a custom or tradition with which you want to be more acquainted.

A number of these have been selected for brief explanation; others are shown with the page of reference. Transliterations are rendered in their usual accepted form; they are in turn given in the author's transliteration.

The following abbreviations are used: A = Ashkenazic; H = Hebrew; pl = plural; pr = pronounce; S = Sephardic; Y = Yiddish.

AFIKOMON. S — Afikoman, H — אֲפִיקוֹמָן; pr — Ah-fee-ko-mawn.

The broken piece of Matzah hidden at the beginning of the Seder for use after the meal. *See* YACHATZ, page 408.

ALIYAH. A — Aliyoh, H — עֲלִיָּה; Y — Aliyeh; pr — Ah-lee-yaw.

The word aliyah means *going up*, and has general reference to going up to the Torah (on the pulpit) to recite the blessings. (Blessings are on page 316). Those summoned to the Torah are called up by the word, "ya-ah-mod — let him stand" with the number of the honor and often the Hebrew name of the person mentioned.

AMEN. A — Omayn, H — אָמֵן; pr — Aw-mayn.

The word Amen means *May it be so*, and is recited or stated by a congregant or congregation after the reading of specific prayers, or at the end of every paragraph of the Kaddish. It implies the acceptance by the worshiper of the prayer recited. Some authorities say that the three Hebrew letters forming the word, AMN, stand for the Hebrew phrase "Ayl Meh-lech Ne-emon (אֵל מֶלֶךְ נֶאֱמָן) — God is the True King," which is recited at the beginning of the Sh'ma.

AMIDAH.   A — Amidoh, H — עֲמִידָה; pr — Ah-mee-dah.

Amidah means *standing* and refers to the Eighteen Benedictions or the Sh'moneh Esray, as the prayer is called in Hebrew. The prayer is included in every one of the three daily services and in every holiday service. The first three and the last three of the benedictions form the basis of every Amidah. Between these are included specific references to the Sabbath or holiday being observed. In the traditional synagogue the Amidah is first recited in silent meditation and then (except at the evening service) is repeated by the Cantor.

AROVOH.   S — Aravah,   pl — Arovos,   S — Aravot,   H — עֲרָבָה, pl — עֲרָבוֹת; pr — Ah-raw-vaw.

A willow branch attached to the lulov, and used together with the esrog on Sukkos. Also, a bundle of about five willow twigs used at the Hoshanos ceremony on Hoshana Rabba. *See* HOSHANOS. *See also* HOSHANA RABBA.

ASARAH B'TEVET.   A — Asoroh B'Teves, H — עֲשָׂרָה בְּטֵבֵת; pr — Ah-saw-raw B'tay-vays.

The tenth day of the month of Teves — a fast day, commemorating the laying siege upon Jerusalem by the Babylonians in the year 586 B. C. E.

ASERES HA-D'VORIM.   S — Aseret Ha-Devarim, H — עֲשֶׂרֶת הַדְּבָרִים; pr — Ah-seh-rehs hah-d'vaw-reem.

The Ten Commandments. *See* page 309.

ASEHRES Y'MAY TSHOOVAW.   A — Aseres Y'may T'shuvoh, S — Aseret Y'may Teshuvah, H — עֲשֶׂרֶת יְמֵי תְּשׁוּבָה; pr — Ah-seh-rehs Y'may T'shoo-vaw.

The Ten Days of Repentance, beginning on Rosh Hashanah and ending with Yom Kippur.

BAAL KORAY.   S — Baal Koreh, H — בַּעַל קוֹרֵא; pr — Bah-ahl Ko-ray; or

Baal Kriah. A — Baal Krioh, H — בַּעַל קְרִיאָה; pr — Bah-ahl K'ree-aw, Y — Bahl Krieh.

The Baal Kriah or Baal Koray is the man who reads the Torah in the traditional synagogue. He is an expert in his field and has usually had many years of experience as well as a full understanding of the Torah.

Bar Mitzvah. H — בַּר מִצְוָה; pr — Bar Mitz-vah.

A Bar Mitzvah literally is *a son of the commandment* and refers to the time, at thirteen, when a boy assumes adult religious responsibility. This includes participation in the required quorum to hold public worship (Minyan), donning the Tefillin (Phylacteries) in the traditional synagogue, and a conscious acceptance and recognition of his faith and people. The term also refers to the ceremony held in the synagogue on the Sabbath following the young man's thirteenth birthday, generally determined by the Hebrew calendar.

Bas Mitzvah. S — Bat Mitzvah, H — בַּת מִצְוָה.

Literally, *a daughter of the commandment*. While there is no traditional ceremony marking the arrival at the age of religious maturity for a young girl, many synagogues have instituted Bas Mitzvah ceremonies in which the young girl is given recognition similar to the boy who reaches the age of thirteen.

Bedikas Chometz. S — Bedikat Chametz, H — בְּדִיקַת חָמֵץ; pr — B'dee-kahs Chaw-maytz.

Searching for the leaven — this refers to the custom of searching for leaven on the eve before Passover. To avoid the recitation of a blessing in vain, bits of bread are usually placed in strategic places so that they may be "found."

When the first day of Pesach falls on a Sunday, this ceremony is performed on the preceding Thursday night.

Ben Zochor or Sholom Zochor. A — Ben Zochor, S — Ben Zachor, H — בֶּן זָכָר pr — Ben Zochor.

This is a home gathering on the Friday evening following the birth of a son. Literally, the words mean "a male child" or "welcome, male child." Songs and prayers and refreshments consisting of sweets and *nahit* (chick peas) comprise the evening's festivity.

B'nai B'rak. S — Benei Berak, H — בְּנֵי בְּרַק; pr — B'nay B'rahk.

The town mentioned in the Haggadah where the rabbis expounded the Exodus story all through the night. *See* page 202.

Brochoh (B'rochoh). S — Berachah, H — בְּרָכָה; pr — B'raw-chaw.

A benediction or a blessing recited before one performs an act For example, Hamotzee prayer is the b'rawchaw one recites before partaking of bread.

Bris. S — Berit, H — בְּרִית; pr — B'rees.

The ceremony of circumcising a male child on his eighth day is called *bris*, and literally means a covenant or contract. It refers to the covenant God made with Abraham. Participants include the Mohe (specialist who performs the circumcision), sandek, the person who holds the child, and kvater, or the godfather who customarily carries the child to the sandek.

B'sawmeem. A — B'somim, S — Besamim, H — בְּשָׂמִים; pr — B'saw-meem.

Spices placed in Spice Box for use in the Havdalah ceremony on Saturday night.

Chag Ha-Aviv. A — Chag Ho-Oviv, H — חַג הָאָבִיב; pr — Chahg Haw-aw-veev.

The Festival of Spring. Another name for Passover.

Chag Haw-aw-seef. A — Chag Ho-Osif, S — Chag Ha-Asif H — חַג הָאָסִיף; pr — Chahg Haw-aw-seef.

The Festival of Ingathering or *Harvest.* The agricultural name for Sukkos.

Chag Ha-Bikkurim. S — Chag Ha-Bikkurim, H — חַג הַבִּכּוּרִים; pr — Chahg Hah-bi-koo-reem.

The Festival of First Fruits. The agricultural name for Shovuos.

CHAG HA-KATZIR. A — Chag Ha-Kotzir, H — חַג הַקָּצִיר; pr — Chahg Ha-kaw-tzeer.

The Festival of Reaping or Cutting. Another name for Shovuos.

CHAG HA-N'TEEOS. S — Chag Ha-Neteeot, H — חַג הַנְּטִיעוֹת; pr — Chahg Hane-tee-os.

The Festival of Planting. Another name for Chamishaw Awsawr or Tu Bi-Shevat.

CHAHG SAW-MAY-ACH. A — Chag Somayach, S — Chag Samehach, H — חַג שָׂמֵחַ.

This is the greeting used on all holidays, and means happy holiday. See GOOT YOM TOV, page 394.

CHAGIGAH. A — Chagigoh, H — חֲגִיגָה; pr — Chah-gee-gaw.

The name of the added offering in Temple days. It is symbolized by the egg in the Seder service.

CHALLAH. pl — Challot. A — Challoh, pl — Challos, H — חַלָּה, חַלּוֹת; pr — Chah-law, Chah-los.

Bread twists or braided loaves used on the Sabbath as well as during the holidays. For the rounded Challah custom on Rosh Hashanah see page 7.

CHAMISHAH ASAR BI-SHEVAT. H — חֲמִשָׁה עָשָׂר בִּשְׁבָט; pr — Chah-mi-shaw Aw-sawr Bi-Shevat.

The fifteenth day of the month of Shevat, the New Year for Trees. Also known as TU BI-SHEVAT, pronounced Too Bi-Shevat.

CHANUKAH. A — Chanukoh, Y — Chanikeh, H — חֲנֻכָּה; pr — Chah-noo-kaw.

The Feast of Lights, the Festival of the Dedication (commemorating the Maccabean victory over the Syrian Greeks in 165 B. C. E.).

CHAROSES. S — Charoset, H — חֲרוֹסֶת; pr — Chah-ro-sehs.

The mixture of apples, wine, and nut meats, symbolic of mortar, used in the Seder.

CHOL HAMOED (A and S). H — חוֹל הַמּוֹעֵד; pr — Chohl Hah-moh-ayd.

The Intermediate Days of Sukkos and Pesach.

CHOMETZ. A — Chometz, S — Chametz, H — חָמֵץ; pr — Chaw-maytz.

The word means *leavened* or *soured*, and refers to the Passover holiday, on which the Jew is enjoined from eating foods containing leaven.

FEER KASHES. Y — פיר קשיות; pr — Feer Kah-shehs.

Literally, *four questions*. Chanted or recited by the youngest son, these questions are a highlight of the Seder service. *See* page 197.

GESHEM (A and S). H — גֶּשֶׁם; pr — Geh-shem.

Rain. The service for Rain on Shemini Atzeres. *See* page 73.

GELILOH. S — Gelilah; H — גְּלִילָה; pr — G'lee-law.

Rolling. The honor of rolling the Torah after the reading service.

GOOT YOM TOV. Y — גוט יום־טוב; pr — Goot Yohm Tov.

This is a popular holiday greeting and means *happy holiday*. *See* CHAHG SAW-MAY-ACH, page 393.

HADASIM (pl of Hadas, A and S — Hadas). H — הֲדַסִּים; pr — Hah-dah-seem.

Myrtles. Myrtle branches attached to the lulov and used together with the esrog on Sukkos.

HAFTORAH (HAFTARAH). A and S — Haftorah, Haftarah, H — הַפְטוֹרָה, הַפְטָרָה; pr. Hahf-taw-rah.

The Haftorah is the portion from the Prophets set aside for the particular day. Like the Torah, which has a definite portion each week in the synagogue service, the Prophets, too, have been included in the weekly Sabbath service. The Haftorah is usually preceded by blessings and is succeeded by the chanting of five other appropriate blessings. A Bar Mitzvah boy usually includes the Haftorah and blessings as part of his first public performance. *See page 317.*

HAGGADAH. A — Haggodoh, S — Haggadah, H — הַגָּדָה; pr — Haggadah.

Literally, *telling, narration.* The Haggadah is the book which tells the story of the exodus from Egypt and contains Biblical passages, midrashic interpretations, prayers and psalms dealing with the Festival of Freedom. *See pages 187–252.*

HAGBOHOH. S — Hagbahah, H — הַגְבָּהָה; pr — Hag-baw(-haw).

Raising up. The honor of raising the Torah after the reading service.

HAKAWFOS. A — Hakofos, S — Hakofot, H — הַקָּפוֹת; pr — Hah-kaw-fos.

Processions of the Torahs on Simchas Torah.

HALLEL (A and S). H — הַלֵּל; pr — Hah-layl.

Praise. Refers to six Psalms (113–118) recited on festivals and New Moon days.

HAMOTZIE. H — הַמּוֹצִיא; pr — Hah-mo-tzee.

He who brings forth. The blessing over bread.

HATIKVAH. A — Hatikvoh, S — Hatikvah, H — הַתִּקְוָה; pr — Hah-tik-vaw.

Literally, *The Hope.* It refers to the song written by Naftali Hertz Imber, adopted by Jewish people and sung before the creation of the State of Israel. It is now the national anthem of Israel. The last three lines were changed from the original, following the establishment of Israel.

כָּל עוֹד בַּלֵּבָב פְּנִימָה,

נֶפֶשׁ יְהוּדִי הוֹמִיָּה,

וּלְפַאֲתֵי מִזְרָח קָדִימָה,

עַיִן לְצִיּוֹן צוֹפִיָּה.

עוֹד לֹא אָבְדָה תִקְוָתֵנוּ,

הַתִּקְוָה שְׁנוֹת אַלְפַּיִם,

לִהְיוֹת עַם חָפְשִׁי בְּאַרְצֵנוּ,

בְּאֶרֶץ צִיּוֹן וִירוּשָׁלָיִם.

Kawl od ba-lay-vawv p'nee-maw,
Neh-fesh y'hoo-dee ho-mi-yaw,
Oo-l'fah-ah-say miz-rawch kaw-dee-maw,
Ah-yeen l'Tzi-yon tzo-fi-yaw.

Ohd lo aw-v'daw sik-vaw-say-noo,
Ha-tik-vaw sh'nos ahl-pah-yeem,
Lih-yos ahm chawf-shee b'ahr-tzay-noo,
B'eh-retz Tzi-yon vee-Roo-shaw-law-yeem.

HAVDALAH.　H — הַבְדָּלָה, Y — Havdawleh; pr — Hahv-daw-law.
　　Separation. The synagogue and home ceremony on Saturday night after sundown, marking the end of the Sabbath.

HAZKORAS NESHOMOS.　S — Hazkarat Neshamot, H — הַזְכָּרַת נְשָׁמוֹת;
pr — Haz-kaw-rahs n'shaw-mos.
　　The *Yizkor* or Memorial Service on the last morning of every holiday. Literally, remembrance of the souls. *See also* YIZKOR, page 408.

Hefsed Merubeh (A and S). H — הֶפְסֵד מְרוּבֶּה; pr — Hehf-sayd m'roo-beh.

Great loss. A term used in connection with *Shivah*, the period of mourning. *See also* Shivah, page 404.

Hoshana Rabba. A — Hoshano Rabbo, H — הוֹשַׁעֲנָא רַבָּה; pr — Hoh-shah-naw rah-baw.

The seventh day of Sukkos. This 21st day of the month of Tishri has added characteristics of *Yomim Noroim* (Days of Awe). Special prayers, called *Hoshanos* (O God, save us!) are offered in the synagogue. The bundles of the willow-twigs, besides the lulov and its accessories, are used in the ceremonials of the day. *See* Arovos. *See also* Hoshanos.

Hoshanos (pl of Hoshano). A — Hoshano, S — Hoshana, H — הוֹשַׁע נָא; pr — Ho-shah-naw.

A name derived from the refrains to prayers, beginning or ending with *Hoshano*, while the willow-twigs are being used in the ceremony. *See* Arovos. *See also* Hoshana Rabba.

Imberlach. Y — אימבערלאך; pr — Eem-behr-lahch.

A ginger cookie.

Kaaros (pl of Kaaroh). S — Kaarot (pl of Kaarah), H — קְעָרוֹת; pr — Kah-ah-rohs.

Plates. Containers for charitable contributions following the Mincha (afternoon) service before Kol Nidre.

Kaddish. A and S — Kaddish, H — קַדִּישׁ; pr — Kah-deesh.

The word means *holy* or *sacred*, and refers to the doxology recited in memory of a departed member of the family. This particular Kaddish is called Kaddish Yawsom (קַדִּישׁ יָתוֹם) or Orphan's Kaddish, and offers praise of God and His sanctity. Other forms in the service include Kaddish Shawlaym (קַדִּישׁ שָׁלֵם) or Complete Kaddish, recited at completion of a service; Chatzi Kaddish (חֲצִי קַדִּישׁ) or Half-Kaddish, which introduces the Amidah and a few other prayers; and the Rabbawnawn Kaddish (קַדִּישׁ דְּרַבָּנָן) or that which is read after study of rabbinic sources.

KAPPOROS. S — Kapparot, H כַּפָּרוֹת; pr Kah-paw-rohs.

Literally, *forgivenesses, ransom.* An old traditional custom of symbolically transferring one's sins to fowl on the evening before Yom Kippur. This ceremony is reminiscent of the sacrifices brought to the Temple at Jerusalem. Instead of fowl, rooster for male and hen for female, money (coins amounting to the number 18 — *see* page 42) is used for this ceremony, and the money is later distributed to the poor and needy.

KARPAS. H — כַּרְפַּס; pr — Kahr-pahs.

Literally, *parsley;* but *see* page 188.

KASHES (Y). H — קוּשְׁיָה, pl — קוּשְׁיוֹת; pr — Kah-shehs.

Questions. Refers to *Dee Feer Kahshes,* The Four Questions, asked by the child at the Seder. See, FEER KASHES, page 394.

KIDDUSH. H — קִדּוּשׁ; pr — Kee-doosh.

The blessing over the wine. There are many kinds of Kiddush prayers, such as those for the Sabbath, the holidays, and Rosh Hashanah.

KOHAYN, KOHEN. H — כֹּהֵן; pr — Ko-hayn.

Priest. Refers to the first honor in the Torah reading service. Also, to one of the three Matzos used in the Seder. The Kohen also conducts the *Pidyon Haben* ceremony. *See* page 402.

KOHANIM (pl of Kohen). H — כֹּהֲנִים; pr — Ko-hah-neem.

Priests. Refers generally to *Birkas Kohanim,* Priestly Benediction.

KOSHER. A — Kosher, S — Kasher, H — כָּשֵׁר; pr — Kaw-shayr.

Ritually prepared. It is generally related to the dietary laws and their observance.

LAG BO-OMER. S — Lag Ba-Omer, H — ל"ג בָּעֹמֶר; pr — Lahg Baw-Oh-mehr.

The thirty-third day of the Omer. See page 265.

LATKES. Y — לאַטקעס; pr — Laht-kehs.
Pancakes; usually of potatoes, served on Chanukah.

LAYVEE, LEVI (A and S). H — לֵוִי; pr — Lay-vee, pl — L'viyim,
H — לְוִיִּם; pr — L'vee-yeem.
Levite. Refers to second honor in the Torah reading service. Also, to one of the three Matzos used in the Seder.

L'CHAYYIM (A and S). H — לְחַיִּים; pr — l'chah-yeem.
The toast, meaning *For Life.*

L'SHONO TOVO. A — L'shonoh Tovoh, S — Leshanah Tovah,
H — לְשָׁנָה טוֹבָה; pr — L'shaw-naw To-vaw.
The New Year greeting. *See* page 6.

LECHEM ONI. H — לֶחֶם עֹנִי; pr — leh-chehm oh-nee.
Bread of affliction: another designation for Matzah.

LULOV. S — Lulav, H — לוּלָב; pl, A — Lulovim; pl, S — Lulavim,
H — לוּלָבִים; pr — Loo-lawv.
Palm branch, used together with the esrog on Sukkos.

MACHZOR. A and S — Machzor, H — מַחֲזוֹר; pr — Mahch-zor.
The Machzor is the holiday Siddur or Prayerbook, and the word means *cycle*. There are two kinds, the High Holy Day Machzor and the Yom Tov Machzor (which contains the prayers for the three pilgrimage festivals, Pesach, Shovuos, and Sukkos).

MAFTIR. H — מַפְטִיר; pr — Mahf-teer.
Maftir means *concluding* and is the last honor offered in the Torah reading service. When a Bar Mitzvah is called to the Torah for the first time, this honor is usually accorded to him. *See* HAFTORAH, page 394.

MALCHUYOS. S — Malchuyot, H — מַלְכֻיּוֹת; pr — Mahl-choo-yos.
Kingship or *Sovereignty.* Refers to the first of three divisions of the Musaf (Additional) service on Rosh Hashanah. *See* SHOFOROS, ZICHRONOS.

MANDLEN.   Y — מאַנדלען; pr — Mahnd-lehn.

Almonds. Also, a sort of fluffy *croutons* served in soup.

MATZAH.   A — Matzoh, pl — Matzos, H — מַצָּה; pr — Mah-tzaw.

Unleavened bread used on Pesach.

MAZAL Tov.   A — Mazol Tov,   H — מַזָּל טוֹב; pr — Mah-zawl
Tov.

Good luck is the meaning of this common expression. It is used at all happy occasions, such as births, weddings, and Bar Mitzvahs.

MEZUZAH.   A — Mezuzoh,   S — Mezuzah,   H — מְזוּזָה; pr —
M'zoo-zaw.

The parchment scroll on the doorpost of a house. *See* page 365 for the home consecration ceremony.

MI SHEBAYRACH (MEE SHEBAYRACH) (A and S).   H — מִי שֶׁבֵּרַךְ;
pr — Mee she-bay-rahch.

Literally this phrase means *May He who blessed* and refers to the blessing recited in the traditional synagogue for one who has been called to the Torah. There are special "Mee Shebayrachs" for the sick as well as for the naming of new born girls in the synagogue on the Sabbath following birth.

MINYAN.   A — Minyon, S — Minyan, H — מִנְיָן; pr — Min-yawn

The word minyan means *number* or *count*, and has reference to the minimal quorum of ten male adults (above the age of thirteen) required to conduct a public service. This practice is followed in all traditional synagogues.

MITZVAH — A — Mitzvoh, H — מִצְוָה; pr — Mitz-vaw.

Literally, *command*, in the sense of observing one of the Biblical or Rabbinical commandments. In daily use, it has developed the meaning "good deed." For example, you have heard people say, "It is a mitzvah to do so and so." Actually one does perform a good deed when complying with a commandment.

Mohel. A and S — Mohel, H — מוֹהֵל; pr — Mo-hayl.

The mohel is the specialist who circumcises boy infants. *See* Bris.

Mogen Dovid. S — Magen David, H — מָגֵן דָּוִד; pr — Maw-gayn Daw-veed.

Literally, *Shield of David*. The symbol is a hexagram (six points) comprised of two equal triangles. It is used on many religious items and is recognized as the Jewish star.

Moror. S — Maror, H — מָרוֹר; pr — Maw-ror.

Bitter herbs, used in the Seder service.

Nachas. S — Nachat, H — נַחַת; pr — Nah-chahs.

Literally, *delight*, the word has a much gentler connotation, such as spiritual satisfaction. It is usually, though not exclusively, referred to as joy from children.

Neshomoh Yesayroh. S — Neshamah Yeterah, H — נְשָׁמָה יְתֵירָה; pr — N'shaw-maw y'say-raw.

Additional Soul. Refers to allegorical description of Jewish spirit on Sabbath. *See* page 314.

Olov Hasholom (Olov Ha-Sholom). S — Alav Hashalom, H — עָלָיו הַשָּׁלוֹם; pr — Aw-lawv hah-shaw-lom. Feminine H — עָלֶיהָ הַשָּׁלוֹם; pr — Aw-leh-haw hah-shaw-lom.

Used when the name of a departed is mentioned, meaning *Peace be unto him*, in the sense of "God rest his soul." In the case of a departed woman the phrase is "Awlehaw hah-shaw-lom," *Peace be unto her*.

Oneg Shabbat. A — Oneg Shabbos, H — עֹנֶג שַׁבָּת; pr — Oh-neg Shah-baht.

The Friday eve get-together in which the Sabbath spirit permeates is called Oneg Shabbat or literally, *Delight of the Sabbath*.

Pesach. S — Pehsach, H — פֶּסַח; pr — Pay-sahch.
The Festival of Passover.

Pidyon Ha-Ben. A — Pidyon Habayn, H — פִּדְיוֹן הַבֵּן; pr — Peed-yon ha-behn.
Redemption of the first born son is a ceremony held on the thirty-first day of birth. The ceremony includes the participation of a Kohen (a Jew descended from the priestly family) who redeems the son for the fee of five silver dollars, and the father who offers to redeem the child. If either the mother or father of the son is of the Kohen or Levite families, the ceremony is not held.

Purim. H — פּוּרִים; pr — Poo-reem.
The *Feast of Lots.*

Rosh Hashanah. H — רֹאשׁ הַשָּׁנָה; pr — Rosh Hah-shaw-naw.
New Year, literally, "head" of the year.

Rosh Hashanah L'ilonos. S — Rosh Hashanah L'ilonot, H — רֹאשׁ הַשָּׁנָה לְאִילָנוֹת; pr — Rosh Hah-shaw-naw L'ee-law-nos.
New Year for Trees. See Chamishah Asar Bi-Shevat, page 393.

Sandek (A and S). H — סַנְדֵּק; pr — Sahn-dehk.
Godfather, at a Bris or Circumcision.

Seder (A and S). H — סֵדֶר; pr — Say-dehr.
Order. The order of the home ceremony on Passover eve.

Sefer Hachayyim (A and S). H — סֵפֶר הַחַיִּים; pr — Say-fehr Hah-chah-yeem.
Book of Life. Refers to the prayers on Rosh Hashanah and Yom Kippur.

Sefirah. A — Sefiroh, H — סְפִירָה; pr — S'fee-raw.
Counting. Refers to counting of the 49 days between the second night of Passover and Shovuos. *See* page 265.

SELICHOS. S — Selichot, H — סְלִיחוֹת; pr — S'lee-chos.

This is the name of the midnight service on the Saturday night before Rosh Hashanah. Where three days do not elapse between the specific Saturday night and Rosh Hashanah, the service is held on the preceding Saturday night. The same name is applied to special penitential prayers of fast days, including special days preceding Rosh Hashanah, as well as the days between Rosh Hashanah and Yom Kippur.

SEMICHAH. A — S'michoh, H — סְמִיכָה; pr — S'mee-chaw.

This word means *ordination*, and refers to the document and ceremony of authority to serve as rabbi. It is usually conferred at the end of a prescribed course of study established by recognized seminaries.

SEUDAH. A — Seudoh, H — סְעוּדָה; pr — S'oo-daw.

"*A festive meal.*" Refers usually to the feast on the day of Purim or the Sabbath afternoon repast. *See also* SHOLOSH SEUDOS, page 405.

SHABBAT SHALOM. H — שַׁבָּת שָׁלוֹם; pr — Shah-baht Shah-lom.

"*A Peaceful Sabbath*," the Sabbath greeting. The modern Hebrew equivalent of the Yiddish, *Goot Shabbes*, Good Sabbath.

SHABBOS. S — Shabbat, Y — Sha-behs, H — שַׁבָּת; pr — Shah-baws.
Sabbath.

SHADDAI (A and S). H — שַׁדַּי; pr — Shah-dai.
Almighty.

SHALACH MONOS. S — Shalach Manot, H — שַׁלַּח מָנוֹת; pr — Shah-lach Maw-nos.
The sending of gifts. Refers to the Purim custom.

SHAWLOSH R'GAWLIM. A — Sholosh R'golim, S — Shalosh Regalim, H — שָׁלֹשׁ רְגָלִים; pr — Shaw-losh R'gaw-leem.
The Three Pilgrimage Festivals.

SHEMINI ATZERES.   S — Shemini Atzeret, H — שְׁמִינִי עֲצֶרֶת; pr — Sh'mee-nee Ah-tzeh-rehs.

The Eighth Day of Assembly, eighth day of Sukkos. It is also considered a רֶגֶל בִּפְנֵי עַצְמוֹ, a Festival, separate and distinct from Sukkos.

SHEVORIM.   S — Shevarim, H — שְׁבָרִים; pr — Sh'vaw-reem.

Broken sounds. One of the three kinds of sounds of the shofar, three short blasts.

SHIVAH.   A — Shiv'aw, S — Shiv'ah, H — שִׁבְעָה; pr — Shee-veh.

Shivah means *seven*, and refers to the seven day period of mourning observed after the passing of a close relative. The period includes the Sabbath, although no mourning is permitted on that day or on holidays. The day of burial and the last day of this period need not be observed in their entirety. If part of these days are observed, they may be considered as full days. When a death occurs on the eve of a holiday, followed by burial, then at least one hour of Shivah must be observed, after which the entire period of mourning is cancelled. The secondary period of mourning is called Sheloshim or *Thirty*, and deals with the days following the original seven until the thirtieth day. In many cases, in the event of substantial monetary loss (*hefsed merubeh*) three days of mourning are considered as Shivah.

SHIVAH ASAR B'TAMMUZ.   A — Shivoh Osor B'Sammuz, H — שִׁבְעָה עָשָׂר בְּתַמּוּז; pr — Sheev-aw Aw-sawr B'Sah-mooz.

The seventeenth day of the month of Tammuz. A fast day. *See* page 362.

SHEMONEH ESSRAY.   H — שְׁמֹנֶה עֶשְׂרֵה; pr — Sh'moh-neh ehss-ray.

See AMIDAH, page 390.

SHOCHET.   H — שׁוֹחֵט; pr — Sho-chayt.

Shochet means *slaughterer*; it refers to the expert who has the knowledge as well as the skill to slaughter animals and fowl in accordance with Jewish law. He has proved his ability not only by experience but has received authority, called Kabbalah, to perform this service.

SHOFAR. S — Shofahr, H — שׁוֹפָר; pr — Sho-fawr.

The *Ram's Horn*, sounded in the High Holy Day service.

SHOFOROS. S — Shofarot, H — שׁוֹפָרוֹת; pr — Sho-faw-ros.

The third of the three divisions of the Musaf (additional) service of Rosh Hashanah. *See* MALCHUYOS, ZICHRONOS.

SHOLOM or SHOLOM ALAYCHEM. S — Shalom or Shalom Alechem, H — שָׁלוֹם or שָׁלוֹם עֲלֵיכֶם; pr — Shaw-lom, or Shaw-lom Ah-lay-chehm.

The word sholom means *peace*; it is used in greetings and fare-wells. The expression Shawlom Alaychem is a traditional greeting, *Peace be unto you*, to which the person greeted responds in the inverted order, Alaychem Shawlom or *And to you, peace*.

SHOLOM ZOCHOR. S — Shalom Zachor, H — שָׁלוֹם זָכָר; pr — Shaw-lom Zo-chor.

See BEN ZOCHOR, page 391.

SHOLOSH SEUDOS. S — Shalosh Seudot, H — שָׁלֹשׁ סְעוּדוֹת; pr — Shaw-losh S'oo-dos.

Three festive meals. Refers to the Sabbath afternoon repast, the third of the three customary Sabbath meals.

SHOVUOS. S — Shabuot, H — שָׁבוּעוֹת; pr — Shaw-voo-os.

The Feast of Weeks.

SIDRA (Sedrah). H — סִדְרָה; pr — Seed-raw.

The word means *order* (and in this sense is related to Siddur or prayerbook and Seder, because all deal with a specific order of service); it refers to the portion of the Torah read each Sabbath.

SIMCHAH. A — Simchoh, H — שִׂמְחָה; pr — Sim-chaw.

Simchah means a joyous affair or event. The word itself means *rejoicing*, as for example Simchas Torah (*Rejoicing of the Torah*).

SOFER. H — סוֹפֵר, pr — Soh-fayr.

The word means *scribe* and is related to the word book. It refers to the man who through piety, ability, and experience writes or copies Torahs, Tefillin, Mezuzos, and Gittin (*divorces*).

SUKKOS. S — Sukkot, H — סֻכּוֹת; pr — Soo-kohs.
The Feast of Tabernacles.

TAANIS ESTHER. S — Taanit Esther, H — תַּעֲנִית אֶסְתֵּר; pr — Tah-nees Ehs-tehr.
Fast of Esther. See page 363.

TAL (A and S). H — טַל; pr — Tahl.

Dew. The prayer for dew recited during the Musaf (additional) service on the first day of Passover. *See* page 176.

TALMUD. H — תַּלְמוּד; pr — Tahl-mood.

The word Talmud means *study*, but it relates exclusively to the gamut of rabbinic creativity during a five hundred year period until 500 C. E. It is called the Oral Law (the Torah or Bible is the Written Law) because from the days of the Bible the laws and interpretations were handed down orally and were recorded only centuries later. Included in the six general categories which comprise the Talmud are legalistic, religious, historical, ethical, economic, and social records of our people.

TASHLICH (A and S). H — תַּשְׁלִיךְ; pr — Tahsh-leech.

The custom of symbolically casting sins into a river or lake on the first day of Rosh Hashanah. *See* page 6.

TEFILLIN. H — תְּפִלִּין; pr — T'fee-leen.

Phylacteries worn by traditional Jews during the morning weekday service. The cases or cubicles, one for the forehead called Shel Rosh and the other for the arm called Shel Yahd, contain Biblical inscriptions on parchment. The four passages from the Bible appear on *one piece* of parchment for the phylactery Shel Yahd and on *four separate strips* for the Shel Rosh. You can see four separate sections on the latter phylactery. The passages are from the following sources: Exodus

13:1–10, Exodus 13:11–16, Deuteronomy 6:4–9, and Deuteronomy 11:13–20. The straps are called Retzuos. On the side of the phylactery for the forehead you will notice the Hebrew letter "שׁ" — "SH" in relief. This letter, plus the knot in the straps for the Shel Rosh, plus the knot on the strap of the Shel Yahd, combine to form the Hebrew word שַׁדִּי — Shaddai or Almighty.

The idea behind the use of the Tefillin is that the mind (Shel Rosh), the heart (adjacent to the Shel Yahd), and the hand, or deeds, are together directed to the higher ideals of Godliness and to the performance of noble deeds.

TEKIAH.   A — Tekioh, H — תְּקִיעָה; pr — T'kee-aw.

Shofar blast.

TEKIAH GEDOLAH.   A — Tekioh Gedoloh, H — תְּקִיעָה גְדוֹלָה; pr — T'kee-aw G'do-law.

Shofar blast. One of the three kinds of Shofar sounds, one continuous blast. Gedolah means great and refers to the long blast sounded at the end of each group of sounds and also the sound to mark the end of Yom Kippur.

TeNaCH.   A and S — Tanach, H — תְּנַךְ; pr — T'nach.

A contraction of three Hebrew words, each letter being the first of a main division of the Bible. T means Torah or Pentateuch, N stands for Nevieem or Prophets, and Ch means K'sooveem or Writings. *See* section, "Books of the Bible."

TERUAH.   A — Teruoh, H — תְּרוּעָה; pr — T'roo-aw.

Alarm. One of the three kinds of Shofar sounds, the nine short staccato blasts.

TORAH.   A — To-roh, H — תּוֹרָה; pr — To-raw.

Torah has broad as well as narrow connotations. The word itself means *Law* or *Instruction*. In its narrow sense, it is the Pentateuch or the Five Books of Moses. In a larger sense, it includes the entire Bible as the Written Law, and in a still wider significance, it means the Oral Law or Talmud, as well as Jewish culture and concepts in general.

YAAMOD (A and S). H — יַעֲמוֹד; pr — Yah-ah-mod.

Let him rise. The word which summons one to recite the Torah blessings. Usually succeeded by either the Hebrew name of the person called or by the number of the honor.

YACHATZ (A and S). H — יַחַץ; pr — Yah-chahtz.

Breaking the Matzah. The breaking of the middle of the three Matzos and hiding it for the Afikomon. *See* page 389.

YISROEL. S — Yisrael, H — יִשְׂרָאֵל; pr — Yis-raw-ayl.

Israel. Refers to the Jewish people as in the phrase "Children of Israel" or to the State of Israel.

YIS-R'AY-LEEM. A and S — Yisre'elim, H — יִשְׂרְאֵלִים.

Israelites. Refers especially to all Jews who are neither Kohanim (Priests) nor Leviyim (Levites).

YIZKOR. H — יִזְכּוֹר; pr — Yiz-kohr.

Yizkor means *He will remember.* It is the special memorial service conducted in the synagogue four times per year, Yom Kippur, Sukkos, Pesach, and Shovuos. Another well known name for this service is Hazkoras Neshomos or *Remembering the Souls*. *See* page 396.

YOM HAZIKORON. S — Yom Hazikaron, H — יוֹם הַזִּכָּרוֹן; pr — Yom Hah-zee-kaw-ron.

Day of Remembrance. The biblical name for Rosh Hashanah.

YOM HA-ATZMAUT. A — Yom Ho-Atzmous, H — יוֹם הָעַצְמָאוּת; pr — Yom hah-ahtz-mah-oot.

Israel's *Independence Day*, celebrated on the 5th of Iyar, second month in the Jewish calendar, counting from Nisan.

YOM KIPPUR (A and S). H — יוֹם כִּפּוּר; pr — Yom Ki-poor, also YOM HAKIPPURIM, יוֹם הַכִּפּוּרִים.

Day of Atonement.

ZICHRONOS. S — Zichronot; H — זִכְרוֹנוֹת; pr — Zeech-ro-nos.

Remembrances. The second of the three themes of the Musaf (additional) service of Rosh Hashanah. *See also* MALCHUYOS, SHO-FOROS.

Z'MAN CHAYRUSAYNU. S — Zeman Chayrutenu, H — זְמַן חֵרוּתֵנוּ; pr — Z'mahn Chay-roo-say-noo.

The Festival of Our Freedom. The festival of Passover, commemorating the exodus from Egypt.

Z'MAN MATTAN TOROSAYNU. S — Zeman Mattan Toratenu, H — זְמַן מַתַּן תּוֹרָתֵנוּ; pr — Z'mahn Mah-tahn To-raw-say-noo.

The Festival of the Giving of our Torah. The festival of Shovuos, commemorating the receiving of the Torah on Mt. Sinai.

Z'MAN SIMCHOSAYNU. S — Zeman Simchatenu, H — זְמַן שִׂמְחָתֵנוּ; pr — Z'mahn Sim-chaw-say-noo.

The Festival of our Rejoicing. The festival of Sukkos rejoicing with the ingathering of the harvest; also rejoicing with the Torah.

Z'MIROS. S — Zemirot; H — זְמִירוֹת; pr — Z'mee-ros.

Melodies. The songs which are sung at the Sabbath table.

Hebrew Names for Your Children*

BOYS

Abba — Father   אַבָּא

Abiram — Exalted father   אֲבִירָם

Abner — Father of light   אַבְנֵר

Abraham — Father of a great nation   אַבְרָהָם

Abram — Exalted father   אַבְרָם

Absalom — Father of peace   אַבְשָׁלוֹם

Adam — Earthborn, name of first man   אָדָם

Adiel — Ornament of God   עֲדִיאֵל

Adlai — God is justice   עַדְלִי

Aharon, Aaron — Very elevated, Mountainous   אַהֲרֹן

Akabyah, Akaviah — [In] God's steps   עֲקַבְיָה

Akiba — Step, steadfast   עֲקִיבָא, עֲקִיבָה

Alexander — Helper of man, Man-defender   אֲלֶכְּסַנְדֶּר

Amos — Burdened, A bearer of God's message   עָמוֹס

Amram — An exalted nation   עַמְרָם

Ari, Aryeh — Lion   אֲרִי, אַרְיֵה

Ariel — Lion (hero) of God   אֲרִיאֵל

Arnon — Constant sounding, roaring of a stream   אַרְנוֹן

---

* The transliteration of most of the names in this section, owing to their Biblical origin, is in the Sephardic. For this reason, the letter ב is rendered as *B*, as it is in the English translation of the Bible, though we pronounce it as *V*. The letter י is generally transliterated as J, though we pronounce it as *Y*. Some of the newly coined names in use in Israel have been added to this list.

Baruch — Blessed   בָּרוּךְ

Benjamin — Son of my right hand, Son of my old age   בִּנְיָמִין

Ben-Ammi — Son of my people   בֶּן־עַמִּי

Ben-Zion (Ben-Tzion) — Son of Zion   בֶּן־צִיּוֹן, בֶּנְצִיּוֹן

Bezalel (Betzalel) — Under the shade, protection of God   בְּצַלְאֵל

Boaz — In him is strength   בֹּעַז, בּוֹעַז

Caleb — Dog-like faithfulness   כָּלֵב,

Carmel — Vineyard, Fertile   כַּרְמֶל

Cathriel — Crown of God   כַּתְרִיאֵל

Chanoch, Enoch — Initiated, Dedicated, Taught   חֲנוֹךְ

Chayyim (Chaim) — Life   חַיִּים

Chiram (Churam) — Most noble   חִירָם, (חוּרָם)

Dan — He judged   דָּן

Daniel — God judged, God is my judge   דָּנִיאֵל, דָּנִיֵּאל

David — Beloved   דָּוִד, דָּוִיד

Dob, Dov — Bear   דּוֹב

Eleazar — God has helped   אֶלְעָזָר

Eli — Elevation, Majesty   עֵלִי

Eliezer — Help of God   אֱלִיעֶזֶר

Elijah — My God is Yah, My strength is God   אֵלִיָּה, אֵלִיָּהוּ

Elisha — Sight of God, Salvation of God   אֱלִישָׁע

Elkanah — God has redeemed, God has acquired   אֶלְקָנָה

Emmanuel, Immanuel — God is with us   עִמָּנוּאֵל

Ephraim — Twin fruitfulness, Fruit, Posterity   אֶפְרַיִם

Ethan — Firm, Perpetuity, God is very ancient   אֵיתָן

Ezekiel — God will strengthen   יְחֶזְקֵאל

Ezra — A helper   עֶזְרָא

GABRIEL — A man of God, Strength of God   גַּבְרִיאֵל

GAD — Fortune, Troop, Assembly   גָּד

GEDALIAH — God is great   גְּדַלְיָה, גְּדַלְיָהוּ

GERSHON, GERSHOM — A stranger there   גֵּרְשׁוֹן, גֵּרְשֹׁם

HOSHEA, HOSEA — He has saved, Deliverance   הוֹשֵׁעַ

HEMAN, HYMAN — Faithful   הֵימָן

HILLEL — He praised, Praise   הִלֵּל

IRA — A watchman, A guardian   עִירָא

ISAAC — He will laugh, Laughter   יִצְחָק

ISAIAH — God saved, Salvation of God   יְשַׁעְיָה, יְשַׁעְיָהוּ

ISRAEL — As a prince, he prevailed with God   יִשְׂרָאֵל

ITHAMAR (ITTAMAR) — Island of palms, Like a palm tree   אִיתָמָר

ITHIEL — God is with me   אִיתִיאֵל

JACOB — He held the heel, Supplanter   יַעֲקֹב

JARON — May he sing   יָרוֹן

JEREMIAH — Exalted of God   יִרְמְיָה, יִרְמְיָהוּ

JESSE — My gift, Gift of God, God exists   יִשַׁי

JOAB — God is (my) father   יוֹאָב

JOCHANAN (JOHN) — God is gracious, God-favored   יוֹחָנָן, יְהוֹנָתָן

JOEL — The Lord, Yah, is my God   יוֹאֵל

JONAH — Dove   יוֹנָה

JONATHAN — God gave, God's gift   יְהוֹנָתָן, יוֹנָתָן

JOSEPH — He adds, He increases   יוֹסֵף, יְהוֹסֵף

JOSHUA — Help belongs to God   יְהוֹשֻׁעַ

JOSIAH — God supports   יֹאשִׁיָה, יֹאשִׁיָהוּ

JUDAH, JEHUDAH — God be praised   יְהוּדָה

KALONYMOS, KALMAN — Beautiful law, A good name   קָלוֹנִימוּס, קַלְמָן

LAADAN — For delight   לַעֲדָן

LAEL — Belonging to God   לָאֵל

LEMUEL — Devoted to God   לְמוּאֵל

LEVI — Attached, Companion, My joining   לֵוִי

MANASSEH — He made to forget   מְנַשֶּׁה

MARNIN — Causing to sing   מַרְנִין

MATTATHIAS — Gift of God   מַתִּתְיָה, מַתִּתְיָהוּ

MEIR — Light bearer   מֵאִיר

MENACHEM, MENAHEM — Comforter, Consoler   מְנַחֵם

MICHA, MICAH — Who is like God?   מִיכָה, מִיכָהוּ, מִיכָיְהוּ
Humble, Poor

MICHAEL — Who is like God, God-like   מִיכָאֵל

MORDECAI — Taught of God, Pure myrrh   מָרְדְּכַי

MOSES, MOSHEH — Extracted, drawn from the water   מֹשֶׁה

NAAMAN — Very pleasant, Beautiful   נַעֲמָן

NADAB — Generous   נָדָב

NACHMAN — Comforter, Consoler   נַחְמָן

NACHUM — Comfort, Penitent   נָחוּם

NATHAN — He (God) gave   נָתָן

NISAN — Flight, Miracle   נִיסָן

NOAH — Rest, Repose, Consolation   נֹחַ

NOAM — Pleasantness   נֹעַם

OZER — Helper   עוֹזֵר

PINCHAS, PINCUS — Mouth of serpent, Mouth   פִּינְחָס, פִּנְחָס
of charmer, Bald-face

PESACH — Lame, Limping, Born on Passover   פָּסֵחַ, פֶּסַח

RAANAN — Fresh, Fertile, Green, Luxuriant   רַעֲנָן

RAPHAEL, REPHAEL — God has healed   רְפָאֵל

REUBEN — Behold a son   רְאוּבֵן

RON — Sing   רוֹן

SAUL — Asked for, Prayed for   שָׁאוּל (שׁוֹאֵל)

SHALOM — Peace   שָׁלוֹם

SHELOMO, SOLOMON — Peaceful   שְׁלֹמֹה

SHEMARIAH — Safe keeping of God, God has   שְׁמַרְיָה, שְׁמַרְיָהוּ
guarded

SHEMUEL, SAMUEL — Heard by God   שְׁמוּאֵל

SHIMEON, SIMEON, SIMON — Gracious hearing   שִׁמְעוֹן

SHIMSHON, SAMSON — Little sun, Distinguished   שִׁמְשׁוֹן

SIMCHAH — Joy, Gladness   שִׂמְחָה

TOBIAH, TOBIAS — God is good, Goodness of God   טוֹבִיָּה

URI, URIAH — My light, Light of God   אוּרִי, אוּרִיָּה

URIEL — Light of God   אוּרִיאֵל

YIGAEL — He will be redeemed   יִגָּאֵל

YIGAL, YIGEAL, He redeems, He will redeem   יִגְאָל, יְגָאֵל

ZADOK (TZADOK) — Just, Righteous   צָדוֹק

Z'AYB — A wolf   זְאֵב

ZECHARIAH — The Lord has remembered   זְכַרְיָה, זְכַרְיָהוּ

ZEMACH (TZEMACH) — Sprout, Growth   צֶמַח

ZVI (ZEVI, TZEVI) — Gazelle, Beauty, Glory   צְבִי

GIRLS

ABIBAH, AVIVAH — Spring   אֲבִיבָה

ABIGAIL — My father (God) brings rejoicing   אֲבִיגֵיל

ADAH, ADA — Ornament   עָדָה

ADINAH (ADELA, ETHEL) — Delicate, Dainty, Noble   עֲדִינָה

AHAVAH — Love   אַהֲבָה

ALEXANDRA — (feminine of ALEXANDER),   אֲלֶכְּסַנְדְרָה
     Helper of man

ARNONAH — (feminine of ARNON), Constant   אַרְנוֹנָה
     sounding, roaring of a stream

ATHALIA — God is exalted   עֲתַלְיָה

BATHIAH, BITHIAH — Daughter of God   בַּתְיָה, בִּתְיָה

BERACHAH — Blessing   בְּרָכָה

BERURYAH, VALERIA — Chosen by God   בְּרוּרְיָה

BINAH — Understanding   בִּינָה

CHABIBAH, CHAVIVAH, — Beloved, Darling   חֲבִיבָה

CHANNAH, ANNA, HANNAH — Grace, Favor   חַנָּה

CHAVVAH, EVE — Life, Living   חַוָּה

CHAYYAH — Life, Vita, Animal   חַיָּה

CHULDAH — World, Weasel   חֻלְדָה

DALIAH — A branch   דָּלִיָה

DAVIDAH — (feminine of David), Beloved   דָּוִידָה

DEBORAH — A bee   דְּבוֹרָה

DINAH — Judgment, Justice, Avenged   דִּינָה

EDNAH, EDNA — Delight, Pleasure, Rejuvination   עֶדְנָה

EMUNAH — Faith   אֱמוּנָה

ESTHER — A star, Happiness   אֶסְתֵּר

ETHIAH, ETHYAH (ETTA) — With God   אִתְיָה

GEULAH — Redemption   גְּאוּלָה

HADASSAH — A myrtle   הֲדַסָּה

ISCAH, JESSICA — A covering, Observant   יִסְכָּה

JAEL — Mountain-goat   יָעֵל
JAFFAH, YAFFA — Beautiful   יָפָה
JEDIDAH — Beloved, Amiable, Friend   יְדִידָה
JESSIE — Help, Salvation   יֵשַׁע
JONINAH — Little dove   יוֹנִינָה
JUDITH — (feminine of JUDAH), Praised, a Jewess   יְהוּדִית

KINNERETH — Gennesareth — sea of Galilee   כִּנֶּרֶת

LEAH — Weariness, Languid   לֵאָה

MARGALITH, MARGARET — Gem, Jewel, Pearl   מַרְגָּלִית
MARNINAH — (ferminine of Marnin), Causing to Sing   מַרְנִינָה
MAXIMAH — Enchantress, Charming, Fascinating   מַקְסִימָה
MARTHA — Mistress, Lady   מָרְתָה
MEIRAH — (feminine of MEIR), Light bearer   מְאִירָה
MENUCHAH — Rest, Quietness   מְנוּחָה
MICHAL — Book, Stream   מִיכַל
MILCAH, MALKAH — A queen   מִלְכָּה, מַלְכָּה
MIRIAM — Bitterness — given at the time of   מִרְיָם
     the Egyptian bitterness
MENACHEMAH — (feminine of MENACHEM), Consolation   מְנַחֲמָה

NAAMAH — Pleasant, Pleasing, Agreeable   נַעֲמָה
NAOMI — (My) pleasantness   נָעֳמִי
NECHAMAH — Comfort, Consolation   נֶחָמָה

ORAH — (feminine of URI), Light אוֹרָה

PENINAH — A pearl, A jewel פְּנִינָה

RAANANNAH — (feminine of RAANAN), Fresh, רַעֲנָנָה
Fertile, Green, Luxuriant
RACHEL — An ewe-lamb, A sheep רָחֵל
REBECCA — Captivating through beauty רִבְקָה
RINNAH, RINNA — Rejoicing, Singing, Song רִנָּה
RONI (RONNY) — Sing רָנִּי
RUTH — A friend, Friendship רוּת

SARAH — Princess of a multitude שָׂרָה
SARAI — My princess שָׂרַי
SHEBA — Seven, An oath שֶׁבַע
SIMAH — A treasure סִימָה
SIMCHAH — Joy, Gladness שִׂמְחָה
SHULAMITH — Peaceful, Perfect שׁוּלַמִּית

TAMAR, TAMARAH — Palm tree תָּמָר, תִּמְרָה
TOBAH — Good טוֹבָה

ZEHAVAH, AURELIA, GOLDIE — Golden זְהָבָה
ZEMIRAH — Song of Joy זְמִירָה
ZEPHIRAH (TZEFIRAH) — Dawn, Break of the morning צְפִירָה
ZIBIAH, TZIVIAH — (feminine of ZVI), a lovely woman צְבִיָּה, צִבְיָה
ZIPPORAH (TZIPPORAH) — a little bird צִפּוֹרָה
ZIVAH — Brightness, Beauty, Splendor זִיוָה

Index of Songs and Melodies